The Book of
LONDON

WEIDENFELD & NICOLSON
LONDON

The Book of
LONDON

General Editor MICHAEL LEAPMAN

CONTENTS

'It is difficult to speak adequately or justly of London.
It is not a pleasant place; it is not agreeable, or cheerful, or easy,
or exempt from reproach. It is only magnificent.'

HENRY JAMES 1843–1916

PART 4

A Place to Work

PAGE 197

PART 5

A Place to Enjoy

PAGE 255

The Makers of London

Glossary of Place Names

Further Reading

Index

Contributors

Acknowledgements

Preface

Knowing a city is not just a question of observing its component parts, or even of understanding how they work and what they signify. You need an awareness of what was there before and of how and why it developed as it did. This is why many Londoners do not know London and most visitors gain only a superficial impression of it. The object of this book is to fill that gap, for residents and visitors alike. Much more than a guide book, it is a practical, authoritative and comprehensive aid to appreciating, understanding and enjoying one of the world's most intricate cities.

This intricacy is in part reflected in the number of contributors – twenty-seven in all, listed on page 319 – and their range of interests and expertise. Nearly all are Londoners but in one sense that has made their work more challenging: those of us who live in the city take much for granted, yet many of our assumptions are wrong and our impressions incomplete. The writers' task has been to discard the legends and reveal the actuality. I am grateful to them for their ready grasp of the basic concept of the book and for complying with it so precisely, while strengthening it with their own insights. In particular, Andrew Saint's introductory section on the growth of London is a *tour de force* that sets the tone and standard for what follows. Geoff Howard's striking colour photographs have captured the essence of present-day London, Susan Haskins laboured long in research libraries to find the original prints, maps, black-and-white photographs that illuminate the text and Harry Green, the designer, performed a masterly juggling act in creating a book that is both elegant and accessible. Thanks must also go to Ralph Hyde at the Guildhall Library and David Bentley and the Department of Urban Archaeology at the Museum of London for friendly and helpful advice and to the latter also for providing us with up-to-the-minute, unpublished information on the archaeology of Roman London; and to John Mitchell and Bob Monks for the informative maps.

The structure of the book is essentially the work of Brigid Avison. She and Emma Way pulled together all the diverse strands, in both the practical and the creative sense, during the production period. It has been a cooperative project, involving the skill of many others apart from those named. My thanks to all of them.

Within the text we have used small capital letters to denote places of particular importance or interest.

MICHAEL LEAPMAN
General Editor

THE GROWTH OF LONDON

The reasons for London's individuality are not difficult to grasp. It was and remains the one city of the western world which, from its ancient beginnings to the present day, with hardly an interruption, has fulfilled every major urban function: largest city of a great and populous nation; capital city; royal seat and cultural mecca; financial and commercial centre; and international port. No other city can boast this record of national continuity and hegemony. Paris comes the closest, but it never had shipping or commerce on London's scale. Other places, even Rome, became great as capitals of city-states, then declined, only to revive in recent years. Inexhaustible London has alone retained its appetite for growth and power for nearly two millennia.

It is a muddled, unplanned city. It grows without much forethought, taking advantage of puffs in prosperity. Its complex form and scarcely coordinated facilities drive the efficiency-minded to distraction, but afford devious pleasure to the initiated. Its municipal government is the despair of every generation of Londoners. Localism is strong, services are divided among a medley of boroughs and statutory authorities. National governments will never leave their capital alone or take proper responsibility for it. These basic conditions of London life are symptoms of an age-old, three-cornered conflict, often submerged but as strong today as it ever has been. The tireless forces battling for dominance are government and law in Westminster and Whitehall; finance and trade in the City; and the aspirations of those who live and work in London. From the ups and downs and compromises of this conflict have emerged not only the institutions but also the physical fabric of the city: more curious and eccentric than rational and efficient; some-

times ugly, often picturesque, diverse, bewildering, frustrating; needing patience to understand and to love.

LONDINIUM: THE FIRST FOUR CENTURIES

Most great cities claim a precise foundation date; London, true to the empirical traditions of its long history, has none. But it is fairly certain now that London was never a Celtic settlement. It began as a new Roman town, established immediately or soon after the Emperor Claudius's invasion of Britain in AD 43.

Why was 'Londinium' (the name may derive from a Celtic word meaning fierce) built where it was and how did it so quickly eclipse Colchester, the first Roman capital? Trade and topography hold the key. When Julius Caesar mounted his punitive expedition against the Celtic chieftains of Britain in 55 BC, he described the south-east as densely inhabited, prosperous, cattle-rearing country. Since then, seaborne trade between Britain, Gaul and the Roman Empire had expanded; among exports were skins, slaves, dogs, corn, cattle, iron and even gold and silver. All this had to be shipped in and out. The Thames provided access to the more developed areas of the interior. It also barred the way to any invader coming from the Kent coast, as both Julius Caesar's and Claudius's armies did. It had to be fought for and crossed, and the natural place to do so was as far east as possible. The river was broader and shallower than it is today, with marshy tracts on both banks. Teddington, Brentford, Chelsea, Westminster and London Bridge have all been suggested for Julius Caesar's point of crossing, with Chelsea a seductive choice because of a scatter of military equipment found in the river there. As for the Claudian army, the very location

An impression of the forum, the social and commercial centre of Roman London. Excavations show that it was on Cornhill, roughly in the centre of the present-day City.

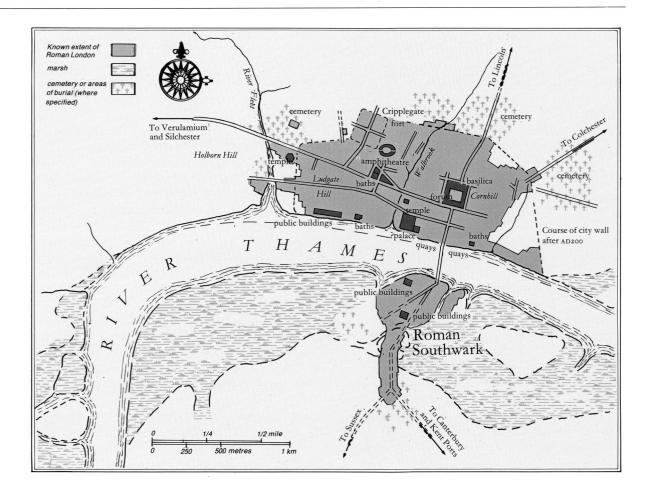

Known extent of
Roman London

marsh

cemetery or areas
of burial (where
specified)

To Verulamium
and Silchester

To Lincoln

cemetery

Cripplegate
fort

cemetery

Holborn Hill

River Fleet

To Colchester

temple

amphitheatre

Walbrook

cemetery

Ludgate
Hill

baths

basilica

forum

Cornhill

public buildings

baths

temple

Course of city wall
after AD 200

?palace

baths

quays

quays

RIVER   THAMES

public buildings

public buildings

Roman
Southwark

To Sussex

To Canterbury
and Kent Ports

0   1/4   1/2 mile

0   250   500 metres   1 km

Roman London

'Londinium' is now one of the most intensively studied cities of the Roman world. Every building boom in the City offers the chance of excavation and the basic structure of Roman London and the location of its major buildings are clearer now than ever.

The Thames was perhaps twice the width it is today, and its tributaries, the Walbrook and the wider-mouthed Fleet, could be used by small boats. The Romans pushed back the river frontage, in order to construct a sequence of quays and jetties, which stretched either side of London bridge. The early city sprang up in the sloping area to their north, bounded by the Walbrook on the west. Its major monuments were a forum and basilica (later rebuilt to cover an area some 200 yards square) straddling what is now Gracechurch Street, and a large palace on the site of Cannon Street Station.

By the late first century the city stretched well west of the Walbrook. The Thames-side baths at Huggin Hill, fed by clear spring water, and a smaller bath suite north

of Cheapside were both started by them, though later enlarged, and the amphitheatre in Guildhall Yard, discovered in 1988, is thought to be second century.

London reached its early peak of prosperity in about the middle of the second century, at about the time the Cripplegate fort in the suburban Barbican area was being constructed. Some fifty years later came the great city wall, ditched, gated and crenellated, and taking in the fort at its north-west corner. The wall's irregular landward line was to define London for more than a thousand years, and it is now certain that a riverside wall was added during the fourth century.

Traces of Roman occupation stretch beyond the circuit of walls, chiefly along the lines of communication. Southwark, as the means of approach to the bridge, was a flourishing suburb. Extensive cemeteries for both cremation and burial have been found in the east near the Colchester road and in the west on either side of the Fleet valley, where parallel roads led to Westminster (an ancient river crossing and site of one or more Roman villas). But the basic street pattern of the City of London today is not Roman but Saxon, interrupted and overlaid by many later changes.

of London Bridge makes this the most plausible crossing point, though many experts now favour Westminster. What is certain is that by about AD 50 a permanent bridge close to the line of the present London Bridge had been thrown across the river from a spit of gravel on the Southwark side to firm, rising ground on the north bank. Here London grew up, initially between the foot of the bridge and the eastern edge of the little Walbrook stream. This site promised well for growth, as the experienced Roman engineers and planners spotted. It could expand north, east and west, up to and beyond the low eminences represented today by Cornhill and the site of St Paul's. The settlement lay close to an existing road network and strategically near the borders of four important tribal territories. In addition, the surrounding land was fertile.

London developed then as a commercial settlement and entrepôt, not as a military or tribal centre. Whatever immediate strategic value it had, declined as the Romans extended control over much of England. Not that the city ever lacked a military presence; many of Roman London's surviving tombs commemorate soldiers. The rapid prosperity which made it Roman Britain's most flourishing city, 'famous for the number of its business-men and traders', as Tacitus says, also turned London into a military target during Boudicca's uprising of AD 61. Suetonius Paulinus, arriving too late to defend the unwalled city, was obliged to evacuate it. London was sacked and burned before Boudicca could be defeated. But it buoyantly recovered from this catastrophe, as it was to do from another devastating fire some sixty-five years later.

After Boudicca's rebellion Colchester lost status, and in due course London became the official seat of Roman government in Britain. The procurator or chief financial administrator was already stationed there in the wake of these events, while the governor probably moved down in the late first century to a palace whose site is now overlaid by Cannon Street Station. So began the pattern whereby finance and commerce have taken practical and psychological precedence in London over affairs of state and administration. This tradition has had incalcul-able impact on British history.

London reached its first apogee of Roman prosperity in about the mid-second century, but then seems to have stagnated. By this period it possessed a spacious public forum stretching across what is now Gracechurch Street, with a basilica for official use – the largest Roman building known north of the Alps – along one side. There were ample public baths, and a twelve-acre fort had been built in the Cripplegate area, clear of the main cluster of population. All these were durable buildings, faced mainly in ragstone from Kent. The city itself consisted of streets whose lines have now mostly vanished, bordered by low houses chiefly of timber with wattle and daub infill and thatched or tiled roofs. Many interiors boasted garish plaster on the walls and green glass in the windows, while the best had mosaic pavements.

The population was of all types: chiefly first-generation immigrants from provinces of the Empire or Romanized Celts, working as merchants, craftsmen, officials, seamen, soldiers or slaves. They were united by Roman administration and by the Latin language, which was widely written as well as spoken. Life was competi-tive, commercial and eventful. The wharves, spreading along the river east and west of the bridge, were vital to the city's welfare, bringing in wine, oil and pottery and taking out corn and many raw materials. There were entertainments of all kinds, many no doubt held in an amphitheatre recently located in Guildhall Yard. Wor-ship embraced not only the official Roman deities but also Celtic ones and, in later centuries, some of the popular cults from the east. One such was Mithraism, as the dramatic post-war discovery of the Walbrook Mithraeum with its exotic sculptures, attests. Christian-ity was another, though it made scant impact during the Roman period.

Around AD 200 a city wall was built from the Tower area round to the mouth of the Fleet river. Encompas-sing more than the built-up area, it may at first have seemed an imposing extravagance. But as Roman power fragmented, it proved its worth. After years of peaceable obscurity, London reappears in the history books from the late third century, when strains began to beset the empire. For short periods coins were minted in London, and it even acquired the name Augusta in recognition of its importance. Several emperors, including Constantius Chlorus (whose relief of London in 296 prompted the first known depiction of the city, on a commemorative medallion), visited London to reorganize the administ-ration of Britain and bolster defences against marauders. In due course the city wall was strengthened with bastions and a new line was even added along the river. But by the end of the fourth century the citizens were faring badly. A damaging raid in 369 may have started the rot. People began to drift away, while those who remained seem to have taken deserted areas into cultiv-ation. The *coup de grâce* occurred in the decade after 401, when troops were progressively withdrawn from Britain to defend Italy. Thereafter London fell into decay. Economic activity collapsed, the waterfront was allowed to silt up and an impoverished population was left to eke out a living in a town whose circumstances and history are shrouded in mystery for more than two centuries.

MEDIEVAL LONDON

The walled area of London was never a proper mid-Saxon town. But recent excavations show that an alternative Saxon London did exist from the seventh century, in the shape of trading and manufacturing sites close to the river along the Strand, between the Roman city and Westminster. This loose ribbon development foreshadowed events four hundred years later when Edward the Confessor, the penultimate Saxon king, transferred his residence to Westminster and started rebuilding a small abbey there on a grand scale. In this way, suburban Westminster became (at first in tandem with Winchester) the seat of national government. Hence developed the historic tension, palpable still, between an inward-looking centre of authority at Westminster and the ebullient, unruly, trade-oriented City of London. In due course the lines of transport between London and Westminster became means of mediation and dialogue between them, with the trades of administration, law and information clustering around Whitehall, the Strand and Fleet Street.

But first there had to be security enough for the ancient city's fortunes to revive. This began in the late ninth century as London came within the orbit of Alfred's Wessex, survived bouts of renewed piracy (including, if the story is credited, the breaking down of London Bridge by the questionably sainted Olaf in 1014) and got into its stride after the Norman Conquest. By then the enclosed city was again London's undisputed nucleus, with a street layout quite different from the Roman plan and a thriving pattern of trade. To contain and defend it, the Normans built the core of the Tower of London at the eastern end of the circuit of walls and two long-vanished strongholds, Baynard's Castle and Montfichet's Tower, at the west end in the Blackfriars area.

The special characteristic of medieval London was not its strongholds but its churches and parishes. Christianity returned to London in 604, when King Ethelbert founded St Paul's Cathedral. Few very early churches are known, but in the eleventh and twelfth centuries they proliferated. In time there were over a hundred churches and parishes, more than in any comparable European city. They reflect a strong pattern of localism in London life, as does the system of city wards dating back to the same period. At first most churches were humble, simple structures, which later Gothic ambition embellished with towers and aisles. Today, the tiny St Ethelburga's, Bishopsgate, best conveys the atmosphere of the local city churches once so common.

In contrast, the great churches and abbeys of medieval London were symbols of private munificence or monas-

One of the earliest known views of London shows the Tower in the fifteenth century. Behind it, London Bridge is crammed with houses. The man writing in the White Tower is Charles, Duke of Orléans, taken prisoner at Agincourt in 1415 and held in the Tower for 25 years. The picture illustrated a book of his poems.

tic ambition and laid claim to a loftier style of architecture to match. The nave of St Bartholomew the Great is the noblest example of such a Norman foundation, begun in 1123 with royal support by the former 'courtly parasite' Rahere as the kernel of a hospital and priory in a sordid quarter of London. A little later, when the Gothic style arrived from France, came the circular nave of the Temple Church, to be followed by Henry III's proud reconstruction of Westminster Abbey. Southwark Cathedral, formerly a priory, is another prominent extra-mural survival of this class. Though these churches remain as witnesses to London's ecclesiastical wealth, they are a mere fragment of what has been lost, like the monasteries of Blackfriars, Whitefriars, Charterhouse and Holy Trinity, Aldgate, and above all Old St Paul's itself, rebuilt magnificently between 1220 and 1340. Of secular Gothic building on this plane of artistry we have today only Westminster Hall, reconstructed between 1394 and 1402 by Henry Yevele and Hugh Herland with a sumptuous oak roof of unparalleled scale.

Secular organization in London marched apace with the parish system from the twelfth century. The constant cry of the city's rich men, as in all medieval communities, was for self-government and exemption from arbitrary

London in 1561

Maps of pre-Elizabethan London must be constructed from painstaking research, but from the 1550s, contemporary maps improve. This one derives from a map published in Germany in 1572, itself based on a more detailed survey of some ten years earlier. London has changed little since the Middle Ages.

At this date, Elizabeth I has been on the throne three years and has yet to consolidate her position. London remains largely within its walls, though to the west the population has long spilt out around Smithfield and Fleet Street. Ribbon development links the City with the royal enclave of Whitehall and Westminster and members of the nobility vie for the convenient and spacious plots between the Strand and the river; the original Somerset House, built by Edward VI's ill-fated Lord Protector, is among these. On the south bank, Southwark and Bermondsey stretch south and east of London Bridge. They are thriving suburbs, reliant on milling, brewing, inns and the rough beginnings of the Elizabethan entertainment industry. The medieval palaces of two great prelates, those of the Archbishop of Canterbury at Lambeth and of the Bishop of Winchester at Southwark stand clear of the city in proud independence, a reminder of the political power of the sixteenth-century clergy. To the north, development is starting to edge into the Spitalfields area.

In the City itself, the main arteries of communication run east–west. All roads are irregular. The widest, like Eastcheap and Cheapside, are often blocked with market stalls, while others have permanent free-standing buildings in the middle. Densest of all is London Bridge, whose many pontoons are needed to withstand the weight of its houses. So soon after the abolition of the monasteries in the 1530s, the sites of the various religious houses have not yet all been engulfed. Austin Friars, Holy Trinity Priory, Whitefriars, Bridewell, and the 'Convent Garden' north of the Strand are among those still recognisable. Dominating the City is the medieval St Paul's Cathedral, which lost its spire after being struck by lightning in 1561. The ancient square mile is bounded not only by its well-maintained and gated wall, but by a ditch which runs from Aldersgate to the Tower. On the west the Fleet River performs the same function, while doubling as a sewer. Along the Thames, houses and warehouses come down to the water's edge, with few inlets or jetties for mooring except Queenhithe. Only the wall and the Tower of London itself give the impression that London is organized or planned in any modern sense.

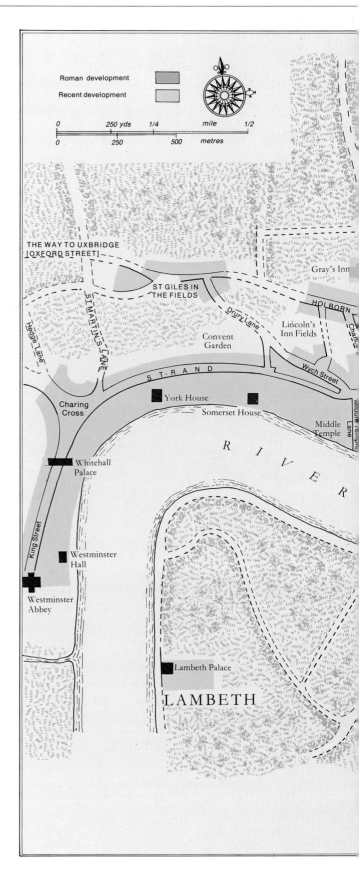

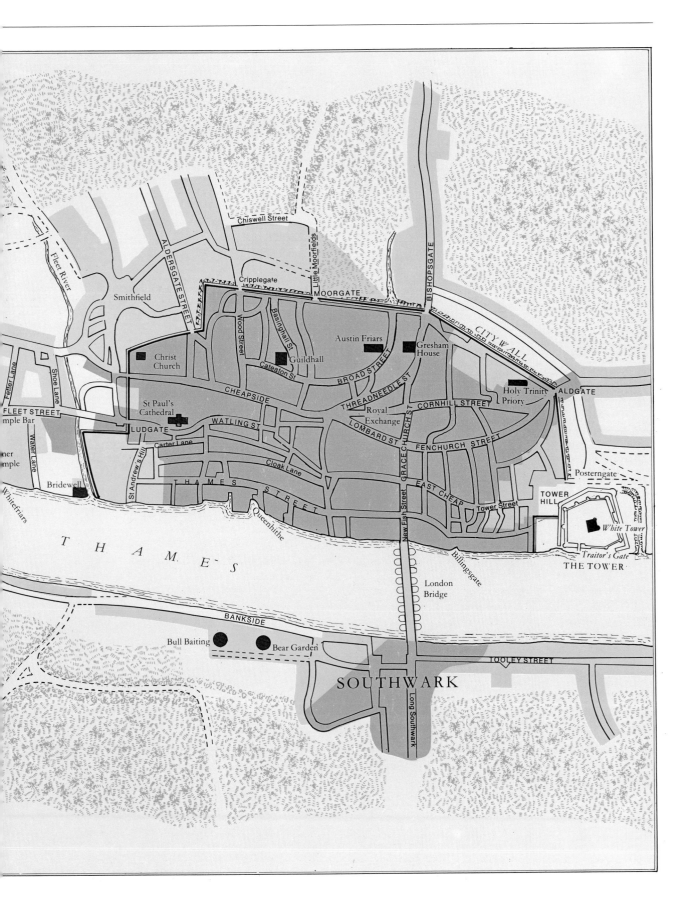

Chiswell Street

Fleet River

ALDERSGATE STREET

Cripplegate

Little Moorfields

MOORGATE

BISHOPSGATE

CITY WALL

Smithfield

Wood Street

Basinghall St

Austin Friars

Gresham House

Christ Church

Guildhall

Cateaton St

BROAD STREET

Holy Trinity Priory

ALDGATE

Fetter Lane

Shoe Lane

CHEAPSIDE

THREADNEEDLE ST

CORNHILL STREET

FLEET STREET

St Paul's Cathedral

WATLING ST

Royal Exchange

Temple Bar

LUDGATE

Carter Lane

LOMBARD ST

GRACECHURCH ST

FENCHURCH STREET

Water Lane

Inner Temple

Cloak Lane

EAST CHEAP

Posterngate

Whitefriars

Bridewell

THAMES STREET

New Fish Street

Tower Street

TOWER HILL

Queenhithe

Billingsgate

White Tower

Traitor's Gate

THE TOWER

T H A M E S

London Bridge

BANKSIDE

Bull Baiting

Bear Garden

TOOLEY STREET

SOUTHWARK

Long Southwark

taxation. It was achieved in fits and starts, brought on usually by the weakness of kings or their need for money. London took advantage of the civil war between Stephen and Matilda to inch towards the status of a 'commune' in about 1140. Then, by means of a bargain with Richard I's brother John in 1191, the city acquired its first mayor, Henry Fitzalwin. When John himself became king, got into difficulties with his barons and was pressed into signing Magna Carta, London was able to wrest further independence. Twenty-four aldermen began to advise the mayor and in time came to represent defined city wards. So evolved the core of the city's government – a framework restricted to the ancient area and oblivious of the suburbs beyond. A modest guild-hall supplied this rudimentary government's early wants, to be rebuilt more lavishly in the fifteenth century.

Extracting such privileges depended on the power of London's wealth. By the late twelfth century, when William Fitzstephen wrote his colourful panegyric on London and praised its far-flung trading connections, the city was on its way to being one of the great ports of the world. The nature of that trade was always shifting. Fur, skins and slaves were among London's main commodities while the Vikings dominated the seas. Cloth, wine, linen and fish were important once freer exchange with Europe opened up; and after 1100 the export of wool, usually via Flanders, assumed outstanding value. Incoming goods came in either at Billingsgate near London Bridge (rebuilt in stone with a gated drawbridge between 1176 and 1205) or Queenhithe further west, and were regulated from a riverside customs house. The main market street for retailing was Cheapside, which was divided into sections for various goods and attracted craftsmen to the streets around it. Because of its function, Cheapside in about 1245 acquired London's first reliable water supply, piped via a conduit from the Tyburn brook. As in other cities, specialist trades congregated in particular districts – clothiers, for instance, in the Smithfield area where Bartholomew Fair was held.

Credit was crucial to medieval London. The Jews, who arrived with the Normans, specialized in lending to monarchs and merchants alike. After their expulsion in 1290, the Milanese became the acknowledged experts in financing foreign trade. Foreign and native groups among traders and craftsmen tended to live and stick together. In this way late medieval London became a cosmopolitan patchwork, consisting of exclusive communities organized in defence of their interests and dependents. Such in their earliest form were the parish fraternities and the city guilds or livery companies. From the fourteenth century the richer trade guilds started to

devise more effective restrictions for their crafts and better administration of charitable funds and property under their control. Hence began the long tradition of building city livery halls, of which the best medieval survival is that of the Merchant Taylors.

Though nobody can be sure how many people lived in medieval London, it seems likely that the city touched some 40–50,000, perhaps the same as its Roman peak, in the fourteenth or fifteenth century. If so, London was one of the largest cities of Europe but a good deal smaller than Naples, Venice or, above all, Paris. Plague reduced numbers in the 1340s, after which came a lull, to be followed by unprecedented immigration and expansion under the Tudors.

TUDOR AND STUART LONDON

The first trustworthy bird's-eye views and maps of London date from around 1550. By then the city itself, still walled and gated, was dense indeed, with precious few patches of open ground. The times were disturbed, but London was prospering. As a consequence newcomers poured into the city, pressing the population up to some 200,000 by 1600. Owners of ampler properties along the main streets squeezed minuscule tenements in 'courts' on to every available piece of back land, at growing risk to safety and health. London Bridge, the busiest and most valuable thoroughfare of all, was jam-packed with buildings and shops. Most houses were still individual, piecemeal affairs, timber-built, of three storeys at most, long and narrow and with their gable-ends turned to the streets. Retailing, manufacturing and warehousing were carried on for the most part within or behind such houses. Precision crafts like fine metalwork, weaving, document-copying and the new trade of print-setting tended to migrate to the top floors where light was good, whereas noxious or noisy jobs like tanning, slaughtering and stabling took place in yards. As yet few houses had special shopfronts, and storage was consigned to cellars, ground floors and garrets. Coal had become widely available for heating and manufacture by 1500 and its sooty smoke was being cast up into the atmosphere from the myriad stone or brick chimneys put up on new houses or added to old ones.

Since the time of the first mayor the city authorities had striven to regulate buildings and sanitation. By banning thatched roofs and making rules about party walls they had some success against the ever-present threat of fire. But their powers of enforcement were poor and they had to contend with the individualism of ownership and building traditions. Some improvements stemmed from private initiative, like the 'longhouse', a capacious Thames-side public privy built in the fifteenth century by Dick Whittington's executors. Outside the

city limits, the writ of the Corporation did not run. It adopted a dog-in-the-manger attitude towards the suburbs, procuring periodic laws to ban suburban building in its own economic interest, while refusing to extend its boundaries for fear of political dilution. From the later Tudor period monarchs were obliged to take note of crowding and disorder in Westminster as well. A flurry of proclamations and parliamentary acts between 1580 and 1617 addressed these issues – without great effect. The prohibitions on building could always be evaded on payment of a fine, so that they became largely revenue-raising devices for the Crown.

Tudor London covered a broader canvas than the Roman or medieval city. The 'king's works' of Henry VII and Henry VIII, large suburban builders both, were dotted from east to west along the ribbon of the river – the great artery for those whose work lay with boats or who could pay the thousands of watermen plying their wherries along or across it. At Greenwich, far to the east, were the three quadrangles of Henry VIII's favourite palace. Nearby in the hamlets of Deptford and Woolwich he constructed dockyards to build his ambitious navy, so creating the basis of London's larger shipbuilding industry. Blackwall Yard, on the northern bank, opened a little later. From these yards, enterprising sea captains ventured out in search of a wider world of commerce and discovery – Willoughby and Chancellor in 1553 to seek a north-east passage and lay the basis of the Muscovy Company, the East Indiamen from the 1590s and Captain John Smith in 1606 to Virginia. Heavier shipping crept steadily eastwards from the City towards these yards. In 1550 there were big boats at Poplar and Ratcliff. Already these suburbs were taking on the darker characteristics of the future East End,

The coronation procession of Edward VI from the Tower of London (*left*) to Westminster Abbey for his coronation on 19 February 1547. From a painting by Samuel Grimm (1734–94) the Swiss watercolourist. The city appears much as it would have done throughout the medieval period.

John Stow complaining in his *Survey of London* of a 'filthy strait passage, with alleys of small tenements, or cottages, built, inhabited by sailors' victuallers' running most of the way from the Tower to Ratcliff.

Further west, development was more congenial. At Westminster Henry VII added his glorious Lady Chapel to the Abbey. His son improved and embellished Whitehall Palace nearby and, further inland, built St James's Palace in place of a suburban leper hospital. Well up river lay the palace of Sheen or Richmond, reconstructed after a fire in 1499. Beyond comes Hampton Court, started by Cardinal Wolsey, purloined from him by his monarch when he fell from favour and then extended. Hampton Court and St James's Palace were both built in brick, still then a rare and costly material but gradually to become dominant in London. Where kings led, others followed from choice or necessity. Sir Thomas More moved up river from the City to Chelsea in 1520, partly for its comfort and amenities but also for quick access by boat to the royal presence. Most of the mansions and villas which sprang up along the Thames over the next two centuries, such as Sir Thomas Gresham's Osterley, were more than pleasure palaces; they were also rich commuter homes, sited to take advantage of good river transport.

With the turbulent onset of the Reformation, the tone of London turned secular. Church-building stopped abruptly after 1530 and only recommenced when the Great Fire forced it upon the city. The suppression of

London in 1666

The suburban eruption of London was given dramatic impetus by two events early in the reign of Charles II. First came the Great Plague of 1664–5. This unusually prolonged epidemic is estimated to have claimed the lives of 100,000 citizens. Those who could afford it moved temporarily away from the centre. Some doubtless failed to return, finding better and safer accommodation outside the walls.

Then came the Great Fire of September 1666. Almost all of the City of London within the walls was consumed, as well as a sizeable extra-mural district around Fleet Street, Shoe Lane and Fetter Lane. Only the Aldgate and Tower areas of the City escaped. The result was utter devastation of London's densest and most historic core. Ninety per cent of its ninety-seven churches and fifty-one livery halls and perhaps seventy per cent of its houses were destroyed. Among complete losses were St Paul's Cathedral, the Royal Exchange, Christ's Hospital and that grim trio of prisons, Newgate, the Fleet and Bridewell. The Guildhall, though severely damaged, survived to be patched and repaired. The houses at the north end of London Bridge were destroyed, though the structure itself was saved from collapse. Most major buildings were reconstructed under Wren, though the number of churches was much reduced.

The map shows how irregular was the pattern of destruction over the four hundred-plus acres affected. The fire started just east of London Bridge, but prevailing winds fanned it north and west along and often across the narrow, closely packed streets. The masonry city wall and gates appear to have been no obstacle to its progress, though selective demolitions by means of explosion were used to impede its advance.

A hundred years earlier the loss would have been greater. As it was, the Elizabethan and early Stuart expansion of London into Bishopsgate, Moorfields, Smithfield and Holborn and further west into Westminster (see next map) allowed a number of those who had lost their homes to find accommodation nearby. Southwark too escaped, though it was to suffer a devastating fire of its own ten years later. The pattern of the City's commercial life, while inevitably disrupted, was not brought to a standstill. Markets were soon in operation again, and there is no suggestion that the trading centre or the quays suffered as a result of the fire. Nevertheless the Great Plague and the Great Fire marked a turning point. Many citizens never returned to the City, and it never regained its former importance as a centre of population.

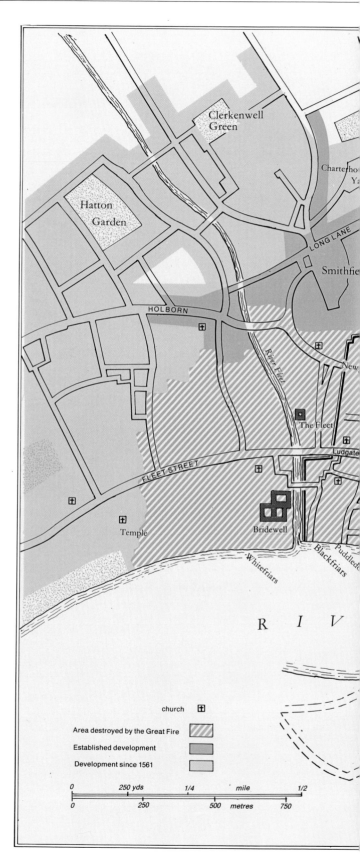

church ⊞

Area destroyed by the Great Fire

Established development

Development since 1561

0   250 yds   1/4   mile   1/2

0   250   500 metres   750

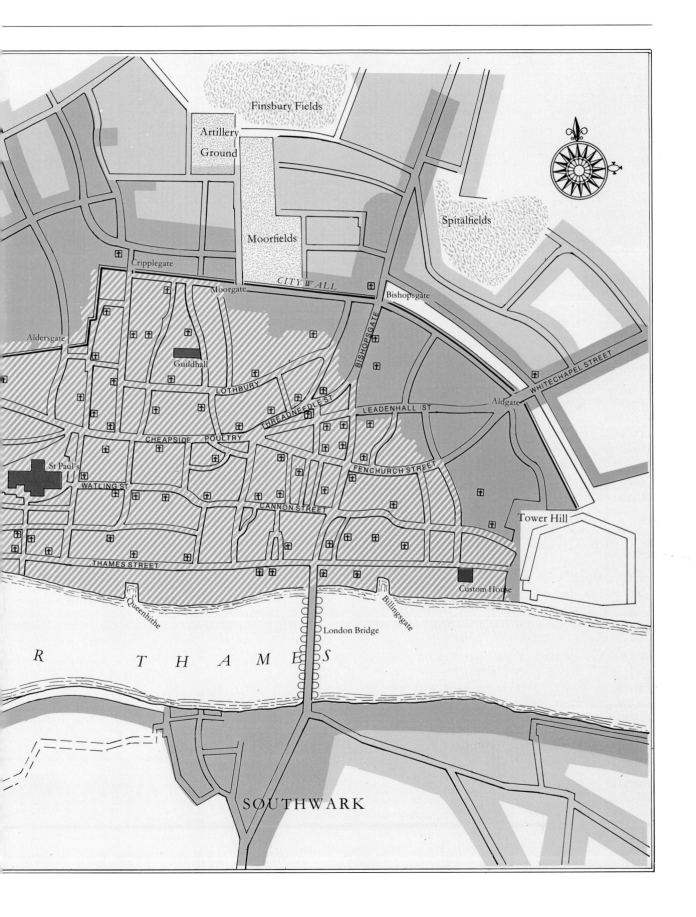

Finsbury Fields

Artillery
Ground

Spitalfields

Moorfields

Cripplegate

CITY WALL

Moorgate

Bishopsgate

Aldersgate

WHITECHAPEL STREET

Guildhall

LOTHBURY

Aldgate

THREADNEEDLE ST

LEADENHALL ST

CHEAPSIDE   POULTRY

FENCHURCH STREET

St Paul's

WATLING ST

CANNON STREET

Tower Hill

THAMES STREET

Custom House

Queenhithe

Billingsgate

London Bridge

R   T   H   A   M   E   S

SOUTHWARK

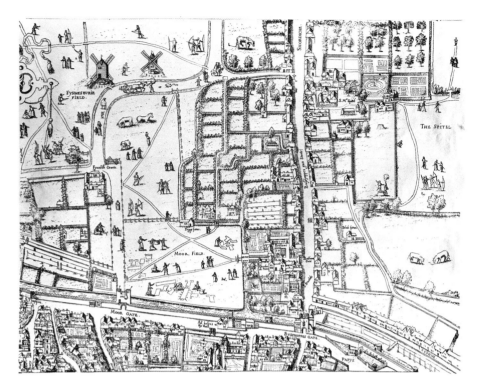

LEFT One of only two remaining sheets of the oldest surviving map of London, drawn in 1559. It shows Bishopsgate and Moorgate, two of the northern gates of the City, whose wall is bounded by a moat. Laundresses are at work in Moorfields and there are two windmills in Finsbury.

RIGHT Inigo Jones's drawing of his Banqueting House in Whitehall, completed in 1622, one of London's most admired buildings. On the left is Whitehall Gate, an entrance to the old palace.

London's religious houses had profound effects. Some, like Charterhouse and Bermondsey Abbey, became homes of the newly rich, others were turned into schools (Christ's Hospital) or hospitals proper (St Thomas's). But most were either subdivided or destroyed and their generous sites built upon, making overcrowding worse. The Reformation also changed the pattern of property-holding, giving power to a class of commercially inclined Protestant merchants and speculators. Symbolic of this change was Gresham's Royal Exchange (1566–70), the most successful innovation of the Elizabethan city. A meeting place for traders and their backers, it was modelled on the Bourse at Antwerp, where political and religious strife caused the collapse of Europe's former financial centre. In contrast to the livery companies' halls, it pointed to a more open model for business life. It was also the first public building in London to adopt a classical arcade, questionable in northern climates but preferable to the open street where transactions had previously taken place.

Few houses of scale or sophistication were built in the City proper after the Reformation, since rich people now preferred the greater peace, space and health obtainable outside the walls. Instead, the Elizabethan period saw the development of an indigenous mercantile architecture which almost parodied what had gone before, with overhanging storeys, bulging windows and comically carved corbels. Sir Paul Pindar's house from Bishopsgate, preserved in the Victoria & Albert Museum, displays the manner well. The larger London inns also took to this style. As precursors of the modern hotel, they were becoming the focus for passenger travel and long-distance cartage in the new four-wheeled vehicles. It was in the galleried innyards too that the most famous spectacle of the age, the Elizabethan theatre, was born. London's theatres soon found an independent form, while keeping their inn-like quality. Such were the Rose, Globe and Swan in flourishing, suburban Southwark and the Fortune in Finsbury, all built outside the City where public playhouses and entertainments were tightly controlled.

The mode of life that developed in Elizabethan London evolved but did not radically alter under the early Stuart kings and the Commonwealth. People continued to pour in from the provinces and abroad. James I's efforts to limit this met with scant success. One idea of his was to encourage the nobility to spend more time in the country. It was as well for London that he failed, since courtly and aristocratic expenditure contributed to urban prosperity. James and his son Charles I were less adept at bargaining with the City than Elizabeth had been. The tensions that ensued were a factor in precipitating the Civil War, climax of the time-honoured confrontation between Westminster and the City. At the start of hostilities in 1641 the City's leaders were far from united against the King. But a combination of efficient organization by the supporters of Parliament, purging of the Corporation, Protestant mercantile sentiment and financial self-interest pre-vailed. In the end the Commonwealth proved a difficult period, with high taxation and the collapse of court life leaving the city drab and austere. London was quick to welcome Charles II's return in 1660.

In one visible way Charles I's reign did mark a break with the past and that was in standards of street

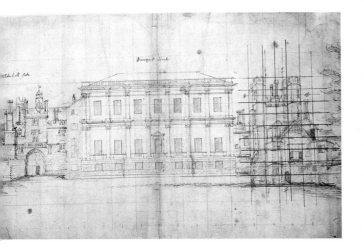

architecture. Inigo Jones, the court architect, had already put Tudor vulgarity to shame with two impec-cable, eye-opening visions of Italian elegance, the Queen's House at Greenwich and the Banqueting House in Whitehall. In the 1630s two speculative developments in Holborn – groups of houses in Great Queen Street and on the west side of Lincoln's Inn Fields – showed what the authority of classicism combined with regular brick fronts might do for high-class housing. But the test of the new architecture was the Piazza at Covent Garden, developed under royal licence from 1631 by the 4th Earl of Bedford. Here Jones supplied a church – cheap, plainly Protestant, but imposing – and three sides of arcaded brick housing to be let on long leases, round an open space for amenity. The result, though never so complete or orderly as it looks in engravings, was the first London square. It was over thirty years before any landowner had the funds or daring to imitate Covent Garden, but it provided a model for Georgian and Victorian leasehold development on great estates.

FROM THE GREAT FIRE TO THE REGENCY

In the later seventeenth century, London emerged from its medieval chrysalis into a city recognizably the one it is today. One devastating event and some subtler insti-tutional changes set off this transformation. The event was the Great Fire of 1666, which destroyed a huge arc from London Bridge northwards and westwards to Fleet Street. The changes were a decline in the City Corporation's power, balanced by the rise of the modern City money market.

The fire, complete and calamitous for citizens at the time, in the long term worked for London's good. No longer could obstructed streets, spewing gutters and stinking cellars be tolerated for want of a viable plan of reform. Since London had to be rebuilt, here was the chance to implement long-term remedies. Ambitious proposals to replan the city were presented by Sir Christopher Wren, John Evelyn and Robert Hooke, but stood no prospect of success; existing property rights, the need to rebuild swiftly and lack of ready money precluded any radical change of layout. But the oppor-tunity for a better infrastructure and improved building laws was fruitfully seized. The reconstructed streets had regular frontages and a set of uniform widths. Pave-ments and gutters were decently defined, proper sewers for rainwater laid down and arrangements for cleansing reformed. The City used the disaster to plan some port improvements, turning the mouth of the stinking Fleet river into a canal with wharves alongside and trying to reorder stretches of the Thames frontage, in the vain hope of competing with the new moorings down river.

The buildings which rose from London's rubble looked dramatically different from their predecessors. They had to be of brick and stone, with storeys of specified heights and walls, floors and roofs of sufficient thickness. These stipulations, the first to be effectively 'policed' by surveyors, were the origins of a system of building control which not only led to the distinctive form of the London terraced house, but also made London in structural terms the safest great city in the world. The models for the new style of sash-windowed, brick-fronted house were not Italian but Dutch, and elicited a neat but undemonstrative street architecture. In the City, little post-Fire housing survives, but its spirit can still be captured in the slightly later terraces of Great Ormond Street (Bloomsbury), Queen Anne's Gate (Westminster) and the weavers' streets of Spitalfields.

To save rebuilt London from banality, some sparks of individuality were needed. The Monument, that bizarre, flame-topped column in commemoration of the Fire, was one. But the City churches, conceived by the energetic Wren and his band of helpers, were the fuller response. Enough of them remain for us to savour their beauty, atmosphere and intelligence. They suggested how a distinctively Anglican church might be planned and decorated, using the best craftsmanship. Above all they stood out for their public presence, as connected incidents in a city still low enough for their towers and Baroque steeples – classical variations on a Gothic theme – to answer one another across the rooftops. Far above

The West End in 1682

By the 1680s the rebuilt City of London was back in business. Charles II needed the City's financiers to retain the precarious Stuart hold on the throne during the years after the Restoration, as much as they needed his support and encouragement after the Great Fire. Yet by the 1680s Westminster, with the advantages of open space and the royal seats of Whitehall and St James's, was expanding so fast that it was beginning to vie with the City as the hub of London.

This map is based on an excerpt from William Morgan's masterly survey of London, Westminster and Southwark, published in 1682 and the most accurate record of London up to then. Next to the river it shows some survivors of the old Strand palaces of the aristocracy, including Northumberland House and Salisbury House; another of the series, York House, has just been replaced by streets and terraces developed by the dubious Nicholas Barbon. On the Strand itself is the New Exchange (1608–9), a high-class shopping centre. Whitehall Palace to the south is still the centre for royal administration. Next to it is St James's Park, newly landscaped in the French taste. At its western edge, St James's Palace became the prime royal residence in Westminster after Whitehall Palace burnt in 1698.

North of the line of the Strand are the new developments: Covent Garden, laid out on the Earl of Bedford's freeholds in the 1630s and, north and west, the Restoration squares that carried on the Covent Garden tradition. These include Leicester Fields, Soho Square and, most ambitious of the set, St James's Square, instigated by the Earl of St Albans in the 1660s. It has its Wren church of St James's Piccadilly to the north, still being built in 1682, and its market to the east. The grid of streets laid out round these squares provides for regular plots with terraced houses in the post-Fire manner. Along Piccadilly, a new line of noble mansions replaces those of the Strand. They consist of Burlington House; Clarendon or Albemarle House, which succumbed to new streets soon after 1682; and Berkeley House, later Devonshire House. Elsewhere, Leicester House and Newport House are further grand residences but the latter, like York house and Clarendon House, is soon to disappear.

The large open space near Charing Cross is the Royal Mews, to the east of which stands the medieval St Martin's-in-the-Fields. Further north, St Giles's parish is becoming well built up, with Drury Lane and Long Acre past the peak of fashion they had enjoyed in the early Stuart period.

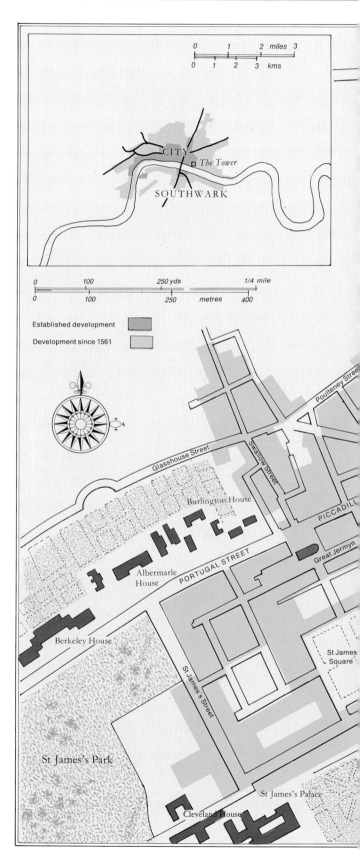

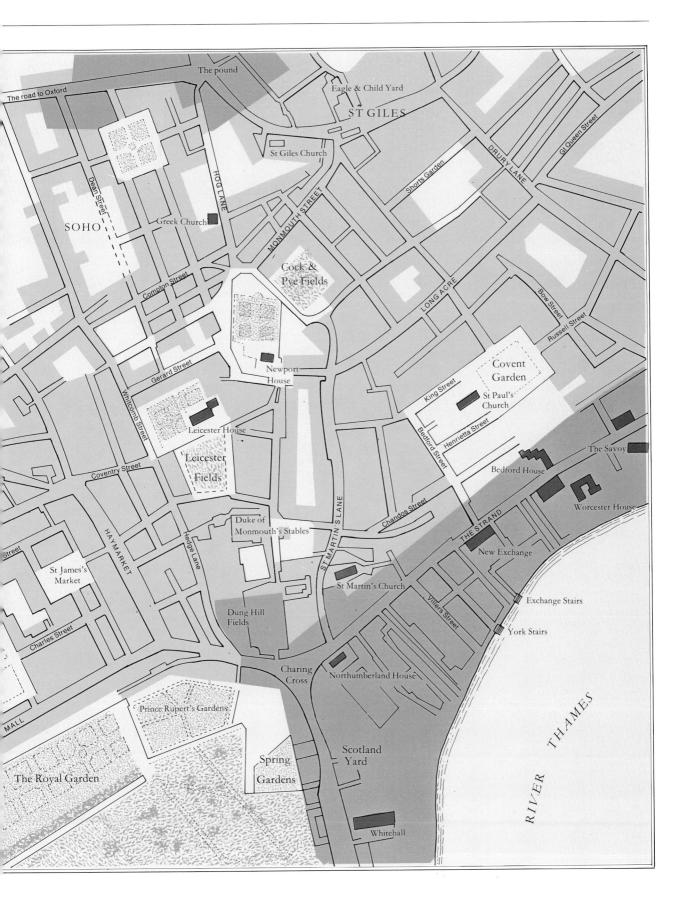

The road to Oxford

The pound

Eagle & Child Yard

ST GILES

St Giles Church

SOHO

Dean Street

HOG LANE

DRURY LANE

Gt Queen Street

Shorts Garden

Greek Church

MONMOUTH STREET

Compton Street

Cock & Pye Fields

LONG ACRE

Bow Street

Russell Street

Gerard Street

Newport House

Covent Garden

Whitcomb Street

King Street

St Paul's Church

Leicester House

Henrietta Street

Bedford Street

Coventry Street

Leicester Fields

Chandos Street

Bedford House

The Savoy

ST MARTIN'S LANE

Worcester House

HAYMARKET

Hedge Lane

Duke of Monmouth's Stables

New Exchange

Street

St James's Market

St Martin's Church

Villers Street

Exchange Stairs

Charles Street

York Stairs

Dung Hill Fields

Charing Cross

Northumberland House

RIVER THAMES

MALL

Prince Rupert's Gardens

Spring Gardens

Scotland Yard

The Royal Garden

Whitehall

everything rose St Paul's Cathedral, majestically rebuilt by Wren between 1675 and 1711, its Franco-Italian dome a symbol of an urban sophistication to which London could at last lay claim.

The rebuilding of the City proved a struggle. The Corporation, in financial straits since the Commonwealth, could regulate much but initiate little and had to rely upon the Crown not just for the help of experts like Wren but also for money from coal dues to fund

The Monument, in a 1798 engraving. Erected in 1677, it was designed by Wren to commemorate the Great Fire – hence the bronze flames at its summit. The church beyond it is Wren's St Magnus-the-Martyr.

reconstruction. In the event much of the City population, alienated by the twin disasters of plague in 1665 and fire in 1666, did not return. From the time of the Fire, the Corporation gradually lost credibility as London's natural government, though it long controlled some extramural activities like markets and the river.

This situation left merchants freer to focus on their main concern – business. The relative stability of Charles II's reign saw a revolution in the arts, wiles and disciplines of City finance, with the introduction of joint-stock companies, the growth of house and marine insurance, the beginnings of stockbroking and the rise of a recognizable banking profession. As always, the credit requirements of kings and governments did most to precipitate these changes. The modern, money-orientated city may be said to date from the founding of the Bank of England in 1694, in response to a demand for war funds from William III. By this time London, boosted by a fresh influx of skilled Protestant immigrants, was beginning to surpass Amsterdam as Europe's leading centre of trade. Many banking, insurance and broking houses sprang up, to be checked but by no means stopped by the South Sea Bubble 'crash' of the 1720s. At first these new businessmen foregathered in city livery halls, merchants' houses, or in the fashionable coffee houses of the post-Fire City, of which Lloyd's was one. It was long before they built offices for themselves.

The West End was the focus of fashionable London after the Great Fire. Grand houses appeared along Piccadilly and Pall Mall, and spacious districts with better amenities than the rebuilt City sprang up round the new squares of St James, Bloomsbury, the Red Lion, Leicester Fields and Soho. St James's, with its palace, its royal park (the first generally open to Londoners) and its square was the especial haunt of the court whores, fops and literati. Hence London spread north-westwards, encroaching after the accession of George I into Mayfair and Marylebone. After building began on the Grosvenor family's hundred acres of Mayfair, the biggest single freehold yet developed, London rapidly reached Hyde Park and there for a time was checked.

A mile or so to the west lay the village of Kensington, where a humble square grew up in the shadow of the suburban palace taken in 1689 by William III for his health. The early Georgian court was still peripatetic. Nobles, office-holders, functionaries, servants and hangers-on had to move around between Whitehall, St James's, Kensington, Kew, Hampton Court and Windsor, depending on circumstances and seasons. (Greenwich, which Charles II started to rebuild, was now off the circuit, having been replaced by a naval hospital after his death.) Most people obliged to be near the court tended for these reasons to rent lodgings. This encouraged a pattern of living whereby few but the very rich owned freeholds and many well-off families took simple town houses for only brief, seasonal periods. In these conditions the lucrative but perilous business of leasehold development and tenure fell into the hands of a specialized class of landlords, agents, surveyors, building craftsmen, solicitors and mortgagors – experts in the methods pioneered by the enterprising Nicholas Barbon after the Restoration. Since few of them were highly capitalized and all were subject to fluctuations in credit and demand, building tended to proceed piecemeal. Even the most orderly squares as yet boasted no uniformity of elevation.

The Georgian West End was far from exclusive and polite. Living conditions allowed little segregation of the classes, even in better districts. Servants lived cheek by jowl with masters and mistresses. Nearby stabling had to be provided, increasingly in a neat 'mews' directly behind the houses. Shops and markets, too, soon pressed close to good residential streets. Oxford Street, for instance, was already the world's longest shopping street by the 1780s, but unprepossessing and ill-regulated, with trades and crafts of all kinds carried on away from the frontage.

In the older districts, Georgian London was perilous indeed. The metropolitan depravity that Hogarth depicted was no caricature; poverty and misery were far worse in the 1730s than in Victorian times. Facilities for education and for the sick, insane or destitute were desperately lacking; many people lived together in a single room; public behaviour was rowdy, criminality pervasive and execution commonplace. The lot of the young was grim. Only one in four London children

London, the Middlesex and the remarkable Foundling Hospital which for a period admitted all children brought to its doors, only to find itself under siege.

Gradually, London became less barbarous. A secular reform movement instigated by the novelist Henry Fielding and his brother, both magistrates, led to some improvements in policing, sentencing and prisons, and more enlightened attitudes towards the causes of social problems. Better lighting, housing and water supply had their effect, as did the slow spread of prosperity and education. The window-shattering practices of radical John Wilkes's champions and the anti-Catholic riots of 1780 proved the last destructive gasps of the notorious London mob. In comparison, Victorian working-class agitation was tame. After the French Revolution, the authorities no longer feared mindless violence but the type of principled organization by artisans represented by the London Corresponding Society, which led to many thousands meeting at Spa Fields in 1816–17. London in the aftermath of the Napoleonic Wars was

could expect to survive beyond the age of five. Child abuse and child labour were rampant, while the old methods of apprenticeship were breaking down.

An influx of cheap gin after 1720 resulted in appalling alcoholism and brought matters to a crisis. Outside the City, responsibility for the poor fell to the individual parishes. For reasons of efficiency and economy, vestrymen came to believe that they should jettison the old traditions of 'outdoor relief' and farming out paupers to private contractors, and build parish workhouses, preferably outside the parish itself. The essentials of this system, despite much change and controversy, survived until workhouses were abolished in 1930. At the time they seemed a step forward – on a par with the rash of suburban hospitals established between 1720 and 1755, including Guy's, St George's, the Westminster, the

London in 1764, from an engraving by Patton. This is one of the best depictions of the City skyline, dominated by the spires of Wren's churches, that was to remain unaltered until the Blitz.

rife with political grievance and fears of spies and repression. But the plight of the poor was less desperate than in former centuries.

Not that Georgian London was all gloom, violence and suspicion. Pleasures, innocent or otherwise, could readily be had if you could pay for them. West End theatres, though still few in number, were an obsessive haunt of the fashionable and the literate, whose ideas about why they were there were often at odds. The Theatre Royal, King's Theatre and Covent Garden offered a farrago of opera, oratorio, serious drama, serious music, musical comedy and sheer spectacle. Such buildings were apt to burn down, so that only Benjamin

Mayfair, St Marylebone and Soho in 1784

During the eighteenth century, the power of aristocratic landowners increased at the expense of the monarchy. During the reigns of the first three Georges, the development of fashionable London became more organized. Owners employed surveyors and lawyers to oversee their estates, while financiers and builders learnt to play the risky game of speculation. The result was increased order, amenity and value at the price of a certain monotony.

The layout of the Georgian West End north and south of Oxford Street demonstrates this at a glance. The alignment of the streets round Hanover Square (1715) carries on unbroken to the hundred acres of the Grosvenor Estate (1720) and less confidently to the Harley Estate round Cavendish Square (1717). The Grosvenor Estate also provides the axis for the plan of the Portman Estate north of Oxford Street, started in the renewed Georgian building boom of the 1760s. There are some awkward joins, as where southern and northern Mayfair meet near Berkeley Square (1739), but the broad picture is of urban order, with good residential streets alternating with open-ended mews for stabling, and a fringe of major shopping streets like Bond Street, Oxford Street, Mount Street and Marylebone Lane. Each development has its church or chapel, but little else in the way of amenity. The square gardens are mostly accessible only to tenants of houses immediately adjacent.

To the west of Mayfair, Hyde Park is protected by a high wall. Tyburn Lane (later Park Lane) runs alongside it up to the gruesomely popular Tyburn Gallows, at the corner of Oxford Street and Edgware Road. Executions were held here until 1783, discouraging fashionable people from living too close.

At its northern extremity, London is neatly defined by the 'New Road' from Paddington, laid out in the 1750s by the government as a bypass. Marylebone is reaching out to it, notably via Portland Place, planned from 1778 by the Adam Brothers at rare width to preserve the view north from Foley House. Fitzroy Square, last of the Adams' speculations, has yet to be built, and Bedford Square, today the most complete and elegant of London squares, lacks its north side. The core of the British Library and British Museum collections are in Montagu House on Great Russell Street, awaiting the neo-classical pile which Robert Smirke will erect for them there in the 1820s.

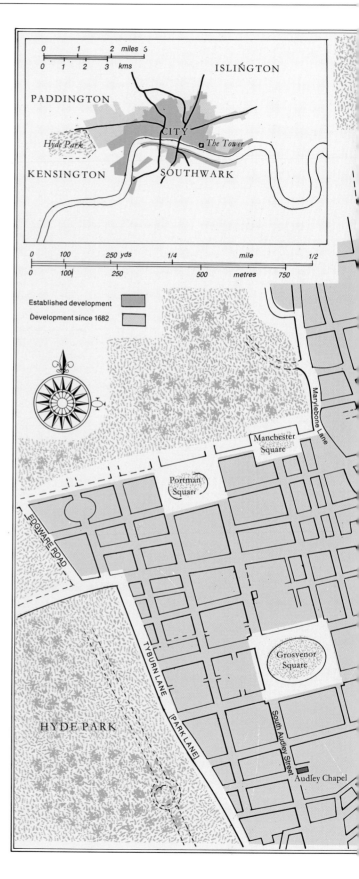

Established development

Development since 1682

Tottenham Court

LAMBS CONDUIT FIELDS

New Road from Paddington

PORTLAND PLACE

PORTLAND ROAD

TOTTENHAM COURT ROAD

Bedford House

Montagu House

Middlesex Hospital

RUSSELL STREET

Wimpole Street

HARLEY STREET

Bedford Square

GREAT

Vigmore Street

Cavendish Square

HIGH STREET

HIGH HOLBORN

Oxford Market

Soho Square

BROAD ST GILES

O X F O R D   S T R E E T

Argyle House

HOG LANE

OOK STREET

Hanover Square

NEW BOND STREET

Wardour Street

Dean Street

LONG ACRE

Grosvenor Street

Conduit Street

ST MARTIN'S LANE

Golden Square

Leicester House

Berkeley Square

SAVILE ROW

OLD BOND STREET

HAYMARKET

STRAND

Burlington House

PICCADILLY

The Royal Mews

JERMYN STREET

Royston House

Charing Cross

Wyatt's Theatre Royal of 1811–12 and Nash's Haymarket Theatre of 1820–1 still convey the intimate scale of the early London playhouses, usually all interior display with little show on the outside. Smart and exclusive clubs of all kinds – political, literary, gaming or purely social – had their heyday in this period, even if the architectural grandeur of the Athenaeum, the Carlton and the Reform along Pall Mall came a little later.

Of pleasure gardens there were two riverside rivals, Ranelagh at Chelsea and the bigger Vauxhall, which after 1750 you could reach either by boat or via Westminster Bridge, the first of five pre-Victorian crossings to smash the monopoly of London Bridge, damage the watermen's trade, and open up Lambeth to development. Suburban inns and spas like Bagnigge Wells and Sadler's Wells were, like Bath, first frequented

survival of the type, Bedford Square, strove for architectural unity across a series of house fronts. Since London street fronts are rarely seen head on or in mutual relation, such drawing-board elevations do not always tell.

One architect above all understood this – the theatrical John Nash. In a burst of invention between 1812 and 1835 Nash replanned a swathe of the West End on behalf of the Prince Regent, later George IV. Its backbone, Regent Street, connected the Prince's elegantly screened Carlton House with the new Regent's Park. Later the scheme was amended to take in the reconstruction of Buckingham Palace, the replacement of Carlton House with a pair of terraces, the layout of Trafalgar Square, and parts of the Strand. Not all this turned out well. Buckingham Palace brought humiliation to Nash's old age, while the workmanship behind his slick stucco

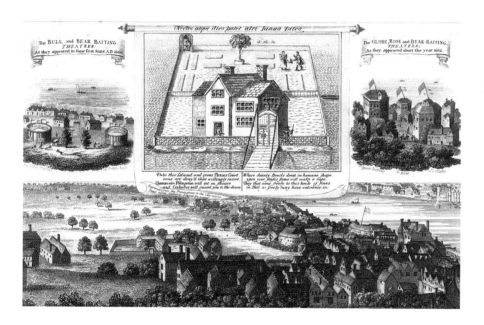

This 1818 print depicts the pleasures, licit and illicit, of Southwark in the mid-seventeenth century. The house at the top is a licensed brothel and the verse beneath it says:
> 'They that come freely to this house of sinne, In Hell as freely may have entrance in.'

for health, then for the entertainments that grew up around them. Further north, Hampstead on its hilltop first attracted Londoners from about 1700 to drink its chalybeate water. By the 1820s it was turning into the city's most picturesque suburb, a resort of poets, painters and intellectuals.

London's high point of aesthetic achievement in city planning came with the Regency. By then methods of estate development and house-building had been refined. Square followed square, street joined up with street. The building boom of the 1760s saw the first inkling of increased architectural ambition in such matters. The Adam brothers' Adelphi project, raised high between the Strand and the Thames, was the conspicuous call to arms. The schemes that followed, like the Adams' own Fitzroy Square or the one intact

fronts often left much to be desired. Yet Nash's ability to know how a block would bulk in profile or a vista would look from a distance bequeathed to London one of its most precious assets. Though Regent Street has been rebuilt the qualities of its line survive, while the villas and terraces of Regent's Park remain one of the great setpieces of Europe. Later developments in the tradition, even lordly Belgravia, seem impoverished in comparison.

Regent Street anticipated the many 'metropolitan improvements' attempted by the Victorians in search of better communications for London. It could only be undertaken by the Crown, since the existing authorities that governed London could not attempt it themselves. The vestries grappled with local duties, but increasingly these were confused by a layer of *ad hoc* authorities, turnpike trusts and sewer commissions whose remit crossed parish boundaries. For major undertakings, Parliament still had the decisive voice.

Thus it was with the provision of churches. A small spurt of activity after 1711 furnished outlying parishes with eight extravagantly Baroque, government-financed churches, among them St Martin's-in-the-Fields and three East End masterpieces by Hawksmoor. Thereafter enthusiasm waned; most new Georgian development was accompanied only by cheap 'proprietary chapels'. Fear of disorder and the growing strength of Nonconformity induced the Government to stir again in 1818. A national Act provided for a large number of cheap churches, of which London acquired some thirty. The better-looking ones were subsidized by their parishes, but many were centrally funded. They largely failed to attract the working classes back to Anglican church attendance and thus to respect for the existing order. Catholics and Nonconformists came to see the campaign as a subsidy for middle-class Anglicanism. In response to pressure, the duties of parishes were clearly split in the 1830s into secular and religious functions. All future church building had to be privately funded.

By 1830 London was at last more than a monotonous succession of streets and houses, with the occasional church to liven things up. In the east, an awesome succession of enclosed docks and stock-brick warehouses signalled the predominance of British commerce, shipping and engineering. Only the prettified remnants of the last-built of these, St Katharine's dock next to the Tower, now bear witness to the scale of these enterprises.

At that time London was not only the biggest city in the world, with a population of about a million in 1800, but also the world's largest manufacturing centre. Warehouses and works fringed the City, though most manufacturing had yet to shift into purpose-built premises. Institutions of government and finance, on the other hand, were now better housed. The Mint, the Custom House, the Post Office and the Bank of England all had their own dignified accommodation, the last in Soane's cavernous masterpiece. Somerset House, built from 1775 onwards, provided a core of ever-expanding government offices. There were new courts of law at Westminster and a formidably Piranesian prison at Newgate. Markets, theatres, hospitals, clubs and schools had all become familiar, specialized types of buildings. The British Museum was in process of acquiring a purpose-built home and a National Gallery was planned for Trafalgar Square. Even the university which London so long lacked had been embarked upon in Gower Street. Georgian London had seen a revolution in its facilities.

— VICTORIAN AND EDWARDIAN LONDON —

When Queen Victoria ascended the throne in 1837, London was still a network of quite parochial communities. Craft and casual workers were far more numerous than factory hands or clerks. The breweries, distilleries, engineering and shipbuilding firms dotted along the south bank of the Thames from Lambeth to Woolwich were the largest employees of skilled labour. The dock companies were their counterpart for casual work: they had no settled labour force but decided from day to day how many hands they required, thus sowing seeds of insecurity and demoralization among the meagre East End houses that grew up around their gates. Most Londoners, male or female, building workers, craftsmen, costermongers, coal-heavers, shopkeepers, street vendors, publicans, laundresses, domestics and prostitutes alike, led restricted, small-scale lives, seldom leaving their locality. Even along the ribbons of settlement put out into the suburban market gardens by the building boom of the 1820s, in Brompton, Kensington, Paddington, Kentish Town, Barnsbury, Islington, Poplar, Kennington and Camberwell, those who walked or rode into town to work were outnumbered by those who supplied their wants locally.

Yet the density and harshness of central London

Fleet Street, linking the City with the West End, has always been one of London's busiest arteries. When horses gave way to motor vehicles, it kept its nineteenth-century character until the 1980s, when tall office towers began to replace the four- and five-storey buildings, and the newspaper offices moved away.

Regent's Park in 1828

A glance at the plan of Regent's Park and its environs shows how the picturesque principles of planning adopted by John Nash revolutionized the whole approach to fashionable development of London's fringes. South of the New (Marylebone) Road is the dense, hard grid of Georgian streets. Beyond it, town and country mingle in a conception of elaborate artifice.

In 1809 the Crown's surveyor drew up proposals for developing Marylebone Park and for linking it with the West End via a new street along the existing line of Portland Place. The Prince Regent (George IV from 1820) chose Nash to translate this scheme into something visually imaginative, although the architect's preferred design was not fully realized. The landscaping of the park itself, the lake apart, was not extensive and had to be supplemented later; the Broad Walk north of Park Square, for instance, was reordered in the 1860s. Architectural pleasures were relegated to the edges, where Nash and his assistant Decimus Burton devised their inventive parade of stucco terraces. But there was more than architecture to the scheme. The Regent's Canal, linking the Grand Junction Canal from the Midlands with the Thames docks, bordered the park and came down to a canal basin behind Albany Street. Here was the scheme's working-class and service sector, which included a barracks, a hospital and other institutions. Entertainment was represented by the Diorama on the east side of Park Square, the unsuccessful Coliseum, and the 'Zoological Gardens' on the unfrequented north side of the park. Missing from Regent's Park at this time are the two exquisite Park Villages created north and east of the barracks.

On the Eyre Estate around St John's Wood, laid out at the same period as Regent's Park, detached and (for the first time) semi-detached houses appear in their own ample plots, and, wherever possible, the roads deviate from the rectangular formula suggested by economy. This approach represents the beginning of the British tradition of picturesque suburbia. It contrasts not only with the dense development to the south but also with the haphazard appearance of such an area as Paddington, still not completely built over. But this was the exception, not the rule. Lord Pratt's growing estate of Camden Town, though well north of London at the time of the map, shows every sign of the conventional grid being patiently filled in as economic opportunity arises. Only Mornington Crescent, begun in 1821 on Fitzroy–Southampton land, conveys an inkling of the new architectural sensibility.

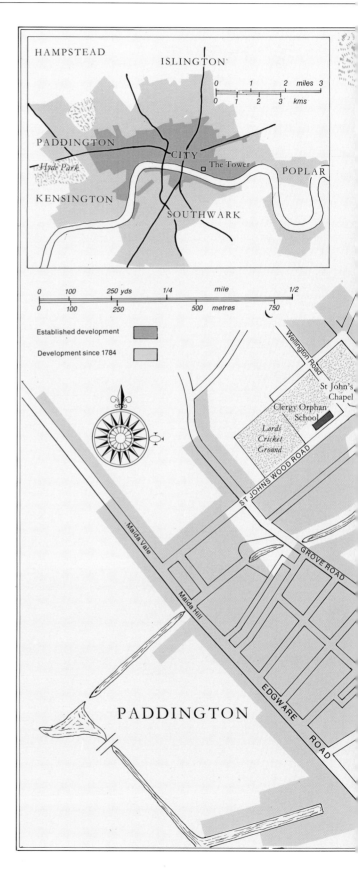

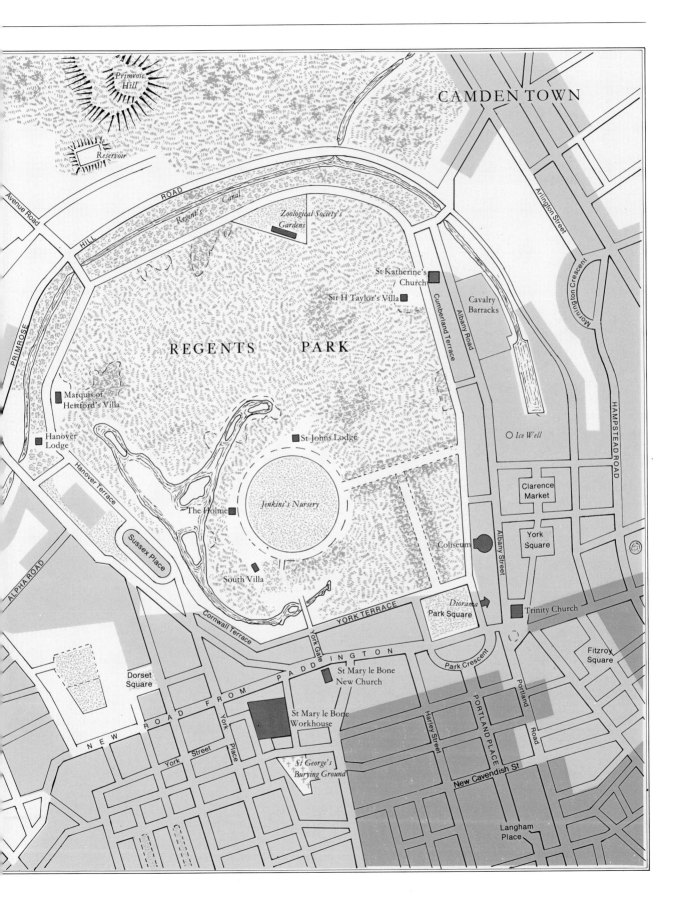

CAMDEN TOWN

Primrose Hill

Reservoir

Avenue Road

Regent's Canal

ROAD

HILL

PRIMROSE

Zoological Society's Gardens

St Katherine's Church

Sir H Taylor's Villa

Cumberland Terrace

Albany Road

Cavalry Barracks

Mornington Crescent

Arlington Street

HAMPSTEAD ROAD

REGENTS   PARK

Marquis of Hertford's Villa

Hanover Lodge

Hanover Terrace

St Johns Lodge

Ice Well

Clarence Market

York Square

The Holme

Jenkins's Nursery

Coliseum

Albany Street

Sussex Place

ALPHA ROAD

South Villa

Cornwall Terrace

YORK TERRACE

Diorama
Park Square

Trinity Church

Park Crescent

Fitzroy Square

Dorset Square

NEW

ROAD

FROM

PADD

York Gate

York Street

York Place

St Mary le Bone New Church

St Mary le Bone Workhouse

St George's Burying Ground

Harley Street

PORTLAND PLACE

Portland Road

New Cavendish St

Langham Place

encouraged those who could afford it to live as far out as possible. More would have done so but for the lack of transport. Georgian Londoners were good walkers because they had to be. After 1815 a haphazard system of short-stage coaches evolved, with high fares and few stops in the centre (where ill-regulated hackney carriages had enjoyed a monopoly since the seventeenth century). From 1833 the horse omnibus or 'box on wheels', a Parisian invention, was sanctioned. More than the railway, it was the omnibus that stimulated the spread of Victorian London. From 1855 the routes of the London General Omnibus Company crept along the main roads, fuelling development wherever they reached. At first these services were too spasmodic to allow better-off people to do without their own stabling. But with the addition of horse tramways, the spread of the hansom cab (precursor of the taxi) and the beginnings of a suburban railway system, the habit of keeping private horses began to die. By the time cars appeared on the streets, private horse-drawn transport for non-commercial use was all but obsolete in central London.

As for the railways, their early effect was to damage London. They struck at the city's heart, before offering it any relief. The first lines of the late 1830s were innocuous enough. Mostly they brought in long-distance traffic to suburban termini at Vauxhall, Paddington and Euston. The nearest to a commuter railway was the successful route from Greenwich to London Bridge.

As competition intensified, the companies raced for positions close to the centre. By 1875 a ring of termini had been created – Paddington, Victoria, Waterloo, Charing Cross, Cannon Street, London Bridge, Fen-

In the mid-nineteenth century, traffic in London Docks was growing rapidly. The new Customs House (*right*), with Smirke's façade, was completed in 1825 and Rennie's London Bridge, in the background, in 1831.

church Street, Liverpool Street, Broad Street, King's Cross, St Pancras and Euston. Many were magnificent monuments to railway engineering, and offered the novelty of luxurious hotel accommodation for the long-distance traveller. But they were extravagant in number and wasteful of space. They caused much destruction of property, particularly slum property, after Parliament started to use its powers over railway routes as a tool of slum clearance. Thus they added to overcrowding elsewhere and also increased traffic in the centre, putting extra pressure on the roads that linked them. The Metropolitan Railway, the world's first underground, finally took shape as a means of linking the railway termini. The first section from Paddington to Farringdon opened in 1863, but it was to be years before the 'Circle', the core of the London underground system, completed the link.

Roads, like railways, were used by the Victorians to destroy London slums, in the idle hope that slum-dwellers would find a better class of lodging elsewhere. The first such attempt was New Oxford Street, smashed through the wretched 'rookeries' of St Giles in the 1840s. Like Regent Street, this task fell to the Crown; but, if such 'improvements' were to continue, London needed a permanent authority to undertake them. In 1855 Parliament created the Metropolitan Board of Works, composed of nominees elected by parishes or district boards. The Board of Works was a step towards representative government for London, but its own idea of its role was more mundane. It possessed at first only basic, unglamorous powers: slum clearance, building regulation, road improvements and main drainage. In due course it took on extra tasks, such as the running of a proper municipal fire brigade under the flamboyant Captain Shaw.

Perpetually short of money, the Board of Works always had a bad press; yet it achieved much for London. Main drainage was its triumph. Savage cholera epidemics had underlined how urgently London needed a complete new system of sewers. After the 'Great Stink' of 1858, when Parliament was overwhelmed by the stench of river sewage, the Board's engineer, Joseph Bazalgette, brought forward a scheme for four great east-west lines of intercepting sewers, two on either side of the Thames, taken out to pumping stations beyond the East End. This huge task of purification was completed in a decade, adding as a bonus the Victoria Embankment from Westminster to Blackfriars on top of the lower northern interceptor.

The Board of Works laboured on until 1889 at its thankless task of reforming London's infrastructure. It could not rehouse those it displaced with its many road schemes. Instead, it relied on limited-dividend housing companies to build the grim but sanitary blocks of 'artisans' flats' dotted about London during its existence. But with housing and mortality as bad as ever, aiming a

road at a slum was plainly no solution. Instead, the railways were pressed to run cheap workmen's trains to the outskirts. Most of the companies resisted, but the Great Eastern Railway complied. After 1885 outer East London, in an arc from Hackney round to Ilford and East Ham, saw a profusion of small, two-storey artisans' houses on cheap land.

The London County Council, taking over from the Board of Works in 1889, pressed on with the policy of dispersal. After 1900 it bought and electrified tramways to lure people out of the centre and embarked on the first suburban municipal housing estates. By then the railways had at last completed an effective suburban network for the middle classes. An explosion of banking, insurance and financial services in the City after 1875 led to a great increase in the number of clerks, well paid enough to travel into work by tram or train, particularly from south London suburbs. Factories too were beginning to move away from the centre as they grew bigger, and voluntary movement and official policy alike began to draw people and jobs out of the centre. Inner London reached its peak of population at $4\frac{1}{2}$ million in 1901.

The eruption of late Victorian building was by no

Holborn Viaduct, opened in 1869, typified the robust and confident approach of Victorian designers to the new industrial arts. The two statues on the north side, seen here as the viaduct neared completion, represent commerce and agriculture. On the other side are science and fine arts.

Central London in 1891

London is at its densest in the 1890s. The Victorians have transformed the infrastructure of the city but failed to divest it of any of its teeming multitudes. Aldgate, Spitalfields and Whitechapel are crushed by unremitting immigration of the poor and a long tradition of casual employment and there are pockets of grim poverty and overcrowding in the district of Holborn.

In south London, the ancient origins of Southwark and Bermondsey can still be discerned by the irregular streets and plethora of lanes and yards. Tanning, brewing and distilling abound in these districts and other industries, notably printing, are steadily crossing the river to join them. Further west, Lambeth and Kennington show how promisingly they at first developed after 1750, with smart terraces lining the wide, straight roads built from the new Georgian bridges at Blackfriars, Waterloo and Westminster, converging at St George's Circus.

But by 1890 the whole area is in decline. Prime culprits for this are the railways. The lines into London Bridge (1836) and Waterloo (1848) have caused only slight damage, though the environs of both stations have suffered social decline. More destructive have been the extensions of the 1860s over the river from London Bridge to Charing Cross and Cannon Street, and from the south over Blackfriars Bridge to Holborn Viaduct and Farringdon. Similar encroachments into the central area can be seen at Fenchurch Street (1841) and the twin stations of Broad Street (1865) and Liverpool Street (1874). As well as increasing population densities by demolishing much property and blighting more, the termini have generated extra road traffic which has been met with new arteries such as Southwark Street, Commercial Street, Farringdon Road and Holborn Viaduct. A more beneficial road improvement is the Victoria Embankment, laid out by the Metropolitan Board of Works from Westminster to Blackfriars over the new sewer and underground railway, and extended into the heart of the City by Queen Victoria Street.

By 1891 most of Victorian London's public buildings are complete. The rebuilt Houses of Parliament face St Thomas's Hospital, ousted from Southwark by the railway. Officialdom is accommodated in purpose-built palaces around Whitehall; the Law Courts, completed in the 1880s, confirm the Strand as the centre of legal business, and the City Corporation is just completing a market-rebuilding programme. The Corporation's other great building project, Tower Bridge, is in progress, finally to be opened in 1894.

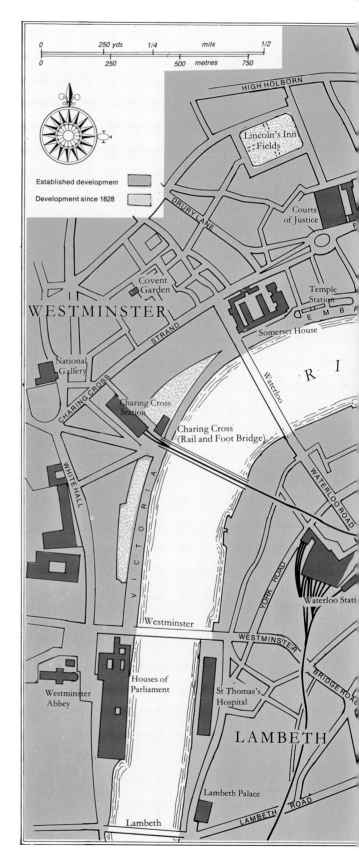

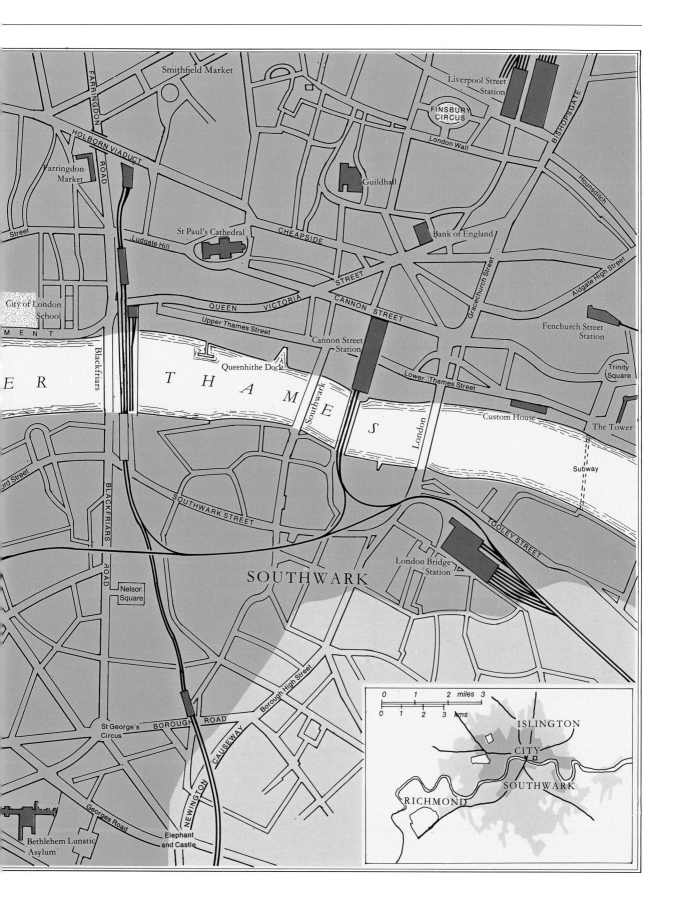

Smithfield Market

Liverpool Street
Station

FINSBURY
CIRCUS

London Wall

FARRINGDON ROAD

HOLBORN VIADUCT

BISHOPSGATE

Hounsditch

Farringdon
Market

Guildhall

Street

St Paul's Cathedral

CHEAPSIDE

Bank of England

Ludgate Hill

Gracechurch Street

Aldgate High Street

City of London
School

QUEEN   VICTORIA

Upper Thames Street

CANNON   STREET

STREET

Fenchurch Street
Station

M E N T

Blackfriars

Queenhithe Dock

Cannon Street
Station

Southwark

Lower   Thames Street

Trinity
Square

R I V E R   T H A M E S

London

Custom House

The Tower

Subway

BLACKFRIARS ROAD

SOUTHWARK STREET

TOOLEY STREET

SOUTHWARK

London Bridge
Station

Nelson
Square

St George's
Circus

BOROUGH   ROAD

BOROUGH HIGH STREET

NEWINGTON CAUSEWAY

Georges Road

Bethlehem Lunatic
Asylum

Elephant
and Castle

0   1   2 miles 3

0   1   2   3   kms

ISLINGTON

CITY

SOUTHWARK

RICHMOND

means confined to the suburbs. In the interests of sanitation, improvement and 'progress', swathes of earlier London were demolished. With a confidence born of technological advance and imperial achievement, most Victorians felt that anything they built would be superior to what it replaced. There were no organized campaigns to rein in urban redevelopment. Calls to preserve old buildings began to be heard towards the end of the century, but they were few and feeble. Had they been as effective as they became in the twentieth century, we might have fewer not only of the more banal aspects of the Victorian building legacy but also of its more enduring monuments – the libraries, public baths, cemeteries, schools, hospitals and even the pubs of London.

Central to this building endeavour was a sense of moral purpose. The Victorians were gripped by a terror of the London slum and of the contagion – physical, psychological and political – that might flow from it. Pockets of slum property were everywhere, but it was the East End which after 1880 held the imagination, with its single-class population, its patterns of casual employment and criminality, and its concentration of immigrants, above all poor Jews from Eastern Europe. Many piecemeal efforts were made to tame the East End. The Church of England reformed its system of parish extension in the 1840s with East London in mind. The late Victorian East End became a laboratory of social service, with secular and religious bodies alike founding settlements or missions as diverse as Toynbee Hall, Oxford House and the People's Palace. The School Board for London, zealously carrying out the pledge of elementary education for all wrung from Parliament in 1870, scattered its tall outposts throughout the East End, while in the 1890s the LCC built its first and by far its

biggest housing scheme at Boundary Street, Bethnal Green, in place of a notorious slum. Pockets of open space were created, to make up for the area's lack of parks and squares. Policing the East End was a major preoccupation of the Metropolitan Police, whose establishment in 1829 with powers over a wide area had helped to unify London.

Not that East Enders proved incapable of self-help. The Jewish communities, for instance, mostly resisted the blandishments of respectable West End synagogues, preferring to remain independent congregations. Unions too, formerly strongest among craft workers like the printers of Clerkenwell, spread in the 1880s among the dockers and gasworkers of the East End. The great Dock Strike of 1889 and its aftermath did much to shape the pattern of working-class politics in London – always more complex than elsewhere in Britain. After a brief revolutionary phase culminating in the violence of 'Bloody Sunday', the Trafalgar Square demonstration of November 1887, workers and reformers established an uneasy alliance that led to the creation first of the Progressive Party on the School Board and the County Council, and later of the London Labour Party.

As the largest and richest city in the world, Victorian London fascinated visitors with its extremes of life style, its diversity, its curious administration, its overcast climate and its unselfconscious ugliness. In some ways it compared poorly with other cities at the turn of the century. Its great public buildings, like the Law Courts in the Strand and the Foreign Office in Whitehall, were dispersed and ill-sited. The great exception was Barry and Pugin's Palace of Westminster, whose setting and lacy silhouette furnished the perfect theatre for the Mother of Parliaments. Only 'South Kensington', that un-English concentration of cultural and educational

In the second half of the nineteenth century, such three-storey (including basement) brick terraces proliferated around London, but not all had long front gardens like these in Camera Square, Fulham.

institutions set up at Prince Albert's instigation after the Great Exhibition of 1851, could claim an overall plan. But the educational hopes and architectural ambitions of South Kensington were marred by hand-to-mouth funding and changes of mind, leaving an axis visible only from above and a masterpiece at either extremity: at the north end, that strange, oversized Victorian jewel in Hyde Park, the Albert Memorial; at the south end, Waterhouse's magnificent, multi-coloured Natural History Museum.

London's record for services in 1900 was mixed. Its system of sewage disposal led the world and was in the process of transforming the capital's health. But water supply remained in private hands and was much complained of. Buildings, generally speaking, were properly built and safer from fire than those in other cities. Almost all chimneys burnt polluting Newcastle coal and most streets and houses were lit by coal gas, no less filthy and supplied according to district by different companies. A few rich residential neighbourhoods boasted electric lighting but, because of legislative mistakes and a reluctance by the companies to go into poorer areas, electricity spread slowly. It was just coming into commercial use, notably for traction on the tramways and the deep-level tubes, of which the first fragment opened between Bank and Stockwell in 1890, to be followed by a proliferation of lines between 1900 and 1907, so creating the core of the central underground network. West End theatres, music halls, shops and hotels were ablaze with the new incandescent lamp. If few of these could rival Paris at its most elegant, the very number and vitality of London's attractions made it the most cosmopolitan of cities. People of every race and nation, from foreign potentates to the young Mahatma Gandhi, flocked to London to spend, to study, to buy, to look and to live.

For despite the daily spectacle of poverty, London was emerging at the start of this century as a more liveable place. The shopkeepers, clerks and artisans who rented the ubiquitous two- and three-storey stock-brick terraces of the minor suburbs, living for the most part lives of ordered respectability, fared better than their parents had done, with access to elementary education and some possibilities for further technical and commercial training. A step or two up, with money enough for more than a single servant – probably female, as male servants were vanishing now – families could choose from the old-fashioned streets of four- or five-storey houses that stretched west to Earl's Court and beyond; or the semi-detached, art-wallpapered houses of suburbs like Bedford Park; or the 'mansion blocks' of flats of the West End, Maida Vale and Kensington which, after 1885, took over as the most convenient way to live closer

in. Above this level, the plutocratic houses of Mayfair and Belgravia, tied to the social rituals of the London season and therefore fully occupied for only part of the year, retained their appeal up to the First World War, despite signs that the life style they represented could not last for ever.

——— TWENTIETH-CENTURY LONDON ———

Between the World Wars, London resolved itself into two cities: the core – volcanic, turbulent, self-renewing as ever, with its tarnished necklace of residential districts, rich and poor, around it; and, beyond, the lava flow of 'semi-detached London', creeping out over Middlesex, Essex, Kent and Surrey, lapping round towns and villages on its path.

Inner London was governed until 1965 by a two-tier system of metropolitan boroughs and the London County Council. The boroughs, created in succession to the old vestries in 1900, were small enough to sustain local loyalties. They never had sufficient powers to make much political impact, but many built fine town halls for themselves. Some – mostly Labour-controlled boroughs such as St Pancras, Finsbury, Bermondsey, Woolwich and Poplar – had vigorous bursts of municipal activity aimed at providing better housing, health care and public assistance. Poplar in particular earned praise and notoriety for its stubborn generosity towards its many poor residents.

The LCC was a different matter. Created as a sop to London's municipal pride in 1889, it inherited the tasks of the old Board of Works but acquired others along the way. In its heyday, under Labour control between 1934 and the late 1950s, it seemed the natural institution of government that London had always lacked. Directly elected and housed in stately headquarters at County Hall in plain and bold sight of Parliament, the LCC ran London's education, its major roads, its sewage disposal, its fire brigade, its building regulations and much of its public housing and parks. Its administration was respected and free from corruption, while its politicians tended to put the provision of services above party antagonisms. It prided itself upon being a model of local government.

Yet in some respects the LCC was flawed. It never controlled many vital services, like the public supply utilities or the Port of London. Others, including hospitals and transport, it ran only in part or for a time. Above all, the size of the area which it controlled was too small from the beginning. In 1965 it was replaced by the Greater London Council, covering a wider area. But by that time the outer areas of London, mainly Conservative-controlled, were strong and resented the new body. The political tensions between Labour inner

North-West London in 1938

This map shows the growth of the Wembley, Willesden, Ealing and Acton areas of Middlesex just before the Second World War. From the opening of the Grand Union Canal in 1814, linking London and the Midlands, the district had become riddled with transport systems. At first they ignored the area through which they passed, but by 1910 the railways had made large local inroads. Ealing liked to call itself the 'Queen of the Suburbs' on account of its high-class Victorian commuting population.

The various railway and engineering works (including, by the First World War, the germ of west London's lucrative aircraft-parts industry) created local employment and a proliferation of two-storey artisans' terraces in Harlesden and Willesden. A few, more thoughtful, types of planned development followed. In 1901 Brentham became the site of Britain's first co-operative garden suburb. Along similar lines, the London County Council in 1912–20 built one of its four early municipal 'cottage estates' at Old Oak Common. Tenants here had employment chances at the Great Western carriage works, at Wormwood Scrubs Prison (opened 1890), or at the Hammersmith Hospital (1905); after 1920 they could commute from East Acton Station. The Old Oak Estate spawned successors to its south and west.

Western Avenue, started in 1921, was introduced to relieve the congested road to Oxford; the North Circular was the capital's first attempt at a peripheral relief road. Both attracted faience-clad factories of the electric age, especially where road and railway ran close together; most famous is the Hoover Factory at Perivale (1932–3). Industry grew around Park Royal, the venue for the Royal Agricultural Show in 1903–4, and later a centre of munitions manufacturing during the First World War. A happier attempt to promote a suburban exhibition site was made at Wembley Park. There the Metropolitan Railway had vainly tried in the 1890s to encourage suburban traffic by laying out pleasure grounds. In 1924–5 Wembley became the site of the British Empire Exhibition, thereby acquiring a permanent stadium and, later, other sports facilities of an international standard.

Amidst this complex transport network there was still ample room until the 1930s for acres of low-density housing, leaving space for gardens, schools, parks, sports grounds, golf courses, allotments and other amenities. By 1939 the essential texture of these western suburbs – still recognizable today – had been fixed.

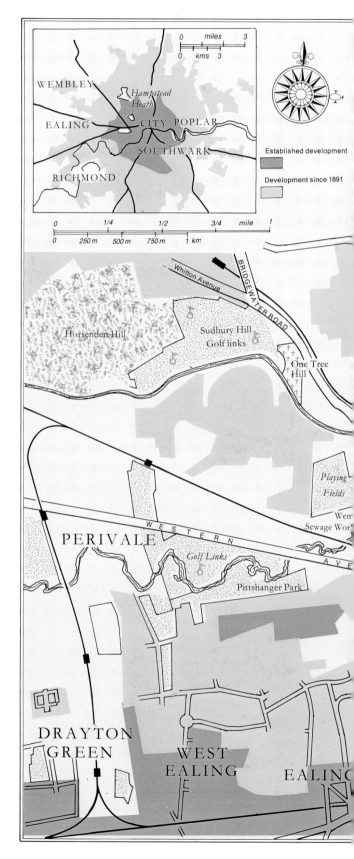

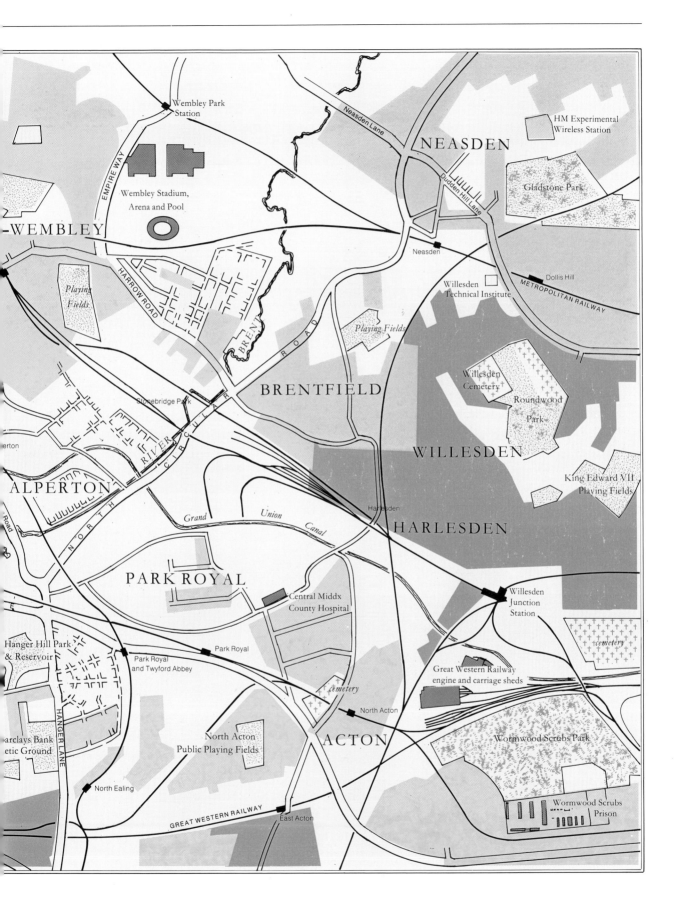

WEMBLEY

Wembley Park
Station

EMPIRE WAY

Wembley Stadium,
Arena and Pool

NEASDEN

Neasden Lane

Dudden Hill Lane

HM Experimental
Wireless Station

Gladstone Park

Neasden

Dollis Hill

METROPOLITAN RAILWAY

Willesden
Technical Institute

Playing
Fields

HARROW ROAD

ROAD

BRENT

Playing Fields

Willesden
Cemetery

Roundwood
Park

Stonebridge Park

RIVER

CIRCULAR

NORTH

BRENTFIELD

WILLESDEN

King Edward VII
Playing Fields

ALPERTON

Grand

Union

Canal

Harlesden

HARLESDEN

Willesden
Junction
Station

PARK ROYAL

Central Middx
County Hospital

cemetery

Hanger Hill Park
& Reservoir

Park Royal

Park Royal
and Twyford Abbey

Great Western Railway
engine and carriage sheds

HANGER LANE

cemetery

North Acton

Wormwood Scrubs Park

Barclays Bank
etic Ground

North Acton
Public Playing Fields

ACTON

North Ealing

GREAT WESTERN RAILWAY

East Acton

Wormwood Scrubs
Prison

and Conservative outer London contributed to the failure of the GLC, which survived only until 1986. London today has no metropolitan government as such. Instead it has the expanded boroughs created in 1965, together with that odd if colourful anachronism, the City Corporation.

Outer London too has its own history and order. Towns of staunchly independent character, such as Bromley and Harrow, far from being absorbed in the suburban tide, have redeemed its monotony. Some – Croydon is the best example – have learnt urban rapacity for themselves and become thriving commercial centres, with the economic prosperity and visual impoverishment that implies. Nor has the twentieth-century spread of London ever been restricted to

Middlesex, well served by successive suburban extensions of what in 1933 became a unified underground system under the single management of London Transport, became the *locus classicus* for inter-war housing. The variety of development in such places as Kingsbury, Pinner, Stanmore, Wembley (venue for the British Empire Exhibition of 1924) and Southgate showed that English individualism could endow even the smallest plot and the dullest road with a picturesque touch. Yet the commuters' insistence on their own houses and gardens, in preference to flats, destroyed Middlesex as a rural county. Almost too late, the LCC helped to save other counties by devising a Green Belt around outer London in the late 1930s. The Green Belt has often been breached, not least by the LCC's own 'out-county estates'

The tradition of map-making continues; this 1988 view of the City of London by Norbert Ceulemans combines the virtues of aerial photography with cartographic skills.

suburban housing. Industry, always greedy for cheap open space, was concentrating around areas like Hendon, Willesden and Tottenham by the First World War. It went on to line the Great West Road, Western and Eastern Avenues and the North Circular Road with the factories of the electric age – slick offices in front and plain sheds behind. The Ford Motor Company opened its Dagenham plant in 1931, saving the LCC's enormous Becontree housing estate from disaster. Small firms, always the lifeblood of London industry, brought prosperity to swathes of suburban London between the wars, softening the effect of world depression.

of the post-war period, but it mostly remains and has done much to redeem and define modern London.

In the centre, there was a gradual shake-out of industry between the wars, leaving dressmaking and furniture-making in the East End and printing, watch-making and jewellery in the City and Clerkenwell as the chief concentrations of skilled manual work. This was the heyday of the London daily newspaper, with the *Telegraph* and *Express* resplendent in overweening headquarters on Fleet Street itself, and the presses of their rivals, notably the Harmsworths' *Daily Mail*, roaring away in back streets behind. It was the era, too, of the department store. Oxford Street, with Selfridges as its flagship, boasted the biggest variety of shops. Special excursion trains brought suburban shoppers in to Kensington High Street's trio of stores: Barkers, Derry and Toms (with a roof garden) and Pontings. Newspapers, shops and, above all, the cinema reflected the growing American tenor of London life. Americans increasingly owned or invested in London businesses, while American styles and habits influenced work and leisure, dress and architectural fashion. Though London banned skyscrapers, the bigger scale and style of the new stone banks, offices and flats of the City and West End had an American rather than a European feeling.

War, long expected, came to London again in 1939. It was feared that air raids would virtually obliterate the city. In a gigantic operation the LCC evacuated most of the capital's children, only to find them seeping back when the raids did not materialize. When the bombs did fall in 1940–1, they proved London's worst trial since the Great Fire. The physical damage was uneven – devastating in the East End and City, comparatively slight in the West End. On top of the discontinuities and poor maintenance of wartime, it made a shabby city shabbier still. The planners saw their chance and decreed a new post-war London, lower in density at the centre, freed from polluting industry and with plenty of space for growing families. Those who did not want to stay could find a fresh life in a ring of New Towns beyond the Green Belt.

Post-war planning in London proved cumbersome and rigid. Areas like Stepney and Poplar long remained waste lands. The flats that eventually replaced the broken little East End terraces may have had better accommodation, but they looked less friendly and discouraged neighbourliness. In the City, enthusiasm for comprehensive redevelopment combined with institutional niggardliness turned the precincts of St Paul's into a failure of the imagination, while the more adventurous and fashionable Barbican development became a fortress-like enclosure. Yet there were some successes. The Festival of Britain, with the handsome and permanent Royal Festival Hall at its centre, gave fresh impetus to London's cultural life and promised something better than austerity. The LCC's estates at Roehampton showed that public housing could be attractive if the site was right and sufficient care was taken with appearances and planting.

Gradually London recovered. Buildings were restored or replaced and the grainy, sooty city of the 1940s became decent again. The property boom of 1958–64 led

the way back to prosperity, raising London office rents to among the highest in the world. Few white-collar jobs had ever been lured away and many more were being created: the future of central London lay with office and service employment. Tourism, never negligible but scarcely organized until now, began to be exploited as a means of revenue. Hotels – of scant architectural merit – were built with government subsidies to meet this new demand. Meanwhile, the docks dwindled rapidly. Until the mid-1960s big boats would come up above Tower Bridge into the Pool of London; but, with containerization, merchant shipping stayed further and further down river. Docks closed in swift succession, until even distant Tilbury was in trouble. All along the river the waterfront decayed. With more produce coming into London by road, the position of the central markets was now illogical. The fruit and vegetable trades deserted Covent Garden Market in the late 1970s, leaving the shell of its buildings to be converted into tourist shops. Billingsgate Fish Market followed suit, though Smithfield still has a central presence for its meat.

For a time in the 1970s it looked as though London might succumb to a combination of urban motorway mania and comprehensive redevelopment. The threat passed (though not before damage was done) largely through the protests of a new breed of Londoner – the young professional or academic brought up in the suburbs, who found the decaying Victorian or Georgian terrace houses of Camden Town, Islington or Camberwell cheap, charming and serviceable places to bring up a family. This 'gentrification' took up the slack caused by the migration of artisan families to the outer suburbs. Twenty years after the process began, values have so increased that the subdivision of houses, which the previous generation was undoing, is again in evidence, as aspiring couples find they can afford only flats.

Today London is in the throes of a new boom, set off by the deregulation of financial markets in 1986. Cranes are silhouetted against the skyline behind St Paul's. The impetus to build high, unwisely indulged for a brief period in the 1960s, is with London again. Developers rampage around the city, looking for old railway sidings to devour. The docks are alive once more, not now with ships but with a muddle of little vernacular houses, light industrial sheds and brassy office blocks. Warehouses are converted into riverside apartments at prices which no docker or railwayman could contemplate. For the first time for many centuries, the pendulum of fashion is moving east. Whether it can be sustained when the tax incentives for going in that direction are removed is unclear. What *is* certain is that London retains the same rapacious appetite for growth and rebirth that it had when the first London Bridge was built.

London Today

How can London be defined at the end of the twentieth century? Mobility today is such that any physical boundary is largely meaningless, although an estimate of the population in 1987 gave London 6.77 million residents. Just two features offer some sense of containment. One is the M25, completed in 1987 and already overloaded; the other is the Green Belt. Created in the 1930s, this safeguards some fifty-five square miles of countryside from development and has rescued outer London from the worst excesses of megalopolitan land-hunger. But the capital's gravitational pull has long leapt far beyond the Green Belt and the communities of the 'Home Counties'. Led on by escalating house prices and accelerated rail services, many people now travel in daily from Portsmouth, the Cotswolds, Bristol, the Midlands and even South Yorkshire. Once the Channel Tunnel is complete in 1993, regular commuting from the Pas de Calais and beyond is certain.

The Greater London boundaries set in 1965 have no demographic or economic basis. Within them, thirty-two boroughs struggle for a sense of their identity. But there is no clear community of interest between Barking in the east and Hillingdon in the west. Closer in, dense building, double-decker buses (no longer all red) and traffic congestion are the norm, and at the very centre the tiny, opulent City of London, with 340,000 workers by day and 4,700 residents at night, still asserts that it alone is the true London.

London's centre of gravity may now be moving east. West London has been losing skilled jobs faster than other parts of the city, as the painful transition from blue-collar to white-collar employment continues. Meanwhile, land shortages and tax incentives have emboldened developers to tackle the arid industrial legacy of the Thames estuary. Thamesmead, a bleak municipal township on the Erith marshes, was the forerunner. In the 1980s the Docklands Development Corporation was charged with transforming swathes of rotting riverside from London Bridge eastwards. It is already plain that the infrastructure and architecture of this vast enterprise leave much to be desired. Derelict land elsewhere is in equal demand. Various road schemes are proposed as short-term palliatives, but London needs massive renovation of its public transport system if it is not to become a more dangerous and costly city. Yet despite this London is plainly thriving, its residents still identify themselves as Londoners and its 24.3 million visitors prove its place as the most successful international city in the world.

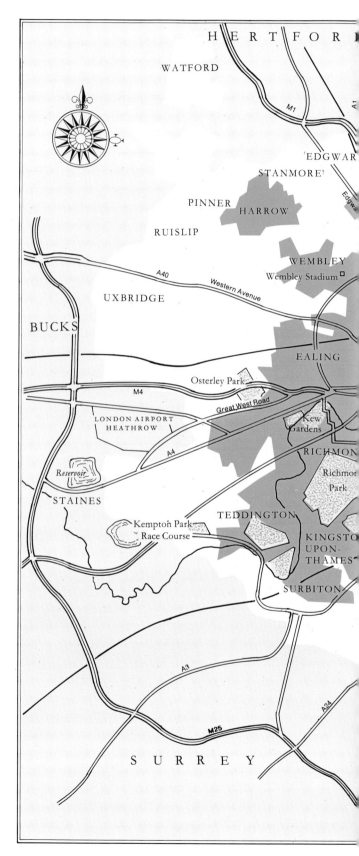

H I R E

ENFIELD

COCKFOSTERS

Epping

Forest

LOUGHTON

E S S E X

A10

EDMONTON

WOOD
GREEN

Alexandra Palace

MUSWELL
HILL

POTTER'S
BAR

WALTHAMSTOW

ROMFORD

A12

Archway

Hampstead
Heath

HAMPSTEAD

STOKE
NEWINGTON

LEYTON

ILFORD

HORNCHURCH

UPMINSTER

CAMDEN

STRATFORD

Regent's Park

King's Cross
Station

Mile End Road

WEST
HAM

BARKING

DAGENHAM

Paddington
Station

CENTRAL
LONDON

The
Tower

Rotherhithe
Tunnel

Commercial Road

R I V E R

A13

Hyde Park

Blackwall Tunnel
City Airport

ISLE
OF
DOGS

T H A M E S

Dartford
Tunnel

Victoria
Station

Waterloo
Station

BERMONDSEY

Old Kent Road

WOOLWICH

GREENWICH

TNEY

WANDSWORTH

PECKHAM

LEWISHAM

Shooter's Hill

ELTHAM

A2

DARTFORD

imbledon
ommon

DULWICH

SIDCUP

A20

WIMBLEDON

MITCHAM

CRYSTAL
PALACE

BROMLEY

K E N T

M20

A21

CROYDON

SUTTON

A23

M25

Established development

Development since 1938

| 0 | 1 | 2 | 3 | miles | 5 |

| 0 | 1 | 2 | 3 | 4 | 5 | kms |

M23

41

CHRONOLOGY

43	Emperor Claudius invades Britain and forces Thames crossing at or near site of London
c.50	First London Bridge thrown across Thames
61	Sack of London by Boudicca
c.125	Major fire
c.200	City wall built
c.288–326	Coinage first issued from London
296	Relief of London by Emperor Constantius Chlorus
401–10	Legions leave Britain. London starts to decline
604	St Paul's Cathedral founded by King Ethelbert
c.900	New City of London street plan
1065	Westminster Abbey, rebuilt by Kind Edward the Confessor, consecrated
1078	Tower of London commenced by Gundulf, Bishop of Rochester, for William the Conqueror
1176–1205	London Bridge rebuilt in stone for first time
1191	Henry Fitzalwin becomes first Lord Mayor
1197	Control of Thames in London area passes from Crown to City
1215	King John concedes important municipal freedoms to London
1348–9	Major epidemic of Black Death kills many Londoners
1381	Peasant's Revolt. Riots in London, Wat Tyler killed at Smithfield
1411–44	Guildhall rebuilt
c.1515	Beginnings of major naval dockyards and ship-building at Deptford
1535–40	Dissolution of monasteries and start of influx of population into London
1570	Royal Exchange opened
1580–1617	Proclamations against suburban building
1582	First pumped water supply from wheel under London Bridge
1599	Globe Theatre built in Southwark
1605	Guy Fawkes's plot to blow up Parliament discovered
1613	New River brings more reliable water supply to London
1630–7	Development of Covent Garden
1641	Civil War begins, with London in hands of Parliament
1660	London welcomes restoration of Charles II
1661–3	Lincoln's Inn Fields Theatre and Theatre Royal open
1665	Great Plague
1666	Great Fire of London
1670s	Intensive post-Fire rebuilding
1676	Southwark badly damaged by fire
1680s	Origins of modern insurance and banking in City
1694	Establishment of Bank of England
1711	Rebuilding of St Paul's Cathedral completed; Act for Rebuilding Churches passed
1720s	Building boom in West End
1720–53	'Gin Lane' period, and beginnings of social reform movement in London
1750	Westminster Bridge opened
1756	New Road from City to Paddington completed
1758–62	London Bridge cleared of houses
1759	British Museum inaugurated in Montagu House, Bloomsbury
1763	Start of renewed building boom
1774	First comprehensive London Building Act
1780	Anti-Catholic 'Gordon Riots'
1783	Newgate Prison opens and executions at Tyburn discontinued
1802	West India Dock, first enclosed docks in the world, opened

1807	Experimental gas lighting in Pall Mall
1812	Nash's Regent Street commenced
1816–17	Civil disturbances: Meetings at Spa Fields
1820s	Building boom: Belgravia, Bloomsbury, Regent's Park and Brompton in development
1826	University College, core of University of London, founded
1829	Metropolitan Police established under government control. First omnibus service
1834	Palace of Westminster burnt
1836–7	Railways reach central London at Euston and London Bridge
1837–41	Seven suburban cemeteries created. Churchyard burials prohibited
1843	Thames Tunnel, first underwater tunnel in the world, completed from Wapping to Rotherhithe
1848	Great Chartist demonstration at Kennington
1851	Great Exhibition in Hyde Park
1855	Metropolitan Board of Works set up
1860–75	Bazalgette's main drainage scheme executed by Board of Works
1865	Metropolitan Fire Brigade established
1870	School Board for London begins work
1883	First effective Cheap Trains Act encourages working-class commuting
1886–9	Social unrest, including dock strike and demonstrations
1888	Jack the Ripper murders
1889	London County Council set up
1890	First deep-level tube opened
1894	Tower Bridge completed
1894–1900	First major municipal housing estate built by LCC at Boundary Street, Bethnal Green
1900	London boroughs replace vestries and district boards
1901	Maximum recorded population for inner London of 4.5 million
1904	LCC takes over London's educational services
1909	Port of London Authority takes control of docks
1924	British Empire Exhibition at Wembley
1926	General Strike
1933	London Passenger Transport Board set up to unify London's transport system
1936	Beginnings of Green Belt policy
1939	Greater London reaches its maximum population of 8.5 million
1940–1	Blitz
1943–4	Patrick Abercrombie's County of London Plan and Greater London Plan lay down principles for post-war rebuilding
1946	New Towns Act provides for towns to relieve London
1951	Festival of Britain
1952	Town Development Act reinforces dispersal of Londoners
1956	Clean Air Act ends London's smogs
1965	LCC and Middlesex County Council replaced with Greater London Council. Larger London boroughs created, ILEA becomes education authority for inner London
1976	National Theatre building opened on South Bank
1982	Completion of Thames Barrier
1986	Abolition of Greater London Council. Deregulation of financial markets
1990	ILEA abolished – Education becomes responsibility of London boroughs

THE
AREAS OF
LONDON

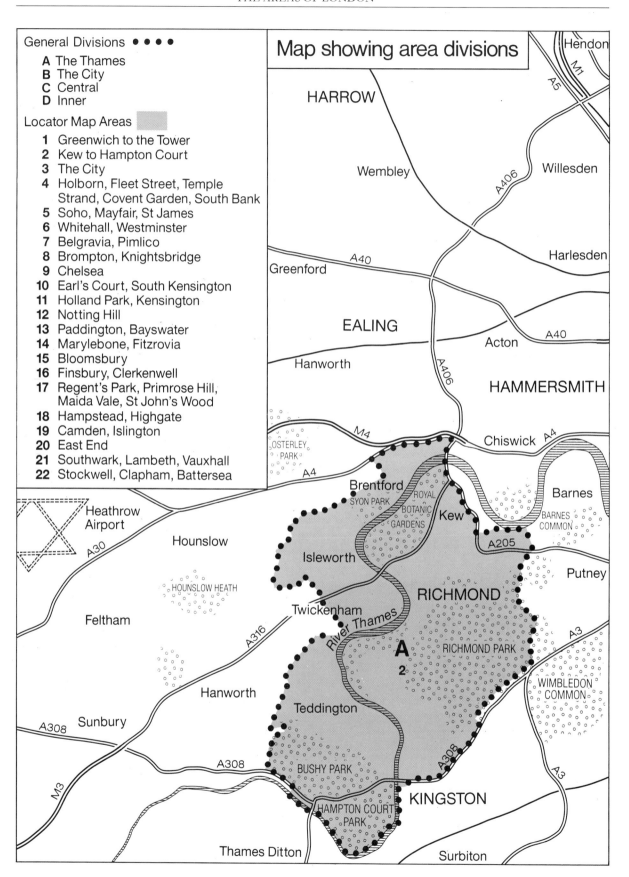

Map showing area divisions

General Divisions ● ● ● ●
- **A** The Thames
- **B** The City
- **C** Central
- **D** Inner

Locator Map Areas

1. Greenwich to the Tower
2. Kew to Hampton Court
3. The City
4. Holborn, Fleet Street, Temple Strand, Covent Garden, South Bank
5. Soho, Mayfair, St James
6. Whitehall, Westminster
7. Belgravia, Pimlico
8. Brompton, Knightsbridge
9. Chelsea
10. Earl's Court, South Kensington
11. Holland Park, Kensington
12. Notting Hill
13. Paddington, Bayswater
14. Marylebone, Fitzrovia
15. Bloomsbury
16. Finsbury, Clerkenwell
17. Regent's Park, Primrose Hill, Maida Vale, St John's Wood
18. Hampstead, Highgate
19. Camden, Islington
20. East End
21. Southwark, Lambeth, Vauxhall
22. Stockwell, Clapham, Battersea

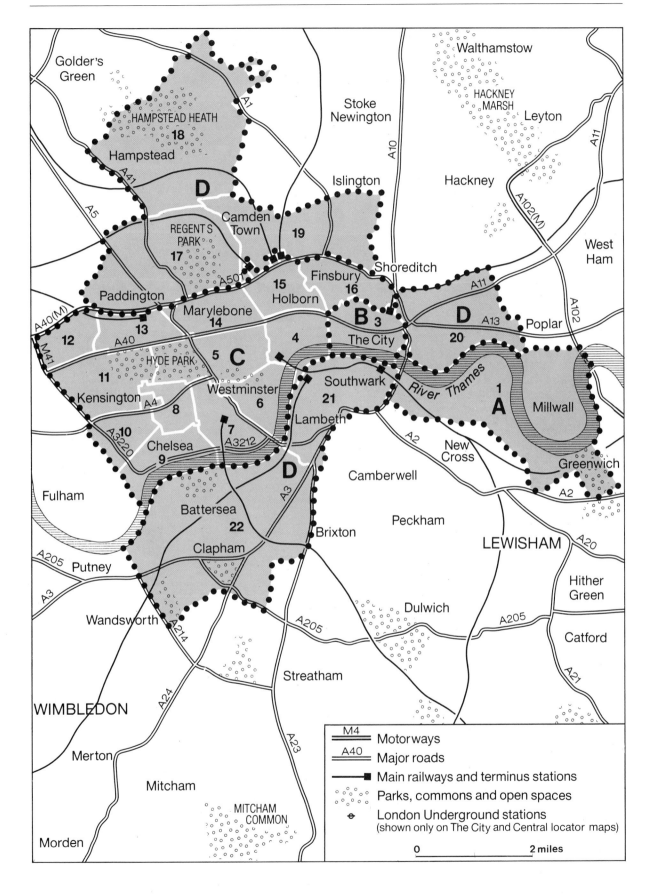

Golder's Green

Walthamstow

HAMPSTEAD HEATH

HACKNEY MARSH

Leyton

18

Hampstead

Stoke Newington

A1

A41

D

Islington

Hackney

A5

West Ham

REGENT'S PARK

Camden Town

19

17

A501

Finsbury

Shoreditch

A11

Paddington

15

16

D

A40(M)

Holborn

B

A13

Poplar

M41

12

A40

Marylebone

3

The City

20

A102

13

14

4

The City

HYDE PARK

5   C

Westminster

1

11

A3220

8

Southwark

A

Millwall

River Thames

Kensington

A4

6

21

10

7

Lambeth

Greenwich

Chelsea

A3212

Battersea

D

New Cross

A2

9

Camberwell

Fulham

22

A3

Peckham

A2

A205

Clapham

Brixton

LEWISHAM

Putney

Wandsworth

A3

A214

A205

Dulwich

Hither Green

Streatham

Catford

A205

A24

WIMBLEDON

A21

Merton

A23

Mitcham

MITCHAM COMMON

Morden

	Motorways
M4	
A40	Major roads
■	Main railways and terminus stations
° ° °	Parks, commons and open spaces
⊖	London Underground stations (shown only on The City and Central locator maps)

0   2 miles

THE THAMES

The Thames does not get into the first division of rivers of the world for length, volume or spectacular scenery. But it is possibly the most famous because for centuries it was the front door, main street and administrative offices of the city that became a great imperial and commercial power. London grew naturally on the river that was the gateway to Europe and the city's *raison d'être*, trade.

In the beginning of London, when the Romans arrived, the argument *ex silentio* is that there was nothing there except a few wandering hunters who have left only traces. If you came by sea, as invaders and traders to Britain had to, the quickest and easiest way into the heart of the country was to float your boat on the tide sixty miles up the Thames to the first safe landing-place. In those days before it was embanked and canalized, the Thames was at least a thousand yards wide at high tide (two hundred yards today), an inland sea with islands, marshes and no solid ground on which to land. London grew on two little hills on the northern, less swampy, bank of the Thames that provided the first dry landing-place for ships. In one of the many improbable folk etymologies for London it derives from the Celtic *Llyn-Din*, 'the hill by the pool'. The Thames is the second oldest surviving place-name in Britain, after Kent, and is derived from a conjectural British (Celtic) root element, *teme-*, meaning either simply 'river' or more specifically 'dark river'.

As well as a main road, the Thames was a barrier to travellers. The first roads, such as Watling Street, ran to London as the first place upstream where the river could be crossed. From the beginning London was a port, an entrepôt, and a place for mariners and traders (see *The port of London*) – an identity that has changed only in the twentieth century. Now as you approach the river from the sea, you pass through ten miles of obsolete docks which for centuries were the mouths of what became the greatest commercial city in the world. They culminate at the Pool of London, where the big ships could go no farther because of London Bridge.

The docks are being transmogrified, though there are still miles of industrial wasteland where the great ships were parked at the end of the street only fifty years ago. The river has been bridged and tunnelled and embanked many times, and is now barriered at Woolwich to prevent flooding in freak conditions. For most of its life the Thames was the lavatory as well as the high road of London, and in the 1960s became a dead river because of industrial pollution. It has been cleaned considerably since then and every year salmon are reported to be coming back to it – but, if you fall in, you might still die of poisoning even if you do not drown.

The Royal Naval Hospital, now the Royal Naval College, was built in the early eighteenth century to designs by Wren. It was devised in two sections to avoid obscuring the Queen's House, visible between the two halves in this painting by Canaletto

— FROM GREENWICH TO THE TOWER —

If you take the old river route to London, you come to a great S-bend. On the cusp of the second curve on the left or southern bank stands a spectacular congeries of buildings by England's finest architects. There is the grand square of the ROYAL NAVAL HOSPITAL by Wren, Hawksmoor and Vanbrugh, with the duty officer standing on the river steps to salute you, if you are in a Royal Navy ship. Framed through their classic quadrangle is the QUEEN'S HOUSE, designed by Inigo Jones for James I's Queen, Anne of Denmark, and the rest of what is now the NATIONAL MARITIME MUSEUM. Above them on the hill of Greenwich Park stands Wren's ROYAL OBSERVATORY, the home of the Greenwich meridian and Greenwich mean time.

Greenwich is the gateway to London. The name means either 'green village' in Anglo-Saxon or 'green reach' in Old Norse. The Danish fleet camped here from 1011 to 1014, besieging London and murdering their hostage Alphege, the Archbishop of Canterbury. On this bend in the river, Humphrey, Duke of Gloucester, the brother of Henry V, built Bella Court in 1427, considered by contemporaries to be the finest house in England. He was a cultivated magnate and his private library was left to Oxford University to become the nucleus of the Bodleian Library. Henry VI took his palace over and renamed it Placentia, the pleasant place. It became the favourite palace of the Tudors, and the birthplace of Henry VIII, Mary I and Elizabeth I. Here Raleigh is said in folk legend to have laid his cloak over a puddle to save Elizabeth getting her feet dirty. Here Elizabeth revived the Maundy ceremony, washing the feet of the poor (after they had been washed by three other people first) and many other historic or fabulous events of that turbulent century took place.

Tudor Placentia was a complex of castellated buildings around three quadrangles approached by a massive river gatehouse. In the Civil War the Parliamentarians tried unsuccessfully to sell it and then, having stripped it of its famous paintings and furniture, made it a biscuit factory. James I settled Greenwich on his Queen Anne and built her the Queen's House. Charles II at the Restoration decided to rebuild the old river palace and John Webb completed the western block; but money ran out. William and Mary abandoned the river palace and engaged their best architects to build the Royal Naval Hospital for old sailors and what became the Royal Naval College.

The park on the hill was laid out to designs by Le Nôtre and Wren built the Royal Observatory and FLAMSTEED HOUSE for the first Astronomer Royal. Greenwich became the centre of the world for navigation and chronometry: the prime meridian is marked by

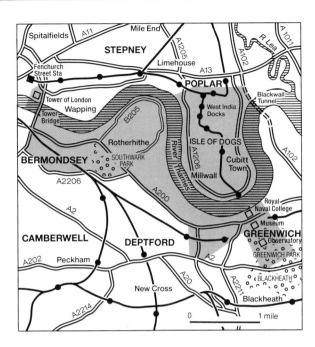

a brass rail inlaid in concrete. Over the next three centuries the area became a large London suburb, with a famous view of the city from the hill, and a place for outings by river or by the first London railway, opened in 1838. But it retains its connections with the sea. The *Cutty Sark*, the old tea clipper, stands in dry dock on the river front, beside *Gipsy Moth IV*, in which Sir Francis Chichester circumnavigated the world solo.

The best view of Greenwich is from the ISLE OF DOGS on the north bank opposite. Its name is first recorded on a map of 1588. It is not an isle but a peninsula made by a great loop in the Thames; and the connection with dogs is mythical (King Charles II is unpersuasively alleged to have kennelled his little spaniels there). Unworldly onomasticians suggest the name may be a corruption of the Isle of Ducks. The most likely explanation is that it was a contemptuous nickname for the people who lived there.

It is in the thick of up-market development, as property companies erect expensive flats with a river view and newspapers quit Fleet Street. Beneath the rising towers of Canary Wharf lies the heart of old dockland, the Millwall Docks and the West India Docks. Cubitt Town was built in the 1840s as cheap housing and cramped recreation for the rapidly increasing army of dockers; and the pedestrian tunnel under the Thames to Greenwich was dug to let dockers cross over from the south bank. The DOCKLANDS LIGHT RAILWAY, opened in 1987, runs from here to Tower Hill without drivers, to carry the new residents to their work in the City. Behind the modern bustle on the Isle of Dogs stands Hawksmoor's church of St Anne, Limehouse, the

River Transport

The Thames has been the high street of London for most of its history, the main road for carrying passengers and goods across town. Wheeled transport and bridges took most of the traffic away from the river; but recently the dense road and rail congestion has returned some of it to London's old main thoroughfare. It is used by a variety of private pleasure boats propelled by engine, sail and arm power, by water buses taking tourists on sightseeing tours, by barges carrying heavy, inexpensive cargo (for example the sludge vessels that carry London's treated sewage to dump in the Barrow Deep opposite Foulness) and by a scheduled water bus service that opened in 1988 and may attract enough passengers to stay afloat. If bigger ships want to come into central London the bascules of Tower Bridge have to be raised, increasing the headway from 28 feet to 140 feet.

Until fifty years ago the London river was its main artery, creating special kinds of vessel and many different professions of watermen and rivermen. The first Thames boats that can be reconstructed from archaeology and the texts are the Roman merchantmen, with a permanent mast and a square sail made from linen or hides, capable of four knots in normal conditions. By the time of the Roman occupation the average *navis oneraria* rated 50 tons.

By the nineteenth century the Pool of London was full of ocean-going vessels and the lighters and little boats that unloaded them. Thames sailing barges, with hinged masts, flat bottoms and square sails, were once as characteristic of the river as feluccas on the Nile. Some of them went to Dunkirk in 1940 to help evacuate the British army and a few are still in use. As a matter of course royals travelled between their riverine palaces by royal barges and the monarch still employs a bargemaster and royal watermen, though these days they have to ride on the back of the royal coach. The last royal barge, built in 1689, appeared on the tideway in 1919 to carry George v and Queen Mary to a peace pageant. It is now laid up in the National Maritime Museum. Nobles and other magnates, and the City livery companies, had their own ceremonial barges, manned by liveried oarsmen and as gilded as the *Bucentaur*s of the doges of Venice.

Commercial passengers who wanted to cross the river or the town had to take a wherry with up to six oars, or a double-sculler. The prudent or timorous disembarked above London Bridge and rejoined their boat on the far side, below the rapids that fell four feet at low tide between the piles of the bridge. You shouted 'oars' when you needed transport. A visiting Frenchman, misapprehending that he was being taken to a brothel, was shocked by the blatancy of the English.

Thames watermen survive, driving diesel engines these days. Doggett's Coat and Badge race for them is the oldest annual contested sporting event in the world. Thomas Doggett, an Irish comedian and a staunch Hanoverian Protestant, who used the watermen to ferry him to the pleasures of the South Bank, introduced the prize in 1715. The race, usually held at the end of July, is from London Bridge to Cadogan Pier, Chelsea, nearly five miles, and the winner gets a red coat, breeches and cap, and a silver arm badge.

Transport on the Thames is largely ceremonial and for pleasure these days, but it is the vestige of a huge commercial past. There are occasional madcap schemes for building a motorway above or underneath the Thames; but the odds are that the river will continue to be used for light transport and pleasure, as Londoners turn their backs on the traffic jams in despair.

A paddle steamer at a jetty in Chelsea opposite the Adam and Eve pub, before the river was embanked.

St Katharine's dock at its opening in 1828. Some of the warehouses still exist as part of the tourist amenity into which the dock has been converted.

OVERLEAF The Waterman's Arms, a Victorian pub, became fashionable in the 1960s for its nostalgic music-hall evenings. Then it was surrounded by decaying warehouses, but two decades later the Isle of Dogs itself came into vogue and the warehouses were replaced by expensive private housing with river views, such as the apartments being built on the left.

dockers' church, with a west tower like a great ship under easy sail, once a landmark for mariners coming home to the Port of London.

Circumnavigating the Isle of Dogs on the way to London, on the left is Deptford, a decaying suburb ripe for some of the money that is being spent on the opposite bank. It was founded by the Tudors as their naval dockyard, and great ships were built there for the next three centuries, as long as sail ruled the Thames. Deptford was the original home of Trinity House, still the lighthouse authority for England, Wales, the Channel Islands and Gibraltar. It started as a religious society for retired pilots and other old seafarers in the Middle Ages, and was given a charter by Henry VIII in 1514.

Next on the south bank, left hand, is Rotherhithe, another fossil from Britain's maritime past, when the world and ships were smaller. Today it is decaying warehouses and neglected housing estates. But the Black Prince had his fleet built here and one of the earliest London docks (the only one on the south bank) was here. This became the Surrey Docks, specializing in trade with the Baltic and Scandinavia, i.e. a lot of timber. They burned for weeks during the Blitz and were finally closed in 1970. Some offices and apartments are being built here, but not as rapidly or extensively as on the opposite bank.

As the returning mariner (or, these days, tripper on pleasure boat) swings round the last bend below London into Limehouse reach, the City slips into view. The dome of St Paul's no longer dominates the town like a bubble floating overhead, but it is still visible through the encircling thicket of towers, like matchboxes on end. Early travellers noted in wonder the mass of shipping

and masts below London Bridge, so thick that it seemed as though you could walk from bank to bank of the London river without getting your feet wet. On the south bank is Bermondsey, the *ei* or marsh of someone called Bermond, recorded as early as 708 and used by Dickens as an example of the worst slums created by the Industrial Revolution. On the north bank Shadwell and Wapping, only a century ago celebrated landfalls for sailors, are today being redeveloped as the City overflows eastwards.

The first bridge across the Thames, on the eastern boundary of the old City, is TOWER BRIDGE. It was opened in 1894 and its bascules still have to be raised to let big ships up river. Its hydraulic machinery, now electrified, is open as a museum of Victorian engineering. Beyond the Victorian Gothic towers of the bridge is the Pool of London, the original harbour and dock, and the TOWER OF LONDON itself, guarding the river approach. Today it is the most popular tourist attraction in the United Kingdom, notorious for the length of the queues to get into it and the romantic garrulity of the Beefeaters (superannuated soldiers in Tudor uniforms who live in the Tower and act as guides). It is one of the oldest buildings in the kingdom and the most historic, for centuries soaked in battles, blood, decapitation and power struggles. He who held the Tower held London: it was the key piece on the medieval chessboard.

Remains of the Roman bastion and part of the Roman wall survive, and William the Conqueror built a temporary fort here immediately after the Battle of Hastings, to awe his reluctant subjects. Later he converted it into stone as the central White Tower, with four sides of different lengths and four quite different turrets on top. The lop-

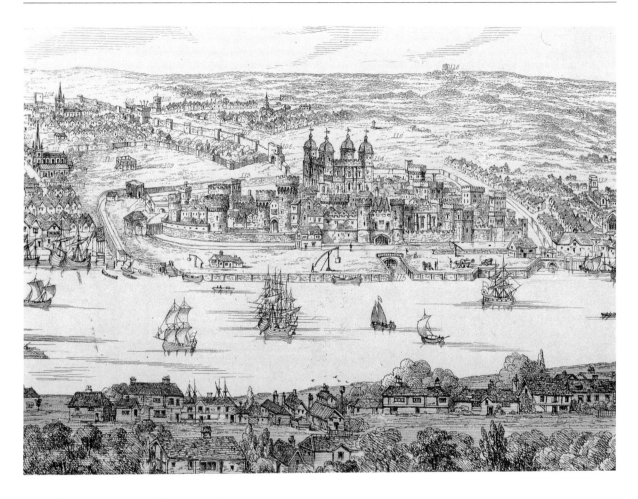

In the sixteenth century there were still fields to the north of the Tower. The village of Whitechapel is behind it, leading to Aldgate, the main entry gate to the walled city from the east.

sided designer was Gundulf, an emotional monk from the Abbey of Bec in Normandy, who was the most celebrated architect of churches and fortresses of the age. It was called the White Tower because some of the stone was limestone imported from Caen to reinforce the feeble local mudstone and because it was originally whitewashed. It is the most perfect medieval fortress and palace in England, with St John's Chapel on the second floor, still a royal chapel, a prime example of Norman architecture. In the beginning the only entrance to the keep was on the south side facing the river, fifteen feet above ground, so that the ladder could be pulled up if unwelcome Saxon visitors called.

Subsequent building monarchs added to its fortifications until Edward I completed the outer wall, enclosing an area of eighteen acres. Unsuccessful monarchs tended to get locked up in the Tower. For six turbulent centuries it was at the centre of English politics, particularly during the struggle between John and his magnates, the Wars of the Roses and the Tudor revolution. In its time the Tower has played many parts, because it was the strongest castle in the kingdom: fortress, palace, state prison as late as the Second World

War, the royal armouries, the first mint, the first zoo (the polar bear used to swim in the Thames), the first public record office, the original royal observatory, the home of the crown jewels, which are still there. James I regularly staged animals fights there. Spies were shot in the outer ward in the First World War and Rudolf Hess was locked up in the Tower in the Second.

Big guns removed its impregnability in the seventeenth century and the blood spilled there by the Tudors destroyed its attractions as a palace. It is still technically a royal palace but, unsurprisingly, no monarch since James I has chosen to live there. The Yeoman Warders, with their nightly Ceremony of the Keys (when the West Gates, the Middle Tower and the Byward Tower are locked in one of the oldest military ceremonies in the world), and the resident Governor and Lieutenant, maintain the royal pretence. But the Tower today is run by the Department of the Environment as a successful museum of the chapters of England's past.

── FROM KEW TO HAMPTON COURT ──

The western, upstream stretch of the London river is the side for soft living, away from the stink and business of the city, but within easy reach by the river that was for fifteen centuries the main road of the capital. In the twelve miles from Kew to Hampton Court the Thames winds past three old royal palaces, the fossils of two others, numerous grand houses and expensive suburbs that prefer not to consider themselves part of London, and some lush riverine vistas that have not been wholly blotted out by the urban sprawl.

Kew today is shorthand for the ROYAL BOTANIC GARDENS, one of the oldest and most famous centres for the study of plants in the world. It has also been the home of a pleasure garden for Londoners since the seventeenth century. The three hundred acres of lawns and trees and exotic plants jutting out into a neck (or kew) of the Thames have been popular resorts for kings and courtiers for centuries, but they became the site of the favourite royal palace for several of the Hanoverians. The only palace still standing is the Dutch House, a funny little (by palatial standards) three-storey house of red bricks laid diagonally in Flemish bond. This replaced the White House, another Hanoverian palace, and George III lived a life of almost bourgeois bliss here, as well as it being his refuge, out of the public eye, during his periodic fits of madness. He commissioned James

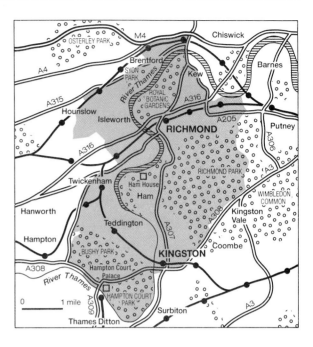

Kew Palace, built in 1631 of red brick in the Dutch style that was then gaining popularity. Originally it was a private mansion, known as the Dutch House, but George III moved here in 1802 when he had his former residence, the nearby White House, demolished.

Wyatt to build a castellated palace in the Gothic style beside it which, perhaps mercifully, was never finished.

The gardens, laid out for Queen Caroline of Anspach (George II's consort), were heavily altered by Lancelot 'Capability' Brown around 1770 and became famous under the unofficial directorship of Sir Joseph Banks. In 1841 they were handed over to the nation. The classical temples, follies and pagoda were designed by Sir William Chambers, who was employed to instruct the future George III in architectural draughtsmanship. Today Kew is an expensive residential suburb. Eighteenth-century houses surround the green, where cricket is played in the summer, and the church of St Anne.

On the north bank opposite is BRENTFORD, where travellers to the west crossed the Brent. Here was also a ford across the Thames. Brentford is run-down working-class, distracted by motorway and airline traffic, but no longer by barges, though the Grand Union Canal linking London and Birmingham runs into the Thames here. On the site of the old water works there are tower blocks of flats and the Kew Bridge Engine Trust, exhibiting historic steam pumping engines. Brentford is a famous name in the evolution of democracy in Britain. It was here that the electors of Middlesex persisted in returning John Wilkes as their Member of Parliament in a series of rowdy eighteenth-century elections, in spite of having his election continually annulled by Parliament.

Next on the north bank (more or less, as the Thames meanders in loops) comes another great house, a square, stone, embattled, turreted quadrangle with a lead lion passant on top of it. SYON HOUSE looks like yet another royal palace and it nearly is, having been the London home of the Percys, Dukes of Northumberland since 1594. They still live there, but in 1965 it became a garden centre. The grounds were laid out by Capability Brown and you can see London's heronry in their trees.

Next on the north bank lies ISLEWORTH, a posh riverside village, notable for the London Apprentice pub, which has been a river resort for Londoners since the fifteenth century, and for the ingenuity with which the parish church of All Saints has been rebuilt inside the shell of its fourteenth-century predecessor, burnt down in 1943.

The river swings round to Richmond, the only London borough with land on both sides of the Thames, surrounded by open spaces including the 2500 acres of RICHMOND PARK, the largest urban park in Britain. Richmond's cachet is due to yet another royal palace. It was originally called Sheen and from the twelfth century the English kings and their attendant flocks of courtiers, monks and statesmen had a salubrious retreat here, upstream from the dangerous capital. When the old palace was burned down in 1499, Henry VII rebuilt it and renamed it Richmond after his earldom in Yorkshire.

It became a favourite palace of the Tudors: Henry VIII

Hampton Court, built for Cardinal Wolsey, is the sole Tudor palace near London to have survived with its surrounding gardens virtually intact.

OPPOSITE One of Richmond's newest developments, on a fine riverside site by the bridge, is this commercial scheme by Quinlan Terry. Some consider it an appropriate homage to Georgian classicism, others condemn its artificiality.

was born here, Elizabeth died here. The contemporary drawings show a cluster of onion domes, and visitors from Chaucer onwards spoke of the creaking of the weather vanes. All that remains today is the gateway on the Green, carrying the arms of Henry VII, and the restored buildings of the Wardrobe. Around this has proliferated a large London borough, notable for its carefully restored river front and the famous view from Richmond Hill, more suburban sprawl than wooded vale today.

Next on the north bank is MARBLE HILL HOUSE, an eighteenth-century Palladian villa set in Thames parkland, built for George II's mistress, now open to the public. So is HAM HOUSE, on the south bank, the sleeping beauty of stately homes and a perfectly preserved Jacobean mansion and garden, little changed since John Evelyn and Horace Walpole visited it.

In the middle of the Thames lies Eel Pie Island, an oddity in a river whose islands are called aits or eyots. As its name suggests, this has been a place of raffish popular resort since before Dickens visited it and sent his characters there. On the north bank is STRAWBERRY HILL, Horace Walpole's Gothic Revival fantasy, now a teacher training college. And so to Teddington, the first lock on the Thames and a major watermark because here the tideway ends.

On the south bank is KINGSTON-UPON-THAMES, the next outer London borough, well-off because of its situation by the upstream Thames and green fields, and now a busy shopping-centre. Its name records that it was the coronation place for the Saxon kings of England and their reputed coronation stone is preserved outside the Guildhall.

As the river swings north again, in the great loop lies HAMPTON COURT palace and park, the last of London's river palaces and one of the grandest secular buildings in Britain. It was built by Cardinal Wolsey, the son of an Ipswich butcher who rose by wits and ambition to become Henry VIII's chief minister, as an outward and visible sign of his rise. He started it in 1514, in the green fields upstream from London, but within half an hour's fast rowing from the centre of power and danger. When Wolsey fell in 1529, partly because of his monarch's jealousy and frustration at not getting his way, Henry took over and finished the red brick Tudor palace. Wren rebuilt the eastern wing for William and Mary in neo-classical style. This side was badly damaged by fire in 1986, but is being rebuilt. Today Hampton Court provides grace and favour flats for forty-five royal pensioners, widows and children of distinguished men who have done the state some service, or, as William IV described it, 'the quality poor-house'. It is also one of the most popular tourist attractions in the country.

The Thames Bridges

Twenty bridges from Tower to Kew —
(Twenty bridges or twenty-two) –
Wanted to know what the River knew,
For they were young and the Thames was old,
And this is the tale that the River told:

The count was uncertain even in 1911, when Kipling wrote his 'Prehistoric Song' for C. R. L. Fletcher's *A History of England*. It depends on whether you count the footbridges at Hungerford, Richmond Lock and Teddington Lock (yes), and the abandoned piers of former bridges as at Blackfriars (no). Today there are thirty-four bridges between Tower Bridge and Hampton Court Bridge, that is in Greater London. They carry commuters from the southern dormitory suburbs across the Thames by rail, motor, bicycle and foot to their jobs in central London and back again in the rush hours. The traffic jams caused by the river crossing may seem intolerable, but they are nothing like as bad as they were for the many centuries when there was only one bridge.

Starting down river is Tower Bridge, London's best-known, opened in 1894, dominating the Tower with its two Victorian Gothic towers. These are not just ornamental blots on the landscape, but contain the machinery that operates the bascules or drawbridges that are raised to allow a headway of one hundred and forty feet. They are made of steel clad with stone in order to support the great weight, and have lifts to carry pedestrians to the high-level footbridge, now open as a museum.

Until 1750 London Bridge was the only bridge over the river in London. The first one was built by the Romans shortly after their arrival, at first probably a bridge of boats, a few yards downstream from the modern bridge. The stone one that replaced the previous wooden bridges in 1176 became one of the wonders of the medieval world, for spanning such a fierce tidal ebb and flow in the heart of a great city. It had houses, shops and a church built along either side of it, looking like the Ponte Vecchio in Florence, and decapitated heads of traitors were displayed on the spikes of the fortified gates at either end to encourage visitors from the south. In 1831 this old ruin and hazard to navigation was replaced by a granite bridge of five arches designed by John Rennie. Increasing traffic led to this being replaced in 1973 by the present bridge of three huge flat arches made of concrete. Rennie's bridge has crossed the Atlantic to America, where it now spans Lake Havasu in Arizona.

Londoners had to wait until 1750 for a second bridge over the Thames, at Westminster. Bridging the river was controversial because it threatened the privileges and livelihoods of such powerful interests as the City Corporation and the watermen. The Industrial Revolution bridged the barrier many times, allowing the Victorian megalopolis to spill its suburbs along the south bank. By 1850 London was a city along both banks of its river, although the centre remains firmly on the north.

Southwark Bridge (1912) replaced Rennie's early nineteenth-century three-arch, cast-iron bridge, with the

London Bridge in 1616 was still essentially the old twelfth-century stone bridge, heavily built up, as it was to remain for another one hundred and fifty years. Traitors' heads are displayed above the southern entrance arch on the far right.

largest central span ever made of iron. Southwark Causeway on the south side was used by Wren when he crossed the river to supervise the building of St Paul's. Blackfriars Bridge by William Cubitt (opened in 1899) replaced an eighteenth-century predecessor. The pulpits on the bridge commemorate the religious house that lent its name to the west end of the old City.

Waterloo Bridge by Sir Giles Gilbert Scott (opened in 1945) is an example of post-war concrete and Portland stone functionalism. It replaced another Rennie early nineteenth-century bridge with nine elliptical arches and Doric columns, described by Canova as 'the noblest bridge in the world'. Hungerford Railway Bridge was opened in 1864 to carry trains from the south-east into the new West End terminus of Charing Cross. The nine-span, wrought-iron lattice girders are functional rather than pretty, but the footbridge beside it gives a spectacular distant prospect of the City on the bend of the Thames.

Westminster Bridge, cast-iron with seven arches, was opened in 1862, to replace its 1750 predecessor. There had been a ford at low tide from the royal enclave at Westminster from earliest times (the river is still fordable by a tall man here). There was a horse ferry owned by the Archbishop of Canterbury at Lambeth Palace: he was paid £21,025 compensation when the first bridge was built. On old Westminster Bridge on 31 July 1802 Wordsworth wrote 'Earth has not anything to show more fair'.

Lambeth Bridge, a five-span, steel-arch bridge painted in red and brown, replaced a suspension bridge of 1862 and before that the Archbishop's ferry on which Oliver Cromwell's coach and horses sank and Mary of Modena and the infant Prince James escaped in 1688. Vauxhall Bridge, five steel arches on granite piers, connects Pimlico and Lambeth, and replaced the dangerous cast-iron bridge of 1811, originally called the Regent's Bridge. It was freed from tolls in 1879. When it opened in 1859 Victoria Railway Bridge was the widest railway bridge in the world, providing ten lines to Victoria Station. Chelsea Bridge, suspension, in 1934 replaced an earlier suspension bridge with cast-iron towers of 1858.

Albert Bridge (1873), a quaint hybrid of cantilever and suspension, is a precarious bottleneck for motor traffic. It is a pity it could not have been left as a footbridge. Battersea Bridge, dirty old iron of 1890, replaced the old wooden bridge of 1772 that transformed Chelsea into a little town and was much painted by Whistler and Turner. Wandsworth Bridge, three spans of steel-plate girder cantilevers, in 1940 replaced the first bridge of 1873. From 1729 until Westminster Bridge was opened, Putney Bridge was the first bridge across the

Hungerford Bridge, in the foreground, seen from the Savoy Hotel, was completed in 1864 to carry trains from the south into Charing Cross Station. Beyond it in this 1920 photograph are Westminster Bridge, in its surviving 1862 version, and the 1861 Lambeth Bridge, rebuilt in 1932.

river west of London Bridge. It was wooden with twenty-six spans, charged a toll and presented a serious obstruction to navigation. It was replaced by Bazalgette's five-span granite bridge in 1886. Since 1845 it has been the start of the Oxford and Cambridge University Boat Race (see *A London calendar*).

Hammersmith Bridge, distinctive for its frivolous pylons and pavilion tops, is another gateway to the south-west suburbs by Bazalgette. Opened in 1887, it re-uses the piers and abutments of the bridge of 1827, the first suspension bridge in London. Chiswick Bridge, 1933, three concrete arches faced with Portland stone, marks the finish of the Boat Race. Kew Bridge, three stone spans, is officially called the King Edward VII Bridge because he opened it in 1903. It replaced a wooden bridge with seven arches of 1759. Twickenham Bridge is a wide concrete traffic-carrier of 1933. Richmond Bridge, 1777, with its five arches and parapet, is one of the most handsome across the Thames. It replaced the earlier horse ferry, and was a toll bridge until 1859.

There is a footbridge at Teddington Lock, where the tide is stopped. Kingston Bridge, five stone arches, was opened in 1828, replacing a wooden bridge that had been there since the early Middle Ages and made Kingston an important crossing place. Like many of the London bridges it charged a toll until 1870. There is still a ferry at Hampton, but there has been a bridge there since 1753; the first one had seven spans of timber and was the largest Chinoiserie bridge ever built. It was replaced by an iron bridge for the rising suburbs of Surbiton and Kingston in 1865. The present Hampton Court Bridge, of reinforced concrete with stone and brickwork facing, replaced it in 1933.

THE CITY OF LONDON

The City is at once the most historic and the most aggressively modern part of the capital. London started here almost two thousand years ago and until the eighteenth century the 'Square Mile' (in fact, 677 acres) was London's principal residential area, as well as the centre of commerce and finance. Yet the City we see today is largely the product of three relatively recent building booms: in the 1860s and 1870s, the 1950s and 1960s and, still under way, the 1980s and 1990s. Aside

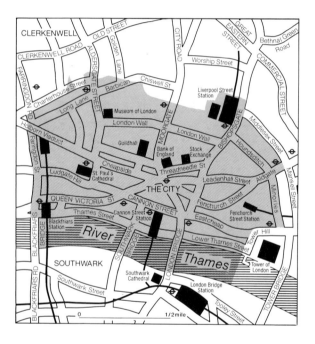

from Wren's churches and St Paul's Cathedral, virtually nothing remains of the City erected after the Great Fire and even the Victorian City is becoming increasingly hard to find.

The transformation of the City's role took place during the nineteenth century. Until then business was relatively small-scale. Bankers, merchants and brokers had their offices in domestic buildings, often living literally above the shop. Two developments changed the scale of their operations out of all recognition: the Industrial Revolution and the rapid expansion of the British Empire. The finance required to build the new factories was partly raised by the City's banks and on the Stock Exchange; the raw materials of the Empire were sold on the City's commodity markets and exchanges. By 1850 the City was becoming a major centre of international finance and trade.

To function efficiently, the City's flourishing institutions (banks, insurance companies, discount houses, commodity exchanges) required larger and more suitable accommodation. Property values were rising, fuelled by the City's increasing commercial importance. The time was ripe for redevelopment.

The great rebuilding of the 1860s and 1870s destroyed almost every trace of the City of Wren and the Georgians. Houses, churches, half-timbered coaching inns, all vanished – only about one in five of the City's buildings in 1855 was still standing in 1901. In their place came new commercial buildings and an improved road system, with new thoroughfares and old ones widened. The new purpose-built offices, the world's first, were for the most part imposing classical or neo-Gothic structures, often lavishly ornamented and decorated – outward expressions of the City's increasing wealth.

The City's inhabitants disappeared at the same time. The population fell from 128,000 in 1851 to 51,000 thirty years later, and to 27,000 in 1901. Land in the City was too valuable for houses and the City's workers began to commute to work on the new suburban railways.

The City's population has continued to fall steadily for most of this century, reaching 14,000 in 1921, 9000 in 1939, and a low point of 4000 in 1971, many of them resident office caretakers. There has been a modest increase to about 5300 in 1989, largely as a result of the construction of the Barbican. But, even so, most of the City's streets, packed by day (some 300,000 people are employed here), claim scarcely a handful of residents. By night they are largely deserted.

Demand for more, and more sophisticated, office space has likewise fuelled the more recent building booms. In the 1950s and 1960s, planners favoured slab-like office blocks which, many critics now argue, did much to destroy the unique character of the City by breaking up the dense medieval network of narrow streets and tight-knit buildings that the Victorian rebuilding had mostly preserved. Ironically, many of these blocks are now threatened with demolition. One reason is that they are ill-suited to contemporary office design, with its emphasis on information technology. But equally significant are the substantial profits that can

OPPOSITE Rapid modernization in the City has not altered the reality of commuters fighting their way to work on a wet morning, here along Queen Victoria Street near Bank Underground. The church is St Stephen Walbrook, described by Pevsner as 'amongst Wren's most playful spires'.

be made from up-to-date, space-efficient developments on the same site, despite the cost of demolition and rebuilding.

'Big Bang' is probably the most important single explanation for the City's current phenomenal redevelopment boom (see *The business of money*). During 1987 and the first half of 1988 planning permission was granted for 20 million square feet of office space – not far short of one-third of the City's existing stock of offices. The scale of many of the new projects far exceeds anything previously attempted. The mammoth BROADGATE complex near Liverpool Street Station, to be completed in 1991, consists of 14 independent buildings, providing 3.5 million square feet of office space.

The design of the new generation of building devel-

guards and cameras indicates. Whole blocks of streets, shops and alleys with a diverse history, character and contemporary life are being obliterated, to be replaced by monolithic structures whose overall effect has been described as 'corporate North American': a bland international style that robs the City of its individual character and makes it look just like any other financial centre.

THE HEART OF THE CITY

The streets immediately around the Bank of England are the commercial heart of the City and the area least disturbed by recent development. Three important buildings – the Bank, the Royal Exchange and Mansion House – face each other across a crowded junction,

George Dance the Elder's Mansion House, completed in 1753, today retains its original façade, although the interior has been much altered. This print dates from 1783.

opments generally shows some verve and imagination. Architects are using a variety of materials and colour, and the ubiquitous grey concrete of the 1960s has vanished. One particular benefit is the attention devoted to the spaces between the buildings. Imaginative use of fountains, greenery, courtyards and the provision of shops, wine bars, restaurants and so on, help create an attractive environment that encourages people to stop and pass the time.

On the debit side these new developments are, at best, semi-public spaces, as the presence of private security

modest in size compared with the public spaces of many other European capitals; but then the City has never favoured grand squares and avenues.

The BANK OF ENGLAND hides behind a forbidding blank exterior wall, which is virtually all that remains of the neo-classical offices designed by John Soane in 1788. The rest of the building was remodelled in the 1920s, but Soane's colonnaded Bank Stock Office, designed for the transaction of public business, has recently been reconstructed and forms an impressive introduction to the new Bank of England Museum. Exhibits explain its development as the nation's central bank. Gold is displayed in the central Rotunda – as near as visitors get to the millions stored deep in the underground vaults.

Between the Bank (traditionally nicknamed the Old Lady of Threadneedle Street) and the Royal Exchange (see *The business of money*), Threadneedle Street leads to the over-emphatic 330-foot concrete tower of the STOCK EXCHANGE (1972). Since 'Big Bang', trading has all but vanished from the floor and as a result a visit to the public viewing gallery, despite films and interactive displays, lacks excitement.

The massive NATIONAL WESTMINSTER TOWER (Richard Seifert, 1981) looms over Old Broad Street. The most interesting approach is along Adams Court, which leads to a small square with seats and a fountain directly at the base. From the top of the Tower there are views deep into the City's commuter hinterland. Architectural assessment gives way to statistical awe: 600 feet tall, 21 lifts (including five double-deckers), 100,000 tonnes of concrete, 12,000 square metres of windows.

Running east from the Bank interchange, Lombard Street, named after the North Italian merchants and bankers who settled in London in the thirteenth century, is full of banks, for the most part occupying imposing late nineteenth- and early twentieth-century buildings, their signs hanging from the façades. Tucked in the triangle formed with King William Street is ST MARY WOOLNOTH (Nicholas Hawksmoor, 1716–27). The exterior is severe, remarkable for its Corinthian columns inset from the corners, the interior majestic, with some fine wood carving. Edward Lloyd, founder of Lloyd's of London, is buried here (see *Lloyd's of London*).

An intricate network of narrow alleys runs around and between Cornhill (site of a medieval grain market), Lombard Street and King William Street. In St Michael's Court, close to Wren's St Michael's, Cornhill, is the Jamaica Wine House; now a pub, it was opened as a coffee house in 1688 and patronized by merchants involved in the West Indies trade. Simpsons, in nearby Ball Court, is an eighteenth-century chop house. Rothschilds Bank has its headquarters (1963–5) in narrow St Swithin's Lane: faced in black granite, the offices look on to a small courtyard.

MANSION HOUSE is the official residence of the Lord Mayor. Built in the mid-eighteenth century by George Dance the Elder, it looks somewhat like a country mansion set down by mistake in the middle of London's traffic. The main entrance is through an imposing classical portico. The interior, much altered over the years, contains a series of grand ceremonial rooms, notably the Ball Room and the Egyptian Hall, where banquets and receptions are held. The Lord Mayor's Show starts from here (see *Ceremonies*).

TOWARDS ST PAUL'S

Two roads, Queen Victoria Street and Poultry, run approximately west from Mansion House. The area between them is occupied by an ornate 1870 office block known as the Mappin & Webb building and an assortment of small-scale Victorian shops and offices. This has in recent years been the subject of controversy, starting when the property developer Peter Palumbo submitted plans to demolish the entire site and create a new plaza, MANSION HOUSE SQUARE, with a 290-foot office building by the modernist architect Mies van der Rohe as its focal point. Enthusiasts argued that London deserved a building by one of the masters of twentieth-century architecture. A 'great glass stump' was the reaction of the Prince of Wales in one of his first contributions to architectural debate.

The square itself was justified as a much-needed breathing space in the core of the City; Wren himself had proposed similar plazas and this twentieth-century version would provide an exciting area for ceremonial and public activities. It would also open up new views of Mansion House, Wren's St Stephen Walbrook (one of his finest interiors) and Lutyens's Midland Bank (1924–39). The counter-argument was that the existing Victorian buildings respected the tight-knit character and human scale of the City landscape, to which Palumbo's plaza was quite alien. Following a long public enquiry, planning permission was refused.

Poultry leads into Cheapside, the shopping centre of medieval London; *ceap* was Old English for market. You bought milk in nearby Milk Street, fish in Friday Street (Friday was a meatless day) and got your shoes repaired in Cordwainer Street. Half-way along is Wren's elegant (but much restored) St Mary-le-Bow, home of the celebrated Bow Bells, a landmark in an otherwise workaday street.

GUILDHALL, a few streets north of Cheapside, is the centre of the City's unique system of government, with origins in the twelfth century. In charge of the Corporation's affairs is the Court of Common Council, whose members are the Lord Mayor, 24 Aldermen and 133 elected Common Councillors representing 25 wards (areas) of the City. Elections are held every December, although most Councillors are returned unopposed; candidates do not stand on a party political ticket. The Corporation's responsibilities include health and social services, police and street-cleaning, but it also devotes much effort to fostering the City's economy. It maintains four Thames bridges, runs housing estates – several beyond the City's boundaries – and maintains 8000 acres of parks and open spaces, including Epping Forest and Burnham Beeches. The Lord Mayor, who is chosen from the Aldermen and serves for a year, plays an

Devastation and Reconstruction

On two occasions – following the Great Fire of 1666 and in the aftermath of the Second World War – London's planners and architects have been offered the chance to start afresh: to remodel the capital on more spacious lines, to create the drawing-board city of their dreams.

THE GREAT FIRE

The fire started on 2 September 1666 in a house in Pudding Lane, just north of Billingsgate Fish Market, when Thomas Farrinor, the King's baker, failed to bank down his oven properly at the end of the day's work. The flames took hold, slowly at first, then, fanned by a brisk east wind, ever more rapidly, racing through the close-packed timber buildings, swallowing homes, shops, churches and one famous City landmark after another: the Royal Exchange and St Paul's Cathedral, the Guildhall and Old Bailey, the Temple. When, after four days, the fire finally died, four-fifths of the City lay in ruins. By a miracle, only nine people lost their lives. As the inscription on the Monument, the official memorial to the Fire, puts it: 'For in a small space of time the city was seen most flourishing, and reduced to nothing.'

the King in support. Within days of the end of the fire, the young Christopher Wren, then better known as an astronomer than as an architect, met the King to discuss his grand reconstruction scheme. Wren's new city would have been based on a geometric grid of intersecting avenues, with a triumphal arch at the foot of Ludgate Hill below the rebuilt St Paul's, a massive forum around the Royal Exchange and, along the river, a 'Grand Terras with Public Halls'. It was a utopian vision that owed little to the pressing need to revive the City's

ABOVE Wren's ambitious plan for rebuilding London after the fire, including turning the Fleet River into a canal, was never put into effect. Instead, the city was rebuilt largely along the pattern of the old streets.
LEFT This contemporary painting of the Dutch school shows the fire at its height. Pepys, from across the river, saw 'one entire arch of fire from this to the other side of the bridge and in a bow up the hill above a mile long'.

To begin with, there was virtually no organized fire-fighting. Only on 4 September, after Samuel Pepys (having buried state papers and his wine and Parmesan cheese in his garden) had alerted Charles II's court, were fire-fighting teams set up and houses demolished to form fire-breaks. The Duke of York directed operations, with

shattered economy and rather more to Wren's studies of architectural theory and his visit to Paris the previous year.

Wren's plans, plus five more proposals, including an Italianate scheme by the diarist John Evelyn, were shelved. Immediate reconstruction was the City

Corporation's priority and it was unwilling to delay while grandiose schemes were prepared. A six-man commission was appointed to supervise the rebuilding. Timber was banned in favour of stone or brick. Houses were to follow standardized designs, with two, three or four storeys, depending on their position and the class of person occupying them. Some streets were widened, and one new thoroughfare (now King Street and Queen Street), from Guildhall to the river, was constructed, but the old street pattern was largely preserved.

By the late 1670s rebuilding was more or less complete, except for St Paul's and the parish churches. These were Wren's responsibility as Surveyor of the King's Works. The City skyline he created, punctuated by the graceful steeples of his churches and dominated by the magnificent dome of his cathedral, remained for more than two centuries and only vanished for good when the Luftwaffe's bombs rained down.

THE BLITZ

The Blitz on London began on 7 September 1940. The German planes, on average 160 of them, returned on each of the next 75 nights except one. After a brief respite, the raids continued until 11 May 1941. With his invasion plans frustrated by the failure to defeat the Royal Air Force during the summer of 1940, Adolf Hitler was determined to knock the commercial and administrative heart out of the capital and take revenge for British raids on German cities.

Some 30,000 civilians were killed and many more wounded. Although hardly a district remained un-scathed, the East End, the City and Westminster suffered the most. By November 1940, forty per cent of Stepney's houses had been damaged or destroyed. Following the final raid in May 1941, when the House of Commons, Westminster Abbey, the Law Courts, the Mint and the Tower of London were all hit, one-third of the capital's streets were blocked and 155,000 families were without gas or electricity.

The lack of official preparations was soon revealed. The fire service was disorganized, air-raid shelters were inadequate and unhygienic, rest centres for the homeless ill-equipped. Some 350,000 people took refuge in Underground stations each night. Morale, especially in the East End, plummeted and did not rally until early 1941, when systematic fire-watching was enforced and welfare services were improved.

The City suffered its worst night on 29 December 1940. The Guildhall and many of the remaining Wren churches were left in ruins, the narrow streets around St Paul's were destroyed, most of the Barbican and Moorgate vanished; over 1400 separate fires were

started. But, despite receiving two direct hits, St Paul's survived amid a ring of flames to become a symbol of the nation's will to resist.

Peacetime reconstruction began gradually, hampered by economic difficulties and shortages of materials. National policy, enshrined in the two Abercrombie Plans of 1943 and 1944, gave priority to public housing and factories, and Londoners were encouraged to move to the New Towns established in the countryside beyond the capital.

Thousands of people took refuge from the German bombs in Tube stations but even these were not totally secure. On the morning of 11 January 1941 more than one hundred people were killed in this direct hit on Bank Station in the City.

In the City, a third of it consisting of bomb sites, rebuilding had to await the lifting of restrictions on office construction in the early 1950s. The Holden–Holford Report (1947), commissioned by the Corporation, provided the blueprint for over twenty years of comprehensive redevelopment and improvement. Speed and commercial convenience were the main criteria, as they had been after the Great Fire, and little attention was paid either to aesthetic considerations or to the City's history and traditions. The end result was unimaginative and dispiriting; a sprouting of formula office blocks – rectangular, medium height, often set back from the street with a paved, windswept plaza. The object of the plazas was to let in daylight and maintain a conservative ratio of ground area to accommodation, but they produced a sterile and uninviting environment. A major programme of road construction led to the demolition of a number of historic buildings that had survived the War and, notably along the river, involved the destruction of the City's ancient street pattern. London's present skyline has neither the classical elegance of Wren nor the modern drama of Chicago or New York. A second chance had been lost.

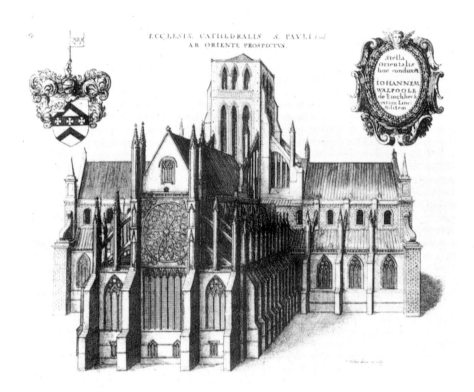

ECCLESIÆ CATHEDRALIS S. PAVLI
AB ORIENTE PROSPECTVS.

The medieval St Paul's Cathedral from the east. It was destroyed in the Great Fire and replaced by Wren's masterpiece.

OPPOSITE Old Change Court is one of the post-war pedestrian precincts built around St Paul's Cathedral – an amenity for lunching office workers in fine weather, but architecturally bland.

important role as the City's ambassador, travelling abroad on diplomatic and business missions and receiving state and other important visitors.

The Guildhall dates from the early fifteenth century, but was twice largely rebuilt, following the Great Fire and the Blitz; the façade is late eighteenth-century. The Hall itself is the scene of the Lord Mayor's Banquet, given each November to honour the outgoing Mayor and usually attended by the Prime Minister. It is 52 feet long and 49½ feet wide and decorated with the banners and arms of the City Livery Companies; figures of Gog and Magog, legendary giants, stand at the west end. A modern extension to the Guildhall houses a library with an excellent London collection, and a clock museum.

South of Cheapside, Queen Victoria Street, built 1867–71 with the District (Underground) Line underneath, is perhaps the most dispiriting of the City's main thoroughfares. Among a series of unimaginative twentieth-century buildings, Bucklersbury House (completed 1958) typifies the worst of post-war architecture: a dull four-storey slab with three six-storey spurs. A bare paved space in front contains an inaccurate 'reconstruction' of a Roman Temple of Mithras uncovered during the building: it was moved from its original site, only the ground plan is shown and some modern materials were used.

Attractive lanes run between the west end of Queen Victoria Street and St Paul's. In Blackfriars Lane, named after the Dominicans (or Black Friars) who settled here in the thirteenth century, is the seventeenth-century Apothecaries' Hall, built around a quiet court. After the monks left in the sixteenth century, actors moved in: two theatres were built in Playhouse Yard and Shakespeare may have owned a house in Ireland Yard. Printing House Square is the former home of *The Times* and *The Observer*. Wardrobe Place marks the site of the Great Wardrobe, a warehouse where medieval monarchs stored armour, robes and furniture. In Dean's Court is Wren's Deanery, a building of simple elegance.

ST PAUL'S CATHEDRAL

Even today, when several skyscrapers tower above it, Wren's masterpiece remains the focal point of the City skyline. The approach is along Ludgate Hill to the west front, with its twin towers and two-storeyed portico, but the view is interrupted by the 1960s' Juxon House. The river walkway, by the new buildings of the City of London School, offers a commanding view of the dome.

The cathedral, the fifth on the site, took only thirty-six years to build. There was some difficulty in getting the clergy to agree a design. Wren submitted three plans and was not happy with the design finally accepted; fortunately, he was able to make radical modifications during construction.

The nave, dark at first, draws the visitor forward to the crossing, suffused with light, then on to the choir,

with its fine wood carving by Grinling Gibbons and ironwork by Tijou, and the High Altar. A stone set in the floor of the crossing marks Wren's burial place in the crypt beneath. The inscription reads: *Lector, si monumentum requiris, circumspice* – 'Reader, if you seek his monument, look around you'.

Visitors climb to the Whispering Gallery to test the freak acoustics and enjoy the magnificent view down to the nave and chancel. The frescoes are the work of Sir James Thornhill – Wren would have preferred mosaics. A further climb leads to the exterior Stone and Golden Galleries, the second just below the lantern, ball and cross. This ascent reveals some of the mechanics of Wren's design. There are in fact two domes, not one, since from inside the cathedral the exterior dome would have appeared too high. A brick cone between the two domes supports the weight of the lantern.

The area immediately to the north of the cathedral, including the churchyard and an intricate pattern of narrow streets and courts, was devastated during the Second World War. Much was expected of the PATERNOSTER SQUARE development, planned by the architect William Holford in 1956 and erected between 1961 and 1967. Its large precinct and smaller courtyards, interspersed with shops and cafés, and with offices above, were planned as a pleasant meeting-place for office workers and tourists. The intention was laudable; the result is generally regarded as disastrous. The main

precinct was too large (and too windy) to be inviting, the buildings weathered badly, the shops were unexciting. Above all, the square diminished the impact of the cathedral. As elsewhere in London, recent redevelopment plans have provoked, and been delayed by, vigorous public debate about appropriate architectural styles in historic areas.

Beyond Paternoster Square to the west lies OLD BAILEY. The Central Criminal Court, topped with a statue of Justice, occupies part of the site of the notorious Newgate Prison, demolished in 1902. The road widens to accommodate the crowds who came to watch the public executions in the nineteenth century. Further west is Holborn Viaduct, built in the 1860s to bridge Farringdon Street; the statues on the ornate bridge are to Commerce, Agriculture, Science and Fine Arts.

——— SMITHFIELD AND THE BARBICAN ———

The core of Smithfield market is housed in a grand, covered, iron market hall designed by Horace Jones, as were Billingsgate and Leadenhall markets. It has been

Originally, Smithfield was the site of a well-known horse market, although other livestock was also sold there, and was used for public executions until the gallows were moved to Tyburn in Henry IV's reign. In the early nineteenth century live cattle were still bought and sold at Smithfield market. In 1855 they were moved to Islington but Smithfield remains London's wholesale meat market.

London's principal meat market since 1868, handling over 150,000 tons annually. Fleets of refrigerated lorries arrive from about eight o'clock each evening. Unloading – or 'pitching' – is complete by five o'clock in the morning, when the market opens for business, and all is quiet again by midday. Several local pubs have licences to open early for the benefit of market workers.

Facing the market buildings, St Bartholomew's Hospital – Bart's to every Londoner – is the oldest of the capital's hospitals (founded 1123 by a monk named Rahere) and still among the largest (see *Medicine*). ST BARTHOLOMEW-THE-GREAT, which Rahere also founded, is likewise London's oldest church, with an atmospheric Norman chancel and nave. Nearby, 41 Cloth Fair is a rare seventeenth-century survival.

In a redevelopment east of Bart's, the façades of Little Britain's Victorian warehouse are being retained, but the street's Dickensian atmosphere has vanished. Postman's Park, one of the City's numerous pockets of green, takes its name from the nearby General Post Office; the park was formed in 1880 from several churchyards.

LONDON WALL, planned as the southern, commercial fringe of the Barbican development, has become a case-study in rapid obsolescence. Six virtually identical slab office blocks were built in the 1960s and 1970s alongside a dual carriageway, with a 35-storey 'sentinel block' at the east end. Pedestrians used a 'traffic-free zone', a windswept high-level walkway with a scattering of shops. The result, nowadays regarded as alienating, was at least a considered attempt to create a coherent urban landscape. Redevelopment to provide the high-tech offices of the 1990s promises riches. By early 1989 one block had already been demolished and it seems likely that the others will soon disappear. Terry Farrell's Alban Gate, the first of the replacements, straddles the road, with a distinctive curved roof-line, two open-air atriums and façades in grey, red and pink.

The BARBICAN was the Corporation's largest piece of post-war planning, inspired by the ideal of recreating a living City. Planned in the late 1950s and completed in the early 1970s, the development combines high-density housing (some 2000 flats, maisonettes, houses and luxury penthouses) with spacious landscaped gardens and a two-acre ornamental lake designed to provide visual interest and a sense of intimacy. Sections of the Roman wall and the restored parish church of St Giles Cripplegate, burnt out in 1940, have been incorporated. Three 43-storey tower blocks mark the skyline, but there are also many low-rise terrace blocks. People and traffic are segregated; pedestrians use the nineteen-foot-high podium, while traffic circulates underneath. The Corporation has largely failed in its original aim of attracting ordinary office workers to live in the City. Rents, initially quite modest, have increased and the properties now change hands for high sums.

Within the Barbican development are the Guildhall School of Music and Drama, halls of two Livery Companies – the Ironmongers and the Barbers – the City of London Girls' School and an Arts Centre, opened in 1982. There are two theatres, the London home of the Royal Shakespeare Company, as well as a concert hall (base of the London Symphony Orchestra), art gallery, cinema and library. These, together with restaurants, informal exhibition spaces and, in summer, open-air cafés and events, draw crowds of visitors.

THE EASTERN EDGE

When it is complete in 1991, the colossal BROADGATE development will cover 29 acres, enveloping the platforms and tracks at Liverpool Street Station. (The late Victorian façade of the Great Eastern Hotel and part of the glass and cast-iron roof of the train shed will be preserved.) Broadgate represents up-to-the-minute office architecture. The centrepiece is Broadgate Arena, where plant-decked balconies look down on to shops and restaurants and a skating rink, converted in summer into an arena for outdoor entertainments. At night, with lights streaming down from the glass walls of the surrounding offices and skaters swirling, the effect is electric.

South along Bishopsgate are two of the City's oldest churches. The Great Fire just missed tiny ST ETHELBURGA'S which largely dates from the fifteenth century; its walls are built of rubble and ragstone. ST HELEN'S, set in a small churchyard, maintains an active evangelistic ministry among City workers. Originally part of a thirteenth-century Benedictine nunnery, the church has a double nave – one for the nuns, the other for parishioners.

Just beyond St Helen's is the headquarters of Standard Chartered Bank (1985). The entrance is a large landscaped atrium, with waterfalls, streams, trees and plants. Opposite, underneath the National Westminster Tower, stands another bank equally characteristic of its age: Gibson's National Provincial Bank (1864–5), surmounted with statues and containing a handsome banking hall.

To the east of St Helen's, on the corner of Leadenhall Street and St Mary Axe, are the P&O and Commercial Union buildings (1964–9), among the best of the City's 1960s' architecture. Opposite is Richard Rogers's dramatic headquarters for LLOYD'S (1986), whose six satellite towers with their exposed metal pipework and vast 200-foot barrel vault of sparkling glass aroused enormous controversy. A visitor centre, reached by the exterior lifts, describes the development of Lloyd's from origins in a City coffee house to the centre of the international insurance business. From viewing galleries, visitors look down into the Underwriting Room (known always as the 'Room'), where business is transacted (see *Lloyd's of London*).

To the east, Leadenhall Street leads to Aldgate, a busy traffic junction poised between the City and the East End: an uneasy meeting-point of wealth and deprivation. New commercial developments overshadow ST

Avis, refused all payment for his work.

Immediately west of Lloyd's is LEADENHALL MARKET, housed in a cheerful cast-iron building of 1881, with a mixture of shops and restaurants. There has been a market here since the fourteenth century (see *Markets*).

Below Fenchurch Street, narrow streets descend to the Thames. In ST OLAVE'S, Hart Street (Dickens's St Ghastly Grim in *The Uncommercial Traveller*), Samuel Pepys and his wife Elizabeth were buried; the fifteenth-

The hay market in Whitechapel High Street was still functioning in 1927 and the horse-drawn wagons in the foreground illustrate the demand for it. This corner of Leman Street was where East Enders rallied in October 1936 to forestall a march by Fascists. The church is St Botolph's Aldgate, by George Dance the Elder, just within the City boundary.

OPPOSITE Three ages of City architecture. On the right, Wren's spire of St Dunstan-in-the-East; in the foreground the neo-classical Custom House, completed in 1817; behind them, two modern landmarks, the Lloyd's Building and the Nat West Tower.

BOTOLPH'S, rebuilt by George Dance in the 1740s, where the crypt serves as a centre for homeless people.

CUTLERS GARDENS (Richard Seifert, 1982) is an extensive office development built largely on the site of fortress-like eighteenth- and nineteenth-century East India Company warehouses. Four warehouses were retained (although gutted internally), as well as the original ground plan. Arcades, courtyards, gardens and fountains help create a human scale; but conservationists mourned the loss of the 'greatest industrial elevation in London'.

The streets around Houndsditch (so called because dead dogs, among other refuse, were buried there) used to contain many Jewish businesses, now largely vanished. Concealed in a small courtyard off Bevis Marks is the SPANISH AND PORTUGUESE SYNAGOGUE, built in 1701 in a plain style. The architect, a Quaker named Joseph

century church survived the Great Fire, but was badly damaged in the Second World War. Lovat Lane, St Mary-at-Hill (with its Wren church of the same name) and Idol Lane are all quiet streets. A small garden has been made in the ruins of Wren's St Dunstan-in-the-East. His MONUMENT, erected 1671–7, commemorates the Great Fire; 202 feet tall, it is 202 feet distant from the spot where the fire started.

Along Lower Thames Street the 1870s' façade of Billingsgate is being retained, while the interior is converted to offices; the fish market, still under Corporation control, moved to Docklands in 1982. Next door the CUSTOM HOUSE, headquarters of Her Majesty's Customs and Excise, has a fine nineteenth-century river frontage, designed by Robert Smirke to replace an earlier building which partially collapsed. It is a fitting monument to commerce, the City's life blood.

Wren's Churches

Eighteenth-century views of the City of London show a marvellous skyline pierced by many towers, spires, cupolas and domes. That vision has been obliterated in our own time, amid some controversy.

The genius responsible for creating it was Christopher Wren (1632–1723). While at Oxford, Wren assisted in dissection and anatomical studies; subsequently he became a Fellow of All Souls and in 1661 at the age of 29 was appointed Professor of Astronomy. As a scientist Wren knew the pioneers of the new experimental learning. By 1660 he was involved in architectural debate, and designed buildings at Cambridge and Oxford in 1663 and 1664. In 1665 he travelled to France to study the 'Fabrick of Paris', as he had been consulted on the repair of old St Paul's Cathedral in London, and wished to see the achievements of French masters.

The Great Fire of 1666 gave him a unique opportunity to demonstrate his architectural skills and within a few days he presented a scheme for rebuilding the City to the King. Although Wren's ideas were never realized, his designs for the City churches were, and they represent one of the most remarkable achievements of any architect at any time. Money was levied by raising a tax on coal coming into the Port of London and a Rebuilding Act of 1670 provided for the erection of churches and the merging of parishes in order to reduce the number of buildings compared with the churches before the Fire. The tax was used to pay only for the shells of the churches: all fittings had to be provided and paid for by the parishes.

Wren was appointed Surveyor-General of the King's Works by special favour of Charles II in 1668–9, and his office began work in earnest on the design of the churches erected after 1670.

Sites were awkwardly shaped or very confined and mostly quite small. Wren had to plan for Protestant worship as opposed to the old Catholic forms, so spaces had to be created for a largely static congregation which

LEFT St Mary Aldermary in 1839: the tower is derived from the early sixteenth-century church destroyed in the Fire.
ABOVE St Stephen Walbrook, perhaps Wren's finest interior.
OPPOSITE St Bride's in Fleet Street: an 1840 view.

would be seated during the long sermons. The City churches were for parish use and parochial life was important: attendance at church was virtually obligatory, so the churches were well used. Because sites were often cramped, little elaboration was lavished on the exteriors: the furnishings inside were more important. Towers were usually plain until the upper stages which were meant to be seen from afar, over the roof-tops. Such showy structures reflected a release from Puritan rigour, re-established the presence of the Church of England and embellished the City in a manner worthy of a great capital to vie with European rivals.

The City churches were rebuilt under the direction of Wren, Robert Hooke and Edward Woodroffe; Wren seems to have delegated much of the detail to others, but retained control over the designs, approving parts where necessary. Fifty-two churches were erected under Wren's aegis, but it is clear that many architectural details and the internal fittings were designed by the master craftsmen who made them. Wren (who was knighted in 1673) had imbibed architectural influences from a number of sources: he was familiar with the precedents of Classical Antiquity and with the works of Serlio, Palladio and other masters, but he also knew the stunning inventions of the Italian Baroque architects from illustrations. St Vedast, for example, has a spire much influenced by the work of Borromini. Other influences were Netherlandish and French (Perrault's east front of the Louvre had a profound effect on Wren's architecture, for its motifs recur in his work).

Many of these churches were subsequently altered, or destroyed when they were declared redundant in the last century. In the eighteenth century people began to leave the City to reside elsewhere and parish life declined. By the 1830s many churches were empty, a phenomenon described by Dickens in *The Uncommercial Traveller*. The first proposal to destroy churches was made in 1833, and in 1860 the Union of Benefices Act resulted in the demolition of several churches and the sale of sites to raise funds for building new churches elsewhere.

In an attempt to brighten up remaining churches, several underwent drastic renovation. In 1899 the Church decided to destroy ten more Wren buildings and three were pulled down. In 1919 a further nineteen were listed for demolition, but opposition hardened and architectural arguments began to prevail; the House of Lords defeated the Measure in 1926. Most of the remaining churches were damaged or destroyed in the Blitz and the worst cases of damage were not rebuilt.

After 1945 the parishes were again reduced in number and many churches became associated with Guilds, shedding their parochial functions. City churches are oases of peace in the hubbub of daily life: some are used for quiet contemplation, others offer regular religious services, others host concerts and debates.

The most interesting surviving Wren churches are:

ST BENET, Paul's Wharf, Upper Thames Street, 1667–83.
ST BRIDE, Fleet Street, 1671–4.
ST JAMES GARLICKHYTHE, Garlick Hill, 1676–82.
ST LAWRENCE JEWRY, Gresham Street, 1671–9.
ST MAGNUS THE MARTYR, Lower Thames Street, 1671–6.
ST MARGARET LOTHBURY, 1686–90.
ST MARGARET PATTENS, Rood Lane, 1684–7.
ST MARTIN LUDGATE, Ludgate Hill, 1677–84.
ST MARY ABCHURCH, Abchurch Lane, 1681–6.
ST MARY ALDERMARY, Bow Lane, 1681–2.
ST MARY AT HILL, Lovat Lane, 1670–6.
ST MARY LE BOW, Cheapside, 1670–3.
ST MICHAEL CORNHILL, 1670–2.
ST PETER-UPON-CORNHILL, 1677–81.
ST STEPHEN WALBROOK, 1672–9.
ST VEDAST, Foster Lane, 1695–1701.

CENTRAL LONDON

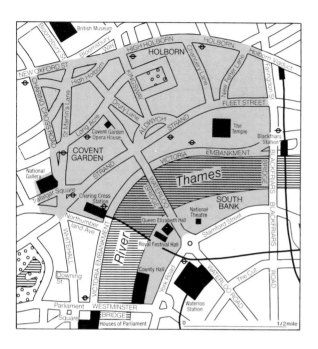

HOLBORN

In summer at lunchtime Lincoln's Inn Fields are almost rural. Sporty lawyers bat tennis balls back and forth while less sporty ones laze on benches beneath the full-blown plane trees, watching, slumbering or swotting up on a brief wrapped in red tape. The café does brisk trade, as do the street-corner ice-cream sellers. The atmosphere is peaceful and controlled; for this is legal land. Nearby are Lincoln's Inn and its suppliers – Wildy the law bookseller lurks over the southern entrance, while Ede and Ravenscroft of Star Yard are busy making wigs for bench and bar. The Seven Sisters pub in Carey Street drones with legal gossip.

The Fields are a jealously guarded sanctuary from the noise and hurry of central London, protected by generations of lawyers. In the fourteenth century, the green space was waste land used as a playground by legal students of Lincoln's Inn. In 1613, the application by one Charles Cornwallis to build a house prompted a remarkable piece of early urban control. The legal community lobbied to stop 'unnecessary and unprofitable buildings' filling up 'that small remainder of ayre'. For two decades they battled with various developers, finally reaching a compromise: William Newton was permitted to build his houses around the Fields, as long as the central part 'for ever and hereafter be open and unbuilt' (see *Noble squares*).

The peace enjoyed by such residents as half a dozen Lords Chancellor and the architect John Soane (1753–1837), whose house is now a museum, was in stark contrast to busy Holborn, the road to the north. Here a unique row of Tudor half-timbered houses survives and, behind them, parts of the small Staple Inn and Barnard's Inn. Holborn Viaduct, hurtling across the former river Fleet into the City proper, is a Victorian triumph decorated with Victorian virtues – Commerce, Agriculture, Science and Fine Arts – opened in 1869 by Queen Victoria.

TEMPLE

Stretching down to the river from Fleet Street, a labyrinth of silent squares forms INNER and MIDDLE TEMPLE, two of London's four Inns of Court. At the river end, great iron gates protect Inner Temple's huge, immaculate garden. A narrow, gloomy walk, Middle Temple Lane, separates one Inn from the other, its street door slammed shut and locked every night. Inside, the lamplighter lights gas-lamps at dusk; and on Sundays the unwigged judges, barristers and students sing lustily at Matins in Temple church (see *Lawyers and courts*).

More than Gray's Inn with its gardens or Lincoln's Inn with its collegiate buildings, the Temple sustains a medieval legal atmosphere. From the Middle Ages until the eighteenth century, the powerful lived in a parade of fashionable palaces here, just as they did in the Strand; those of bishops were known as 'inns'. In 1185, the London branch of the Knights Templar, who protected pilgrims on their way to Jerusalem, moved from Holborn to the riverside. They built the circular Temple church and an adjoining monastery, funded by the donations of the devout. Coveted by jealous monarchs, their London land became Crown property at the Dissolution and was leased in perpetuity by the Benchers, the senior member of the Inns. Today the Purbeck marble effigy of Robert de Ros and those of other Knights Templar, lie serene in the church. The magnificent garden, laid out on land created when the river was embanked, was from 1888 until 1913 the site of the Royal Horticultural Society's major annual show, until it

OPPOSITE Legal London has for centuries centred on the strategic neighbourhood between the City and Westminster. The Inner Temple, whose lawns stretch up to the Strand from the Embankment, is one of the four Inns of Court where much of the nation's law is practised. Law students are required to have been accepted by one of the Inns as a condition of attending Bar School.

moved to the Royal Hospital to become the Chelsea Flower Show.

FLEET STREET

The name Fleet Street conjures a collage of images: the smell of black ink, thundering presses, bales of newsprint, vans hurtling to catch late trains, night-time deadlines and daytime news-hunting. Like lawyers, journalists hovered between the City and Westminster, feeding on both (see *The Press*). The most striking newspaper building left on Fleet Street is the glossy 1931 headquarters of the *Daily Express*, but plenty of other press memories persist. Punch Tavern is where *Punch* was conceived in 1841; Lutyens designed the headquarters of Reuter and the Press Association in 1935. Dr Johnson's house, where he lived from 1746 to 1759 and wrote his dictionary, still stands in Gough Square.

Such spiritual needs as journalists have are served by St Bride's church, one of Wren's most admired, set back south of Fleet Street and hard to see from it – or indeed from anywhere (see *Wren's churches*). A church has been on the site since at least the sixth century, and before that a Roman villa. Remains from these former buildings and from the church's later history are displayed in a small museum in the crypt. Further west at no. 17, on the same side of the road, is another historic structure, the seventeenth-century PRINCE HENRY'S ROOM, once the main oak-panelled room of an inn, it is now open to the public.

TEMPLE BAR, a majestic Wren archway, used to mark the border between the City and Westminster at the point where Fleet Street becomes the Strand. It was removed in 1878 as a traffic obstruction. Just beyond it,

on the Strand side, are G.E. Street's Royal Courts of Justice, known as the LAW COURTS, London's last great Gothic public building, opened by Queen Victoria in 1884, when the courts moved here from Westminster Hall. A slum had been cleared to make way for it and more clearances created Aldwych and Kingsway, which culminates grandly in Bush House, built as offices from 1925–35 but, since 1940, home of the BBC World Service.

COVENT GARDEN

Covent Garden piazza hums with life seven days a week. Keen shoppers pick over craftsmen's stalls piled high with hand-made toys, fancy inlaid buttons, hand-marbled paper, expensive knitwear, bold ethnic jewellery and old silver. Others explore old market halls to find Noel Coward's slippers in the Theatre Museum or jump on to old red London buses in the Transport Museum. Young people window-shop outside fashion boutiques; friends meet in pavement restaurants. Street

A similar fate could have befallen Covent Garden a few years later, were it not for the zeal of its residents and conservationists. Instead, the former fruit and vegetable market was transformed into a self-conscious, heady mixture of Continental square, smart shopping arcade and street fair. It recalls the area's heyday, when actors and writers gossiped in coffee houses and late-night audiences poured from the theatres to pick their way home through moonlit cartloads of cabbages, apples and strawberries arriving from the country for next day's market. Here Samuel Johnson and James Boswell first met at the home of the bookseller Thomas Davies. The actor David Garrick lived here, his memory perpetuated by the GARRICK CLUB (1860 – see *Gentlemen's clubs*).

The area's present bustle contrasts with the monastic calm that prevailed when it was in fact a convent garden, providing food for Westminster Abbey. After its Dissolution in 1540, the land was given to the first Earl of Bedford. As London expanded the fourth earl came to

entertainers – acrobats, magicians, buskers, break-dancers – turn the cobbled area in front of St Paul's into an open-air theatre.

This is the heart of rejuvenated Covent Garden, whose vivacious atmosphere has infected the surrounding streets as far as the theatres of ST MARTIN'S LANE but has not quite reached the cosy bookshops of CHARING CROSS ROAD – nor, at its north end, the ungainly 35-storey CENTRE POINT (completed 1967), the West End's tallest office tower, an aberration of 1960s planning notorious for standing empty for nearly a decade while the owner exploited a tax loophole that made this the most profitable course.

Covent Garden in Regency times was devoted to pleasure and commerce, as it is today. The colonnaded buildings to the north, and their dignified neighbours, were then fashionable residences and are now expensive offices.

recognize the rent potential. To overcome Charles II's reluctance to allow building over the area he tactfully employed the King's favourite architect, Inigo Jones. Inspired by Italian piazzas, in 1631 Jones began the first residential square in London, adorned by his ST PAUL'S CHURCH, known as the 'handsomest barn in England' because of its plain internal structure. The portico outside, supported by classical columns, set the tone for the rest of the piazza, and to an extent does so still.

To amuse residents, the first THEATRE ROYAL was built in Drury Lane in 1663 (see *Theatre*). The present classical building by Benjamin Wyatt, completed in 1812, has a striking hall and foyer. In 1732 John Rich brought his theatre down from Lincoln's Inn Fields and built the first Covent Garden OPERA HOUSE, for which Handel wrote a string of oratorios. It was replaced first in 1809 and then in 1858 by E. M. Barry's version, today being refurbished.

When the court moved from Whitehall to St James's, the piazza emptied of society. The remaining stragglers fled when the fifth earl won a licence for a market for flowers, fruits and herbs in 1670. The tone plummeted. Cheap entertainment, gambling dens, prostitutes, Turkish baths and cheap lodgings lurked behind the elegant façades. The north-west of St Giles was worst, an area of slums where the Great Plague had started in 1664, taking its toll here of more than a thousand lives a month. In the nineteenth century the markets expanded, given order by Charles Fowler's inspired Central Market (1831), Barry's Floral Hall (1860), the Flower Market (1891) and the Jubilee Market (1904).

Now the slums have gone and a more wholesome atmosphere prevails, nowhere more so than in NEAL'S YARD, with its dairy, bakery and health food shops. Office rents are among the highest in London – not surprising, with all those attractions on hand. But the return of its erstwhile affluence has not emasculated Covent Garden; its lively, irreverent spirit lives on.

STRAND

The wide, straight Strand is one of the capital's principal arteries and connects its two cities, London and Westminster. Along it are vestiges of all its past fashions. Shops such as Stanley Gibbons, the stamp-sellers who arrived in 1874, continue the tradition of the Earl of Salisbury's New Exchange shopping centre built in 1608. The Adelphi and Vaudeville theatres survive from the days when this street had more theatres than any other. Simpson's harks back to the old coffee-houses and dives: in the 1840s regulars at Simpson's Divan and Tavern tucked into roast beef between games of chess. And the Savoy, designed for the Gilbert and Sullivan impresario Richard D'Oyly Carte in 1889, is still one of the world's grandest hotels.

The Strand was so called because it was the street closest to the Thames. With the City merchants at one end and the king and his courtiers at the other, this bridle path linking two power centres grew in status as London grew, until in the 1830s Disraeli declared it 'perhaps the finest street in Europe'.

The riverside plots attracted bishops and noblemen who built a string of medieval 'palaces'. John of Gaunt, first Duke of Lancaster, lavished £35,000 on the magnificent Savoy House in the fourteenth century. Later Elizabeth I gave her favourites homes here – Sir Walter Raleigh got the Bishop of Durham's mansion. A lone remnant of this grandeur is the watergate of York House, the home of the Archbishop of York and then of

OPPOSITE St Paul's church, built by Inigo Jones for 4th Earl of Bedford in the 1630s, was an integral part of the piazza scheme and heavily influenced by Jones's experience of Italy. It now regularly acts as a backdrop to the succession of crowd-pulling street entertainers.

RIGHT Before Aldwych was constructed in the early years of the twentieth century, Gibbs's church of St Mary-le-Strand provided a more effective focal point for the east end of the Strand than it does today. On the right of the picture, the Gaiety Toilet Club is named after the nearby Gaiety Theatre.

The Adam brothers' Adelphi development (Adelphi is Greek for brothers) was built in the 1770s and pulled down in the 1930s. In the foreground is the water gate of the former Whitehall Palace.

the Duke of Buckingham. It stands well inland in what is now Embankment Gardens. At the other end of the Strand, Somerset House was completed in 1550 and served briefly as a royal residence. It was demolished in 1775 and the present imposing building was completed in 1835. It is used as government offices and as the new home of the Courtauld Gallery (see *Great houses and palaces*).

Close by are two churches that now occupy island sites in the Strand and are thus often confused. The farther east is ST CLEMENT DANES, begun by Wren in 1679, incorporating the tower from an eleventh century church on the site. James Gibbs designed a dainty 'bonnet' for the tower forty years later. It is today the official church of the Royal Air Force. About one hundred yards west, the Baroque ST MARY LE STRAND, completed in 1714, was the first public building Gibbs designed.

In the 1760s the Adam brothers built the elegant and ambitious riverside ADELPHI scheme, an early housing complex mostly torn down in 1931, except for its arches facing the river. Some of the elegant streets that surrounded it have survived, although several of those to its west were lost when Charing Cross station was built in 1863 (see *The rail termini*). Land was gained, however, when Bazalgette claimed the wide embankment from the Thames. In the 1980s the station itself became the site of one of London's boldest developments, including a building by Terry Farrell rising eight floors above the station and hung from ten great arches bridging the concourse. The scheme is completed by Farrell's ingenious walkway connecting Trafalgar

Square to Charing Cross station and Hungerford Bridge, giving access to the South Bank.

CHARING CROSS was the last resting-place of Eleanor of Castile, Edward I's queen, on her way to burial in Westminster Abbey. The Victorian Eleanor Cross in front of the station replaces a medieval original. The oldest monument in the area now is Le Sueur's magnificent equestrian bronze of Charles I at the entrance to Whitehall. The piecemeal creation of TRAFALGAR SQUARE in the 1830s and 1840s, replacing the sprawling royal stables, dramatically opened up the Charing Cross district. On the square's northern side is William Wilkins's NATIONAL GALLERY of 1832–8 (see *Museums and galleries*), in the process of acquiring a western extension on space left when Hamptons furniture store was bombed in the Second World War. When Ahrends, Burton and Kodalek won the competition to design the extension, the Prince of Wales described their effort as a 'monstrous carbuncle' and the job was given instead to the American, Robert Venturi, whose classical design is much less controversial.

On the other side of the gallery, in the corner of the square, Gibbs's ST-MARTIN-IN-THE-FIELDS church, completed in 1724, has become almost a textbook example of Georgian church architecture, although it incorporates elements of earlier churches on the site. On the east side the South African Embassy stares past Nelson's Column (1839–42) and Landseer's gentle lions at the grandiose Canadian High Commission, occupying the much modified premises of the Royal College of Physicians, completed by Sir Robert Smirke in 1827. (The College itself has moved to Regent's Park.)

SOUTH BANK

The South Bank entertainment and arts complex is an outpost of West End theatreland, separated and a bit isolated by the river but handy for Waterloo station. Not everyone likes the concrete fascias and high walkways and there are plans to modify them. Still, in fine weather a near-Continental atmosphere can pervade as musicians busk, people play boule or skateboard, others examine the open-air bookstalls, and patrons of the plays, concerts and films drink on the terraces with their wide river views. In contrast, the subterranean car parks and pedestrian subways increasingly provide shelter for the homeless. The original vision of the South Bank was an expression of the creative mood of optimism that gave birth to the Festival of Britain held here in 1951 to cheer up the British after post-war austerity and to celebrate the centenary of the Great Exhibition of 1851. The mixture of temporary fairs and buildings, erected on derelict land, produced an animated atmosphere and gave birth to a long-term scheme. Robert Matthew and J. L. Martin's Royal Festival Hall, the Festival's only permanent building, was the foundation for what is now the largest arts centre in the world – twice the size, for instance, of New York's Lincoln Center. Five million people visit the complex each year, some forty thousand visit the Royal Festival Hall each week, and the day-long programme of events inside and outside includes one hundred and forty concerts a month. Recent additions include Sir Denys Lasdun's National Theatre, opened in 1976 (see *Theatre*), and the Museum of the Moving Image (MOMI), opened in 1988.

South of the complex, in front of the late-1950s Shell Centre, lie Jubilee Gardens. Beyond them is County Hall, Ralph Knott's palatial headquarters for the London County Council, begun in 1910 but not completed until 1930. The LCC was formed in 1889 as the first single body to run amorphous London; later enlarged as the Greater London Council, it was abolished by Parliament in 1986. Plans for the 2390 rooms and ten miles of corridors include a deluxe hotel in the south section, conference halls in the middle and apartments at the north, with riverside access to ground-floor shops.

SOHO

London without Soho would be like an egg without salt. The pleasure-seeking, licentious character of this ancient and cosmopolitan quarter has been an essential part of the capital's flavour for three centuries. Ironically, many habitués and residents now fear that, with rental values mounting as the sex shops and strip clubs are closed down (they have been reduced from 167 to 10), Soho may lose the other specialist businesses that are among its more respectable attractions. Apart from its many

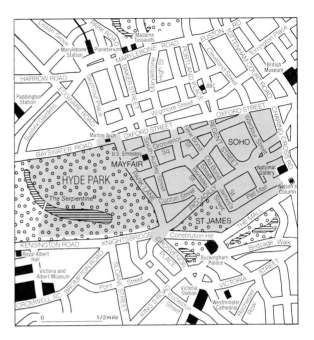

Greek, Italian, French and Far Eastern restaurants, Soho has always been a place to track down exotic cheeses, oils and coffees, rare white truffles, Chinese and Indian spices, and to find those elusive personal services such as alteration tailoring.

Soho now has only a few thousand residents, though more than 70,000 workers pass through it each day and night. The Street Offences Act of 1959 drove prostitutes off the narrow roads and alleys, but they were replaced by ever more garish manifestations of the sex industry in the permissive 1960s. Many of the former brothels have been taken over by production and facilities houses connected with the booming television industry, established in the 1980s close to the traditional home of the film industry in Wardour Street; and several advertising agencies have followed them there.

Soho has always had an ambivalent character: craftsmen and artists side by side with prostitutes and dubious places of entertainment. As early as 1641, a 'lewd woman' named Anna Clerke was bound over for threatening to burn 'houses at So:ho'. The curious name is believed to have derived from an old hunting cry. There is evidence that hunting took place over St Giles's Field, as the land was known before Henry VIII acquired it to make a park for Whitehall Palace. Bits were subsequently sold to various aristocratic developers; the earls of Leicester, Newport and Salisbury are remembered in street names, along with Lord Gerard, whose principal legacy, Gerrard Street, has been dominated by Chinese restaurants and food shops since the late 1950s. They have also colonized Lisle, Wardour and Macclesfield Streets, to form a pedestrian precinct guarded by

Chinese triumphal arches and complete with pagoda-style telephone kiosks.

Packed into a network of narrow streets bounded by Oxford Street, Wardour Street and Charing Cross Road – a street pattern largely untouched by the twentieth century – Soho's raffish character spills out southward to touch Piccadilly Circus, where the young and transient traditionally congregate at the foot of Alfred Gilbert's Eros statue (properly called the Shaftesbury Memorial). Originally designed by Nash as a true traffic circle, it is now partly pedestrianized around Eros, but the handsome London Pavilion building, whose portico was once a symbol of the hub of Empire, has been cleaned and refurbished to make one of the many shopping malls that have been created in the area since the 1970s.

The Soho voltage is less intense by the time it reaches Leicester Square, first laid out in 1635 and now a scruffy

Soho Square, one of the earliest London squares, was laid out before the end of the seventeenth century. For much of the eighteenth century it was among the most fashionable places in London to live.

and incoherent space. Its monumental 1930s' cinemas are a dull replacement for the flamboyant theatres of the 1900s: the Empire with its celebrated promenade, Daly's and the Alhambra, all famous for lavish musical comedies. Before the First World War the square was the hub of London's nightlife and, when the soldiers sang 'Goodbye, Piccadilly; farewell, Leicester Square' in their favourite marching song, they were in truth bidding farewell to an era. Today's theatreland is more scattered, but its heart is in Shaftesbury Avenue, a road driven through Soho slums in the 1880s and named after the philanthropic Earl.

Soho can boast the oldest of London's foreign communities; it was first colonized by Protestant Huguenots driven out of France by Louis XIV's harsh discriminatory laws and, before it developed as London's main restaurant district, it was noted for the making of tapestries and musical instruments. Artists,

poets and writers established themselves there and, later, the quarter (especially Soho Square) attracted medical men; there are still three specialist hospitals in the neighbourhood.

Soho was developed in the seventeenth century by builders and entrepreneurs such as Richard Frith, and Soho Square was one of London's most fashionable addresses until Mayfair was laid out during the eighteenth century. After society moved west, Soho cultivated the spirit of which John Galsworthy, creator of the materialistic Forsyte family, wrote:

'Of all quarters in the queer adventurous amalgam called London, Soho is perhaps the least suited to the Forsyte spirit. . . . Untidy, full of Greeks, Ishmaelites, cats, Italians, tomatoes, restaurants, organs, coloured stuffs, queer names, people looking out of upper windows, it dwells remote from the British Body Politic.'

The first recorded Soho restaurant was the Hotel Sablonière in 1816, but the habit among the more affluent of dining out rather than eating at home did not become established until the 1900s. The earliest restaurant still trading today is Kettners of Romilly Street: founded in 1868, it was a favourite of Oscar Wilde. The ornate, *fin de siècle* Café Royal in Regent Street, another Wilde haunt, has lost its Soho raffishness under the ownership of the Trusthouse Forte hotel empire. In 1900 the literary partnership of G. K. Chesterton and Hilaire Belloc was forged at the Mont Blanc restaurant in Gerrad Street. Literary lunches are still very much part of the Soho scene. Agents, publishers, television producers and authors can be seen discussing new projects at L'Escargot in Greek Street or at the Groucho Club in Dean Street, named quirkily after Groucho Marx, who once said he wouldn't want to join any club that would have him as a member.

In the 1920s and 1930s Soho was famous for drinking clubs, such as Mrs Meyrick's at 43 Gerrard Street. Later the Gargoyle in Dean Street was a magnet for literary and artistic figures. Today, the Colony Club, with its deliberately louche atmosphere, attracts a variety of eccentric characters.

Soho is on the threshold of change, in both appearance and atmosphere. Rupert Street will be largely closed to traffic and the fruit and vegetable market in adjoining Berwick Street tidied into neat street stalls. Its fabric may be better preserved in future, like Covent Garden, but its character may grow less spicy. Soho was permissive before the word was invented.

RIGHT Almost as soon as it was cut through a slum district of the West End in 1886, Shaftesbury Avenue became the heart of London's theatre and entertainment district. Most of its theatres date from the last years of the nineteenth century.

Grand Hotels

What makes a grand hotel? If luxurious appointments and smooth service were the only criteria, some of London's modern, internationally owned temples of tourism and business travel would qualify. But history, an indefinably English style and tradition are an indispensable part of the mix, along with the kind of legends that could only be created by generations of distinguished visitors.

London's grandest hotels are concentrated in Mayfair, with the notable exception of the SAVOY, which celebrated its centenary in 1989 on its original magnificent Thames-side site between the Strand and the river. Its founder was the impresario Richard D'Oyly Carte, who brought Gilbert and Sullivan together and produced their comic operas in the adjoining Savoy Theatre. He engaged Europe's top hotelier, the Swiss César Ritz, to run the Savoy, and Ritz brought in Auguste Escoffier as chef. The Savoy is encrusted with legend and anecdote, from the champagne tycoon who had the forecourt flooded for a Venetian party in 1912 (with Caruso as a singing gondolier) to Frank Sinatra's 15-room suites. Monet painted his views of the Thames from a fifth-floor room; Johann Strauss brought his own orchestra to play and an Italian dishwasher named Guccio Gucci was so impressed by the Savoy's wealthy guests that he went home to Florence to found the Gucci leather goods business. The Savoy was among the first hotels in London to feature lifts – splendid red-lacquered affairs described as 'ascending rooms'. Its plumbed-in washbasins had Oscar Wilde protesting that when he wanted hot water he would ring for it like a gentleman. The hotel has a staff-to-guest ratio of three to one and its extravagant attention to detail is legendary: it even makes its own mattresses.

The Savoy was London's first truly grand hotel, although there were already some imposing establishments at the main railway termini – none more so than the Midland Grand at St Pancras, a pinnacled Gothic fantasy by George Gilbert Scott that is about to be revived as a hotel after decades as British Rail offices. Most of the original railway hotels still exist, though their style and quality has eroded as the districts around them became seedier. Such hotels as London boasted before the railway age were mostly in Mayfair. Pulteney's at 105 Piccadilly (present home of the Arts Council) and the Clarendon at 169 New Bond Street (where Cartiers now stands) were the most fashionable. Others such as Long's, also in New Bond Street, and Limmer's (whose barman, John Collins, invented the gin-based drink that bears his name) at the corner of Conduit Street and Hanover Square, were gloomy places frequented by hard-drinking, sporting squires.

Middle-class families visiting London from the country would generally put up in lodging-houses in the

T. E Collcutt's Savoy hotel opened in the Strand in 1889, on the site of the ancient Savoy Palace. The most desirable rooms and suites here are at the back, with balconies overlooking the Victoria Embankment Gardens and the river.

The Dorchester in Park Lane opened in 1931 as a rival to London's most opulent hotels. This illustration of the extensive lounge area is taken from *A Young Man Comes to London*, a short story written to mark the opening.

Mount Street area of Mayfair, but in 1815 a former royal servant called James Mivart set up a hotel in two houses in Brook Street. In the 1850s it was bought by an ex-butler named William Claridge and, while continuing for some years to be known as Mivart's, soon became popular with foreign royalty. CLARIDGE's was acquired by the Savoy as early as 1895 and was rebuilt in the 1890s by C.W. Stephens, the architect of Harrods; its tradition of patronage by visiting royalty and heads of state remains intact.

The CONNAUGHT, like Claridge's favoured by foreign royals and the British aristocracy, but smaller and more private, is also part of the Savoy group. In the heart of Mayfair, between Grosvenor and Berkeley Squares and dating from 1896, it was originally known as the Coburg. The name was changed in 1917 because of anti-German sentiment during the First World War. It is not as expensive as some larger establishments but carefully guards its reputation of exclusivity; Hollywood stars with publicity retinues are courteously steered towards the Savoy. Less exclusive but also wrapped in a clubby, country-house atmosphere is BROWN's, opened by James Brown in Dover Street in 1837 and later extended back to Albemarle Street.

In 1899, César Ritz opened the ornate CARLTON in the Haymarket. Its frontage echoed that of the neighbouring Her Majesty's Theatre, and one of its pastry-cooks before the First World War was Ho Chi Minh, later the Communist leader of North Vietnam. The Carlton was badly bombed in the Second World War and was replaced by the uncompromisingly modern tower block of New Zealand House.

A second flowering of grand hotel-building took place between the two world wars. Increased taxes after 1920 forced the sale of two great Mayfair mansions, the Duke of Westminster's Grosvenor House and Sir George Holford's Dorchester House. GROSVENOR HOUSE, with its famous art gallery and colonnaded courtyard by Thomas Cundy, was replaced in 1929 by an American-style hotel with tall towers of apartments: a controversial structure in its day. Sir Edwin Lutyens designed the Park Lane frontage which echoes the old mansion's colonnade screen. In the Second World War, Grosvenor House was a meeting place for European resistance leaders and governments in exile; its gigantic Great Room, once a skating rink, is still the largest public room in Europe. It is now the London flagship of the Trusthouse Forte hotel and catering empire.

The Renaissance-style Dorchester House (which had forty bedrooms but only one bathroom) was rebuilt as the DORCHESTER HOTEL in 1930. The reinforced concrete building, faced with crushed marble and insulated with two-inch-thick layers of cork to its rooms, was reputed to be the safest in London during the Blitz. Several members of Churchill's War Cabinet lived there and a Canadian diplomat described the wartime Dorchester as 'a luxury liner on which the remnants of London society have embarked in the midst of this storm'. It now belongs to the Sultan of Brunei and was closed at the end of 1988 for extensive refurbishment.

For sheer fin-de-siècle splendour, caught in a time warp, there is nothing to touch the RITZ, designed by Mewès and Davis in the Parisian style with an arcaded frontage echoing the rue de Rivoli. (Opened in 1906 on the south side of Piccadilly, the hotel had no personal connection with César Ritz, by this time an ailing man.) The beauty of the public rooms, especially the Palm Court – first known as the Winter Garden – and the painted dining-room overlooking the park, captivated Edwardian society. The late Diana Cooper recalled that the Ritz was the first hotel in London to which young unmarried women were allowed to go unchaperoned.

MAYFAIR

The most fashionable address in London for more than two hundred and fifty years, Mayfair faces Soho across Regent Street, the great shopping thoroughfare designed by Nash in 1811, but this geographical boundary is not accepted by all Mayfair denizens. Purists insist that Mayfair – never officially recognized as a postal district – runs no farther east than Bond Street, and there are residents of Albany, the collegiate-style chambers off Piccadilly beloved of writers and wealthy recluses, who would argue that their entrance is in St James's and their back doorstep in Soho. Most, however, accept the view of the nineteenth-century cleric Sydney Smith that Mayfair is a parallelogram bounded by Oxford Street, Park Lane, Piccadilly and Regent Street. Smith believed it enclosed 'more intelligence and human ability ... wealth and beauty, than the world has ever collected in such a space before'.

For the last half-century, however, since many of its town houses were abandoned by their owners on the eve of the Second World War, Mayfair has been only about one-third residential, with the rest given over to office and commercial use. 'Temporary' office permits issued to firms bombed out of the City and elsewhere have somehow lasted for over forty years. Westminster City Council has been attempting to reverse this trend: BROOK HOUSE in Park Lane, built as glamorous apartments in the 1930s but used as offices since 1945, will be the first major building to revert to its intended purpose.

Over the centuries, since associates of Charles II first developed its southern border, Mayfair has boasted an extraordinary mix of residents. The amalgam of Georgian red brick, Victorian terracotta and 1930s' neo-classicism has at different times been home to Clive of India, Beau Brummell, Disraeli, Handel (who composed his *Messiah* in Brook Street), Florence Nightingale, the New York financier J. P. Morgan and leaders of pre-war society like the Mountbattens and Douglas Fairbanks Jr. In the 1970s oil boom Arab sheikhs moved in.

In the eighteenth and early nineteenth centuries it had almost a village air, mingling all talents and social classes. Aristocrats and artisans lived literally back to back in elegant terraced houses whose rear gave access to stables and workshops. A remnant of this social cocktail survives in the working-class flats built west of Duke Street by the first Duke of Westminster. (The ennobled Grosvenor family has owned around 100 acres of Mayfair since the late seventeenth century, inheriting it through an arranged marriage with a 12-year-old heiress, Mary Davies, when the area was swampy meadowland.) At the other extreme are the few remaining lordly town houses of BERKELEY SQUARE. No. 44, designed by William Kent for Isabella Finch and now the Clermont

Club, has one of the most beautiful interiors in London.

Mayfair began as a cluster of grand houses on the northern side of Piccadilly, built on land given to friends of Charles II after the King's restoration in 1660. The first, built for the Earl of Clarendon on a site between present-day Dover and Albemarle Streets, lasted less than twenty years before a consortium of developers, including the Soho builder Richard Frith and the banker Sir Thomas Bond, bought the site and began building speculative housing northwards. The diarist John Evelyn commented waspishly that Bond had demolished Clarendon House to 'build a street of tenements to his undoing'. Bond Street did take years to find occupiers and the consortium went bankrupt.

West of Clarendon House was Berkeley House, built for the Earl of Berkeley and eventually to pass to the Dukes of Devonshire as the rebuilt Devonshire House. This survived until 1925, when the house and its walled courtyard were pulled down in a mass redevelopment uncommonly sympathetic to the character of the area. East, in Piccadilly, two other great houses became BURLINGTON HOUSE, home of the Royal Academy of Arts since 1868, and Melbourne House, later renamed ALBANY and converted into sixty-nine sets of chambers for bachelors.

North and west of those early Piccadilly mansions, all was still rural. North-east of Hyde Park Corner, the notorious May Fair (see *Fairs*) created licentious havoc each spring on a meadow called Brookfield, a site roughly covered today by the attractive but still slightly disreputable alleyways of SHEPHERD'S MARKET. Queen Anne tried in vain to suppress the May Fair, which enjoyed a perpetual charter from James II; it was eventually driven out by the objections of new residents along Piccadilly. (Piccadilly itself, which has its north side in Mayfair and its south in St James's, derived its curious name from the 'pickadils' or collars made by Robert Baker, a tailor who was one of its earliest residents in the 1620s.)

Mayfair developed in three main bursts during the eighteenth century, when its three great squares were laid out: first Hanover, then Grosvenor and finally Berkeley. The last part to gain favour was the north-west corner, near the Tyburn gallows, which were removed in 1783. Houses on PARK LANE, formerly Tyburn Lane, at first faced away from the park; their pretty Regency backs survive here and there amid the cliff-like 1930s'

OPPOSITE Brown's in Dover Street is the least flamboyant of the plush Mayfair hotels. It was established in 1837 by James Brown, a former manservant. The author Rudyard Kipling was a frequent guest.

office and apartment blocks. 'Speakers' Corner' at Marble Arch today maintains an anarchic touch of old Tyburn; the Arch itself, designed by Nash, was moved here from Buckingham Palace in 1851.

GROSVENOR SQUARE was the centre of London high society from its first leases in the 1720s to the outbreak of war in 1939. The Mayfair town house, four or five storeys high, with perhaps fourteen rooms and stables behind it, was designed principally for use during the

Piccadilly in Edwardian times was lined with grand homes, some of them occupied only for part of the year when their wealthy owners were in London for the summer season. The railings in front of Green Park were removed in 1941 to be melted down for armaments.

parliamentary season – winter and spring. For the rest of the year its owners would as like as not be on their country estates. Between the 1930s and 1960s most of the square was rebuilt as flats, with Eero Saarinen's dominating US embassy on the bomb-damaged west side.

The great mansions of Mayfair nearly all fell victim after the First World War to heavy new taxes and a less formal style of life. Dorchester House and Grosvenor House (town house of the Duke of Westminster) were pulled down in the 1920s to be replaced by hotels of the same name. Lansdowne House survives in truncated form as the Lansdowne Club; Chesterfield House in South Audley Street, a masterpiece built by Isaac Ware in 1748 for the fourth Earl of Chesterfield, gave way to a block of 1930s' flats, and Londonderry House, once a great centre for political entertaining, was replaced in the 1960s by an anonymous modern hotel.

The southern end of Park Lane, once resplendent with the mansions of bankers and South African mining kings such as Barney Barnato and Alfred Beit, can now muster only an isolated group of highly decorated

Victorian mansions in Hamilton Place. No. 5, once the home of the Rothschilds, is now *Les Ambassadeurs* club, popular with sheikhs, financiers and lobbyists. The rest of the mansions have been pulled down to accommodate more modern international hotels, investing the area with a bleak aspect, reinforced by the impenetrable HYDE PARK CORNER roundabout. Here, pedestrians are forced underground into a bewildering maze of tunnels beneath Decimus Burton's Constitution Arch, designed in 1825 to complement his park entrance gates but not erected until 1846, when it was surmounted by a statue of the Duke of Wellington. The statue was replaced in 1912 by the present bronze figure of Victory in her chariot. A different statue of the Duke on horseback (1888) stands alongside.

The area is not associated with men's clubs like neighbouring St James's, but two exceptions are the Savile Club, housed in two opulent town houses in Brook Street, and the Naval and Military Club at 94 Piccadilly, at one time the home of Lord Palmerston and usually known as the 'In and Out' from the words on its prominent gateposts.

The Second World War brought destruction to parts of Mayfair, but in the 1960s night-life began to revive with Annabel's in Berkeley Square and, later on, lavishly appointed gambling clubs like the Clermont and Crockford's in Curzon Street. Mayfair is still a magnet for the wealthy shopper: gunmakers Purdey in Mount Street and fine china and glass merchants Thomas Goode in South Audley Street, the tailors of SAVILE ROW (a centre for doctors before Harley Street) and the exclusive shops of Bond Street and the BURLINGTON ARCADE, where uniformed 'beadles' patrol to keep public order. In Mayfair, you have to behave.

ST JAMES'S

London has been described as a masculine city and St James's is its most masculine quarter. It no longer has colonies of bachelor 'chambers' around King and Jermyn Streets, but for two centuries it has been the home of London's oldest and grandest men's clubs. It is a place to browse, shop, lunch and dine rather than to live though, if you crane your neck in narrow Jermyn Street, the home of bespoke shirtmakers, you may spot a few attractive penthouses, and some extremely wealthy people like the media tycoon Rupert Murdoch maintain palatial apartments overlooking Green Park. But its beginnings were grandly residential, after Charles II gave plots of land to associates who had remained loyal throughout his exile.

Henry Jermyn, Earl of St Albans, was the principal beneficiary of Restoration largesse, receiving 45 acres of St James's Fields, on which ST JAMES'S SQUARE was

Gentlemen's Clubs

Food, drink, company and talk were begetters of the London club, though gaming played its part in Georgian times. The splendid nineteenth-century establishments owe their origins to the coffee-houses and taverns in which men met to dispute, indulge their wit and set tables in a roar. A change of manners in the early nineteenth century rendered taverns unfashionable. Eighteenth-century club houses, such as Boodle's and

ABOVE The Subscription Room at Brooks's Club in St James's Street, designed by Henry Holland in 1777, 'decoration far more restrained in distribution and detail than anything by Adam.'

RIGHT Charles Barry's Reform Club in Pall Mall, the second building from the right, was completed in 1841, its façade based on the Farnese Palace in Rome. Beyond it is the Travellers', an earlier work by Barry.

and sited at the corner of Waterloo Place and Pall Mall East, was the first of a series of grand club houses to be erected in the area. (It now houses the Institute of Directors.) Opposite is the Athenaeum of 1830, designed by Decimus Burton, its Grecian flavour reflecting the fashion of its time. Next door is the Travellers' Club (1829–32), designed by Barry to resemble an Italian palazzo, used by gentlemen who had resided or travelled abroad. Perhaps the grandest is the Reform (1837–41), (its distinguished façade is based on the Farnese Palace in Rome) originally associated with those who backed the Great Reform Bill of 1830–2.

The Garrick, near Covent Garden, was founded in 1831 for the patronage of drama and named after the actor David Garrick. Today it is still favoured by theatrical people, as well as writers and journalists. The huge National Liberal Club, with its superb site by the river in Whitehall Place, was designed by Alfred Waterhouse and completed in 1887. Its architectural eclecticism was said to reflect the variety of opinion within the party of Gladstone (whose presence in the form of portraits and statues still dominates the tiled interiors). Conservatives congregate in the Carlton in St James's.

Rising costs and, in some cases, fewer members, made things difficult for clubs in the mid-twentieth century. However, the survivors have gained more members as

Brooks's, set standards and, not surprisingly, were sited in the West End, near the Court. Thus Pall Mall and St James's acquired the main concentrations of palatial club houses. Those with common interests would gravitate to a particular club, so each acquired a distinctive flavour.

The United Service Club of 1827, designed by Nash

club life proves attractive to new generations. Women, too, have been admitted in increasing numbers. Many clubs operate a theoretical ban on discussing business on the premises, and there is still the occasional armchair filled with a gentleman lingering or dozing over *The Times* and a glass of decent port, even if the aroma of fine Havana leaf is rarer these days.

developed in the 1660s and Jermyn Street twenty years later. The square remained a place of aristocratic town houses until the mid-nineteenth century, but has been extensively rebuilt in the last fifty years. NORFOLK HOUSE on the south-east corner, which replaced the Duke of Norfolk's magnificent London home in 1938, was used by General Eisenhower as his headquarters during the Second World War.

JERMYN STREET was also largely rebuilt in this century and suffered bad war damage. Several important Piccadilly buildings back on to it, including Thomas Verity's Criterion Theatre of 1874, recently restored, and the 1936 Simpson's department store, the first welded steel building in London.

Jermyn Street runs through at one end to Haymarket, literally once a market for hay and fodder, and at the other to St James's Street, one of the grandest in London. Haymarket in Victorian times was infamous for its many brothels, but then and now boasted two splendid theatres facing each other: the Haymarket and Her Majesty's. At the southern end the glassy 1960s' tower of New Zealand House rises on the site of the old Carlton Hotel, one of prewar London's finest.

The view down St James's Street from Piccadilly is one of the most exhilarating in London. At its foot is the crenellated Tudor profile of ST JAMES'S PALACE, official residence of England's monarchs from William III to the accession of Queen Victoria, when Buckingham Palace took its place (see *Great houses and palaces*).

The gentlemen's clubs in St James's Street replaced the coffee and chocolate houses for which the street was originally renowned. Next to each other on the east side are White's and Boodles, founded in 1736 and 1762 respectively: facing them is Brooks's, founded in 1764 by William Almack, a legendary St James's host and clubman. Tucked away up little Park Place is the exclusive Pratt's, where only 14 of the 600 members can dine at any one time.

James Lock, the hatters who invented the bowler or 'Coke' hat, together with J. Lobb, the bespoke boot and shoe maker and the venerable wine merchants, Berry Brothers and Rudd, all maintain historic premises in St James's Street, while off it are a couple of secluded and fashionable hotels, Duke's and The Stafford. Facing Piccadilly and Green Park is the arcaded and mansard-roofed RITZ HOTEL, modelled in 1906 after its Paris namesake and bringing a breath of Parisian style to the solemn portals of clubland. Grand mansions once lined the east side of Green Park, but those that survive, like Bridgewater House in Cleveland Row and Spencer House in St James's Palace, are now occupied by companies.

Nearby in King Street is the old-established auction house of CHRISTIE'S, rebuilt after wartime devastation. A pleasing modern architectural note is stuck by the hexagonal stone towers of the *Economist* building (Alison and Peter Smithson, 1962–4), discreetly set back from St James's Street on a raised piazza.

PALL MALL, the broad, elegant street which derives its name from the Italian ball game played by Charles II, is the other great centre of clubland (see *Gentlemen's clubs*). It was originally a street of fine residences. Nell Gwynne, best known of Charles II's mistresses, lived on the site of number 79, now the head office of the P&O shipping group. This is the only piece of land on the south side of Pall Mall that does not belong to the Crown: at Nell's insistence, Charles had the freehold conveyed to her trustees. This was an early assertion of women's rights in a street later to take revenge, barring women from most of its clubs until recent years.

Parallel with Pall Mall and to its south CARLTON GARDENS and CARLTON HOUSE TERRACE are shielded by the club buildings and feel unusually isolated, given their central location. They were constructed by Nash on the site of the lavish Carlton House, built for George IV before he was Prince Regent but abandoned when he became king. Many of the buildings have been altered and some modern offices allowed to obtrude but, despite the parked cars, the enclaves as a whole still possess much of the stately calm that Nash intended. The fine houses remain Crown property and are occupied mostly by public institutions. Many statesmen have lived in them and 4 Carlton Gardens was headquarters of the French resistance in the Second World War: General de Gaulle's defiant message to his people in 1940 is reproduced on a plaque on the wall.

The two terraces are separated by Waterloo Place and DUKE OF YORK'S STEPS, one of London's few imposing public stairways, leading down to The Mall and St James's Park. Between Pall Mall and the Mall are three of London's surviving mansions – Clarence House, still a royal residence, and Marlborough and Lancaster Houses, used for diplomatic and official purposes.

WESTMINSTER

Church, Government and Crown have contributed to making Westminster the grandest and most varied part of the capital. It embraces the qualities that Londoners like to think of as quintessentially theirs: solidity without fuss, good order without overweening discipline, continuity and yet a capacity to surprise. It has a knack of capturing the city's prevailing mood. Photographs from the late nineteenth and early twentieth centuries show its stately buildings blackened by coal

OPPOSITE The cast of the equestrian statue of Richard I, sculpted by Carlo Marochetti for the Great Exhibition of 1851, stands in Old Palace Yard, Westminster.

dust, fitting well with the earnest view the Victorians and Edwardians took of Westminster's sombre responsibilities as the heart of the Empire. Newsreels from between the wars show the buildings blacker still, as bowler-hatted civil servants hurry in and out in their attempts to cope with economic recession and international bellicosity. When they failed, the grimy buildings symbolized the nation's wartime mood.

The passage of the Clean Air Act of 1956 (see *Public health*) made the washing of grubby public buildings worthwhile. Yet there was a school of thought that

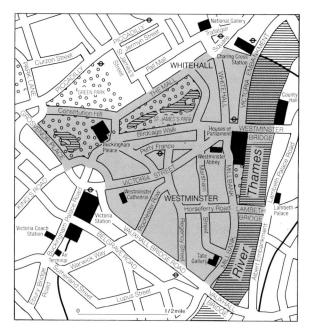

opposed doing this in Westminster, on the grounds that bright red buses in front of smutty black stonework represented London's authentic colourscape: to change it would be akin to straightening the Leaning Tower of Pisa. The forces of cleanliness and light won the day. The Abbey, the Houses of Parliament and the government buildings were restored to the colour in which their architects had envisaged them. The assault on the soot began in the 1960s, when London was escaping belatedly from the shadows of the war years and the long period of austerity that followed. The newly bright buildings of Westminster aptly reflected that.

At the core of the area lies the church built for the monks of WESTMINSTER ABBEY. The Abbey's earliest proven records are tenth-century. Originally its site, the uninhabited Thorney Island, was cut off from the north bank of the Thames by streams. Fresh-water springs and an ample supply of fish were probably the island's main attraction to the monks. Edward the Confessor rebuilt its church – completed just in time for his funeral and,

almost twelve months later, for the coronation of William the Conqueror. Henry III was responsible for the present building, begun in 1245. The Henry VII Chapel was added in 1512 and the west towers finally completed in 1745.

Almost all English rulers since the Norman Conquest have been crowned in Westminster Abbey and most of those that pre-date the Hanoverians are buried there. It contains tombs and other monuments from the thirteenth century on. The building was spared when the monasteries were dissolved; Henry VIII appears to have shown sentiment for its church, in which he and his predecessors had been crowned and his father buried. Technically, Westminster Abbey ceased to exist in 1540 and its former church is now officially the Collegiate Church of St Peter at Westminster; the old name, however, is generally used. The Dean owes direct allegiance to the Sovereign rather than to a bishop and for that reason the church is known as a 'royal peculiar'.

Behind the Abbey, in the old precinct, is an untidy jumble of buildings of varying degrees of antiquity that make up a charming backwater, a retreat from the bustle of Victoria Street and Parliament Square. Entry is through the Abbey itself or Dean's Yard, by its west entrance. Some of these old buildings are used by the church, others let out as prestige offices and many occupied by Westminster School, one of Britain's oldest public schools, founded by Henry VIII (see *A centre of learning*). Church House, the conference centre of the Church of England, is also within the precinct, although its main entrance is on Great Smith Street. Built just before the Second World War, it is a functional building of tedious appearance. Immediately north of the Abbey, but again within its grounds, stands the part-Tudor St Margaret's, the House of Commons church since 1614 and popular for weddings: John Milton, Samuel Pepys and Winston Churchill are among those who have been married in it.

Facing the Abbey across Victoria Street are examples of monumental public buildings from the two ends of the twentieth century. The cavernous Central Hall, built for the Methodists shortly before the First World War, has all the flamboyance of Edwardian architecture. Alongside it, across a brick piazza and a token area of grass, is the squat Queen Elizabeth II Conference Centre, opened in 1986. Beyond that, the neo-Gothic Middlesex Guildhall (1906–13) looks out over Parliament Square, a grassy traffic island surrounded by flagpoles for state occasions with, at the north-east corner, the menacing statue of Winston Churchill, overcoated, glowering at the Houses of Parliament.

The existing buildings known as THE PALACE OF WESTMINSTER stand on a site first chosen as the place of royal residence in the early eleventh century, during the reign of Canute. Following the Norman Conquest William Rufus planned a new, more splendid complex to the north, but only Westminster Hall was built. Henry VIII moved to the adjacent Whitehall Palace in 1532 but Parliament remained at Westminster, usually meeting in the Gothic St Stephen's Chapel, until the disastrous fire

Canaletto's mid-eighteenth-century painting of the Henry VII chapel at Westminster Abbey, built between 1503 and 1512 and one of the Abbey's most admired jewels.

of 1834. Charles Barry won the competition for designing new accommodation for Parliament in 'Gothic or Elizabethan style', aided by the inspired detailing of Pugin. The buildings, which include the clock tower housing the bell 'Big Ben', were completed by 1860 and show both Gothic Revival and superb Victorian craftsmanship at their best. Surviving parts of the medieval palace include WESTMINSTER HALL which, with its fine early fifteenth-century hammerbeam roof, served as the law courts until the late nineteenth century; and Edward III's JEWEL TOWER, now a museum.

The presence of Parliament and Court has influenced the development of Westminster's streets. Late-night sittings of the Commons made it desirable for MPs to have a *pied-à-terre* nearby. Many Georgian houses south of the Abbey, in Barton and Cowley streets, have long provided them with accommodation. In the late

nineteenth century these were supplemented by the large blocks of red-brick 'mansion flats' that are a feature of many streets in the southern part of Westminster. The wealthiest live in a well-maintained group of early Georgian terraced houses in Lord North Street. They are possibly the most prestigious houses in London and they continue around the corner on to the north side of Smith Square. The square itself was once the furnace of British politics when it contained the headquarters of both the Conservative and Labour parties, but in the 1970s Labour moved to Southwark. The former Church of St John, in the centre of Smith Square, is now a concert hall. The Baroque architect Thomas Archer designed it with a tower at each corner, earning Queen Anne's description of it as 'an upturned footstool'.

Between the church and the river is Victoria Tower Gardens, a narrow strip of green from Parliament to Lambeth Bridge. It contains a replica of Rodin's *The Burghers of Calais*, a statue of the suffragette leader Emmeline Pankhurst and a pretty mid-Victorian fountain, lavishly decorated in enamel. Further upstream is the TATE GALLERY, built in 1897 by Sir Henry Tate, the philanthropist and inventor of the sugar cube, to house a national collection of modern art (see *Museums and galleries*). It occupies the site of the nineteenth-century Millbank Penitentiary, the largest prison ever built in London.

WESTMINSTER CATHEDRAL, the most important place of Roman Catholic worship in England, is also on the site of an old prison. The church bought the land, just off Victoria Street at the station end, in 1867, but spent many years agreeing on a design. Cardinal Manning turned down a Gothic blueprint because it would be too like Westminster Abbey. Finally John Francis Bentley's Byzantine scheme was approved, its red brick toning well with the surrounding mansion flats. Inside there is some magnificent marble work and a series of bas-reliefs by Eric Gill depicting the twelve stations of the cross.

Victoria Street was created in the 1860s to provide a route from Parliament Square to the new railway station (see *The rail termini*). It has always been lined with mainly nondescript office blocks and a few apartment buildings, but a block away in Caxton Street, stranded amid the tall offices, is the charming Bluecoat School of 1709, now a National Trust shop. The earliest houses in nearby Queen Anne's Gate date from the same period: it is one of the most pleasing enclaves in Central London, although Basil Spence's modern Home Office building at its junction with Petty France is at odds with the street's eighteenth-century character.

A flight of steps on the site of a former cockpit leads from Queen Anne's Gate to Birdcage Walk, a royal aviary in Stuart times, running alongside St James's

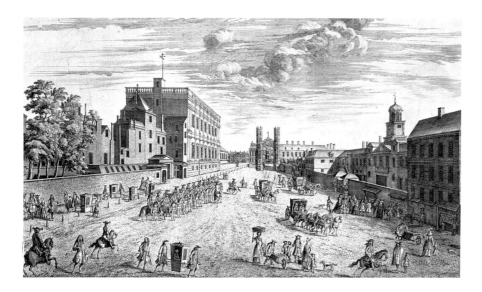

The remnants of Whitehall Palace in 1724, twenty-six years after much of the sixteenth-century palace was destroyed in a fire. The only recognizable feature today is Inigo Jones's stately Banqueting House, dominating the left-hand side of the street.

Park (see *Parks and gardens*). Across the park THE MALL looks as though it was designed as a triumphal entry into BUCKINGHAM PALACE at its western end, but in fact Charles II had the street laid out before the palace became a royal residence (see *Great houses and palaces*). He wanted it as a new venue for the then popular game of *pallemaille* (there are numerous spellings), which involved hitting a ball through a hoop suspended at the end of a long alley; nearby Pall Mall, where it was originally played, had become too crowded. It was not until early this century that the Mall assumed its present grand air, when the Victoria Memorial was sited outside the palace gates and ADMIRALTY ARCH built at the far end, to provide an imposing entry from Trafalgar Square.

WHITEHALL

The English have never taken much to monumental architecture, to landscaped avenues of pompous public buildings. They have rather been piecemeal, pragmatic planners, constructing the key components of their capital as and when needed, shunning accidental opportunities to start again with a clean slate. The broad Whitehall, lined with government offices of varying pedigrees, is the closest London gets to a street specifically designed to overawe and that chiefly at the bottom end, where the Victorian set of government offices – Foreign Office, old Treasury and Cabinet Office – look out over Lutyens's Cenotaph, which stands in the middle of the road.

The street takes its name from the palace built here in

PREVIOUS PAGE One of the classic London views is across St James's Park lake to the back of the buildings on the west side of Whitehall. On the left is the Horse Guards, on the right the Old Treasury (now the Cabinet Office) and Downing Street.

1532 by Henry VIII, who turned it into the largest royal palace in Europe. The Stuarts embellished it until William III decided it was too close to the river and bad for his asthma. He moved to St James's Palace and a few years later, in 1698, much of Whitehall was destroyed by fire, leaving Inigo Jones's magnificent BANQUETING HOUSE (1622) as the most significant memento (see *Great houses and palaces*). Other survivals are Henry VIII's Wine Cellar, sunk beneath the mock-heroic Ministry of Defence Building (completed 1959) in Whitehall Gardens; fragments of the real tennis court in Downing Street; and, facing the Victoria Embankment, part of a riverside terrace built by Wren.

The guards defending the palace were stationed on its north approach, the site of the present Horse Guards, built for George II by William Kent and John Vardy. The guard is still mounted daily, defending nothing but an extensive parade ground where, in June, the ceremony of Trooping the Colour marks the official birthday of the sovereign (see *Ceremonies*).

The pavement between the Horse Guards and Downing Street is one of the most trodden tourist routes in London. Visitors, having watched the guard changing, walk down to see the Prime Minister's house. Downing Street was named after Sir George Downing, who spent some of his youth in the American colonies and was the second person to graduate from the fledgling Harvard College; he returned to England to fight for Cromwell in the Civil War, became an MP and, after the Restoration, rounded off his varied career as a courtier. He bought the land and built the street in 1680. No. 10, where the Prime Minister traditionally lives, and no. 11, the home of the Chancellor of the Exchequer, are two of the four houses surviving – though much altered – from the seventeenth century. They are unimposing from the outside but no. 10 has a much larger building at the rear and a walled garden.

At the northern end of the old Whitehall Palace, accommodation was reserved for the kings of Scotland on their visits to London, until 1603 when the crowns were united under James I. This accounts for the name of the short street, Great Scotland Yard, between Whitehall and the river. It is known best as the earliest headquarters of the Metropolitan Police. Their founder Robert Peel, then Home Secretary and later twice Prime Minister, secured accommodation for them here in 1829. In 1870 much larger headquarters were built further south and called New Scotland Yard. In 1967 that name was transferred to the latest police headquarters in Victoria Street, and the handsome 1890 complex, re-named the Norman Shaw Buildings after their architect, was converted into offices for MPs.

The government buildings further north in Whitehall are older than those at the south and less grandiose. Dover House (the Scottish Office) and Gwydyr House (the Welsh Office) are pleasant Georgian town houses. Robert Adam's stone screen (1761), outside the old Admiralty building, is one of the highlights of the street. Just north of it, the Whitehall Theatre – for many years associated with farces – signals the end of Whitehall as the sober street of government, a metamorphosis confirmed by the row of souvenir shops on the other side of the road.

BELGRAVIA

Belgrave Square has lent not just its name but its character to Belgravia, the area bounded by Knights-bridge, Sloane Street, Grosvenor Place and Victoria Station. It is a mixed blessing. The square's grand houses in creamy stucco, not so much formal as pompous, spread their chaste blandness into the surrounding streets and terraces, setting a polite but lifeless tone.

It would have been different when the houses were erected in the 1820s by Thomas Cubitt, that pioneer of inner-city development (see *The makers of London*), on a former swamp belonging to Lord Grosvenor, one of whose other titles was Viscount Belgrave. George IV had commissioned John Nash to transform nearby Buckingham House into a grand palace and this made the area desirable for the rich – precisely the market Cubitt had in mind. The newly built Belgravia would have been bustling with domestic activity as callers came and went and servants busied themselves with making life comfortable for their employers. Today the houses, still part of the Grosvenor Estate, serve mainly as embassies and the offices of professional and charitable institutions. A few in neighbouring EATON SQUARE and CHESTER SQUARE survive as single dwellings but many others have been broken up into apartments.

Some high-class shops and a few modern hotels, designed to blend unassertively with their environment, occupy the narrow streets between Belgrave Square and Sloane Street. In one of them, Motcomb Street, the powerful Doric columns of the PANTECHNICON, built in 1830, are anything but unassertive. The building was modified in the 1960s behind its original façade. Now an arcade penetrates it, leading to a courtyard containing Geoffrey Wickham's uncompromisingly modern fountain, erected in 1971.

In the early eighteenth century Jonathan Swift wrote of watching haymaking in the marshy area just south of Hyde Park, then known as the Five Fields. People picking their way across, taking a short cut to Chelsea, would sometimes fall prey to footpads. In 1776 Richard Tattersall opened his first horse stud and sale room on the northern edge of what is now Belgrave Square. It became the headquarters of the Jockey Club. (Tattersall's, now in Newmarket, is still an integral part of British horse racing.) Cubitt solved the Five Fields drainage problem in the thriftiest possible way by taking the clay topsoil and using it for bricks, replacing it with earth from the area east of the Tower of London, where St Katharine's dock was being created.

The first ST GEORGE'S HOSPITAL had been built facing Hyde Park Corner in 1734. The present building on the same site was designed in 1827 by William Wilkins, architect of the National Gallery. It stayed a hospital until the 1970s and, after standing empty for some years, is now being converted into a hotel, preserving Wilkins's imposing façade.

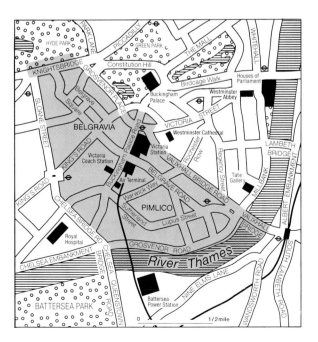

The mews behind the Belgravia squares used to be the stables and carriage houses for the stately homes in front and to some extent still serve that purpose. Long limousines edge down the narrow spaces between buildings to their private or commercial garages. Other old garages and stables have been converted into desirable small houses, on a scale more in tune with modern requirements than the mansions on the squares. The mews are more pleasant to stroll through than the main streets. In Old Barrack Yard, between Wilton Crescent and Knightsbridge, some nineteenth-century military houses have been well preserved, along with what is said to be the Duke of Wellington's mounting block. On the corner of the yard and Wilton Row is a picturesque gem of a pub, the Grenadier, which attracts a fashionable clientele.

PIMLICO

The district immediately to the south-east was also developed by Cubitt, some twenty years later. Until then Pimlico had been mostly market gardens. The curious name may have derived from a tavern and pleasure garden, near what is now Victoria Station, which sold Ben Pimlico's Nut Brown Ale, a popular brew in the seventeenth century.

Cubitt spent over a decade amassing the property for this further development, which for a time was known as South Belgravia. He signalled his commitment to the project by establishing his main London workshop by the river on a site now occupied by Dolphin Square. Calculating no doubt that the market for top-of-the-range housing was finite, he lined most of the streets with terraces of tall, narrow dwellings for the middle class – among the first of a rash of such developments in the inner suburbs. The area bounded by Warwick Way,

Belgrave Road, Lupus Street and Sutherland Street still looks today much as Cubitt planned it.

Yet, while Belgravia itself began and stayed fashionable, Pimlico soon went into a decline. Middle-class families moved to the further suburbs and the houses were broken up into single-room units. In part this was due to the erection of Victoria station in 1860 as the terminus for trains from south of London (see *The rail termini*).

The hinterlands of all the main London termini were blighted in the late nineteenth century by the conversion of nearby housing into cheap hotels and lodgings for transients. Some streets of Pimlico, especially Belgrave Road, are still lined with small hotels, now catering mainly to tourists from overseas. But since the 1960s most of Cubitt's houses have been reclaimed for the middle class and Pimlico again ranks among London's more desirable residential areas. A small but lively outdoor market in Tachbrook Street, at its junction with Warwick Way, draws people from all over South London, especially on Saturdays.

One block east, the broad Vauxhall Bridge Road links the Thames bridge with Victoria Station. On the right-hand side, beyond the Queen Mother Sports Centre, is one of the most admired of recent housing projects, the Lillington Gardens Estate, completed in 1971. Its red-brick facing and irregular projections, as well as the absence of high-rise towers, distinguish it from the concrete blocks that typified public housing in the 1960s. The Victorian Gothic church of St James the Less – also, unusually, in red brick – has been retained in the scheme and now serves as the headquarters of the Red Cross Society. It was designed in 1860 by G. E. Street, whose most prominent London work is the Law Courts in the Strand.

The southern stretch of Pimlico, between Lupus Street and Grosvenor Road, contains further characteristic examples of twentieth-century architecture. Starting from the west, the Churchill Gardens Estate, one of the first public housing projects built in London after the Second World War, set a pattern for its successors, with its mix of high and low-rise blocks, some terraced houses and shops on the street frontage.

East of it on Lupus Street is Pimlico School, a startling, mainly glass structure, whose ground floor is set below street level. Finished in 1970, it was not universally admired and has not been emulated. Between it and the river stands DOLPHIN SQUARE, equally an object of architectural controversy. Built in the 1930s as the largest apartment complex in Europe, it has been criticized for its unimaginative monolithic quality. The interior is more interesting. The public restaurant has been pleasingly restored Art Deco style, and diners have a view over one of London's best indoor swimming pools. The flats command high prices and, being so close to Westminster, are popular with Members of Parliament.

Between Dolphin Square and Vauxhall Bridge, overlooking the river, are two examples of 1960s and 1970s luxury apartment buildings. Right by the bridge is the earlier of the two, Rivermill House, an understated and unobtrusive rectangular block – very different from its flamboyant neighbour, Crown Reach, with its curious curved roofline. Crown Reach presents a virtually blank face to Grosvenor Road, strengthening its fortress-like security arrangements. It opens out on the river side, inaccessible to outsiders, giving its wealthy residents views over Nine Elms – sadly for them, not the most inspiring of London river frontages.

KNIGHTSBRIDGE

The typical Knightsbridge resident lives in a large flat in one of the red-brick-lined canyons west of Sloane Street and shops at Harrods and Peter Jones. She is wealthy, smart, conventional, confident and a bit of a snob. So is Knightsbridge.

The heart of Knightsbridge lies at the junction of Brompton Road, Sloane Street and Knightsbridge itself. Today it is a bustling Mecca for shoppers pouring from the Tube station to flood the designer boutiques and classy department stores. For centuries it was a small, outlying village where the roads from London to Kensington and Fulham went their separate ways.

Knightsbridge takes its name from the bridge that crossed the Westbourne. It is said, on no evidence at all, that two knights fought a duel there. The village was a dangerous spot, so plagued with highwaymen that travellers would return to London from Kensington in

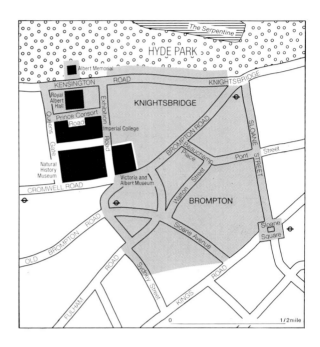

parties for protection. It was also notorious for its pubs – Pepys caroused at the World's End. Cattle markets were held on Knightsbridge Green, now reduced to a narrow passageway.

Knightsbridge began to expand in the middle of the eighteenth century. Handsome terraces sprang up along the Brompton Road turnpike. Land to the north and south which had been chiefly walled nursery gardens was sold for housing development. In 1780 SLOANE STREET was sliced south through land owned by Lord Cadogan, Sir Hans Sloane's son-in-law, to Sloane Square. To the west, architect and builder Henry Holland created HANS TOWN. Jane Austen stayed with her brother at 23 Hans Place. The houses, some of which survive, were attractive, three-storey terraces, with the notable exception of Holland's own country villa with gardens landscaped by his father-in-law Lancelot 'Capability' Brown.

Hans Town was almost completely redeveloped in the 1880s in the new red-brick, domestic style. The ornate cocktail of influences was epitomized by Sir Osbert Lancaster as Pont Street Dutch. Cadogan Square and the curving Lennox Gardens were built at about the same time. Amongst all this Knightsbridge red, St Columba's Church of Scotland, built in the 1950s to replace its bombed predecessor, stands out like a bloodless sore thumb.

Sloane Street itself is a dusty and, for most of its length, dull thoroughfare. The Cadogan Hotel, where Oscar Wilde was arrested, and the 1970s' Danish Embassy are worth a glance on the west side, the gardens of Cadogan Place on the east (open to residents only) are restful if uninspiring. SLOANE SQUARE, the most Parisian of London squares, begging for café tables at its centre, is noteworthy for the Royal Court Theatre and the splendour of the 1930s' department store, Peter Jones.

Development of the area between Brompton Road and Knightsbridge began in the 1820s. The houses were mostly more modest than Hans Town and went through a period of working-class occupation. Now thoroughly gentrified (and exceptionally well-served with pubs), charming Trevor Square, Montpelier Square and their attendant streets and mews make a village-like residential oasis.

RUTLAND GATE, opening on to Knightsbridge, consists of grander, Victorian houses now mostly converted to flats, like so much of the district. Rutland Court in Rutland Gardens is a handsome mansion block designed by Delissa Joseph in 1920. KNIGHTSBRIDGE BARRACKS (for the Household Cavalry) stand between Knightsbridge itself and Hyde Park. The present barracks, dominated by a tower block, date from 1959 and are by Sir Basil Spence.

BROMPTON

Brompton is smart with no heart. A good address, bordered by Knightsbridge, Kensington and Chelsea, it has absorbed the character and architecture of all three districts but failed to find a distinctive style of its own.

Broom Farm was a scattered hamlet of market gardens until speculative building began in the late eighteenth century, in and around Yeoman's Row, one of the oldest streets in the district. On the other side of Brompton Road, elegant Brompton Square was begun in 1821–35 by the prolific local builder James Bonnin. It was an instant success and remains unspoiled today. T. L. Donaldson's HOLY TRINITY church next door, built at the same time, is now largely hidden from view by

BROMPTON ORATORY, built in the face of opposition from the vicar of Holy Trinity.

The Oratorians – members of the Roman Catholic community of St Philip Neri – first arrived in Brompton in 1853. Their Italian Renaissance-style house of that year forms part of the group; the splendid Baroque Oratory, by Herbert Gribble, was added some thirty years later and contains several huge late seventeenth-century marble statues of the Apostles, originally in Siena Cathedral. Ennismore Gardens Mews, one of the prettiest and most extensive examples of a London mews, lies just behind the Oratory.

The Thurloes (a collection of streets, squares and mews) and Alexander Square, designed by George Basevi and built between 1820 and 1840, were another successful venture and proved instantly popular with gentlemen, professional people and members of the armed forces. William Hazlitt lived at 4 Alexander Place while a law student. Today the squares and streets form a peaceful and attractive backwater behind South Kensington Tube station.

Among Basevi's other work in the area are two of the most desirable and elegantly stuccoed streets in Brompton, Pelham Crescent and Egerton Crescent. His employer was the major local landowner, the Smith's Charity Estate, founded in the seventeenth century to relieve the plight of captives held as slaves by Turkish pirates.

Egerton Crescent lies at the centre of an area newly christened Brompton Cross to give identity to an otherwise formless patch of London. To the east, it is bounded by Beauchamp Place, a modest terrace dating from the 1820s but now a chic street packed with fashionable shops and restaurants. Walton Street, on the southern boundary, is going the same way. On the corner of Brompton Road and Sloane Avenue, the

Harrods began as a small grocer's shop in 1849 but its present huge terracotta-faced store, with a frontage of some 200 yards along Brompton Road, was completed in 1905, shortly before this picture was taken. The top four floors were originally luxury flats but were incorporated into the trading areas as the store's reputation and business grew.

entertaining and eccentric MICHELIN BUILDING, dating from 1911 and newly refurbished, now houses The Conran Shop, descendant of Sir Terence Conran's first Habitat which started life next door.

The south-west corner of Brompton is dominated by vast 'dwellings' built at the turn of the century to house the poor. To the north-west, on either side of Kensington Gore, lie the two monuments to Queen Victoria's consort Prince Albert: Sir George Gilbert Scott's magnificently flamboyant Gothic ALBERT MEMORIAL faces Francis Fowke's more restrained ALBERT HALL. The latter is rather overshadowed by Norman Shaw's seven-storey Albert Hall Mansions, dating from 1879. On the other side of the Hall are the 1967 Royal College of Art and the enchanting Royal College of Organists, 1875. Neighbouring Queen Alexandra's House was built in 1883 to house one hundred female students studying at the various colleges and museums in the area.

CHELSEA

The life of Chelsea is carried along two main arteries, both congested: King's Road and the Embankment. Between these rampant highways cluster the Georgian and Victorian houses that have always given the residents an excuse for clinging to Chelsea's old title of 'village'. Before the Embankment was opened in 1874 it was indeed 'the village by the river', its cottages and taverns tumbling down the eroded banks of the Thames. Flowery twin monuments of nude water sprites stand on either side of Albert Bridge, not very appropriate memorials to Sir Joseph Bazalgette, the Embankment's superb engineer (see *The makers of London*). Nearby is an

interesting Victorian dwelling: Norman Shaw's Swan House, for which he employed Flemish domestic architecture to redress the balance of old English. The name-Swan House harks back to the old Swan Inn, formerly at the end of Swan Walk, to which Samuel Pepys once came for a 'naughty' evening but found it closed.

Where Lower Sloane Street runs into Chelsea Bridge Road two other types of Chelsea architecture confront each other in stark contrast: on the left the modern Chelsea Barracks; on the right the splendid ROYAL HOSPITAL for Chelsea Pensioners, with their military uniforms, pipes and sticks. Built in 1682 on the initiative of Charles II by Sir Christopher Wren, its great hall is the dining-room for some four hundred Pensioners, though they were for many years banished to their cubicles because of bad table-manners. It is said that Nell Gwynn persuaded Charles to support the old soldiers who 'never die' but have nowhere to live. In the garden stands Grinling Gibbons's bust of their benefactor, known to them as 'Old Charlie Boy'.

The imposing early nineteenth-century Duke of York's headquarters on King's Road was erected as a foundation for soldiers' children, by the same royal duke whose mistress was to traffic in army commissions. Its style is severely classical, well calculated to instil fear of God and the King. Children of Hill House prep school (in youth attended by Prince Charles) can sometimes be seen on the playing-fields. It may appear curious that Chelsea, first famed as a 'haunt of ancient peace', should attract military installations, the latest being the NATIONAL ARMY MUSEUM at the corner of Royal Hospital Road and Tite Street; they were probably drawn by the Royal Hospital. Round the corner is St Wilfred's Convent. It looks aggressively modern and seems an odd neighbour for the old ghosts of Tite Street: playwright Oscar Wilde and painters John Singer Sargent and Augustus John.

Chelsea has an academic as well as a military tradition. The Royal Hospital was the site of the first Chelsea College; founded to educate Anglican clergy, it ran out of money. Today's college buildings (part of King's College, London) are on the north side of King's Road, the furthest west, near Chelsea's western boundary, being the fine eighteenth-century STANLEY HOUSE. An earlier owner was William Hamilton, antiquarian and secretary of Lord 'Marbles' Elgin, and it is still decorated with casts of the Parthenon frieze.

The oldest mansion in Chelsea stands on the Embankment by Battersea Bridge. This is the fifteenth-century

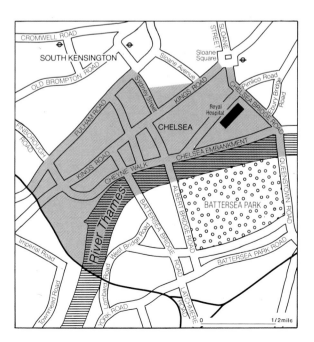

OPPOSITE Chelsea Harbour is one of London's most spirited modern developments. Its pastel-coloured office and residential buildings, capped with fanciful roofs and overlooking a 75-berth marina, give it a Continental feel.

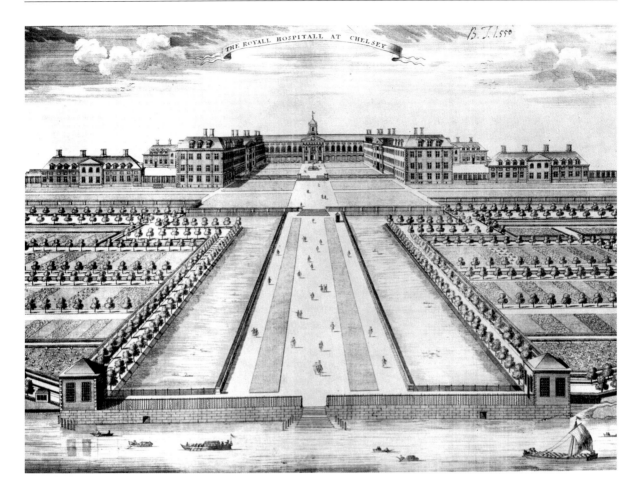

THE ROYALL HOSPITALL AT CHELSEY

Wren's Royal Hospital at Chelsea was completed in 1692. Today the access to the river from its gardens is interrupted by Chelsea Embankment. The grounds are the site of the Chelsea Flower Show each May.

CROSBY HALL, owned for a time by Sir Thomas More in the City at Bishopsgate, sold by him and moved bodily to Chelsea in 1910. More, who lived at what later became Beaufort House, is Chelsea's only indigenous saint, so Crosby Hall was re-erected just west of All Saints, also known as Chelsea Old Church, records for which go back as far as 1290. More's first wife is buried in All Saints, the More Chapel having escaped the 1941 fire bomb that all but destroyed the church. It was devotedly restored and reconsecrated in 1953. In nearby Cheyne Row is the Catholic church dedicated to him. Between the Old Church and Crosby Hall glimmers ROPER'S GARDEN, laid out by the borough in memory of More's favourite daughter Margaret and embellished with statuary and twenty-four welcome benches.

Henry VIII, whose Lord Chancellor More was until executed for treason, would visit him by royal barge. So attractive did Henry find 'the sweet air of Chelsey' that he built himself a new manor house in the area of Cheyne Walk, Oakley Street and Chelsea Manor Street. Elizabeth I spent part of her girlhood there and became disturbingly involved in the love-romps of Henry's widow Catherine Parr and Thomas Seymour. More's

confiscated estate was to have eighteen subsequent owners, including the Duke of Beaufort and Lord Cheyne, until it was run down and Beaufort House was demolished by Sir Hans Sloane in 1740. (He made amends by creating Chelsea's Physic Garden.) Sloane also owned Henry VIII's Chelsea Manor, which was pulled down after his death in 1753, the collection of antiquities that it housed having been bequeathed by him to the nascent British Museum (see *Museums and galleries*).

It was in the eighteenth century that Chelsea acquired its beautiful riverside houses in CHEYNE WALK, now among the most sought-after in London. When royalty and the nobility left, the gentry moved in and in far greater numbers. Some of these houses still retain their elegant iron gates, hoods and balconies. Plaques abound, though not recording all the nineteenth-century celebrities; the area appealed to artists in particular, helping to lay the basis of Chelsea's reputation as a bohemian quarter. J. M. W. Turner, master painter of Thames sky and water, died at no. 119; while James McNeill Whistler, American creator of nocturnes, died at 72 after trying nos 21, 96 and 101, beside four other Chelsea addresses. Earlier Chelsea inhabitants whose homes have vanished were the writers Jonathan Swift, John Gay and Tobias Smollett.

Today along CHELSEA REACH there are brave attempts to recapture the atmosphere of Old Chelsea. The borough has opened the small Cremorne Garden on the site of the former extensive pleasure-ground. An original cast-iron entrance gate, complete with four bronze lions' heads, has been reinstated. East of Cremorne's little pier, dense with seagulls, are the friendly, gently nudging houseboats that have been moored for years beside Battersea Bridge. West along Lots Road after the power station – a splendid brick Edwardian dinosaur – is the ultra-modern world of CHELSEA HARBOUR. This 20-acre marina, with its 75-berth yacht harbour, might have been designed by some latter-day Palladio for the Italian nobility. Certainly its belvedere, wine bars, studios, shops, apartments and walkways, all painted white and sea-blue or in pastel colours to produce an effect of perpetual sunshine, give a feel of abroad. The streamlined yachts have names like *Coco* and *Posy*, differing as much from the old house-boats as a limousine from a battered station wagon.

A return to King's Road via World's End – the original pub being named after Chelsea's last but one

tollgate – raises a historical problem. How did the secluded 'village by the river' become the bohemian *rive gauche* of the 'naughty nineties' and after? Chelsea's earlier artists were far from raffish. Turner lived incognito, John Martin was patronized by the Prince Consort, the sculptor William Theed contributed to the Albert Memorial, a copy of Holman Hunt's *Light of the World* hangs in St Paul's, Daniel Maclise painted the Wellington and Nelson frescoes in the House of Lords. No bohemianism there.

The bohemian idea was introduced and sustained by a series of changes: a general feeling of *fin de siècle*; the coming of the Chelsea Arts Club to 93 Old Church Street in 1891 (it is still there) with the flamboyant Chelsea Arts Balls (see *Fairs and festivals*); the mushrooming of studios in Flood Street, Tite Street, Jubilee Place, Glebe Place; the Pheasantry Club in King's Road – now a restaurant behind its portico of caryatids and chariots; the avant-garde Royal Court Theatre; the Chelsea Set with its sub-species of Sloane Rangers; the King's Road Saturday parades. As the idea grew, people remembered various precedents: high jinks in Cheyne Walk where Rossetti had painted his mistress, his 'dear Elephant' from Royal Avenue, while Swinburne, poet of the 'roses and raptures of vice', read aloud from de Sade or slid naked down the banisters.

In Thomas More's day the King's road was a field path. Widened but closed to the public by Charles II (perhaps visiting Nelly in Fulham) and reopened in

Cheyne Walk in the last years of the nineteenth century, taken from Beaufort Street. From the right, Beaufort House (nos 91–4) was built in 1771. The white building beyond is the seventeenth-century Lindsey House and further on no. 104 still advertised itself as the Greaves boat-building firm, run by the father of the artist Walter Greaves, who lived there until 1897.

1830, it filled up with nursery gardens and florists – Tryon Street, a present-day side street, was Butterfly Alley. Fulham Road in the days of Chelsea's palaces had also been flowery, boastintg a nobleman's 'neat seat'; later it regressed to a workhouse, then progressed to St Stephen's Hospital. Modern King's Road is not yet quite impassable, but Chelsea Embankment is another matter. Monstrous juggernauts make a stroll along Cheyne Walk alarming, except where riverside public gardens shelter the walk from the highway. The novelist Henry James, used to take 'beguiling drives' in his wheelchair all along the Embankment. Today he would be dead before he reached Albert Bridge.

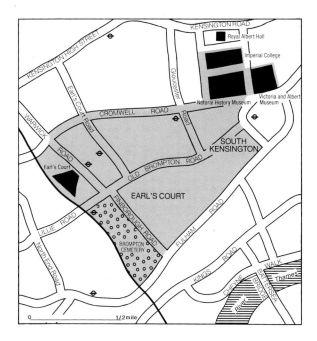

EARL'S COURT

Earl's Court defies consensus. To admirers, it is the nearest the capital has to offer to New York – vibrant, varied, open all hours, international. For others, it is the sleaze centre of London, full of second-rate hotels and third-rate pubs and fast-food joints; noisy, shabby, the focal point for every drop-out and undesirable.

It was not always so. Earl's Court never achieved the status of its neighbours, Kensington and Chelsea, but its grand houses and even grander mansion blocks attracted their fair share of rich residents. Away from the din of Earl's Court Road, they still do. The area takes its name from the court house of the earls of Warwick and Holland, lords of the manor. Earl's Court manor house and farm stood roughly where the underground station stands today. The first area to be built upon, starting in the 1820s, was a little triangle tucked into the corner of Earl's Court Road and Cromwell Road. Once a slum, it is now a peaceful enclave of pretty two- and three-storey houses, a conservation area called Earl's Court village.

Earl's Court's major development, in the latter half of the nineteenth century, followed a pattern already familiar in Brompton and South Kensington. Tall rows of houses spread east, west and south of Earl's Court Road. Most of the houses on the Redcliffe Estate were designed for affluent gentry, with the exception of Redcliffe Square, which had even grander houses with two staircases, and Ifield Road, where residents were mostly plebeian. The large, dull houses to the west attracted some stars – Ellen Terry at 33 Longridge Road, Compton Mackenzie and his sister, Fay Compton, at 1 Nevern Square. Earl's Court Square is the most interesting and varied patch. In late Victorian Philbeach Gardens, St Cuthbert's Church has an abundance of fine

OPPOSITE Earl's Court has long been bed-sitter territory and in the 1950s became the habitat for the shifting population of short-term young visitors from Australia and New Zealand. It retains much of that character although the cultural mix has broadened: hence the Arabic writing on the TV shop sign.

Arts and Crafts furnishings.

Developers to the east of Earl's Court Road met a growing resistance to big terraced houses and began to build, instead, the handsome, red-brick mansion blocks which give Earl's Court its flavour today. Houses in Harrington and Collingham Gardens, by the prolific partnership of George and Peto, represent the extreme point of the late Victorian domestic revival with elements from every variety of Northern European street frontage.

Warwick Road is dominated by the EARL'S COURT EXHIBITION CENTRE. The present building dates from 1939 but the exhibitions began fifty years earlier with an American extravaganza starring Buffalo Bill and Annie Oakley. Another building of note is the circular western entrance to Earl's Court Tube station, a classic piece of 1930s' London Transport architecture.

The grand houses began to be divided as early as the First World War and it did not take long for the area to be christened the bed-sit jungle. Cromwell Road became the start of the main road west out of London, passing Heathrow Airport. In 1955 work began on the huge West London air terminal (now redesigned into flats and a supermarket). This, plus the 1960s' tourist boom, led to even more old houses being turned into cheap hotels.

By the early 1960s Earl's Court Road had acquired a new title – Kangaroo Valley. Australians and other Commonwealth visitors made a beeline for the area because of its cheap accommodation and the Overseas Visitors' Club, which started life as a residential home from home but grew. The Antipodeans have mostly moved on but other itinerants have taken their place.

SOUTH KENSINGTON

There is more than a hint of grandiose pomposity about most of South Kensington. To the north, museums and colleges dominate the landscape. The residential southern half consists chiefly of handsome terraces and squares built for Victorians with a high sense of their own self-importance. Such lively street life as there is huddles round the Tube station. This noisy, traffic-clogged patch, with its cheap restaurants and small shops, estate agents and scruffy hotels, is oddly out of step with the rest of the area.

The museums area was developed between 1856 and 1914 on land bought from the profits of the 1851 Great

Gloucester Road was largely residential until the District Line came in 1868, converting it into a busy commercial street. The Piccadilly Line was extended here in the early years of the century, when this picture was taken. The station (far left) is little changed today.

Exhibition (see *Museums and galleries*). Houses were built to help finance the various colleges, museums, concert halls and centres of learning planned for the plot. Three new roads were laid out over land that had been largely used for nurseries: Cromwell Road, which ran west and was named after a house on the site said to have been lived in by Oliver Cromwell, and Queen's Gate and Exhibition Road, which both cut south from Hyde Park.

Most of the houses were ornate five-storey, Italianate, stuccoed terraces with up to nine bedrooms apiece. The major builder in the area was Charles James Freake, a publican's son and one of the most important speculative builders of the time who, at one point, employed about four hundred men.

The houses attracted a high class of resident – the Duke of Rutland (and Freake himself) lived in Cromwell Road. Exhibition Road housed various noblemen as well as the politician Joseph Chamberlain, while Prince's

Gate could boast Lord Baden-Powell, Field Marshal Earl Haig and President Kennedy's father Joseph Kennedy when he was ambassador.

Today the houses are almost all flats, hotels or embassies. Some relief from this decayed grandeur comes from William Butterfield's pretty, un-English St Augustine's Church and Bute Street, a low-rise shopping street near the station, rebuilt in the 1950s and 1960s. The Norfolk Hotel, right by the station and dating from the late 1880s, reinforced an early tendency to build hotels in the area or to convert terraced houses into lodging houses. Gloucester Road also attracted its fair share of hotels round the station. Red-brick Bailey's, built in 1875, was the first and proved popular with Americans – an 1891 guide praised its 'cosy, homelike atmosphere'. Today, it is overshadowed by Seifert's tall Forum Hotel (1971–2) and the more retiring Gloucester Hotel, built about the same time.

Onslow Gardens, Onslow Square and the surrounding mews and streets form the prime residential area of South Kensington. Built on Smith's Charity land from about 1845, mostly by Freake, the elegant houses attracted a good class of buyer – then and now; William Thackeray at 36 Onslow Square, Prime Minister Bonar Law at 24 Onslow Gardens. Clareville Grove, to the north of Old Brompton Road, is a pretty and intimate enclave of villas which grew up in the first half of the nineteenth century.

The Boltons is the residential centrepiece of the western half of South Kensington. The two facing crescents of large, elegant, stuccoed houses with gardens and a church in between were designed by George Godwin, architect and surveyor to the Gunter Estate. The award-winning Bousfield Primary School, on the crescents' northern tip, was built in 1956 on the site of Beatrix Potter's home. Reminders of earlier settlements straggling along Fulham Road survive in Georgian Seymour Walk and The Billings, a pretty oasis of two-and three-storey cottages dating from the 1840s.

HOLLAND PARK

High points in London's topography have traditionally attracted the wealthy and creative. Campden Hill in Holland Park is no exception. It has the last privately owned country house in central London – Aubrey House, tucked behind solid iron gates at the junction of Aubrey Road and Aubrey Walk. J. M. W. Turner painted sunsets from the gardens in precipitous Campden Hill Square, while Campden Hill Road at the turn of the century was a centre for literary parties. Edward Linley Sambourne, a Victorian illustrator, lived at 18 Stafford Terrace and his house has been preserved by the Victorian Society as a perfect time capsule of the 1890s.

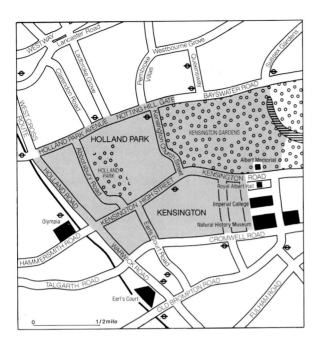

Campden House on Campden Hill was a fine Stuart mansion built in 1612. Queen Anne lived in it while still a princess. It burned down in 1862. This drawing was done in 1647.

The nineteenth-century historian Lord Macaulay, seeking healthy air for his asthma, lived his last years on the crest of the hill in one of a cluster of large, handsome houses inhabited by the nobility and known collectively as 'The Dukeries'. Today the road where they stood, confusingly called simply Campden Hill, ends in the grounds of the post-war Holland Park Comprehensive School (see *A centre of learning*). Rising steeply from Notting Hill Gate and falling more gently to the bustling shops of Kensington High Street, Campden Hill is today the home of many politicians and public figures, as well as families who have deep roots there. (Aubrey House has been in the Alexander family since the 1870s.)

At the green heart of Holland Park lies the remnant of Holland House, a Jacobean mansion built for Sir Walter Cope, James I's Chancellor of the Exchequer, which gave the district its name and cultural tone (Cope's son-in-law became first Earl of Holland). The house was famous for gatherings of eighteenth- and nineteenth-century political and literary figures. In 1952, after severe war damage, it was acquired by the London County Council. In summer it is used for open-air concerts and plays and there is a restaurant in the grounds.

Some of late Victorian England's most successful painters, sculptors and architects settled where Holland Park meets Kensington, in Melbury Road, Holland Park Road and Addison Road. The architect William Burges designed 29 Melbury Road for himself as 'a model residence of the fifteenth century'. Its extraordinary medieval profile dominates a road otherwise much run to seed. In nearby Holland Park Road stands the plain red-brick LEIGHTON HOUSE. Built for Frederic Leighton, the only English painter to be given a peerage, it contains the remarkable Arab Hall, decorated with brilliant tiles from the East. There is now an adjoining art gallery. (See *Homes of the famous*)

Holland Park's most exotic building is 8 Addison Road, sometimes known as 'the Peacock House'. Built in 1906 by Halsey Ricardo for the store magnate Sir Ernest Debenham, its walls, roof and much of its interior are clad in dazzling blue and green tiles, an astonishing sight amid the surrounding drab villas. When it was built, its back garden stretched to the edge of Holland Park itself. Today houses intervene. The most fascinating modern (1962) building is the Commonwealth Institute, at the southern edge of the park near Kensington High Street, with its great sweeping roofs and engrossing displays.

KENSINGTON

The Royal Borough of Kensington has always been genteel, the favoured territory of retired expatriates and colonels' widows living in cavernous flats off Gloucester Road and the wide, Italianate Queen's Gate.

'The old court suburb', as the Victorian editor Leigh Hunt dubbed it, took its regal tone originally from William III, who bought the Earl of Nottingham's Jacobean mansion and had it remodelled by Sir Christopher Wren, converting it into KENSINGTON PALACE as a retreat from smoky Whitehall. It was here that Princess Victoria of Kent was born in 1819 and where, eighteen years later, she was summoned in her nightgown to be told she was Queen.

KENSINGTON GARDENS, which adds so much charm to the views from Palace Gate and Queen's Gate, was originally the Palace's private estate. Its 275 acres seem imbued with the spirit of childhood, from the secluded Flower Walk, where pre-war nannies used to wheel their charges, to the Peter Pan statue and the carved Elfin Oak at the Bayswater end of the Broad Walk.

Kensington was a Victorian creation, laid out almost entirely in the latter half of the nineteenth century, although Kensington Square, tucked secretively behind Barkers' store, dates from William III's reign. It was surrounded by fields until 1840. A village had existed around St Mary Abbots church since medieval times and Kensington High Street retained a small-town character until it was dramatically widened in 1902 and its picturesque little shops swept away to build department stores. (In the 1820s and 1830s, William Cobbett, author of *Rural Rides*, ran a seed and nursery business on the site of what is today High Street Kensington underground station.)

Now the grand department stores, all founded by local drapers – Barkers, Pontings, Derry and Toms – have fallen victim to rising land values and the proximity of Oxford Street. Barkers continues to trade on two floors, but its building is now the editorial office of the *Daily Mail*. Derry and Toms next door, with its roof garden, has also been made into offices.

To the east of Barkers' site, two grand country houses, Kensington House and Colby House stood for two centuries before the explosion of late-Victorian development; they were replaced by the red-brick mansion flats and houses of Kensington Court. Purpose-built flats were invented in Kensington with Albert Hall Mansions (1879) and nearby De Vere Gardens, where Robert Browning and Henry James were near neighbours for a time at nos 29 and 34 respectively. Most of Kensington High Street's remaining Georgian terraces were pulled down in the 1930s to build bland apartment blocks.

Blandness is characteristic of Kensington. The stucco and red-brick terraces and squares between Kensington High Street and Cromwell Road – large tracts of them once cultivated as market gardens by the Berkeley Square patissier James Gunter – convey solid Victorian virtues but little personality. Edwardes Square is an exception, with its low late Georgian houses encircling an immense central garden.

No one could accuse Kensington Palace Gardens of

OPPOSITE Holland Park's imposing stucco terraces have remained fashionable since they were built more than a century ago. Cushioned by its proximity to Kensington, the area has not suffered the inner-city depradations of neighbouring Bayswater and Shepherd's Bush.

In 1860, the date of this photograph, Kensington still had something of a village feel to it. The narrow, winding High Street was soon transformed by the arrival of the Underground in 1868 and John Barker's first drapery store two years later, presaging its development as a major shopping street.

lacking individuality. This secluded private road was built on the old kitchen gardens of Kensington Palace, and each house designed by a distinguished architect (Charles Barry, Decimus Burton, Sydney Smirke, T. H. Wyatt) to fulfil the fantasies of wealthy industrialists and financiers. Today, most of the surviving houses with their ornamental battlements and towers are foreign embassies. No. 2 Palace Green, at the southern end, was designed by Thackeray for himself in neo-Georgian red brick ('the reddest house in all London', he boasted). It is now the Israeli Embassy. Ironically, the first country to buy diplomatic territory in Millionaires' Row was the Soviet Union, in 1930. It acquired no. 13, opposite the banking Rothschilds – and has long outstayed them.

NOTTING HILL

The area of north Kensington known as Notting Hill has always been one of extreme social and economic contrasts. They are still apparent today on descending the northern slope of Ladbroke Grove, where the fine stucco terraces and crescents of the south give way to peeling back streets in the shadow of the railway bridge – an area further blighted since 1970 by the elevated Westway motorway link.

Divisions of wealth and poverty were more dramatically marked in the nineteenth century, when fashionable upper-middle-class homes were going up on the new Ladbroke estate, a stone's throw from a reeking

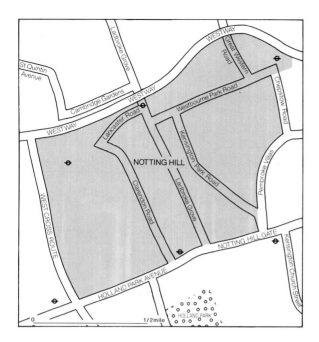

slum known as the Potteries, which in turn was only separated by a road from the aristocratic 'Dukeries' of Campden Hill. The Potteries might well have been named the Piggeries, because the brickfields and tile kilns established there in the 1830s were soon being inundated by pig-keepers displaced by residential development in Tyburnia, a mile or so to the east. In 1849, after a raging cholera epidemic, municipal engineers found 130 people and 3000 pigs to the acre there.

Pig-keeping did not cease altogether until 1894 and this, together with the extension of the Metropolitan Railway from Paddington to Hammersmith in 1864, kept the colonizing gentry firmly at bay. In 1902 the social reformer Charles Booth found in Sirdar Road, Notting Dale, poverty of 'as deep and dark a type as anywhere in London'. Notting Dale is the old name for the district towards Shepherd's Bush, while Notting Hill describes the area north of Holland Park Avenue; Notting Hill Gate is the stretch of high street connecting Bayswater Road to Holland Park Avenue. A turnpike gate once stood here at the junction with Kensington Church Street, then a twisting country lane connecting the gravel pits of Notting Hill's principal industry to Kensington village.

The north of the old Potteries remains a largely working-class district today, though most of the narrow streets running into Holland Park Avenue have been expensively gentrified. The past is evoked by Pottery Lane and one surviving brick 'bottle' kiln, the last of its kind in London, standing in Walmer Road near the Earl of Zetland pub.

On the estate developed by James Weller Ladbroke in

the 1840s, and its neighbour the Norland ('North-land') estate, solid bourgeois comfort was the keynote from the beginning. 'Ladbroke upholds the proper dignity of the English middle classes', wrote a commentator in 1910. With their stucco villas veiled by lilac and acacia, the streets radiating from Ladbroke Grove still exude a countrified charm after the heavy urban terraces of Paddington and Bayswater. Indeed, a farm remained in the area as late as 1880.

Even more surprisingly, before Ladbroke Grove was built northward up its hill in the 1840s, a $2\frac{1}{4}$-mile racecourse called the Hippodrome encircled the site. It opened on 3 June 1837 and was described as 'a racing emporium more extensive and attractive than Ascot or Epsom, with ten times the accommodation of either'. Alas, its builders had not reckoned with the heavy clay soil, which became waterlogged in bad weather. Its last public meeting was held in June 1841, after which a tide of stucco rapidly covered the area.

Today, only a drab slit of a street called Hippodrome Place commemorates the racecourse project, though the famous PORTOBELLO ROAD street market owes its origins to gipsy traders who came primarily to buy and sell horses at the Hippodrome. Antique dealers began to gravitate here at weekends in 1948, when the old Caledonian Market in Islington was closed. Portobello Road owes its Spanish name to Porto Bello Farm which once stood at its northern end, so called in honour of a naval victory in the Gulf of Mexico in 1739. At its southern end stand the solid, dignified dwellings of Pembridge Villas. In a studio here (now replaced by a garage), William Frith painted his famous Victorian

The gate at Notting Hill was erected in the eighteenth century to extract tolls for the Uxbridge Turnpike. This painting portrays the area about a hundred years later.

set-pieces, *Derby Day* and *Paddington Station*. Not far away, in Pembridge Road, Britain's first race riots erupted in 1958 against Caribbean immigrants who had moved into the cheap lodgings of north Kensington. By 1966, however, the annual August Notting Hill Carnival was established: though still controversial among some residents, it is now the biggest ethnic carnival in Europe (see *Carnivals*).

Notting Hill Gate was extensively redeveloped in the late 1950s, its high street widened and its warren of old shops, pubs and slum dwellings to the north and west replaced by modern commercial buildings and an eighteen-storey apartment tower. It has gone up in tone and price. Today's immigrants will find few cheap lodgings there.

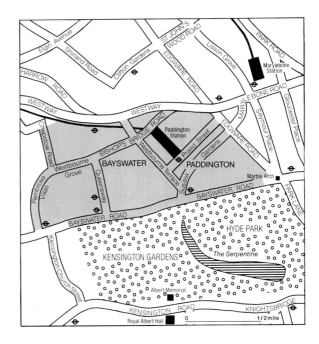

—— PADDINGTON AND BAYSWATER ——

The axis of Paddington, once a village famous for its dairy herds, shifted abruptly westward with the coming of the Great Western Railway in 1838. The district around the station has retained a transient character ever since, typified by seedy hotels and cheap tourist shops. Paddington Green, the original heart of the parish (whose church, St Mary's, is the burial place of the actress Sarah Siddons), is only a sliver of its former self under the shadow of Westway.

Paddington has been in the vanguard of many transport revolutions. London's first omnibus service started here in 1829, from Paddington Green to the Bank of England; the one-shilling fare included a newspaper. In 1863 the first Underground line, the Metropolitan, opened from Paddington to Farringdon, and sixty-two

years earlier the Paddington and Grand Junction Canal was opened, linking Uxbridge to the capital. Its prosperity faded when the Regent's Canal opened in 1820, running through to the Thames via Camden Town, Islington, Hackney and Limehouse (see *Canals*). The canal basin is being developed as a £350 million waterfront centre of offices, shops and apartments – a symbol of Paddington's new status in the West End property market.

The arrival of the railway transformed the land once farmed by three twelfth-century brothers called de

Paddington Green, where the Edgware Road joins the Harrow Road, was the centre of the village of Paddington when this print was drawn in the eighteenth century. Today it is overwhelmed by the link road to the M40 motorway that soars and roars above it.

Padinton or de Padintune and subsequently owned by the abbots of Westminster (the Church Commissioners still control large sections). Within ten years from 1840 the market and nursery gardens of Paddington and its southern neighbour, Bayswater, were covered in handsome terraces and squares of four- and five-storey, porticoed houses in white and cream stucco. (One curiosity is the façade of 23–24 Leinster Gardens, which is just that – a façade hiding the underground railway cutting.)

City merchants and professional families moved in the 1830s and 1840s into wide, tree-lined streets like Sussex Gardens (then Grand Junction Road) and Westbourne Terrace, built above a stream running into the Serpentine in Kensington Gardens. But the area began to deteriorate when Paddington station went up in 1851, and again after the Second World War, suffering from bomb damage and negligent landlords.

The hinterland of Praed Street (whose Cornish name commemorates one of the first canal company directors, Sir John Praed) was built for artisans and railway workers and still looks a poor relation of the grandly planned squares and terraces around it. On a windowsill in St Mary's Hospital, overlooking Praed Street, Alexander Fleming discovered penicillin mould growing in a saucer in 1927.

Development west of Edgware Road and north of Bayswater Road was inhibited by the shadow of the Tyburn gallows, even after their removal in 1783. Connaught Place, a surviving Regency enclave with charming balconies and canopies, was built during the Napoleonic wars, followed by Connaught Square, Connaught and Kendal Streets and the rest of the attractive small-scale exercise in town planning known as Tyburnia. It is now, more prosaically, the Hyde Park Estate and a very expensive place to live, worthy of the fictional Forsyte family who flourished around here in John Galsworthy's saga.

Going west down the straight Roman line of Bayswater Road, just past Lancaster Gate underground station is a startling symbol of the 1980s. Christ Church, a once distinguished yellow-brick structure of 1855, has been partly demolished and a modern apartment house bolted on to the remnants of its tower and spire.

Another famous church near Paddington Station, Thomas Cundy's Holy Trinity in Bishop's Bridge Road, has been demolished to build a block of flats. West of Queensway, however, a mixture of faiths – Greek Orthodox, Jewish and Anglican – continues to flourish in Moscow Road and St Petersburg Place. (Names around here, including the terracotta, turreted Coburg Hotel, commemorate a visit to London by the Russian and German sovereigns in 1814.)

Since the 1930s Bayswater Road has lost many of its imposing stucco frontages facing the park, but the house in which J. M. Barrie wrote *Peter Pan* is still there at number 100, one of a pair of pretty Victorian villas. The enchanting Peter Pan statue, sculpted by Sir George Frampton in 1912, stands a short walk away, in Kensington Gardens.

Bayswater, as its name suggests, was noted for its springs, wells and conduits, some supplying fresh water as far as the City. The district has always been an intriguing mixture of raffishness and Victorian respectability. A house in Porchester Gardens was the first private dwelling in London to be lit by electricity (in 1879), while the Swan and Black Lion pubs in Bayswater Road are relics of the eighteenth-century turnpike.

Whiteley's, London's first department store, began life in 1863 as a drapery shop in Westbourne Grove, then a fashionable shopping street. It moved in 1911 to a grand domed building in Queensway after William Whiteley, a Yorkshire-born businessman who called himself 'The Universal Provider', was shot dead in his office in 1907 by a man who believed himself Whiteley's illegitimate son. The store ceased trading in 1981, but the building has been restored and developed as the shopping and social hub of a neighbourhood now so cosmopolitan as to be unrecognizable, except for the 1936 QUEEN'S ICE CLUB, from Whiteley's heyday.

FITZROVIA

North of Oxford Street and west of Tottenham Court Road, Fitzrovia is a residential neighbourhood shifting to business use. The name is a twentieth-century invention, mockingly coined by literati from the Fitzroy Tavern, a pub favoured by Dylan Thomas, George Orwell and other writers of the 1940s and 1950s.

Fitzroy was the family name of the Stuart earls of Southampton, descended from an illegitimate son of Charles II. In the seventeenth century the Southampton estates covered most of present-day Fitzrovia and the area was built up mainly in the mid-eighteenth century. Its buildings were substantial, but London's rapid expansion soon brought more desirable dwellings in Marylebone. The well-to-do moved west and Fitzrovia's houses were split into small flats rented by immigrants, craftsmen and, later, artists and writers.

Whistler and Sickert had studios in Fitzroy Street as did William Coldstream, W.P. Frith and Augustus John. George Bernard Shaw lived at 29 FITZROY SQUARE from 1887 to 1898 and Virginia Woolf from 1907 to

OPPOSITE Like the hinterland of most main rail termini, the once-elegant Norfolk Square, a few short steps from Paddington Station, is now lined almost entirely with cheap hotels.

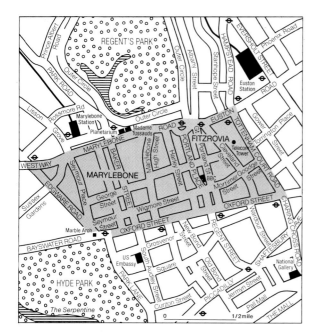

Gothic and High Anglicanism, every inch of its interior walls covered in paintings and mosaics. Dark and silent, the church's great bulk is concealed behind an entrance courtyard modest enough for a small school. Laurence Olivier sang here as a choirboy, and it has provided an incense-scented retreat for generations of exhausted Oxford Street shoppers.

MARYLEBONE

Marylebone comes as near to town planning as London has ever ventured – a grid of Georgian streets, lined with stuccoed houses, their elegant, bland frontages beautifully maintained, their iron-railinged areas always kempt. Behind stand the mews, but no gardens. These are London's most urban houses; they may not charm, but they compel admiration.

John Holles, Duke of Newcastle, bought fields here in 1708, as London spread west. Building went on throughout the eighteenth century, with the streets named after members of the family (Harley, Cavendish) and their country estates. The family's successors, the Portlands and Howards de Walden, still hold the freehold of much of the land, and this continuity has helped to preserve the area's unity and good looks.

The master plan was never quite completed, and in parts has been obliterated. CAVENDISH SQUARE covers an underground car park, while office buildings and the backs of Oxford Street stores fill its southern side. But the grandeur of Harley's original concept can be appreciated on the north side, with it two matching Palladian façades. Between them hangs Epstein's *Madonna and Child*, a surprising but welcome addition to the square.

A fine Robert Adam house (1770) stands on the corner of Queen Anne Street and Chandos Street. Along these and adjoining streets – Harley, Wimpole and New Cavendish – the blue plaques are a rollcall of fashionable artists, busy Victorian architects, composers and men of science and letters. From the mid-nineteenth century doctors moved in, finding the area convenient for hospitals and their wealthy patients. As medical specialization increased they passed on customers to their neighbouring colleagues. At first they lived above their ground-floor consulting rooms, but in this century the living rooms have gone over to professional use.

PORTLAND PLACE retains touches of elegance and has attracted several embassies and high commissions. Portland Place was incorporated into John Nash's triumphal way from St James's to Regent's Park and the end is indeed triumphant, as the street divides to form the two graceful arms of Park Crescent.

Marylebone has four distinguished Georgian

1911. The square has some attractive houses retaining their Adam façades from the 1790s (see *Noble squares*). Nearby, where Warren and Conway Streets meet, is a survival from the early years of the twentieth century, when the Welsh became London's milkmen. Not many of their dairies remain, but this blue-tiled corner shopfront, boldly labelled JONES, is very much of its period.

The Fitzroy area has other such nostalgic corners. Off Charlotte Street, Scala Street commemorates the theatre where *Peter Pan* played every Christmas season from 1945 until its demolition in 1970. Pollock's Toy Museum is on the corner of Whitfield and Scala Streets.

Today corporations have replaced individual artists in Fitzrovia. Independent television producers, foreign television stations, Channel 4 and advertising agencies have their offices here, in the shadow of the 580-foot Telecom Tower, completed in 1964 as a telecommunications centre. They bring business to the many restaurants which cluster at the southern end of CHARLOTTE STREET and in Percy Street. This northern outpost of Soho had long boasted solidly bourgeois restaurants such as Schmidt's and Bertorelli's. They have given way to the designer décors and matching menus favoured by media people. Great Portland Street and Great Titchfield Street, on the west side of Fitzrovia, are the centre of the wholesale fashion trade. There are witty window displays by the suppliers of ribbons, buttons and trimmings, and some small delicatessens and restaurants where the chat is of textiles.

William Butterfield's ALL SAINTS CHURCH, Margaret Street (1850) is an imposing monument to Victorian

Nash's crescent at the north end of Portland Place was designed as a monumental entrance to Regent's Park. The Marylebone Road did not then accommodate today's almost constant flow of east-west traffic, which effectively cuts off the crescent from the Park. Hardwick's Marylebone Parish Church (1817) is in the distance.

churches with a strong family resemblance, though a century separates the youngest from the oldest. The dominant neo-classical features include a columned portico, with a spire or cupola and a plain oblong body with galleries and large, clear windows. ST PETER'S, Vere Place (James Gibbs, 1724) was built by Lord Harley to secure the spiritual wellbeing of his new tenants. Marooned now behind department stores, it is used by an evangelical organization. ST MARYLEBONE PARISH CHURCH (Thomas Hardwick, 1817) provided Nash with a ready-made focus for his York Gate, Regent's Park. ST MARY'S, Wyndham Place (Robert Smirke, 1823) forms part of the Portman Estate's design of squares, circuses, streets and vistas due north of Marble Arch. ALL SOULS, Langham Place (1824) is the only surviving Nash church, restored after bombing in 1940. It stands where his design tripped over Foley House (on the site now occupied by the Langham Hotel), which had rights to a clear view north to the trees. Nash disguised the resultant dog's leg by siting the round portico and slim spire at the head of Regent Street, with the body of the church at an angle. When the BBC built its striking curved and decked headquarters in Langham Place in the 1930s, All Souls became the home of religious broadcasting.

Marylebone Lane and MARYLEBONE HIGH STREET (the heart of Marylebone village from medieval times) follow the course of the Tyburn, a stream which flowed south to the Thames. At the northern end of the High Street, a small garden of rest with benches and flowering cherries marks the site of an earlier St Marylebone parish church, where Sheridan married in 1773 and Charles Wesley and

Byron were baptized in 1778. To the west, in Manchester Square, the Wallace Collection occupies HERTFORD HOUSE, built in the 1770s for the Duke of Manchester. In the 1790s the house was leased by the Spanish ambassador, establishing a connection which lives on in nearby Spanish Place and Roman Catholic ST JAMES'S CHURCH, for English Catholics had worshipped in Spanish Embassy chapels when their religion was in disfavour. The church is Victorian Gothic (Edward Goldie, 1890), with a high-arched nave, a heptagonal apse and flying buttresses.

In George Street, the presbytery links the church to Durrant's Hotel, established in 1921 by combining a row of Georgian boarding houses. For Daisy Ashford, of *Young Visiters* fame, tea at Durrant's was the ultimate in sophistication on a day out in London; today it is more comfortable than chic, but still a convenient place to take tea or stay.

BAKER STREET housed Sherlock Holmes in fiction but in real life accommodates the head office of a different national institution, Marks and Spencer, occupying an entire block. The broad and busy Marylebone Road hosts more household names: Woolworths and British Home Stores have their headquarters here, while MADAME TUSSAUD'S WAXWORKS, and the PLANETARIUM next door, may be identified from a distance by the press of coaches and the queues for admission. Between Baker Street and Edgware Road is another area of Georgian houses set around gardens with London plane trees. Two fine Adam houses (1775–7) grace the corner of Portman Square and Gloucester Place, shaming the banal Churchill Hotel (1970) opposite.

─────── BLOOMSBURY ───────

The name of Bloomsbury – a corruption of Blemunds-
bury, the manor of the Blemunds which stood on what is
now the north side of Bloomsbury Square – has several
associations. The literary one derives from the four
children of Leslie Stephen, including Virginia Woolf
and Vanessa Bell, who occupied a house in Gordon
Square in 1904. The Woolfs lived in Tavistock Square
until 1939 but many members of the 'Bloomsbury set'
did not live in the area. For many Bloomsbury means
culture and learning, dominated as it is by the monumental buildings of the British Museum and the University of London. But in terms of topography, the area
between New Oxford Street and High Holborn to the
south and Euston Road and King's Cross to the north is
characterized by its unique concentration of Georgian
terraces and squares.

On the map the large area between Tottenham Court
Road and the line of Southampton Row and Woburn
Place is conspicuous for the formal regularity of its street
pattern, with all lines on the map meeting at right-
angles. The earls, subsequently dukes, of Bedford
developed this part of Bloomsbury and the Bedford
Estate is largely responsible for the survival of one of the
finest planned aristocratic estates in the capital. The
period pride the Russell family took in this urban
achievement is proclaimed in the names of the area –
Bedford, Tavistock, Woburn, Gordon, Malet, End-
sleigh – each referring to their titles, estates, seats and
connections by marriage.

The ownership of this large slice of London by one
great family with a close interest in its rental value was
responsible for its distinct character. The paucity of pubs
and shops reflects an anxiety to keep the estate respectable, while alterations to the repetitive design of the
standardized houses was not permitted except – as in
Russell Square – where it was intended to keep the
properties fashionable. This is all the more remarkable
as, for Victorians like Ruskin and Gilbert Scott, nothing
could be more boring than the unbroken 'hole in the
wall' architecture of Gower Street. By the 1930s,
however, Bloomsbury's standardized, plain Georgian
family houses seemed a model of urban sanity.

The story begins in 1661 with the laying out of
BLOOMSBURY SQUARE by the Earl of Southampton (whose
only daughter married William, Lord Russell). Bedford
Square dates from 1776, but most of the estate was laid

OPPOSITE Charlotte Street, Fitzrovia's main thoroughfare, has
long been noted for its restaurants of all nationalities and prices.
Trade has been given a fillip by the recent invasion of the area by
advertising agencies and television production houses. The
Telecom Tower (1964) dominates the skyline.

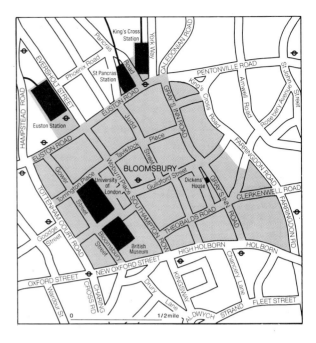

out in the first decades of the nineteenth century, chiefly
by two great speculative builders, James Burton and
Thomas Cubitt. By the beginning of Victoria's reign, the
built-up area had reached the 'New Road' – Euston
Road, originally laid out in 1756.

Nothing survives of the original Bloomsbury Square,
although there are some Georgian houses left and, on
the north-west corner, one of Nash's first buildings,
pioneering the use of stucco. The best square in
Bloomsbury – some would say, in London – is BEDFORD
SQUARE, spoiled only by the traffic roaring down one side
(see Noble squares). Its central garden is still within the
original circular railings and the planting dates from the
early nineteenth century. RUSSELL SQUARE is rather a
disappointment, but Gordon and Tavistock Squares
retain impressive runs of terraces by Cubitt. EUSTON
SQUARE deserves mention but only because the south half
was sold and built over in the 1920s – one of the many
depredations of Georgian London between the wars.

Although outside the Bedford Estate, the part of
Bloomsbury east of Southampton Row is equally interesting and much more complex historically. There are
good squares, like secret QUEEN SQUARE with its hospitals. Some of the earliest surviving houses are to be
found in and around Great Ormond Street and in Great
James Street. Doughty Street, with the Dickens
Museum, largely consists of unbroken late eighteenth-
century terraces. It links two of the most delightful open
spaces in the area, in which a civilized balance is struck
between public and private. At the south end are the
gardens of GRAY'S INN, originally laid out by Francis
Bacon in the early seventeenth century, still open on the

The Rail Termini

Like Paris and Leningrad – but unlike Rome or Vienna – London is remarkable for its large number of railway termini. This was a consequence of the competitive private enterprise that created the railway system, for each company required one or even two stations for its exclusive use. London – again like Paris and Leningrad – is also notable for the number of original nineteenth-century stations still used. Euston, Cannon Street and Blackfriars have been rebuilt, but Paddington, King's Cross and St Pancras survive as three of the great railway monuments of the world.

London's first railway was the London & Greenwich, opened in 1836. Its terminus was LONDON BRIDGE which, owing to railway politics and mergers, expanded to serve two companies: the South Eastern Railway and the London, Brighton & South Coast Railway. A certain amount of the rebuilding of the 1850s and 1860s survives, although hemmed in by modern office towers. The first important railway terminus in London was EUSTON, opened in 1838. Here a heroic architectural gesture was made to celebrate the construction of the London & Birmingham Railway by the engineer Robert Stephenson (son of the railway pioneer George Stephenson). To the north of Euston Square a great Doric gateway was raised to the design of Philip Hardwick. Shortly afterwards this was complemented by a great hall. Neither of these magnificent structures still exists, for they perished when British Railways rebuilt Euston in the style of an airport terminal in 1962. The unnecessary destruction of the 'Euston Arch' – for it could have been moved – was the first important conservation battle for a Victorian building. Its sacrifice was not entirely in vain, for it changed public perception and ensured the survival of other fine stations.

In 1846, during the 'railway mania' when an alarming number of new lines were being promoted, a Royal Commission recommended that no railway should be allowed nearer central London than the line of the 'New Road'. This is why KING'S CROSS lies just along the Euston Road from Euston Station. Opened in 1852, named after a free-standing police station surmounted by a statue of George IV that used to stand nearby, King's Cross was the terminus of the Great Northern Railway, the first main line down the east coast. It consists essentially of two train sheds – originally one for arrivals and one for departures – united by a brick façade in a simple rational classical style, all designed by Lewis Cubitt, a member of the family of builders.

The simple elegance of King's Cross has often been compared with the ornamental extravagance of ST PANCRAS next door – unfavourably by the Victorians but favourably by twentieth-century critics for whom Cubitt's work was closer in spirit to modern architecture than the Gothic revival. Certainly the Midland Railway intended its own terminus, opened in 1868, to outshine King's Cross next door. In terms of both engineering and architecture, St Pancras is superlative – and easy to appreciate because it is today used only lightly. The train shed, by the engineer W. H. Barlow, is a single span of 240 feet – the largest in the world when built – raised above vaults designed for the accommodation of barrels of Burton beer. In front, the railway company placed the Midland Grand Hotel, designed by Gilbert Scott. This lavish essay in the adaptability of Gothic – often erroneously said to be his rejected design for the Foreign Office – is one of the best secular Victorian Gothic buildings in Britain. Executed in red brick and the best materials, it contains a spectacular iron staircase and demonstrates a sensible fusion of architecture and engineering.

At the western end of the New Road lies PADDINGTON and the terminus of the Great Western Railway, opened in 1854. Designed by Isambard Kingdom Brunel, this is possibly the most beautiful of railway sheds, with its three elliptical spans united by two 'transepts'. Brunel, working with the architect M. D. Wyatt, successfully created an iron architecture which was decorative and

yet not at all historical in character: far more sophisticated than the much-vaunted Crystal Palace.

Like all the main termini, Paddington had a grand hotel incorporated into it. For a time these were among the most fashionable places to stay in the capital but they declined, paradoxically, as a result of the railways' increasing popularity. Because the bulk of passengers could not afford to stay at such splendid places, cheap and sometimes squalid hotels were established in the surrounding terraces. This blighted the neighbourhood, deterring the more discerning customers from the station hotels.

In south London, railway competition was more intense and the story more complicated. First to bridge the Thames, in 1860, were the lines into VICTORIA. This is in fact not one terminus but two, side by side: one for the London, Chatham & Dover Railway and one for the London, Brighton & South Coast. (Lady Bracknell in Wilde's *The Importance of Being Earnest*, on being told that Jack Worthing had been found as a baby in the left luggage office on the Brighton line, pronounced: 'The line is immaterial.') The Chatham side's original train shed survives, as does the Grosvenor Hotel (1860–1).

More than most public buildings, railway stations are caught in the conflict between conservation and convenience. It is a three-cornered battle. There are those who want to preserve them as irreplaceable monuments of Victorian industrial architecture; passengers who want them enlarged and modernized to make their journeys less uncomfortable; and British Rail, who want to maximize revenue from their valuable central locations. WATERLOO, terminus for trains to the south-west and the southern suburbs, with its heavy commuter traffic, has sacrificed elegance for efficiency. The smaller CHARING CROSS, serving the south-east, is now the centre of a lucrative development of shops and offices.

Pressures are greatest on stations in the City itself, which for the most part spring into life only in the Monday-to-Friday rush hours. Blackfriars, Holborn Viaduct, Cannon Street and Fenchurch Street have all been incorporated into office complexes. The Blackfriars façade, with its list of exotic European destinations etched into the entrance stonework, was a particularly sad loss. LIVERPOOL STREET, terminus for trains to the east, held out longest, but in the late 1980s that too was buried inside a commercial development, although its fine western train shed (1870) has been retained.

There remains a delightful curiosity, MARYLEBONE. This provincial-looking turn-of-the-century station, tucked off the Marylebone Road, now handles mainly suburban services but it was built as the terminus of the last main line to reach London: the Great Central. The line was a magnificent piece of railway engineering, designed in the 1890s to accommodate Channel Tunnel traffic with a Continental loading gauge. Like the project, most of the line was abandoned – an irony, in view of the disruption caused by attempts a century later to accommodate rail traffic to the reborn tunnel.

OPPOSITE Philip Hardwick's Great Hall at Euston, with a statue of railway pioneer George Stephenson. The hall was demolished in 1962 to be replaced by a more modern facility.

RIGHT Isambard Kingdom Brunel and M. D. Wyatt's majestic ironwork at Paddington, photographed in 1895. Except for the gas lamps and the rolling stock, it is little altered today.

north side. At the other end is MECKLENBURGH SQUARE, notable for its grand eastern terrace of the 1790s with stucco embellishments. Mecklenburgh Square only ever had three sides, like its mirror image, BRUNSWICK SQUARE (now all rebuilt and dominated by the neo-futurist fantasy of the Brunswick Centre), for each looked towards the grounds of the Foundling Hospital inbetween. Here stood the noble institution founded by Thomas Coram, but it was pulled down in the 1920s after London University found the Georgian buildings insufficiently important for its own use – negatively, Bloomsbury's institutions of learning have been responsible for much of the twentieth-century destruction of the area's architectural inheritance. At least the gardens survive for the exclusive enjoyment of children – unaccompanied adults not admitted.

Today, Bloomsbury's grandest buildings are no longer residential. The fine rooms in Bedford Square are largely taken over by publishers and other businesses. Further to the north and east, however, blocks of flats sit within the remains of Georgian town planning. Just north of the wreckage of Regent Square, the late Victorian working-class tenements and post-war council flats around Cromer Street are a reminder that this was an area of desperate poverty in the nineteenth century. Further north again, towards King's Cross – an area formerly called Battle Bridge – the late Georgian terraces around ARGYLE SQUARE have long been largely taken

over by hotels, a consequence of the proximity of the three great railway termini along the Euston Road.

Bloomsbury, however, is more than an object lesson in how the Georgian terraced house could be adapted by speculative builders to meet the needs of both rich and poor. There are many other buildings of interest in the area. Tucked away in the Georgian enclave of Ely Place is ST ETHELDREDA'S CHURCH, a most beautiful piece of medieval Decorated Gothic. Formerly the chapel of the palace of the Bishop of Ely, it has reverted to the Roman Catholic church after many vicissitudes. Georgian places of worship include ST GEORGE's, Bloomsbury, in front of the British Museum, a noble structure by Hawksmoor with an extraordinary steeple based on the tomb of Mausolus at Halicarnassus, topped inconsequentially by a statue of George I. On the corner of Euston Square is the NEW CHURCH of St Pancras by the Inwoods, one of the finest Greek Revival buildings in the country, with its steeple based on the Tower of the Winds in Athens.

Victorian churches include St Alban's, by Butterfield, an Anglo-Catholic mission church originally built in the desperate slums north of High Holborn; the cathedral-like and unfinished church of Christ the King in Gordon Square by Brandon, and the church of the Holy Cross in Cromer Street, another Anglo-Catholic mission in the slums and a dignified expression of Victorian Gothic idealism. The best secular buildings are the Mary Ward Settlement in Tavistock Place, an essay in a 'free style' full of the tricks and symbols of the 1890s, while in Russell Square is a supreme expression of unbridled eclecticism, the HOTEL RUSSELL. This was once complemented by the equally extravagant Imperial Hotel further south, noted for its elaborate Turkish baths. (The modern hotel of that name, on its old site, would better suit a Spanish beach resort.) But even on its own the Russell, Fitzroy Doll's interpretation of early German Renaissance in terracotta, is remarkable enough. Its exhibitionism is rebuked by the sober monumentality of the tower of SENATE HOUSE on the opposite side of Russell Square. This is Charles Holden's 1930s' skyscraper built of Portland stone for the University of London to house the library, administrative offices and the School of Slavonic and East European Studies, and has become the dominant landmark in this varied quarter of London.

St George's in Bloomsbury Way is one of the comparatively few churches by Nicholas Hawksmoor that survive in London. Completed in 1731, its most remarkable feature is the steeple, surmounted by a statue of George I in Roman dress.

OPPOSITE St Pancras is the most pristine of London's Victorian main-line termini, possibly because it is the least used. W. H. Barlow designed the elegant train shed, opened in 1867.

FINSBURY

Although some light industry survives, Finsbury is primarily a hodgepodge of domestic and commercial buildings, with high-rise office blocks dominating its eastern extremities. Two factors have chiefly influenced its development: an abundant supply of fresh water and the proximity of the City.

Much of the area originally comprised Moorfields, a swampy, virtually uninhabited fen or moor immediately north of the City wall. This was drained in the sixteenth century and tree-lined paths were laid. Within easy reach of Cripplegate and Moorgate, these soon became fashionable promenades for Londoners.

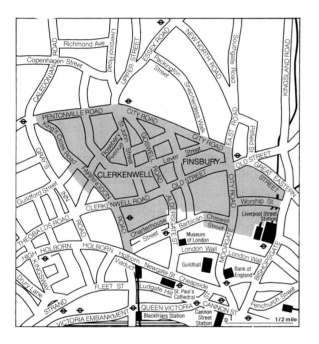

Running along the western edge of Finsbury, the Fleet river was, for long, a major supplier of London's fresh water, but by the Elizabethan period it had already become polluted and an alternative source was essential. To provide this, Sir Hugh Myddelton instigated the New River project, a man-made canal which conducted water from Hertfordshire. This was completed by 1613.

Following the Great Plague and the Great Fire, homeless Londoners camped on Moorfields in makeshift accommodation. Some remained and the urbanization of Finsbury began. Mineral water springs were discovered in various parts of Finsbury during the late seventeenth century and entrepreneurs converted them to health spas. (A fragment of the former Spa Fields remains east of Farringdon Road.) Soon, ancillary amusements grew up around them, Thomas Sadler's 'musick house' becoming one of the most successful; SADLER'S WELLS still survives as an entertainments venue, known in recent years for its opera and ballet companies.

Being outside the City, Nonconformists had greater freedom to express their views in Finsbury and by 1685 a burial ground was allocated to them at Bunhill Fields. John Wesley founded Methodism fifty years later, preaching to vast crowds in the open air. His chapel and house may be visited in City Road.

The parish church of St Luke was built at Old Street in 1733 but, due to instability, most of it was demolished in 1959. The distinctive steeple – in fact an obelisk – and walls have been preserved, looming starkly and somewhat eerily on the north side of the street.

A plentiful water supply led to the establishment of brewers and distillers in various parts of Finsbury. Samuel Whitbread moved to Chiswell Street in 1749 and, although ale is no longer brewed there, most of the

The Temple of the Muses in Finsbury Square was one of London's largest and most famous bookshops when run by James Lackington from 1778 to 1798. By the time this engraving was drawn by Thomas Shepherd in 1828, it was under new ownership.

original buildings survive, some adapted as banqueting suites.

The City Road, an extension to the 'New Road' from Marylebone, was taken through Finsbury in the mid-eighteenth century, heralding complete urbanization. Institutions and hospitals were built along the route and the Finsbury Estate was laid out towards the City, with Finsbury Square, a West End-style development, as its centrepiece. In the present century office blocks have replaced the Georgian houses and this part of Finsbury is virtually an extension of the City. The steepled Triton House on the north side was built between the wars for an insurance company, in typically grandiose fashion. To its south, Finsbury Circus is another former resident-ial development, of a pleasing oval shape, now given over to offices, including the imposing Lutyens House (1924–7).

CLERKENWELL

Overrun for more than a century by light industry and offices, once fashionable Clerkenwell retains exceptional vestiges of pre-Fire London.

Two important monasteries were established at Cler-kenwell early in the twelfth century – St John's Priory and St Mary's Nunnery. A village grew around them to accommodate their servants. In 1371 the Carthusian priory of the Charterhouse was added to the south. Members of the nobility acquired these monastic estates at the Reformation, adapting their domestic buildings to form private mansions.

Clerkenwell remained fashionable until the Great Plague of 1665 encouraged the aristocracy to migrate westward. Merchants took their place, soon to be augmented by Huguenot refugees from France, who were prevented from manufacturing in the City by the protectionism of the trade guilds. The seeds of Clerkenwell's light industrial future were sown at this time.

Nevertheless, Clerkenwell remained primarily domes-tic throughout the eighteenth century and fine Georgian houses were built in many of the ancient streets and squares. During the early years of Queen Victoria's reign what remained of Clerkenwell's open land had been replaced by poor-quality houses separated by mean alleys. Wealthier residents left and many of their homes were converted to light industrial units. Clerkenwell's degeneration to a slum was assured.

The former church of St Mary's Nunnery became Clerkenwell's parish church of St James, but it was completely rebuilt in 1791 and no trace of the ancient monastery remains. ST JOHN'S PRIORY has been more fortunate, its imposing gateway now housing the museum of the revived Order of St John. The twelfth-

century crypt of the priory's church also survives: the rest of the building, however, is modern.

The most spectacular reminder of Clerkenwell's past is THE CHARTERHOUSE. It is the only surviving London example of a monastic complex converted to a private mansion following the Dissolution. Sir Edward North acquired the former priory and, although he demolished its church to build his Great Hall, most of the domestic structures were preserved and may still be seen. In 1611 Thomas Sutton founded a home for male pensioners and a boy's school at the Charterhouse; pensioners remain but the school has been relocated at Godalming, Surrey.

The 1504 gateway of St John's Priory, heavily restored, now houses a museum of the Order of St John. The original priory was burnt down during the Peasant's Revolt in 1381.

CLERKENWELL GREEN, around which the original village was built, had lost its grass and trees by the end of the eighteenth century, but some Georgian houses remain and so does the imposing Palladian structure built in 1782 as the Middlesex Sessions House. Partly due to the poverty of its inhabitants and lack of City controls, Clerkenwell Green evolved in the nineteenth century as a rallying point for political agitators, including the Chartists and Home Rulers.

Clerkenwell may yet regain some of its former fashionability. Already there are encouraging signs of restoration and preservation, particularly around the historic core.

INNER LONDON

REGENT'S PARK

The (Prince) Regent's park, with its dazzling cream terraced houses masquerading as palaces, attracts the rich. That was precisely Nash's intention. Built between 1812 and 1828 on long leases, the properties were designed to bring increased revenues to the Crown as owner in the long as well as the short term.

As Nash himself put it:

'The attraction of open space, free air and the scenery of nature, with the means and invitation of exercise on horseback, on foot and in carriages, shall be preserved or created in Mary-le-Bone Park, as allurements or motives for the wealthy part of the public to establish themselves there.'

Although only eight of the fifty-six villas he envisaged were finally built, his policy proved successful. Mrs Wallis Simpson, for whose love Edward VIII forfeited his crown, lived in a house in Hanover Terrace. So did the author H. G. Wells and the composer Ralph Vaughan Williams. In the 1930s Barbara Hutton, the Woolworth heiress, built Winfield House, now the official residence of the American ambassador. In 1989 expensively restored villas in Prince Albert Road, with parking for up to six cars, were selling for well over £1 million, mainly to overseas investors. Perhaps it is fitting that Sussex Place, one of the original terraces, has been recast, complete with meringue-like domes, into the London Business School.

At the southern end of Albany Street stands the White House, a hotel with nearly six hundred bedrooms much

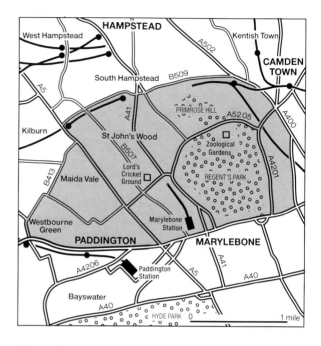

favoured today by the Japanese. In times gone by, as an apartment block with a gentlemen's club, its reputation was racier: but it was always for the wealthy. Except for pockets of further opulence such as PARK VILLAGE EAST AND WEST near Gloucester Gate, this aura of wealth is restricted to the fringe of the parkland itself. A different architecture, atmosphere and life style prevails in the hinterland. In Redhill Street, east of Albany Street, stands a handsome, sturdy, Crown residential develop-

OPPOSITE St John's Wood station dates from 1939. Pleasing and uncluttered, it reflects the superior tone of this always fashionable suburb. The round tower above the station, added more recently, is evidence of increasing property values.
LEFT London Zoo opened in Regent's Park in 1828 and this drawing of the monkey house by James Hakewill depicts it three years later. Today it is one of the largest zoos in the world and among the capital's most popular attractions.

ment of the 1930s, complete with the pediments, weather vanes and classical trimmings which set it aside from what is otherwise a local hodgepodge of public housing.

A fine modern building overlooks the park – the ROYAL COLLEGE OF PHYSICIANS, designed by Sir Denys Lasdun, later architect to the National Theatre. Near Gloucester Gate St Katharine's Church, designed by a pupil of Nash and now used by London's Danish community, stands out against the prevailing cream in startling grey Gothic.

At Hanover Gate another immigrant community worships in a great carpeted prayer hall, free of images and furnishings, under the burnished copper alloy dome of the CENTRAL LONDON MOSQUE. Opened in 1978, it was designed by Sir Frederick Gibberd, after an international competition. Its surprising location – few Moslems live in the immediate vicinity – is due to the land having been donated to the Moslem community by the Crown.

At the south-west corner of the park, the Abbey National Building Society's Art Deco building looms over the top end of Baker Street. Nearby St Cyprian at Clarence Gate, with a fine interior, faces the tight island site of Francis Holland, one of London's best-known independent day schools for girls. At LONDON ZOO in the north-east of the park, architectural highlights are Lord Snowdon's angular aviary; the chunky grey Elephant House by Sir Hugh Casson, a past President of the Royal Academy; the Sobell pavilions for apes and monkeys; the rugged Mappin Terraces and Lubetkin's delightful penguin pool.

PRIMROSE HILL

Primroses have long since vanished, but Primrose Hill escaped development in 1840 and its 216-foot summit today provides a splendid vantage point over the metropolis. Beyond the sloping urban meadow, with its regular mêlée of strollers, joggers and dog owners, lies the city with its distant landmarks – Westminster Cathedral, Big Ben, Euston, the Telecom and Barbican towers, St Paul's Cathedral, even Crystal Palace mast on clear days.

With this busy panorama and the local backcloth of pleasant Victorian terraces, villas and subdued modern flats, it is hard to imagine that the hill was still sufficiently far from polite drawing rooms in the early 1800s for elegant men of society to duel there. The dead and wounded were taken to the original Chalk Farm Tavern in Regent's Park Road. On the site of the old Chalk Farm, this public house was rebuilt in 1853; the adjoining pleasure gardens were built over in the 1860s.

With its pale pink, lemon and sage stucco fronts, trimmed with white like frosted cakes, CHALCOT SQUARE

Primrose Hill in 1895. One of London's smaller open spaces, it was once the haunt of wild animals and footpads, but has been open meadowland since it was cleared of forest in the sixteenth century.

is one of London's prettiest. The houses, now mainly five-storey, along with the curving terraces of Chalcot Crescent and the spacious villas in Regent's Park Road, attracted the professional middle classes. The less socially ambitious moved into the humbler eight-room terraces alongside.

Friedrich Engels, the socialist philosopher, lived for twenty-four years at 122 Regent's Park Road, dying in 1894 at a friend's house (no. 41). William Butler Yeats, born in 1865, spent part of his childhood at 23 Fitzroy Road, where the American poet Sylvia Plath later committed suicide.

After a period of decay, when many houses were sub-divided into bed-sitters, the central leafy location and spacious architecture once again attracted professional people, looking for property which they could afford and then do up. Developers followed, dividing small family homes into smart flats and maisonettes for young people and adding extra floors and terraces.

Yet the area still has social contrasts. Some of the terraces provide low-cost rented housing, and a large development of sheltered flats for the elderly borders the hill. Former railway buildings in Gloucester Avenue have been converted to studios, including those of a film cooperative. Behind many of the terraces lie working mews – Utopia Village, for example, off Chalcot Road, has a recording studio and architects' offices. PRIMROSE HILL STUDIOS, off Fitzroy Road, consists of a courtyard of modest brick artists' quarters with a gilded board listing notable residents such as Sir Henry Wood, the musician and conductor. The upper end of Regent's

Canals

Thistle, Merlin, Serendipity, Icarus with its rusty bike aboard ... all are narrow boats on REGENT'S CANAL, smartly trimmed in maroon and royal blue, tomato and jade. The traditional seven-foot-wide mobile homes still potter quietly along or, lashed to moorings, provide floating *pieds-à-l'eau* for adventurers with a taste for picturesque community living and few possessions.

Despite the magnetic watercolour attraction of Little Venice, and the Camden Lock honeypot with its restaurants, workshops and populous weekend market, the canal provides a curiously calm retreat for Londoners. It runs from the awesome monuments of Kensal Green Cemetery past fishermen squatting under wide green umbrellas, the parkland parade of the London Zoo, gardens of desirable crescents, railway backlands and factories, to Limehouse. Its $8\frac{1}{2}$-mile length is interrupted only by two black tunnels, 273 yards long at Little Venice and 957 yards at Islington. Like today's waterside walkers, the towing horses had here to abandon their barges for the London streets and leave the crew to leg the vessel through. Two men would lie on boards projecting from either side, propelling the barge forward through the pressure of their feet upon the damp brick wall.

Britain's first important canal had been the Bridgewater, built between 1759 and 1761 to carry coal from Worsley to Manchester and Liverpool. The construction of a grand network followed, linking major cities such as Wolverhampton, Birmingham, Oxford and Bristol. In 1801 the Grand Junction Canal reached London at Paddington Basin. It took another eleven years before the final phase, taking the canal east to the Thames, got underway. Once again John Nash played an important role, supporting its construction north of Regent's Park, becoming a major shareholder, and persuading his royal patron to lend his title to the enterprise.

The new waterway had its share of problems. Thomas Homer, the scheme's originator, was caught embezzling nearly £1500. Funds ran dry and a further Act of Parliament was required to raise extra money. The government made a substantial contribution on condition that jobs were created for the unemployed.

Completed in 1820, the new canal involved the construction of twelve locks, the two tunnels and the removal (with compensation) of Thomas Lord's cricket ground to its present site. Success was instant, but brief. The railways came all too soon and took much of the trade. Only twenty-five years after it was opened, the canal's directors were offered £1 million to convert the section between Paddington and City Road into a railway. The joy at such good fortune faded when the promoters failed to raise the cash. Luckily for today's enthusiasts, the canal continued to transport heavy goods such as coal, building materials and explosives, although the last were banned in 1874, after a barge carrying gunpowder exploded, killing crew members, wrecking the bridge to Regent's Park and frightening much of London.

London had other canals during their brief heyday. Some did not connect with the main system from the north but were comparatively short stretches designed to carry goods to land-bound parts of London from the Thames. The Grosvenor Canal, adapted from a former waterworks channel in 1823, attracted warehouses and industry to Pimlico until its basin was covered over to accommodate Victoria Station. The Grand Surrey Canal from Camberwell was not drained until 1971. The Kensington Canal flowed to the river from Kensal Green, where it linked with the Grand Junction: a

The City Basin at City Road, Islington, is the last major basin before the Regent's Canal reaches the Thames at Limehouse. This Shepherd drawing shows it a few years after the canal opened in 1820.

railway was built over it in 1845. Some were 'navigations', cut alongside existing rivers where they were hard to negiotiate, such as the Lea to the north-east and the Wandle to the south-west.

In 1929 the Regent's and Grand Junction Canals became part of the expanded Grand Union Canal, but by then their commercial decline was well under way. Today the surviving canals are run by the British Waterways Board, primarily as leisure amenities. Since the 1960s they have been adapted slowly (because of financial constraints) for the benefit of people who like to potter in boats or walk along the towpath. They provide an unusual perspective on formerly hidden parts of the city.

Park Road provides chic shopping and local rendezvous in the bookshops, patisserie, pubs and wine merchants. Defined by the hill and the railway, Primrose Hill is more self-contained than most areas of London.

ST JOHN'S WOOD

Across Primrose Hill lies St John's Wood, London's prime in-town suburb, its side roads dominated by Italianate and Gothic villas. On the main arteries, however, many have been replaced by sensible, secure, sometimes stylish blocks of apartments, providing a comfortable cosmopolitan environment to the corporate and diplomatic globe-trotter and the families of many Jewish refugees who fled from Central Europe in the 1930s. In the cities they had left, apartments were more familiar than houses, hence the appeal of these recently constructed blocks, close to Central London. They account for the presence of the Liberal Jewish Synagogue in St John's Wood Road, and in part for the cosmopolitan nature of the High Street with its delicatessens, cafés offering temptingly rich cakes, and boutique-style shops selling chocolates, jewellery and expensive fashions.

As the name suggests, the area was once wooded and belonged to the Knights of St John of Jerusalem. Although a road led north to Kilburn Priory from the fields of Lilestone (now corrupted to Lisson in Lisson Grove), the area remained part of the king's hunting ground until the reign of Charles I. Anthony Babington fled into the trees here after the betrayal of his conspiracy to kill Queen Elizabeth I.

By the early nineteenth century most of the land north of the new Regent's Canal was divided between the Eyre and the Harrow School estates, which realized that property would be more profitable than farming in view of Nash's plans for nearby Regent's Park. Eyre's layout was even more radical, abandoning terraced formality for individual houses, single and in pairs, set in the privacy of large walled gardens. Hired hackney carriages and the new exclusive omnibus meant there was little need for stabling or mews.

Professionals and affluent West End tradesmen were attracted to this homogeneous community, as were successful artists and the wealthier denizens of the demimonde. Sir Edwin Landseer, Royal Academician, the renowned Victorian painter of wild life and the man responsible for the lions in Trafalgar Square, had a studio in St John's Wood Road, while Tissot lived in Grove End Road.

The privacy had other attractions. Behind the high brick walls, rich men could come and go as they pleased, whereas in traditionally terraced streets visitors would be noticed. Tissot's mistress lived in Hill Road and Mrs Fitzherbert, the uncrowned wife of George IV, in Prince Albert Road. Prince Louis Napoleon moved in with Harriet Howard in Circus Road – yet crowned Eugénie as his empress. For fifteen years the classic English novelist George Eliot (born Marian Evans) lived with George Henry Lewes on the north bank of the canal in a house later demolished to make way for the railway.

Large houses in Carlton and Clifton Hills and Hamilton Terrace, even if often sub-divided today, retain an air of comfortable individuality and Avenue Road, with its miniature brick mansions, has long been one of London's millionaires' rows. St John's Wood Church, by Thomas Hardwick, faces a dragon-slaying St George at the roundabout near (Thomas) Lord's third cricket ground, headquarters of the national summer game. The

Mansion flats, like these in St John's Wood High Street photographed in 1908, attracted wealthier immigrants from Eastern Europe because they reflected the style of living in many European cities.

modern Mound Stand with its tent-like roof has inspired a rare compliment from one of contemporary British architecture's best-known critics, the Prince of Wales.

This stretch of Regent's Canal, looking east from Warwick Avenue, is today embanked on both sides and lined with houseboats. This photograph dates from before 1905, but some of the villas in Maida Avenue, on the right, are still standing.

MAIDA VALE

Below St John's Wood lies Maida Vale, named after the 1806 Battle of Maida, in southern Italy, where the British defeated the French. The road of that name, lined with solid flats, is an extension of Edgware Road running north from Marble Arch.

The Regent's Canal, opened in 1816, did much to form the character of the area. Unusually for the period, the canal was from early days here treated as a potential amenity with handsome white stucco villas built on the tree-lined roads, Maida Avenue and Blomfield Road, on either side of it. This forms the heart of tranquil LITTLE VENICE, where today traditional narrow canal boats are grouped into a picturesque community of permanent floating homes.

Development did not get properly underway until the 1840s, when the first homes went up on land which the Church had bought in 1185, when it was a farm. The avenues, crescents and gardens are lined with grand terraces, many with porches jutting out on Grecian columns to provide an air of order and confidence similar to that of Pimlico and South Kensington. Randolph and Warrington Crescents were built in 1875

enclosing, as in parts of Holland Park, large areas of communal green space accessible only by residents from their own small back gardens. Gradually stucco gave way to brick apartment blocks and terraces.

Separated from fashionable St John's Wood by the busy road to Kilburn, much of this area, except near the canal, remained for years unfashionable and unmodernized. Now it attracts its quota of the wealthy – bankers, solicitors, financiers – alongside actors, artists and fashion designers. For those with gardens or window boxes to tend, one of London's best-known garden centres and nurseries is at hand, near the canal.

Above Warwick Avenue underground station the spire of the new St Saviour's Church provides a modern focus. Another local spire, St Augustine's, soars even higher off Carlton Vale, over a huge church designed by John Loughborough Pearson in the 1870s. The same architect was later responsible for the handsome brick Gothic Catholic Apostolic Church in Maida Avenue, built for a nineteenth-century breakaway group which believed in the imminent second coming of the Lord. Despite disappointment, the sect soldiers on.

HAMPSTEAD

Hampstead and its neighbour Highgate stand on either side of a still verdant, wooded ridge overlooking the centre of London. The village cores are on or near the top of the two slopes, separated by nearly a thousand acres of heathland, playing fields, parkland, gardens and golf courses. They retain their distinct, essentially Georgian characters as well as their prosperous residents

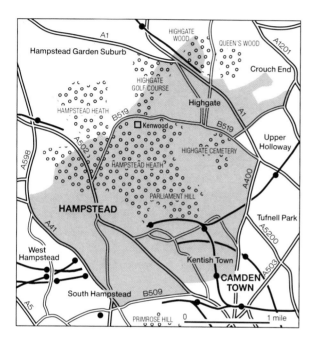

who for centuries have been attracted to the area by the 'sweet, saluterie air', noted by John Norden in 1593, and by the extensive views combined with proximity to the heart of town.

Geography and, over the past one hundred and fifty years, the unremitting use of their citizens' considerable influence and wealth, have spared them the poor sanitation, railways and institutional buildings which blighted the lower lying areas of Highgate New Town, Gospel Oak, Kentish Town and West Hampstead to their south and west. Belsize Park with its rows of stately white-stucco villas, brown-brick mews and the little shops of 'Belsize Village', built by Charles Palmer from 1853 on the site of a mansion house and early eighteenth-century pleasure gardens, also escaped lightly.

Hampstead was originally a Saxon 'homestead': a south-west-facing settlement in the forest of Middlesex around the site of the present mid-eighteenth-century parish church of St John. Even in the middle ages it had satellite settlements or 'ends', at points near its parish boundaries. These still survive as South End, West End (alias West Hampstead) and North End. Near South End and lining Parliament Hill is a hedge and double

ditch mentioned, in a charter dated 986, as separating the manors of Hampstead and St Pancras. North End is still cut off from Hampstead proper by Sandy Heath and retains its hamlet-like atmosphere, its pubs – including the Bull and Bush – and nearby the sixteenth-century farmhouse, Wyldes.

In the early eighteenth century Hampstead quite suddenly became a highly fashionable spa following the discovery of chalybeate springs, still commemorated by a fountain in Well Walk. As Daniel Defoe wrote in 1724, Hampstead 'grew up from a little village, to a magnitude equal to some cities'. A New End developed on what had hitherto been part of the Heath east of the High Street, while to the north building extended through the Heath, along what is now Hampstead Grove and Heath Street to the WHITESTONE POND, the highest point in north London. Many of Hampstead's most distinguished streets and buildings such as Church Row, Fenton House (Hampstead Grove), Burgh House (Newend Square – now the home of the Hampstead Museum), Squire's Mount and Cannon Place date from this period. The popularity of the Wells faded after 1730, as it became a haunt of pimps and prostitutes from London, but Hampstead remained a favoured suburban retreat, especially in the summer, for successful merchants, lawyers, actresses and writers, some of whose homes survive, such as Heath House, facing Whitestone Pond. Leading judges lived in Heath End and Mount Tyndal (since rebuilt), around the eighteenth-century SPANIARDS INN and its tollhouse, mentioned by Dickens in *Pickwick Papers*.

By the early nineteenth century Hampstead was widely regarded as cosmopolitan, healthy and fashionably picturesque, a reputation which attracted writers, poets, intellectuals and artists. Keats House, of 1815–16, was the poet's home during the happy and productive years 1818–20, while John Constable spent his last ten years at the Georgian 42 Well Walk. The 1930s marked Hampstead's artistic apogee, with Moore, Hepworth, Nicholson, Gabo, Kokoschka, Gertler, Mondrian and Gropius associated with the Mall Studios off Parkhill and Tasker Roads and with the influential Isokon Flats (1934) in Lawn Road.

In the nineteenth century Hampstead was linked to London. The development after 1816 of the elegant and little-changed Downshire Hill, with its chapel of St John's, connected South End to Hampstead Town, while in 1826 the construction of Finchley Road across

OPPOSITE The Vale of Health was given its name to celebrate the draining of a malarial swamp at the end of the eighteenth century. Since then it has attracted many notable residents, drawn by the proximity of Hampstead Heath.

Whitestone Pond is the highest point in north London and represents the northern limit of built-up Hampstead. Development crept up to here in the eighteenth century but did not encroach on the expanses of Hampstead Heath beyond.

the middle of the Manor Farm almost joined Hampstead to London's West End. SWISS COTTAGE, a public house in the chalet style, stood by the tollgate near St John's Wood.

Further development on the Manor Farm was stalled for over forty years as a side-effect of the epic struggle of Hampstead's leading citizens to prevent their absentee lord of the manor, Sir Thomas Maryon Wilson, from developing *any* of his lands. The settlement of 1871, which preserved the Heath proper, made possible the development first, in 1878, of Fitzjohn's Avenue, connecting Hampstead Town and Swiss Cottage and, soon afterwards, of West Hampstead, on the other side of Finchley Road. In 1888, the maze of picturesque old alleys separating Fitzjohn's Avenue from the High Street and Heath Street were swept away and replaced by the present red-brick buildings. After 1904 Hampstead Garden Suburb, representing a modernized version of the *rus in urbe* ideal, was created on farmland to the north of the Heath.

The remainder of the twentieth century has seen ever-increasing in-filling, traffic and commercialization. Yet, a few steps behind the boutiques and noise of Heath Street, the core of old Hampstead retains its tranquility.

HIGHGATE

Highgate takes its name from a gate next to the boundary hedge of the Bishop of London's hunting park. To this day the road narrows at the point, by the Gatehouse pub where, until 1876, a gate stood. Highgate owes its growth to the road from Holloway created in the late 1200s as a bypass for the marshy area of Crouch End through which traffic to and from the north had previously passed. The site of the chapel of the hermits who maintained the road until the Reformation is now occupied by the Victorian chapel of Highgate School, founded in 1564 opposite the gatehouse. The dewpond created as the hermits excavated gravel for the road survived until the 1860s and is now commemorated in Pond Square at the heart of the village.

The width and high pavements of the road to the north, now known as Highgate Hill, Highgate High Street, North Road and North Hill, testify to the countless sheep herded through the village over the centuries on their way to the Smithfield meat market. Other relics are the numerous yards off both sides of the High Street, such as Townsend's Yard or Duke's Head Yard, behind which the sheep could graze. Still another reminder of the importance of the road is the number of pubs in Highgate. Some, such as The Angel (High Street), can be traced back to the fifteenth century; some more recent examples such as The Flask (West Hill) and The Bull (North Hill) retain their eighteenth-century appearance.

Since at least the fifteenth century, City merchants and their modern equivalents have lived in Highgate, but in the sixteenth and seventeenth centuries they were joined by the nobility. Lauderdale House, the late sixteenth-century home of Charles II's minister, the Earl of Lauderdale, survives on Highgate Hill, though much altered, with its garden and grounds. Old Hall, of 1691, in South Grove, incorporates part of the country mansion of the early seventeenth-century patron of the arts, the Earl of Arundel. Across the road, the back gardens of 1–6 The Grove, a speculation of 1688, contain remnants of the mansion of the seventeenth-century inventor, the Marquess of Dorchester.

Later in the seventeenth century Highgate, five miles

from London and just beyond the reach of the penal laws, became particularly popular with Quaker friends of William Penn and with Jews. The still splendid CROMWELL HOUSE of 1638, facing Lauderdale House on Highgate Hill, in 1675 became the first house in England to be owned by Jews since their expulsion in 1294. Another house occupied by the same Jewish family, the Mendes da Costas, was the early eighteenth-century Moreton House in South Grove.

A century later this became the home of Samuel Taylor Coleridge before he moved with the Gillman family, who were trying to rid him of his laudanum addiction, to 3 The Grove. Coleridge's legacy is still present in the village through the Highgate Literary and Scientific Institution on Pond Square, founded by several of his friends shortly after his death. It thrives over one hundred and fifty years later as the centre for village history, learning, literature and gossip.

After 1813 an attempt was made to bypass the steep gradient of Highgate Hill with a road and tunnel. When the tunnel, under the spur of land leading to Hornsey, collapsed, it was replaced by a grandiose viaduct or Archway designed by Nash to carry Hornsey Lane above it and give room for the new road below – the first flyover in London. Although the original archway was replaced by a bridge, a little to its north, in 1897–8, the old name has stuck.

Despite ribbon development, and expansion towards Hampstead, Highgate has managed to maintain green buffers against London on almost all its sides. The preservation of PARLIAMENT HILL, KENWOOD (see *Great houses and palaces*) and Fitzroy Farm to the south-west was due to the desire of successive eighteenth- and nineteenth-century earls of Mansfield in Kenwood to have green vistas from their windows. Beyond HIGHGATE CEMETERY (see *Cemeteries*), another open space to the south, lies WATERLOW PARK, presented to Londoners with Lauderdale House in 1889 as 'a garden for the gardenless' by the printer and former lord mayor of London, Sir Sydney Waterlow (see *Parks and gardens*). Behind the yards off the High Street to the east are further precious acres of open space and to the north the Highgate Woods still separate Highgate from Muswell Hill and Crouch End. Westwards again, the Highgate Golf Course, which includes the still recognizable site of the medieval Bishop of London's hunting lodge, separates Highgate from Hampstead.

Highgate has its share of modern buildings; particularly of note are Berthold Lubetkin's revolutionary Highpoint flats I and II built in 1936 and 1938 respectively on North Hill. Traffic thunders along the High Street at all times. But on the whole it has avoided the commercialization that has overtaken Hampstead and retained more of its old families. And on the Green between The Flask and The Grove, in Pevsner's words, 'a more vivid impression of the wealthy London village of the eighteenth century can be gained than anywhere else'.

Nash built the Archway in 1813 to take Hornsey Lane across the new line of the Great North Road near Highgate. In 1897, two years after this photograph was taken, the arch, carrying the road on three shallow spans above it, was pulled down because the gap was too narrow for the growing traffic. It was replaced by today's iron viaduct.

Cemeteries

Burial of London's dead before 1832 was in churches, or in churchyards. In times of pestilence emergency burial-grounds were acquired and, from the eighteenth century, parish burial-grounds were not necessarily beside the churches: sometimes they were patches of ground to be used when church crypts and yards became filled. An example of an 'overspill' ground is that of St Giles-in-the-Fields adjacent to St Pancras Old Churchyard, about a mile from St Giles's church: it contains the extraordinary mausoleum of John Soane.

Small burial-grounds for Dissenters were provided from the seventeenth century, of which the most distinguished is BUNHILL FIELDS by City Road, established on land previously used as a dump for bones from the charnel-houses of St Paul's Cathedral. Bunhill Fields was designated a common cemetery in the Plague Year of 1665 and became a burial-ground for Dissenters afterwards; by 1852 some 120,000 bodies had been interred in the five acres of the cemetery and the ground was closed. It was acquired by the City of London, which restored it for use and contemplation; it contains a remarkable array of tombstones commemorating distinguished Nonconformists.

The overcrowded state of church vaults and church-yards was a scandal for many years, but not until the last century were major reforms enacted by Parliament after a series of cholera epidemics had exacerbated an already appalling state of affairs. As a result of the burial crisis of 1831–2 several joint-stock companies were authorized to establish cemeteries outside the built-up areas of London; these were to be large, well-drained, enclosed, properly managed, with landscaped grounds, and full records were to be kept by law.

The first of these new cemeteries, inspired by the example of Père-Lachaise in Paris, was the GENERAL CEMETERY OF ALL SOULS, KENSAL GREEN, and part of the ground was consecrated in 1833. It contains distinguished Greek Revival chapels and entrance by John Griffith of Finsbury and a remarkable range of tombs, monuments and mausolea set in a landscaped park designed by the Hon. Thomas Liddell. The cemetery acquired fashionable status when Princess Sophia and the Duke of Sussex (children of King George III) were buried in front of the Anglican chapel. The princess is commemorated by a beautiful sarcophagus designed by Ludwig Grüner, artistic adviser to Prince Albert. Many extraordinary monuments add interest to this cemetery.

Once as magnificent as Kensal Green, the SOUTH

All Souls at Kensal Green was the first of the new cemeteries established outside the built-up area in the 1830s. The generous space allowed for elaborate landscaping and ambitious monumental architecture.

METROPOLITAN CEMETERY at Norwood (designed by William Tite and opened in 1837) was also laid out as an English landscaped park in which monuments were to be set. The Gothic chapels have both been demolished, but the Greek Revival chapel by John Oldrid Scott in the part reserved for the Greek community deserves

ABNEY PARK CEMETERY, Stoke Newington (1840) was unusual in that no part of it was consecrated, so it was favoured by Nonconformists. The architect of the thin chapel was William Hosking, but the glories of the cemetery are the Egyptian gates and lodges by Joseph Bonomi Junior, and the planting by Loddiges. Abney

ABOVE The South Metropolitan Cemetery at Norwood, today overcrowded and surrounded by terraced housing, was right on the edge of the countryside when it was built in 1837. The Gothic chapels at the top of the picture have both been demolished.

LEFT Overgrown Egyptian-style catacombs lend a sinister air to the old section of Highgate Cemetery.

mention, as do the mausolea of John Ralli by G. E. Street (1863) and of Eustratio Ralli by Edward Barry (1875).

The London Cemetery Company established two cemeteries: St James's at Highgate (1839) and All Saints at Nunhead (1840). The older part of the ground at HIGHGATE was laid out with serpentine paths on a hill and planted in a luxuriant manner by David Ramsay. Stephen Geary, first architect to the Company, designed a circle of catacombs in the Egyptian taste around an existing Cedar of Lebanon, while J. B. Bunning, who succeeded Geary, added the Egyptian Avenue, with its sinister entrance and other structures. Although most of the individual tombs and mausolea are not so interesting or distinguished as those of Kensal Green and Norwood, Highgate has its fair share of famous dead, but its marvellous planting and extraordinary atmosphere make it the most magical of all London's cemeteries. Its most famous inhabitant, Karl Marx, is in the newer, less evocative section. NUNHEAD CEMETERY, Linden Grove, was laid out to plans by Bunning, who also designed the handsome entrance gate and lodges. The Gothic chapels were by Thomas Little of 1844, but one has been demolished and the other has been damaged by vandals.

Park was an arboretum as well as a cemetery and each shrub and tree was labelled for educational purposes.

BROMPTON CEMETERY, designed by Stephen Geary and Benjamin Baud, was opened in 1840. Baud's design included the classical entrance, formal avenues with arcaded galleries over catacombs and the octagonal Anglican chapel. The enormous amount of expensive structure was far too ambitious and the company quickly got into financial difficulties. It was the only private enterprise London cemetery to be nationalized in the 1850s, when opinion turned against the idea of commercial speculation in the burial of the dead.

Later public cemeteries are on the whole less interesting. An exception is the huge CITY OF LONDON CEMETERY at Little Ilford, opened in 1856 and designed by William Haywood: it has rich and varied planting, chapels in the Flamboyant Gothic style and numerous tombs of quality. A Jewish cemetery, operating from 1761 to 1858, is still visible in Brady Street, Whitechapel. A much larger one, opened in Willesden in 1873, still functions. Cremation became popular in the late nineteenth century: GOLDERS GREEN CREMATORIUM is London's largest and most distinguished architecturally.

CAMDEN TOWN

Camden Town's population and physical environment seem in constant flux. With three of London's main line railway stations ranged along Euston Road to the south, it has traditionally attracted new arrivals as they trudged the streets looking for temporary cheap accommodation and opportunities to make a living, if not quite fortune and fame.

Immigrants from Ireland built a strong community here in the early twentieth century. In the 1950s it was the turn of Greek Cypriots, creating a nucleus of families which again drew subsequent newcomers to the area. Today their presence is evinced in the Greek Orthodox use of a classical Victorian church in Camden Street, the nearby Theatro Technis and a profusion of restaurants. Meanwhile Asians have taken over most of the shops and restaurants in Drummond Street, near Euston station. A fourth community now is that of the young, drawn to London to work, who move into small flats and houses they can just afford as a staging-post on the way to a more settled life elsewhere.

Originally part of the area was a manor or prebend of St Paul's Cathedral, another the property of Charles Pratt, Lord Chancellor, later Viscount Bayham and Earl Camden. In 1790 the two agreed to joint development. The construction of the Regent's Canal thirty years later encouraged industrial as well as domestic building.

Weekend visitors to CAMDEN LOCK market encounter a street scene often reminiscent of the London of Charles Dickens, who spent part of his boyhood in nearby Bayham Street. Bleary-eyed, unshaven men from the local hostel for the homeless slouch on the pavement clutching beer bottles and cans. Zealous young crusaders sell tracts, a street musician performs for small change and some men and women simply beg. Yet a short walk through the market in Inverness Street leads to the handsome Victorian enclave of Gloucester Crescent and Regent's Park Terrace, home in recent years to theatre director Jonathan Miller, and the philosopher Alfred (A.J.) Ayer. Camden Town has always had its quota of intellectuals and artists. The poet Dylan Thomas once lived in Delancey Street and George Orwell in Lawford Road in Kentish Town. The remaining section of Mornington Crescent, now confronted with the massive rear of the 1930s' Greater London House, was known in 1911 for its association with Walter Sickert and the Camden Town group of artists.

The studios of TV-am, the breakfast television company, are in a garage converted with panache by Terry Farrell, the architect of massive post-modernist office developments such as that at Charing Cross. His former partner, Nicholas Grimshaw, who glories in elegant technology, was responsible for the industrial

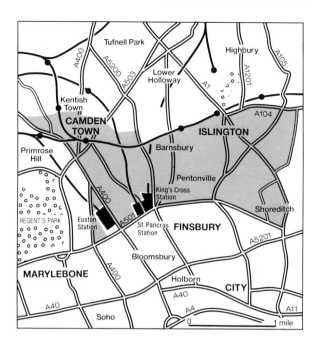

superstore round the corner in Camden Road. Other signs of change include tentative plans to reopen the Round House, a former locomotive shed and more recently a theatre. The old music hall, the Camden Palace, is now a musical nightspot for young Londoners. A large area behind Euston and King's Cross is to be redeveloped, and new premises for the British Library are being built next to St Pancras Station in an area long known as Somers Town.

ISLINGTON

Georgian brick terraces and their Victorian stucco neighbours stretch tastefully in every direction, urbane and elegant but ultimately quite monotonous: this is what the later Victorians were reacting against with the more flamboyant terraces they built in other parts of north London. But from the 1950s onwards Georgian style was once more the rage and Islington became one of the first inner-city areas north of Marylebone Road to attract young, middle-class couples seeking an alternative to the sedate suburbs where many of them had been brought up.

Islington was for years a rural village where Londoners went for fresh air, exercise, archery, custard creams and syllabubs. It contained good pasture land and its farms were noted for dairy produce. Until the eighteenth century the road north of the ANGEL, the first overnight stop for travellers out of London, was renowned for footpads and highwaymen – including Dick Turpin, reputed to have used the forge at Newington Green. CANONBURY MANOR belonged to the de Berners family (hence the name of Barnsbury) and

LEFT Canonbury House was one of Islington's most ancient buildings, dating from before the sixteenth century, and housed many distinguished and noble residents. Today only the tower remains, part of it used by a theatre company.

BELOW The Angel Hotel had been a coaching inn since the seventeenth century and gave its name to this busy road junction in south Islington. The building it occupied in this 1895 photograph has now been put to other commercial use.

later to the canons of St Bartholomew, who built the first tower there. It passed through several noble hands and in the eighteenth century became an apartment house. Oliver Goldsmith, Washington Irving and Ephraim Chambers (of the encyclopaedia), were all residents. Today only the sixteenth-century tower remains and is used by a theatre company – one of several based in Islington, reinforcing its intellectual and arty reputation.

The Angel is still a focus of activity, particularly since the conversion of the derelict Royal Agricultural Hall into the Business Design Centre. Just north of it, CHAPEL MARKET, with its good-value fresh produce, provides evidence of Islington's broad population mix. Prosperous inhabitants of the Georgian terraces queue at the stalls alongside the tenants of the council estates, who include immigrants from Ireland, the Caribbean and Asia, as well as long-established working-class Londoners. North again, Upper Street has developed into a centre for antiques and bric-à-brac, spreading out from narrow CAMDEN PASSAGE, along with fashionable restaurants and wine shops.

The area began to be built up in the late eighteenth century, when London sought room for expansion. Just off Upper Street, Duncan Terrace is a fairly complete row of well-preserved houses from that period. The largest concentration of Georgian terraces and squares, in BARNSBURY and CANONBURY, was built after 1800, when the Regent's Canal was dug through Islington. Canonbury Square was one of the earliest developments. In the 1820s Thomas Cubitt was among those who saw the potential of then rural Barnsbury, to the north of

Islington. The imposing Cloudesley Square and Gibson Square were created then and Cubitt himself was responsible for terraces in Liverpool Road and College Cross. The Venetian-style Milner Square dates from 1841. Good Victorian developments included Alwyne Road and Place, Lonsdale and Thornhill Squares.

The area declined at the end of the nineteenth century, blighted by industrial buildings and slum housing. It seemed that the likeliest fate of most of the old houses was demolition for redevelopment, but in 1963 there was a fierce dispute over the future of the Victorian Packington estate, which Islington Council wanted to destroy. Although most of the estate itself was lost, the dispute established a climate of opinion that ensured the preservation of much of the borough's, and indeed London's, Georgian and Victorian fabric.

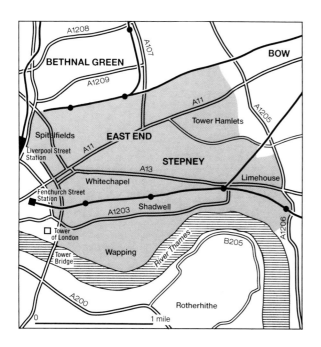

THE EAST END

The Jami Masjid mosque on the corner of Brick Lane and Fournier Street is a powerful symbol of the constant changes in the character of the East End – yet paradoxically it is also a symbol of continuity. In the early years of this century it served as a synagogue – but it was built in 1743 as a church for still earlier immigrants, the Protestant Huguenots who, fugitives from persecution in France, had established a silk-weaving industry here in Spitalfields. The well-proportioned Georgian building is too hemmed in by shops and houses for its grandeur to be appreciated. On both sides of Fournier Street the Huguenots' houses survive, with their plain Queen Anne façades and doorcases that vary from the simple to the grand. Their most distinctive features are the wide-windowed attics, originally used as weaving lofts. At the western end of the street is Hawksmoor's powerful Christ Church, consecrated in 1729, one of several new churches built then to counteract the tide of Nonconformity.

Whitechapel, Spitalfields and Stepney, on the eastern edge of the old City, have traditionally provided a temporary haven for communities in passage in low-cost and often run-down accommodation. Bengali Moslems are the dominant immigrant group today: hence the mosque and the busy Asian shops nearby. A modern mosque, painted gold, with domes and minarets, has been erected on the south side of Whitechapel Road.

STEPNEY

The ancient parish of Stepney extended from Aldgate to Bow and from Hackney to the River Thames. It contained several hamlets set among orchards and market-gardens, but by the middle of the last century had become part of the amorphous, built-up East End. Stepney had a close connection with shipping, and seafaring associations survive, among them the almshouses on Mile End Road erected by Trinity House for 'decayed masters and the widows of such' (see *The poor and homeless*).

Roughly in the centre of the old parish is St Dunstan's church and its enormous burial-ground. Near it are some fine houses in Stepney Green, the late Georgian estate of the Mercers' Company and some late Victorian tenement blocks built to alleviate housing problems among the Jewish community. Today, the population of Stepney is a fraction of what it was and the surviving residential quarters are interspersed with unkempt open spaces.

WHITECHAPEL

Strategically sited to the east of Aldgate, Whitechapel was named after the whitewashed Chapel of Ease that became a parish church in 1320. Other churches were erected later. The seventeenth-century historian John Strype described Whitechapel as a 'spacious fair street, for entrance into the City eastward, and somewhat long … it is a great thoroughfare, being the Essex road, and well resorted unto, which occasions it to be the better inhabited, and accommodated with good inns for the reception of travellers'. It was one of the most important entry-points to the City, and produce from the farms and gardens of Essex passed through it, as well as goods unloaded from ships. It constantly teemed with horse-drawn traffic, creating a maelstrom that is duplicated nowadays on Sundays, when people pour into Petticoat Lane and the adjacent street markets.

In central Whitechapel are the London Hospital founded in 1740 in Whitehapel Road and the Art Gallery of 1901 built in the Art Nouveau style to a design by C. H. Townsend. The gallery concentrates on the collection and exhibition of modern art. There is also the Bell Foundry, an interesting Georgian survival, in which many celebrated bells were cast, including Big Ben and the Liberty Bell. Towards the west end of Whitechapel Road is Bloom's, London's most famous Jewish restaurant, surviving from the time when the Jews dominated the area.

OPPOSITE This fine Georgian building on Fournier Street bears testimony to the successive waves of immigrants drawn to Spitalfields. Built in 1743 as a Protestant church for Huguenots, it became a synagogue and then the Jami Masjid mosque, serving the Bengali community. The attic windows of the adjacent houses were specially designed to give as much light as possible to the weavers who worked there.

SPITALFIELDS

Petticoat Lane, as Middlesex Street was called, was where old clothes, wigs, shoes and other cast-offs were sold. This is in Spitalfields, to the east of Liverpool Street Station and north of Whitechapel: it got its name from the priory of St Mary Spital, the site of which became a teasel-ground cultivated by clothworkers and was later used for archery and gunnery practice (hence Artillery Lane). Spitalfields began to be developed in the seventeenth century, when weavers first settled in the district. The old Archery Ground was laid out for housing and, being just outside the City, Spitalfields became a refuge for Dissenters, and especially for French Protestants, the Huguenots, after 1685.

By 1750 it was densely populated, but dependence on the silk trade created problems. The tone of the area degenerated as the industry declined and by the mid-Victorian period it was unsavoury in the extreme. Attention was focused on the dreadful conditions of Spitalfields and Whitechapel in 1888 during the 'Jack the Ripper' murders and pressure grew to force the State to intervene in slum clearance and improvements in housing.

WAPPING

South of Whitechapel lies Wapping, more intimately connected to the river. The hamlet was noted for boat-building and ancillary activities, and for its many taverns, some of which survive.

At its heart were the London Docks, built between 1800 and 1820; attractive terraces of housing for employees survive at the entrance to Wapping Basin. Today Wapping has acquired a vast new complex of buildings associated with the newspaper industry which moved east from Fleet Street: an increase in noise and traffic, together with a demand for types of eating and drinking establishments foreign to the East End, have attracted some criticism. Many old workhouses have been converted into stylish riverside apartments for these and City workers.

Ancient wooden houses still stood in the East End at the turn of the century. The poverty in Peter's Lane, Spitalfields (above) is shown by the signs advertising rag and bone merchants. In Mile End Road (left) one of the East End's many furniture manufacturers occupies the house on the far right.

Through the centre of Wapping runs Cable Street, linking Royal Mint Street with Limehouse. Mosley's Fascists attempted to march there in the 1930s – partly because of the immigrant population – but were vociferously resisted. Old Cable Street's character has been largely destroyed by post-war redevelopment. The Ratcliffe Highway, joining East Smithfield, Shadwell and Limehouse on a line south of Cable Street, was made famous by the early nineteenth-century Williams murders celebrated by De Quincey in his *On Murder Considered as one of the Fine Arts* (1827). Where the Highway joins Cannon Street Road stands the extraordinary shell of Hawksmoor's St George-in-the-East, damaged in the Second World War, but partly in use.

Further east, by the river, is Narrow Street, Limehouse, where a handsome range of eighteenth-century houses survives, backing on to the north bank of the Thames and including the Grapes public house, with its rear gallery from which drinkers hear the sound of the water slapping against the timbers beneath. Limehouse was another hamlet with pronounced nautical associations: shipwrights, merchants and seafaring men built houses for themselves in that once-salubrious spot. Some Georgian houses still stand in Newell Street, backing on to the churchyard of St Anne, Hawksmoor's third great East End church. Of the thriving Chinese community in Limehouse at the turn of the century virtually nothing survives.

— SOUTHWARK, LAMBETH, VAUXHALL —

The southern bank of the Thames between London and Vauxhall bridges was among the most intensively developed parts of London during the nineteenth century, a dense, grimy amalgam of riverside warehousing and industry, of railway viaducts overshadowing lawless, overcrowded courts and alleys. The railways remain, but the population has shrunk after a century of slum clearance and the commerce dependent on the river has disappeared. Yet behind the river banks, now largely tidied up for tourists and office workers, still lies what is essentially workaday Victorian south London, its street markets and minor industry mixed with vestiges of a still older past.

Southwark is the oldest urban centre on the south bank. The Roman settlement along the road to London Bridge became a medieval borough jealously independent of the City of London. Although much rebuilt, parts of BOROUGH HIGH STREET still retain a recognizably medieval form, with alleys running between narrow house plots. SOUTHWARK CATHEDRAL, shaved closely by the raised nineteenth-century bridge approach, began as the early twelfth-century priory church of St Mary Overie ('over the water'). The heavily restored and

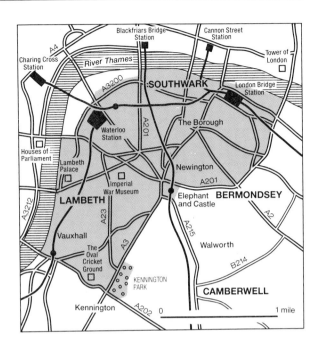

rebuilt exterior is deceptive; the eastern parts are genuine early Gothic work, with a light and spacious retrochoir behind the high altar.

Close to St Mary Overie was the Bishop of Winchester's great riverside palace. Alongside the narrow 'Clink' (named from the Bishop's private prison), the remains of the fourteenth-century great hall are dramatically exposed to view. The west wall, with its inventive rose window, stands to gable height, preserved through the palace's chequered later history as tenements and a warehouse.

Upstream, beyond the swamps undrained until the sixteenth century, the Archbishop of Canterbury built his palace at the little riverside village of Lambeth, a convenient ferry-journey from Westminster. The powerful early Tudor brick gatehouse still guards a conglomeration ranging from thirteenth-century chapel to grand nineteenth-century apartments. Lambeth village itself disappeared beneath later industry; this too has vanished, leaving the High Street as a sad, deserted back lane, sandwiched between the nineteenth-century river embankment and the railway. Lambeth parish church remains as a riverside landmark, with its late medieval stone tower of characteristic Thames Valley type. Deprived of its congregation, it is now a museum of garden history, named after the seventeenth-century royal gardeners John Tradescant and his son, who are buried in the churchyard.

In the countryside were two other medieval centres. The Duchy of Cornwall's present land holdings at Kennington go back to a manor house of the Black Prince. A short ride east was the rich Cluniac abbey of

ABOVE St George's Circus, where the obelisk stands, was the junction of the roads from the new Blackfriars and Westminster bridges at the end of the eighteenth century. The grand building was an 'equestrian and philharmonic academy' erected in 1782, burned down in 1803 and replaced by the Surrey Theatre.

LEFT Waterloo developed as a working-class residential area after the opening of Waterloo Bridge in 1817 and the rail terminus 31 years later. The Cut (originally New Cut) links Waterloo and Blackfriars roads and in 1896, when this picture was taken, was the venue for a busy weekend market.

Bermondsey. At the abbey gates stood the parish church in Bermondsey Street; a few older houses are reminders of the village that once straggled toward Southwark and the Thames.

From the middle ages onwards Southwark attracted all the socially undesirable activities unwelcome in the City: medieval brothels, tanning and soap making, Elizabethan and Jacobean bear and bull rings and the short-lived early theatres of Shakespeare's time along Bankside. They are recalled only by a few street names, as are King's Bench, the Marshalsea and other notorious Southwark prisons.

Philanthropic establishments were less ephemeral: in 1721–4, Thomas GUY'S HOSPITAL was laid out on a generous courtyard plan, and intended 'for that stage of languor and disease to which the charities of others had not reached', as is recorded on Bacon's fine monument to the founder in the hospital chapel. The chief 'other charity' was ST THOMAS'S HOSPITAL, across the road from Guy's until demolished for the railway and moved to a fine array of nineteenth-century buildings in Lambeth. In Southwark a herb garret and a chillingly primitive

early operating theatre (restored as a museum) remain squeezed into the unlikely setting of the attic above the former church in St Thomas Street (see *Medicine: its teaching and practice*).

The framework of modern Southwark and Lambeth was established in the later eighteenth century after the south bank was opened up by new bridges over the Thames. Roads from Westminster and Blackfriars converged at ST GEORGE'S CIRCUS, laid out on the stripfields of the parish common land and dignified by an obelisk in 1771 (since moved to the nearby park). Additional routes followed from Waterloo and Southwark bridges.

Building was slow at first. In 1811 there was still space at St George's fields for the Bethlehem Hospital for the insane, moved from Moorfields (it survives, altered and truncated, as the IMPERIAL WAR MUSEUM). But by 1822 Cobbett complained of two miles of new stockjobbers'

OPPOSITE From the river Southwark Cathedral bears some resemblance to the medieval original, although the exterior and interior have been altered many times, most recently in the nineteenth century.

houses on the way from St George's fields to Croydon. Some of this development was classier than he suggests. Kennington became a superior area: stretches of elegant late eighteenth-century terraces still line the main roads, their respectability sealed in the 1820s by the stately neo-classical church of St Mark at the junction with the new route from Vauxhall Bridge.

Building away from the roads was more expensive. South London has few squares or circuses completed as intended – the OVAL cricket ground at Kennington originated as an unexecuted residential development. An exception is the charmingly secluded Trinity Square of 1823–4, east of Borough High Street.

Meanwhile industry grew with the Port of London and overwhelmed the inner areas. A dour wall of brick warehouses stretched downstream from Vauxhall to the Surrey Docks. Breached by County Hall, then by the post-war South Bank development, the rest stood largely disused from the 1950s. Most disappeared in the building boom of the 1980s. Paradoxically the older riverside buildings have been preserved: the ANCHOR pub on Bankside, and a few eighteenth-century houses directly opposite St Paul's Cathedral. Elsewhere monuments to Victorian commercial pride remain. At Lambeth a small building from the once vast Doulton's potteries, a colourful advertisement for the factory's glazed tiles, peeps out from behind the dull twentieth-century streetscape of the Albert Embankment. Southwark Street, a showpiece cut through the slums in the 1860s, has the former Hop Exchange of 1866 – Southwark was the centre of the hop trade – now offices with a suitably decorated grand entrance. The equivalents in Bermondsey are the Leather Market and Exchange in Weston Street.

The dens of Southwark were prime targets for reformers. Gentrification has not yet emasculated the back streets; shabby fragments of Georgian terraces and Victorian warehouses rub shoulders with prototypes for better working-class housing. They range from tenements such as the early Peabody estate of 1870 in Blackfriars Road to small cottages built under the influence of Octavia Hill (Red Cross Street and Copperfield Street). Later came the attractive Edwardian neo-Regency housing on the Duchy of Cornwall estates at Kennington, still a model of its kind. There were new churches too, but few remain. The best is St Peter, Vauxhall, a noble vaulted building of 1860–4 by J. L. Pearson, complete with vicarage, schools and orphanage to serve the surrounding slums on the site of the old Vauxhall gardens (see *The pleasure gardens*).

The larger improvements of the twentieth century have less character; Vauxhall is filled with anonymous council flats built between the wars and its riverside has been ruined by road widening. The most ambitious clearance took place after 1945 at the ELEPHANT AND CASTLE. This notorious bottleneck owed its name to the public house which stood since the eighteenth century at the meeting of the main roads from Kent and the south coast. Early plans proposed a clean sweep, with a multi-level road junction. Instead, the austere concrete offices by the progressive Hungarian architect Erno Goldfinger look across a double roundabout to an older landmark, the monumental portico of the METROPOLITAN TABERNACLE built in 1859 for the famous Victorian preacher C. H. Spurgeon. It is typical of the muddled compromise of British planning, which has nevertheless been responsible for retaining so much of the diversity of inner London.

The roads to the City from the south, the south-east and the south-west converge at the Elephant and Castle, once a busy coaching inn and today an even busier traffic maelstrom.

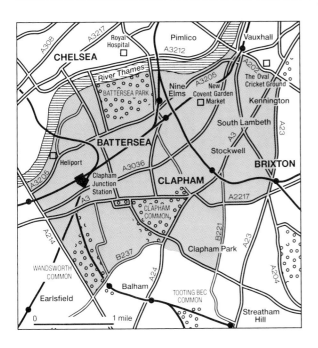

STOCKWELL

The extensive late nineteenth-century development of the Surrey side of the Thames blurred the physical distinctions between the settlements of Stockwell, Clapham and Battersea, as streets of Victorian terraces filled the gaps between the old villages. Today, each retains only vestiges of its former distinctive character. Their Victorian terraces have, since the 1960s, proved popular with young professionals forced south of the river by the high property prices in Kensington and Chelsea. Estate agents and restaurants occupy many of the old small shops forced out of business by the growth of supermarkets and modern shopping centres.

The old isolated hamlet at Stockwell Green, recorded on Rocque's mid-eighteenth-century map, is now un-recognizable. It lost its village atmosphere earlier than its two neighbours, when the first deep underground railway, from the City, had its southern terminus here in 1890. It therefore came to be seen as the outer edge of inner London, and its former individuality was submerged. Today it is a nineteenth- and twentieth-century patchwork of contrasts. West of Clapham Road, middle-class Victorian stucco-trimmed terraces (Albert Square and Lansdowne Gardens are especially complete) rub shoulders with GLC 1960s' brutalism in Lansdowne Way and with the quieter 1980s' cottages of Larkhall Lane. To the east, Stockwell Park, an oasis of small 1840s' villas and terraces around St Michael's church, ends abruptly in the courtyards of Lambeth's forbiddingly dense estate of the 1970s.

Residents of its Victorian houses include several Members of Parliament: although it is marginally less handy for Westminster than Kennington to its north, it has more houses suitable for family living. There are generally two or three MPs living in Fentiman Road, alongside Vauxhall Park, between Clapham Road and South Lambeth Road.

The West Indian immigrants, attracted to neighbouring BRIXTON by low property prices in the 1960s, did not stray far into Stockwell, where prices were higher because of the convenience of the Underground. (The Victoria Line did not reach Brixton until 1971.) The extensive Brixton market is an amenity for the whole area. At the Brixton end of Stockwell Road, the old Astoria cinema (1929) has one of London's most atmospheric interiors: renamed the Academy, it is today used for rock concerts. Another major twentieth-century building is the astonishingly monumental Stockwell Bus Garage (completed 1954) in Lansdowne Way, with its vast concrete shell roof.

CLAPHAM

Clapham's dominant feature is the Common, the largest open space of its kind within the inner suburbs of south London (see *Heaths and commons*). The old village lay a little to the north at OLD TOWN, now spoilt by busy traffic although still with some good eighteenth-century houses. The old parish church of St Paul, rebuilt in the nineteenth century, stands in its churchyard away from the road, on the very edge of the ridge overlooking Battersea. Its memorials bear witness to Clapham's early popularity as a respectable place of residence. William Hewer, Samuel Pepys's clerk, is commemorated here; Pepys died at his house on the north side of the Common.

Along NORTH SIDE there is still a handsome red-brick terrace of the urban type fashionable in London villages in the early eighteenth century, and The Elms, a well-proportioned, detached house built in 1754 on the site of Hewer's larger mansion. By 1800 there were large detached houses all around the Common, country retreats for wealthy City men such as the banker Henry Thornton. Like other richer Clapham residents he also had a town house, but enjoyed his ride to work from his family home on Battersea Rise. The Thorntons were leading members of the Clapham sect, the evangelical campaigners who numbered other Clapham residents such as William Wilberforce and Zachary Macaulay among their members, and whose activities centred on the new church of HOLY TRINITY, built on the edge of the Common in 1774. Its formal galleried interior still conveys the earnestness of that era.

The large houses and their gardens around the Common gave way to more urban developments as Clapham became a suburb. Around the Common an

OPPOSITE Characteristic Victorian terraces stretch from Clapham to Battersea, with modern council flats beyond. Battersea Power Station, with its four assertive white chimneys, was completed in 1935, decommissioned in 1974 and is being developed as an indoor amusement park.

LEFT Holy Trinity Church on Clapham Common, completed in 1776, pictured here in 1845 and little changed today.

especially attractive group is Crescent Grove, off SOUTH SIDE, of 1824, with a stuccoed pair guarding the entrance to an enclave of crescent and terrace, nicely scaled for households of different means. Much more ambitious is the presumptuous mansard-roofed pair of terraces on North Side, flanking Cedars Road, built by the architect-speculator James Knowles in 1860, to announce his grand route through Battersea to the West End. A little earlier Thomas Cubitt had begun with greater success to develop his Clapham Park estate with Italianate mansions intended to impress City businessmen. Impractically large for twentieth-century life, they have nearly all disappeared, and the area around Kings Avenue now provides a bitty but interesting conspectus of municipal housing types: inter-war walk-up blocks, Swedish-modern terraces of the 1950s, early tower blocks of the 1960s.

CLAPHAM JUNCTION, a crossing point for most lines south of London and the busiest rail junction in the country, was built in 1863 midway between Clapham and Battersea. It assumed the name of the former because then Battersea still had chiefly riparian connotations. The station soon became the hub of a lively shopping and entertainment district. Arding & Hobbs is a remnant of its heyday, a rare survival among south London suburban department stores. Originating as a modest drapery, it moved here in 1885 and took advantage of a fire in 1909 to rebuild in its present grand manner. The long-established street market in NORTHCOTE ROAD caters for more mundane needs.

Numerous cinemas and music halls also sprang up: none is still in use as such. The area immediately surrounding the station suffered a prolonged period of urban blight before being developed as a modern shopping centre in the late 1980s.

BATTERSEA

In Rocque's map, Battersea was still a riverside village with low-lying common fields further downstream. The remnants of the old centre are still just recognizable, a backwater reached from Battersea Park Road down the modest High Street. The parish church of St Mary, a neat Georgian preaching box of 1775, stands close to the muddy shoreline – one of the few places where one can still see the Thames unembanked. The church monuments include many to the St John family, lords of the manor in the seventeenth and eighteenth centuries, who also founded the school, now in a range of buildings along the High Street. Overlooking the river in Vicarage Crescent, and surrounded by much later buildings, OLD BATTERSEA HOUSE comes as a surprise: a compact brick house of the type fashionable around 1700, when it was owned by Samuel Pett, a naval official, instruments of whose calling adorn the doorcase.

The larger Battersea of today is a creation of the last 130 years. During the nineteenth century the village became engulfed in riverside industry. In 1851 the population was just over 10,000; by 1901, the year after Battersea became a borough, it had reached its peak of nearly 169,000. At that time Battersea was a working

Heaths and Commons

The commons and heaths scattered about London's suburbs have deeper origins by far than the buildings that surround them, even pre-dating the written record. Accessible now to all as recreational open space, these stretches of meadow, heath or woodland once played a vital part in a rural subsistence economy, providing local inhabitants with grazing land for their animals and fuel for their fires. Such customary rights, held 'in common', were recognized by statute from medieval times, but did not imply ownership of the land itself. That lay with the lord of the manor, who usually had the sole privilege of exploiting the soil – an asset that was to become particularly valuable in the London area in the eighteenth and nineteenth centuries, when there was a constant demand for clay for bricks and gravel for road making.

Apart from their everyday uses, these tracts of uncultivated ground in the London area have a history as rallying points for large crowds. The vast plateau of BLACKHEATH formed a natural gathering place for those travelling to or from Kent and the Continent. The leaders of the Peasants' Revolt of 1381 massed their supporters here before marching on London; Henry V was met here by the Lord Mayor on his return from Agincourt and in 1540 Blackheath was the site of a ceremonial meeting between Henry VIII and his new bride, Anne of Cleves. In the eighteenth century those commons consisting of flat open land provided ideal parade grounds and permanent quarters for the army; there are still barracks on WOOLWICH COMMON in southeast London and on HOUNSLOW HEATH to the west. At Woolwich they remain in a semi-rural setting, although at Hounslow there is nothing left to recall the wild heathland, notorious for robbers and highwaymen, that once stretched around the main roads leading out of London as far as the present site of Heathrow airport. WORMWOOD SCRUBS – once a wood called Wormholt and part of Old Oak Common in the manor of Fulham – is now better known for its prison, but was also used as a military training ground.

Heaths and commons attracted other users. The Elizabethan herbalist John Gerard discovered orchids on the richly varied Hampstead Heath. From the late seventeenth century Hampstead became famous for its mineral springs. In south London visitors were similarly enticed to the attractive commons of STREATHAM and SYDENHAM through the mineral wells discovered nearby. Appreciation of picturesque landscape could lead to improvement: in fashionable CLAPHAM the local residents formed a committee in 1836 to maintain the Common, filling up the gravel pits and reducing its wilder aspects. Wider popularity could result in encroachment and exploitation, as at Hampstead, where copyholders took advantage of their rights to build on the Heath. The fashion for spas died out in the nineteenth century, but by then the open land remaining around London was increasingly appreciated by those eager for a day's escape from the crowded city.

In 1808, Blackheath was not an open meadow but an undulating landscape with bushes, hillocks and a windmill. Even then, it was a popular residential area, and a staging post on the road to Dover and the Continent.

LEFT The pond on Hampstead Heath at the turn of the century, some thirty years after it had been designated a public recreation area.

BELOW A golf course is among the amenities offered at Wimbledon Common. The windmill dates from 1818 but was altered later in that century.

Thousands visited the Easter and Whitsun Fairs on HAMPSTEAD HEATH which began in the mid-nineteenth century, especially after 1860, when the Hampstead Junction Railway provided easy access from the East End, and an obtrusive hotel was built in the once secluded Vale of Health.

By that time many commons around London, as elsewhere, had disappeared. Enclosure Acts extinguishing the rights of commoners had accounted for some. Others, such as Wandsworth and Tooting, had been fragmented by railway lines. Many were so eroded by overuse that formerly cherished rights were of little value. By 1794 the number of cattle put out in spring to graze on KENNINGTON COMMON was so great that the grass disappeared almost at once. SHEPHERD'S BUSH COMMON, once endearingly called Gagglegoose Green, was by 1871 'nothing better than a swamp surrounded by a ditch'.

As London expanded, the pressure to develop all available land increased. Today's commons are not accidental survivals; they exist because of a series of hard-fought campaigns by those determined to preserve Londoners' traditional access to their customary green spaces. The need to improve and increase recreational areas within London focused first on the provision of parks. Kennington Common, the rallying place of the Chartists in 1848, and by then uninviting and insalubrious, was transformed into London's first new public park in 1852.

By the 1860s the large heaths on the edge of the built-up area were under threat. Long-standing battles between conservationists and powerful landlords – Earl Spencer at Wimbledon, Sir Thomas Maryon Wilson at Hampstead – came to a head with the formation of the Commons Preservation Society in 1865 under George Shaw-Lefevre (later Lord Eversley). The Metropolitan Commons Act of 1866, consolidated by later acts which made it possible for local authorities to buy land for recreational use, secured the principle of general public access to all commons in London.

HAMPSTEAD HEATH was acquired for public use in 1871. The modern Heath is however much larger and more varied than the heath of that date, for the diminished common land close to Hampstead was successively enlarged; Parliament Hill, with its splendid panorama over London, was added in 1889; Golders Hill Park, a private estate, in 1898; the woodland of the Heath Extension towards Golders Green in 1904 and Lord Mansfield's fine landscaped park and house at Kenwood in 1927. WIMBLEDON COMMON and PUTNEY HEATH were likewise preserved by an Act of 1871, which set up a board of conservators (still in existence). Here, despite enroachment by a golf course and widened roads, the mixture of rough hilly heath and woodland makes this the best example of 'wild' common land remaining within London.

man's town, the factories lining the riverside broken only by the green stretch of Battersea Park, created from Battersea Fields as the first new public park in London (see *Parks and gardens*). The expanded village had developed into a borough with a staunchly working-class identity, eloquently represented both on the London County Council and in Parliament by the radical John Burns.

The chief change since then has been the disappearance of Victorian industry. Nine Elms, downstream from Battersea Park, was the terminus of the London and Southampton Railway and is still industrial and commercial, but has been entirely rebuilt, starting with the new Covent Garden (fruit and vegetable) Market opened in 1974. The only notable Victorian building remaining here is the floridly decorated BATTERSEA PARK STATION of 1865. In the old village, the factories dominated by the gaunt flour mills near the church gave way around 1980 to luxury flats, a contrast to the utilitarian council buildings nearby, built to relieve overcrowding.

More of Victorian Battersea survives further south: unassuming streets, now being smartened up, arose on the market gardens which once lay around the village. North of Lavender Hill are the distinctive terraces of the self-help working-class Shaftesbury estate, begun in 1872, described by William Booth in 1891 as the area where 'the intelligent portion of the socialism of the district is found'. Further east the showier Park Town estate around St Philip's Square is a fragment of an 1860s' speculation intended to link fashionable Clapham and the West End, which foundered as railway lines overran the area.

On the higher ground, the country lane along the line of St John's Hill and Lavender Hill was built up from the 1860s for middle-class commuters attracted by the railways multiplying around Clapham Junction. This area became the heart of late Victorian Battersea. The church of the Ascension on Lavender Hill, one of James Brook's vast red-brick basilicas, was begun in 1876. Municipal enterprise came with the Library of 1888, then the festive Town Hall of 1892 (now BATTERSEA ARTS CENTRE), the most ambitious civic building of its date in south London. Both are by E.W. Mountford, architect also of the Polytechnic in Battersea Park Road (1891).

The energetic new borough embarked on municipal housing in 1902 with the homely cottages of the Latchmere estate in Burns Road and Reform Road, and continued with larger, less appealing schemes. Council housing was beginning to revert to a friendlier scale in the 1970s (the Greater London Council's Althorpe Grove in the old village) when political change reversed the pattern. Some became private flats: the run-down inter-war St John's estate in the old village was a pioneer conversion. There have been endeavours to brighten others, such as the bleak, unloved ranks of concrete slabs of the late 1960s between the railway and Battersea Park Road; more recently a vast Post-Modernist office building (housing, amongst others, *The Observer* newspaper) has been built by developers on the approach to Chelsea Bridge in Queenstown Road. The most spectacular transformation of the 1990s will be 'The Battersea', an entertainment centre developed within the huge POWER STATION, whose four monumental brick chimneys (1929 and 1944) are Battersea's most familiar landmark.

St Mary's church at Battersea was first recorded in the twelfth century. This view shows it in the early eighteenth century, a few years before it was rebuilt in 1776.

A PLACE TO LIVE

GREAT HOUSES AND PALACES

'I am come from my house to your palace' said Queen Victoria on arrival at a reception given by her friend the Duchess of Sutherland. The monarch had travelled a few hundred yards from Buckingham Palace to what is now known as Lancaster House – a sumptuous mansion used as a government entertainment and conference centre. The remark suggested that a royal palace was merely an aristocratic house writ large, even that it was feasible for the royal residence to be excelled in splendour. A century or so earlier there could have been no comparison, for at the palace had been the Court and that was to a large extent the government of the kingdom.

In 1762 George III and his Queen moved to Buckingham House, formerly a nobleman's home on the edge of town, while the Court stayed officially at St James's Palace. This symbolized the final split between the monarch and real governmental power. The king's 'state' – the pomp and circumstance surrounding him – gradually became another name for nation. The 'Court of St James', to which ambassadors are accredited, persists today as a formality. Royal palaces in and around the capital, as well as what used to be called the 'private palaces' of the nobility, were seats of power, not just grand homes.

Lords spiritual – that is archbishops, important abbots and priors, as well as the richer bishops – rivalled the lords temporal in influence until the Reformation and Henry VIII's Dissolution of the Monasteries in 1536–40. There are fragmentary remains of prelates'

mansions, or 'inns' as they were usually called. The chapel of ELY PLACE can be visited in Holborn and near Southwark Cathedral is a recently exposed gable wall, complete with rose window, of the great hall of WINCHESTER HOUSE. Bishops needed a London base for much the same reason as noblemen, namely to share in the responsibility and spoils of government. Cardinal Wolsey was both Archbishop of Canterbury and Chancellor of England, for example. He built himself a London house in Whitehall as well as a rural seat at Hampton Court. The chief residence of the Primate is still LAMBETH PALACE, with its fine Tudor gate and hall as well as more pretentious buildings by the Victorian architect Blore.

Even when parliament had superseded the Court in importance, the Lords were at least the equal of the Commons, so lords spiritual and temporal needed to be in London for weeks, even months each year. By the eighteenth century there was another reason to have a 'place in town': the social season. The gentlemen enjoyed the delights of balls, gambling, theatre and various diversions of the fashionable world such as the gardens at Vauxhall or riding in Hyde Park. Wives or mistresses could be acquired and entertained, daughters launched into society, influential patrons flattered. But the heart went out of aristocratic mansion-owning society around the time of the First World War, demoralized by the agricultural slump of the 1870s, imposition of income tax in the 1890s and the slaughter

Lambeth Palace in 1682, with Westminster on the opposite bank. Much of the palace, and St Mary's church outside it, are recognizable today.

OVERLEAF Kenwood House, on the edge of Hampstead Heath, was built by Robert Adam in 1767–9 and bequeathed to the nation by the Earl of Iveagh in 1927. Its magnificent rooms are open to the public and contain London's finest small collection of Old Master paintings.

in the trenches. Besides, London was now too crowded and dirty for comfort and there were motor buses in Park Lane.

So the palaces of the nobility largely disappeared. Two of the grandest in Park Lane were demolished between the wars to make way for hotels. Grosvenor House and Dorchester House were as rich as the palaces of Venice and bigger. Their art treasures were of a quality which provided the foundation of many of the great public and private collections of the United States. Grosvenor House had a room full of Rubens' work, as well as superb paintings by Rembrandt and Velázquez among hundreds of old masters. In all, more than a hundred mansions lining Park Lane, Piccadilly and half the squares of London were replaced with hotels, blocks of flats or offices, often only the names remaining. Thus there is still a Devonshire House in Piccadilly – but, instead of William Kent's ducal mansion with its three-acre garden, it contains offices and car showrooms.

Traces remain. The beautiful wrought-iron gates to Devonshire House were re-erected on the opposite side of Piccadilly as one entrance to Green Park. HERTFORD HOUSE survives in Manchester Square, converted at the turn of the century into galleries for the Wallace Collection. The vanished half of the façade of Schomberg House in Pall Mall was actually reinstated in the fifties, though this unique late seventeenth-century design conceals an office block. Wren's MARLBOROUGH HOUSE, though engulfed in nineteenth-century enlargements, retains much of its interior and accommodates the Commonwealth Secretariat.

Similarly concealed is the core of Lord Burlington's house, masquerading as the Royal Academy. The most beautiful mansion of all, Robert Adam's LANSDOWNE HOUSE in Berkeley Square, was mutilated in the 1930s for road widening, yet a few rooms survive in the club of the same name – the best interiors having been sold complete to museums in New York and Philadelphia. DOVER HOUSE in Whitehall was never blessed with such fine apartments, yet at least its columned rotunda survives to act as a vestibule to the Scottish Office. As a representative of great houses in what used to be the countryside around London, overtaken by urban spread in the last century or so, there are the bombed remains of HOLLAND HOUSE, approached in the 1850s through meadows, now in a municipal park. There is the Elizabethan OSTERLEY PARK, transformed by Robert Adam, now owned by the National Trust and administered by the Victoria & Albert Museum. SYON HOUSE at Isleworth, with splendid Adam interiors, is still owned by the dukes of Northumberland, who brought much of the wonderful collection from their London home, Northumberland House, demolished in 1874 to make way for the avenue of that name. HAM HOUSE, by the Thames in Surrey, has survived almost unaltered since the seventeenth century. The home of the earls of Dysart for nearly three hundred years, it is now administered by the Victoria & Albert Museum. Lord Burlington had an exquisite Palladian villa at Chiswick, given by the Cavendish family to the local authority earlier this century. The Cavendishes, dukes of Devonshire, had at least three major houses in and around London in the nineteenth century.

RUNNING A GREAT HOUSE

The organization of life in a large house was complex. Typically the house was arranged with the entrance hall on the ground floor, the rest of which would be taken up with family rooms and perhaps an estate office, and a grand stair which led to state rooms on the first floor and

Chiswick House, a Palladian villa completed in 1729 for the third Earl of Burlington, is today owned by the local authority and open to the public.

family bedrooms on the second. While not so large as the self-sufficient community on the country estate, the nobleman's London household comprised up to fifty servants organized in an increasingly formal and hierarchic way in the nineteenth century.

Most households were run in three departments, under the butler, the housekeeper and the cook – all of whom would have their own room at ground or basement level. Very grand houses would be run by a steward, a sort of managing director. Separation, especially between the sexes, was important: the maids slept in the attics and the menservants in the basement, in particular the footmen who had to answer the door. Physical arrangements varied depending on the size and

shape of house, but conditions were always hard. A parlour maid, who might be only thirteen years old, would be up by five o'clock scrubbing floors, cleaning grates and laying fires – even carrying coal if the junior footman could not be persuaded. She was lucky if she had a few hours off on one afternoon a week. She was paid pennies and never dared misbehave, let alone become pregnant. That would have led to instant dismissal without a 'character' and so no alternative to the workhouse or prostitution.

ROYAL PALACES

The first of London's royal palaces was at Westminster, on the misty isle of Thorney, where Edward the Confessor chose to establish his court. Later in the eleventh century, after the Norman Conquest, William the Conqueror built the TOWER OF LONDON, in the City itself, as both a fortress and palace to overawe his new subjects. The keep, or White Tower, still dominates the area. Other buildings around the baileys are of later date, for the Tower as a whole remained in intermittent use as a palace until Tudor times.

Both the Tower and Westminster were superseded as chief royal residences by palaces now vanished, such as that at Bridewell just west of the City and most notably at Whitehall where, at its height in Elizabeth's reign, the royal apartments, state chambers, government offices, noblemen's residences, gardens, tilting yards and bowling greens covered over twenty acres. Often damaged by fire it was finally destroyed in 1698. Eighty years earlier, Inigo Jones had drawn up plans for a massive Renaissance palace, symmetrical with many courtyards and cupolas. It could be afforded by neither James I nor his ill-fated son Charles I who in 1649 walked to the scaffold from a window of the BANQUETING HOUSE, the only part of Inigo Jones's palace to be built. It is the most perfect early classical building in England with the added attraction of a superb Baroque ceiling painted by Rubens, and it is open daily when not required for official receptions.

Henry VIII had been a great builder, adding to and rationalizing Whitehall, building the magical but short-lived Nonsuch Palace near Cheam, Surrey and Bridewell Palace on the banks of the river Fleet (destroyed in the Great Fire of 1666). He also enlarged his favourite palace, Greenwich, where he had been born. But the palace he built on the site of the suppressed leper hospital of ST JAMES's remains, its lofty towered gatehouse in diapered brickwork looking up St James's Street to this day. The state apartments were refurbished after the Restoration of 1660 and again after a major fire of 1809. From a balcony the monarch is still proclaimed and the Accession Council is held within. Much of St James's

Queen Anne had her main residence at Kensington Palace, shown here in a print of 1707, with the elaborate formal gardens fashionable at that time.

Buckingham House in 1800, some twenty years before John Nash rebuilt it for George IV as Buckingham Palace. The building, dating from 1705, was at this time occupied by the King's mother, and called the Queen's House.

Palace is now taken up with 'grace and favour' residences of retired public, military and court servants of distinction.

The most notable building connected with Henry VIII is HAMPTON COURT PALACE, originally built by his overmighty prelate and chancellor Cardinal Wolsey and given by him to the rapacious king in an unsuccessful effort to stave off disgrace. Henry added a great hall and other apartments which dominate the approach to this palace, together with Wolsey's gateway. Hampton Court was a favourite residence for several monarchs who kept great state there, especially at Christmas. The palace was despoiled during the Commonwealth and redecorated by Charles II whose chief residence, however, was to be the new palace at Greenwich. William and Mary had other ideas. Wishing to rival Louis XIV in all matters, they appointed Christopher Wren to build England's Versailles at Hampton Court. Ambitious plans, which would have meant demolition of nearly all the Tudor palace, were abandoned after Wren had constructed four magnificent ranges around a new fountain court.

Part of the attraction of Hampton Court had been the safe and comfortable approach by river, but it was fifteen miles from London and in later times the physical presence of the monarch was frequently required in the capital: hence the importance of BUCKINGHAM PALACE. By the eighteenth century the monarch no longer presided over ministerial meetings in the closet or 'cabinet' attached to his bedroom; his power had become symbolic. State balls, entertainment of heads of state and the acceptance of public applause from the balcony – all are highly visible functions of the building at the end of the Mall. The original mansion was never sufficiently grand. It was enlarged by the Prince Regent's architect John Nash into an open quadrangle in the centre

frontage of which the Marble Arch was sited – until it was seen to be too small for state coaches.

The interior, with its 650 rooms including Queen Victoria's vast ballroom, is impressive in a vulgar sort of way. George V likened it to a grand hotel. The power of the monarchy's image and of its trappings, many of which are quite modern inventions, is evinced by the fame of the palace façade, created by Aston Webb as recently as 1913.

The wide processional Mall, with the Admiralty Arch at one end facing the gilded Victoria monument at the other, as a preface to the stone-clad and columned palace façade, constituted an Edwardian attempt at imperial grandeur on the Continental scale. Two other London palaces, in late seventeenth-century brickwork, are more typical of the country house image with which most later British sovereigns were more comfortable.

KENSINGTON PALACE is now the home of several royal family members, though its grandest apartments are open to view. It was built by Christopher Wren for William and Mary after 1689, when they bought what had been Nottingham House. With its extensive gardens and park, this was favoured by Queen Anne and the first Hanoverians. But after George II died in his water closet at Kensington Palace, George III preferred Buckingham House.

Even more modest was the palace at KEW, a small Jacobean mansion, the only survival of several royal residences in the area. The house, as well as the famous botanical gardens, is open to the public.

TOWN HOUSES

As the site of the royal court, Westminster was an obvious choice for medieval noblemen deciding where to build their London houses. Certainly there were fifteenth- and sixteenth-century mansions, of which the

The Savoy was one of the earliest of the Strand palaces but in the sixteenth century it was rebuilt as a hospital for the poor. This view was drawn in 1661 – nine years before part of the building was destroyed in a fire. The Savoy Hotel now stands on the site.

only substantial survival is ASHBURNHAM HOUSE, with its fine oak staircase by John Webb, son-in-law and pupil of Inigo Jones; now engulfed in Westminster School, parts of the house can be seen by appointment.

But the favoured residential area was in and around the City. The hall of one courtyard house can be seen today, though not on its original City site. CROSBY PLACE was built on land leased by Sir John Crosby from the formidable Prioress of St Helen's, Bishopsgate in 1466. Later Sir Thomas More owned the building for a while and Sir Walter Raleigh lived there. In 1908, to make way for an insurance company's office, the hall itself was transferred to a site on the Chelsea embankment which had been part of Sir Thomas More's garden.

Pressure on land and increased pollution in the City – the population trebled in Tudor times – together with the desirability of being on the riverside, attracted noblemen and prelates to seek sites for their London palaces on the north shoreline, or 'strand' of the Thames. Large grounds were available and the position was convenient for Westminster and the City by barge.

By Elizabeth's reign most of the clerics had been dispossessed. The seven palaces between the Strand and the river were occupied by courtiers. Most westerly was York House, later the home of George Villiers, Duke of Buckingham. Next was Durham House, former palace of the bishops. Russell House was later replaced by Bedford House north of the Strand. The Savoy was split into a hospital, lodgings and what was said to be England's first glass factory.

Next was Somerset House, the 1540s' palace of the Protector and one of the first major Renaissance buildings in the country. Finally came Arundel House and Leicester House (later called Essex House). All that survives of these great houses is a multitude of street names, the SAVOY CHAPEL, the water gate of York House (now marooned some way from the river, because of the embankment) and SOMERSET HOUSE, rebuilt by Sir William Chambers in the 1770s as one of the world's first purpose-designed office blocks.

Of the houses north of the Strand, in the Covent Garden and Holborn areas, the chief reminder is again street names. Hatton Garden commemorates the residence of one of Queen Elizabeth's more colourful chancellors. In a corner of Lincoln's Inn Fields is NEWCASTLE HOUSE, built in 1685 and later the home of the Duke of Newcastle. The detached brick and stone building of seven floors – including an attic and two basements – was refaced by Lutyens early this century. It is now occupied by the Queen's solicitors.

The much grander mansions of that date, on large sites north of Piccadilly, have mostly disappeared, apart from BURLINGTON HOUSE where the Royal Academy uses William Kent's reception rooms for its smaller exhibitions. Burlington Gardens and Burlington Arcade now occupy what was once part of the earl's garden, as does QUEENSBERRY HOUSE, built in the 1720s for the Duke and Duchess of that name, but now much altered, and long occupied by the Royal Bank of Scotland.

Close to St James's Palace, LANCASTER HOUSE was built in 1825 for the Duke of York, designed by Benjamin Wyatt. In 1913 it was given to the nation by Lord Leverhulme, to house the London Museum – which it did until 1946. Just north of it is BRIDGEWATER HOUSE, one of the later and most impressive of private palaces. Designed by Charles Barry in 1854 in his most vigorous Italianate manner, this stone palazzo has a vast central saloon which had been intended as an open courtyard. The picture gallery was bombed in the last war and never fully restored. Sold by the Earl of

Ellesmere after the war and used as prestige offices, the house has since been restored by a Greek shipping magnate.

Also being refurbished is SPENCER HOUSE, next door to Bridgewater House and with its chief elevation overlooking Green Park. This stone-built Palladian palazzo was completed for Earl Spencer in 1766. To the north of Green Park, in Curzon Street, is CREWE HOUSE, now the Saudi Arabian embassy.

For at least two centuries the centre of London's aristocratic life was St James's Square. In 1756 Horace Walpole described a house-warming. 'The Duchess of Norfolk has opened her new house. All the earth was there last Tuesday.... In short, you never saw such a scene of magnificence and taste.' Norfolk House was demolished in 1938, the LCC declaring that the incomparable Rococo interiors were of no historic interest. Other interiors do remain in the square, notably by Robert Adam at number 20, owned by the Distillers Company. Of similar late eighteenth-century date is LICHFIELD HOUSE by Athenian Stuart, retaining at least one splendid painted ceiling. CHATHAM HOUSE, numbers 9, 10 and 11, also has fine rooms (it is now the Royal Institute of International Affairs), as does the smaller number 7, the Royal Fine Arts Commission's office. The former Byng family home in the north-east corner was latterly the Libyan embassy.

Most such great houses are now in commercial hands, but usually tended with care. Number 44 Berkeley Square was built by William Kent in 1742–4 for Lady Isabella Finch. It has a dramatic and inventive staircase of late Baroque type and its principal room occupies not only the whole first-floor front – the piano nobile – but the second as well. Lady Bel, a spinster, often entertained her friends to cards there, as no doubt did Lord and Lady Clermont a little later. The aptly named Clermont Club is a suitable successor.

Another Kent house, in Arlington Street, reached its apogee of grandeur early this century when, with a ballroom and other additions, its floor area extended to over half an acre. The house has been beautifully restored. Another where a ballroom was added early this century, this time by Lord Derby, is STRATFORD HOUSE, dominating a cul de sac off Oxford Street and now the Oriental Club. Its architecture is often described as being in the Adam style. Two of the most notable Adam houses are Apsley House at Hyde Park Corner and Home House in Portman Square. APSLEY HOUSE was a modest brick building, though with sumptuous interiors, of the 1770s. The Wyatts clad the house in stone, enlarged it and added the portico for the Duke of Wellington. Being the last building on the edge of town before the village of Knightsbridge – the toll gate was outside – it came to be called 'No. 1, London'. Given to the nation in 1947 and opened as the Wellington Museum, there is still a family flat at the top.

ABOVE Apsley House, once known as 'No. 1, London' was built in the 1770s by Robert Adam and modified by Benjamin and Philip Wyatt in 1829, when this print was drawn. It was presented to the nation by the 7th Duke of Wellington in 1947 and is now the Wellington Museum.

LEFT Somerset House in the Strand was designed by William Chambers in the late 1770s as the first purpose-built office block.

NOBLE SQUARES

To be in part composed of 'noble squares' might be taken as a definition of a major European city. In Rome the piazzas were dominated by Baroque palaces and churches, often with a fountain or two, and in Paris urban pride and even military might were expressed in the monumental layout and a central obelisk or arch. By contrast, London's squares usually evolved at the core of speculative housing schemes, albeit often on an aristocratic urban estate. Even so, Continental influence was crucial; London's first residential square was known, after all, as the Covent Garden 'Piazza'.

There was a homegrown precursor in the collegiate quadrangle and even in the courtyards round which most great houses, including many in London, were built until the reign of James I. The 'inns' of lawyers also often surrounded square or rectangular spaces. Lincoln's Inn Fields is sometimes thought of as the first London square, but it was not so much a pre-conceived urban space as the accommodation of the builder, William Newton, to the demands of the Inn's students and other local residents that an open space be preserved in this rapidly expanding quarter of town. That accepted, there was an attempt at unified design in the surrounding house façades, Italianate in a manner influenced by Inigo Jones.

By the time Newton, perhaps the first speculative developer, had embarked upon most of his houses in 1640, Jones had almost completed Covent Garden

piazza for the fourth Earl of Bedford, whose 40-acre estate stretched north from his mansion off the Strand. Today an attractive hive of tourists, the arcaded piazza then consisted of houses 'fitt for the habitacions of Gentlemen . . .'.

After the Restoration of 1660 London grew apace. The Earl of Southampton built 'a little towne' centred on what soon came to be known as Bloomsbury Square, with his own mansion occupying the north side and houses – each 24-feet wide – on the other three. The grand houses fronting it required service blocks behind; stables, mews buildings and also outlying shops and here, for example, a market too – hence the 'little towne'. This set a pattern; for the next couple of centuries, the square was the key urban design unit. Bloomsbury Square is also typical in that this once fine space has been mutilitated by a main road on one side and an overblown 1930s' office block on another, that distract passers-by

OPPOSITE Built in 1775, Bedford Square is a fine survival of late Georgian London. Once the homes of the aristocracy, the terraced houses are today occupied as offices, many by publishers and learned institutions. The embellishments round the doors are in Coade stone, an artificial stone popular at the time.

BELOW Leicester House, in the centre of this print (now the site of the Empire Cinema), was built in the 1630s and Leicester Square was laid out to its south later in the seventeenth century. The equestrian statue of George I was placed there in 1784 and removed in the late nineteenth century after being vandalized.

The Owners of London

Modern London gives few clues as to its owners. A street name here, a certain uniformity there; but property can change hands, making old names redundant, and local authorities can impose as many responsibilities on occupants of attractive streets as old estates ever did. Ownership dates in some cases from many centuries ago; but in others it is constantly changing.

A few major landowners own significant areas of central London. The Crown is the biggest, with 5666 acres of royal parks and palaces, run by the Department of the Environment, together with 350 acres in St James's, Regent Street, Millbank, Kensington Palace Gardens and adjoining Regent's Park, managed by the Crown Estate Commissioners.

The Church Commissioners are large freeholders in Bayswater, Maida Vale and parts of south London, having assumed responsibility for estates owned by the bishoprics. While monasteries were forced to forfeit vast tracts of land at the time of the Dissolution of the Monasteries in the 1530s, bishoprics were not deprived of theirs. Ownership of the manor of Paddington by the bishops of London meant they were well placed to profit from the westward expansion of London in the early

nineteenth century and grand stucco terraces were built on the land as a result. Parts of the Duke of Westminster's Grosvenor Estate, which extends to 300 acres in Mayfair and Belgravia, were being developed at the same time.

Eton College holds land in Hampstead as a result of having been granted the manor of Chalcot (later Chalk Farm) by Henry VI in 1440. The Portman Estate in Marylebone, though now much diminished from its original 270 acres, still occupies part of the Manor of Lileston bought by the Portman family in 1553.

In Kennington, the Duchy of Cornwall still owns 40 acres of what was once a substantial royal manor where the Black Prince built a palace. And in Chelsea the Cadogan Estate extends to 94 acres, covering much of the old manor of Chelsea which came into the family as a result of Charles Cadogan's marriage to a daughter of the then owner, Sir Hans Sloane, in 1717.

Estates such as these are historic; but they are divided from one another and sometimes fragmented by more recent incursions. Land and/or buildings have been sold off to developers; modern pension funds and institutions have invested in ownership of individual office blocks; estates have passed on embarrassing slums to local authorities.

Accurate estimates of the size of estates, whoever the owner may be, are difficult to make. Local authorities

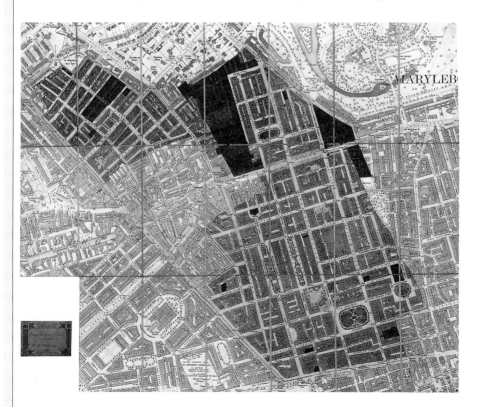

In the late eighteenth century Henry William Portman began to develop his ancestral estate, then on the north-western outskirts of London, which had been in the family since 1553. He built northwards: the map on the right shows the plans for development in 1780. In the next hundred years development had almost reached St John's Wood, as the map on the left shows. (The shaded part is the Portman Estate.) The later streets are more tightly packed – fewer extravagant squares and circuses.

measure the size of their housing developments by the number of units they include. Institutions assess their property portfolios in terms of square footage or value on the open market. The Church Commissioners can reel off numbers of rack rents and ground rents – but not a figure for the number of acres. Indeed, with buildings reaching to dozens of floors, acreage is scarcely relevant: a single tower block of offices can be worth many times a large housing estate.

The variety of forms of tenure makes the situation more confused. Though the great estates own the freehold of their property, in most cases they have sold it on leases of varying lengths. A householder who buys a home on a long lease may pay a price for it that differs little from that of a freehold, but at the end of that lease the property reverts to the freeholder.

Similarly, companies are rarely owner-occupiers of their office blocks, although there has recently been increasing interest from small companies in buying small freehold office buildings on the fringe of the City, both as an investment and to avoid paying large sums each year in rent.

In some cases, continued ownership by an estate has had a welcome affect on an area. Compare Belgravia, a swathe of 200 acres held by the Grosvenor family since 1677, with Pimlico, which it sold off in the 1950s. Pimlico was somewhat run down by that date, but it has

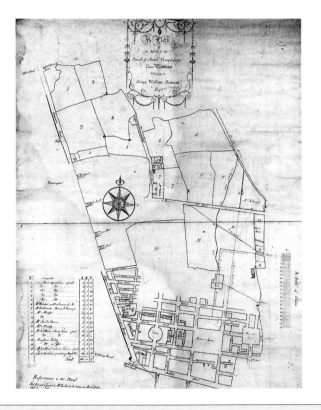

not been enhanced by subsequent piecemeal redevelopment, whereas Belgravia retains its integrity.

On the Hyde Park estate, by contrast, the Church Commissioners destroyed the unity of design by demolition and replacement with large blocks of flats in the 1950s. The gradual sale of their Maida Vale estate has been less damaging, thanks to tighter planning controls.

The most important event in the early history of land ownership in London was the Dissolution of the Monasteries. Until then most of the land surrounding the old City was held by religious foundations, but confiscation and redistribution left it in the hands of various noblemen and allies of Henry VIII.

Those who found themselves in possession of land nearest the City were the first to benefit as it expanded, and common rights over that land were no impediment. When in 1609 the Earl of Salisbury – described by Simon Jenkins in his book, *Landlords to London*, as the first successful property speculator – bought a site where Leicester Square is today, he simply paid a token sum to the parish in compensation for building over common land.

Others came later to land ownership and waited longer for the right moment to begin development. The Grosvenor family became the owners of what is probably now London's best-known estate only in 1677, when Sir Thomas Grosvenor of the Eaton Estate in Cheshire married Mary Davies, heiress to her great-great-uncle's swampy manor of Ebury. Development began in Mayfair 50 years later, but there were no houses in Belgravia until the early nineteenth century.

Concern for the environment was a hallmark of speculations by the great estates – not for any altruistic reason but to ensure that their developments were sufficiently bucolic to attract wealthy tenants. Outside the estates, however, development was unregulated. In the nineteenth-century City, increasing commerce and the disappearance of householders to the suburbs left the area prey to redevelopment by speculators and this has continued in the twentieth century: the buying and selling of the post-war Paternoster Square by property companies, in advance of its scheduled redevelopment, is one example of how quickly land can change hands.

For the most part, however, fragmentation of land ownership has occurred gradually over the centuries. The coming of the railways, the devastation of the Second World War and the development of public-sector housing all helped to change traditional patterns. Given all that, it is surprising how much of the freehold of central London, between Hampstead and the Thames, Kensington and the City, is still held by the estates that originally developed it.

from the good houses on the other two sides.

St James's Fields, developed at the same time for Henry Jermyn, Earl of St Albans, maintained its character as an aristocratic quarter until well into this century. Indeed, despite insensitive alterations in the 1930s, St James's Square still has something of the air of its eighteenth-century heyday. It too was at the centre of secondary streets, three of which issued from the middle of the sides, instead of at the corners as was more usual.

Leicester Square came into being in the 1670s when the Earl of Leicester was licensed to build ranges of houses to the south, east and west of the fields in front of his house. Even in the eighteenth century it was taking on its rather seedy entertainment function. The same fate befell nearby Soho Square, created a decade later. Hog Lane, a service road to its east, was redeveloped in the nineteenth century as Charing Cross Road, a not uncommon reversal – Park Lane is another example –

Berkeley Square, but the massive 1930s' brick blocks, especially that on the east, would discourage any nightingale which might once have sung there.

FASHION MOVES NORTH

Another population surge came at the end of the Seven Years' War in 1763 and this time the bulk of vacant land was to be found on the suddenly immensely valuable estates of the Portlands, Portmans, Cavendishes and Harleys, who named their new streets and squares after themselves – Harley was Earl of Oxford, thus Oxford Street which bounds this area to the south. Both Portman Square and Cavendish Square are still attractive, with impressive central gardens, now mostly used by office workers from the surrounding buildings. A little further west, Bryanston Square (after the Portmans' Dorset house) and its twin Montagu Square, remain largely residential. So does the beautiful Con-

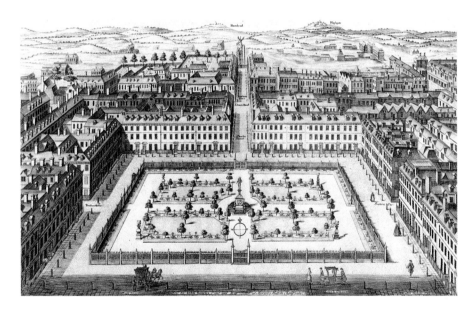

RIGHT Soho Square was one of the most fashionable addresses in London when this engraving was done in 1731, fifty years after it was constructed. Open fields separate Oxford Street from Hampstead and Highgate. The statue of Charles II, removed in 1870, was returned to the square in 1938.

OPPOSITE George Basevi designed Belgrave Square in 1825 as the focal point of Thomas Cubitt's Belgravia development. The pompous, rather cold stucco terraced houses are now used as embassies and as the headquarters of public bodies.

where a peripheral street turns into a thoroughfare and the square becomes almost a backwater. Architecturally disjointed, only numbers 10 and 15 Soho Square survive, but at least the garden has remained with, in the middle, an unlikely wooden Tudor-style arbour and tool shed of the 1870s. Lacking even that rustic touch, Golden Square, also an aristocratic address in the late seventeenth century, has been unable to resist commercial development pressures.

Other seventeenth-century squares were built on the edge of town from Spitalfields in the east to Kensington in the west, but north of Piccadilly became the fashionable area once building began on what had been the garden of Lord Berkeley's former house. A few early eighteenth-century houses remain on the west side of

naught Square further west again, built in the 1820s as one of the first developments in Bayswater. Its name commemorates a royal connection, as had the much more ambitious Hanover Square, built in 1717 (soon after the accession of that dynasty) by a great Whig landlord – the Harleys *et al.* on the other side of Oxford Street were Tories. A handful of houses survive in this, the first of the Mayfair squares.

Two squares, Mecklenburgh and Brunswick, built on the Foundling Hospital estate north of Holborn, share the Hanoverian connection and present-day domination by London University halls. Other Bloomsbury squares, Woburn, Gordon and even the much larger Russell Square, were unfortunate enough to be at least partly engulfed in the university's post-war expansion.

Hanover Square in a painting by Edward Dayes of 1787. Laid out some seventy years before, it was the centre-piece of a large development undertaken principally by the Whig magnate the Earl of Scarborough. The square and its environs immediately became fashionable.

Fortunately, the Russell family kept control of Bedford Square, though recently even they, like the Grosvenors, have had to bow before leasehold enfranchisement legislation. Text books often quote Bedford Square as being the best remaining example of graceful late-Georgian uniformity (see *Georgian terraces*). Bedford Square has a fine central garden with tall plane trees and large-scale shrubberies behind high railings; there is a far greater contrast with the urbanity of surrounding façades than was imagined by the original builders. Here the keyholders are the publishers and other office users occupying the houses.

For two centuries even the Bedford estate has been dwarfed by that of the dukes of Westminster. Twelve-year-old Mary Davies married Sir Thomas Grosvenor in 1677; she was heiress to one hundred acres north of Jermyn's land where a May fair was held, and to four hundred acres of marshy fields which became Belgravia and Pimlico. Grosvenor Square, at the heart of the Mayfair estate, was built between 1720 and 1770. This, the largest of London squares excluding Lincoln's Inn Fields, was the address of aristocrats until well into this century.

The more south-westerly Belgrave Square was developed on drained and consolidated land in the 1820s. Not content with controlling the designs as before, here the Grosvenor estate, by agreement with the builder Thomas Cubitt, oversaw a unified and massive palace-style development of a grandeur to compete with Nash's work for the Prince Regent. The architect Basevi emphasized both the centres and ends of long blocks with bold groups of columns. The detached mansions across each corner were designed by different architects. The big houses, especially on what Oscar Wilde's Lady Bracknell called 'the fashionable side', were the homes of nobility. Now they are mostly embassies.

Cubitt was also responsible for Eaton and Chester Squares, linked to Belgrave Square with fine streets now the homes of the international rich. Less elevated, but by no means inexpensive, are the residential squares to the north and west of the West End. These areas have long been more sought after and more fashionable than those to the south and east, being on higher ground and out of the path of the prevailing winds, which for several centuries were soot-laden. Nevertheless, there are a handful of squares in south London, especially in Camberwell, and at least one architecturally distinguished square in east London, Tredegar Square, in Bow, which has recently been renovated.

ON THE PERIMETER

Kensington Square itself was an isolated forerunner, being built in the 1680s near the new Kensington Palace in a setting that remained rural until 1840. Its nineteenth-century inhabitants included John Stuart Mill and Edward Burne-Jones. It remains attractive as does neighbouring Edwardes Square. Like Campden Hill Square of the 1830s, many of the houses have been reconverted back to single-family occupation. Still subdivided, however, are the rather later and considerably bigger houses of the Earl's Court squares, with their rows of repetitive columned porches in painted plasterwork and brick upper floors. A stone-built Gothic church often fills a good part of the centre of these gloomy places. Others, such as Redcliffe Square, were designed with a street through the middle, so denying them the sense of seclusion so central to the concept of a square.

The architectural tone in Islington is altogether lighter; even the intact neo-Gothic façades of Lonsdale Square are set off by a lavish central garden, well maintained by the council. Starting with Myddelton Square of 1827, near the old Finsbury town hall, a circuit through the several smaller-scale squares of the delightful Lloyd Baker estate leads to a whole series of mid-nineteenth-century squares north of the Pentonville Road – the elegant Cloudesley, the neo-classic Gibson and finally, via Canonbury, recently revived De Beauvoir Square. There is nothing 'villagey' about them, though their gardens, open to the public until sunset, are aglow with daffodils in spring and roses in summer.

Most squares are now listed as being of architectural or historic interest or are at least conservation areas. This means that the architectural unity and the upkeep of the gardens are generally the responsibility of local authorities rather than private landlords. In the post-war period, the square as a civic form has come into its own again. It tames the motor car, for one thing.

GEORGIAN TERRACES AND REGENCY VILLAS

The idea of uniting individual structures behind a continuous elevation, or within a single composition, was not new in the eighteenth century. Indeed, as towns and cities increased in population and building land at their centres became scarce and valuable, it was a logical space-saving development. Medieval town centres had deep-plan houses set side by side, elbowing one another for street frontage and, as early as the 1630s, Inigo Jones had introduced the compositional devices that became the Georgian urban ideal. At his Covent Garden piazza of *c*.1631 Jones had united individual houses behind a uniform and grand palace front; while, a few years later (*c*.1638), for a site in Lothbury in the City of London, he designed an austere uniform terrace embellished with nothing but its correct classical proportions.

These works by Jones and his contemporaries – notably the uniform, pilaster-clad palace fronts of the 1640s and 1650s in Lincoln's Inn Fields and Queen Street, Covent Garden – were to have a profound influence on the architecture of the early eighteenth century. These prototypes have been long demolished,

with the exception of a single house in Lincoln's Inn Fields – Lindsay House of *c*.1640 – and a remarkable pilastered group of the 1650s that survives in Newington Green, North London.

But the ideal of the individual house subservient to the design of the terrace as a whole, which itself was conceived as part of a larger scale urban composition, had to contend with the harsh reality and individualism of the system of financing house building.

The basic building block of this kind of urban design – the individual terrace house – was the product of the speculative builder who, in the early years of the eighteenth century at least, was far from financially stable or aesthetically sensitive. Typically, he was a small-time builder dogged by events beyond his control which could squeeze credit or remove demand for housing. Money and survival were what mattered to the

Nash's Cumberland Terrace in Regent's Park, completed in 1828, is the epitome of a palace-fronted terrace and is among Nash's finest creations. The interior was modernized in the mid-twentieth century but the façade was kept intact.

builders of Georgian London. Consequently, the realization of the urban ideal – uniform terraces judiciously disposed to form squares, crescents, circuses, avenues or streets – was rarely achieved. Virtually every effort in London was hopelessly compromised by the exigencies of speculation.

Left to his own devices, the individualistic speculator of the first half of the eighteenth century would invariably undertake terraces like those that survive in Fournier Street and Elder Street, Spitalfields (both of the 1720s) or in Southampton Street, Bloomsbury or Chesterfield Street, Mayfair (both of the 1740s and 1750s), where the individuality of each building operation is apparent, despite the similarities imposed by the limits of building technology (frontage widths commonly of 20–30 feet reflecting size limits of timber for structural beams). Even those early eighteenth-century streets that do display more uniformity – such as Great James Street in Bloomsbury of c.1722, Lord North Street, Westminster of c.1720–5 and Meard Street, Soho of 1722 and 1732 – lack any attempt to organize the matching elevations into any form of coherent urban composition.

IMPOSING ORDER

It was not until the late eighteenth century, when single speculators tended to undertake larger developments and when estates felt better able to exercise strong control, that rigidly uniform or palace-fronted terraces began to appear regularly in London. A pair of terraces in Percy Street, off Tottenham Court Road, begun in c.1764 on the Goodge estate, are early (though now much altered) examples of uniform terraces articulated to form a lively urban composition with centre and end houses breaking forward and embellished with pedimented porches.

The Adam brothers' Adelphi development off the Strand, built 1768–72 and now mostly destroyed, realized the ideal of a piece of city (small though it was) composed entirely of uniform terraces, each with central and terminal emphasis, while Bedford Square, built on the Bedford estate between 1776 and 1786 under the control of two builders (William Scott and Robert Grews) was the first London square to be formed by four palace-fronted terraces.

However, as with earlier, less formal developments, Bedford Square was still the work of several individual speculators, which accounts for the variety of interior finishes and, perhaps, for some of the solecisms of the

design. For example, the individual front doors are emphasized by Coade stone blocks which make a nonsense of the attempt to merge separate houses into a single palatial composition. Later and in many ways more successful examples of the palace-fronted terrace are the east and south sides of Fitzroy Square (1790–4) designed by Robert Adam and some of the terraces erected in the 1820s under the overall control of John Nash – notably York Terrace of 1822 and Cumberland Terrace of 1828, both in Regent's Park, and Carlton House Terrace, Westminster, of 1827.

For later Georgian terraces, embellished with nothing but their remarkable and sustained uniformity and austerity, the best examples survive on the Bedford estate in Bloomsbury, particularly Montague Street and Bedford Place. Both were erected in 1800 under the overall control of James Burton.

Anxiety about money and bankruptcy flawed the product of the speculative building system. Façades had to look fashionable and appear well wrought of good materials to attract buyers, but concealed work could be skimped and, in theory, no one would be the wiser. Poor quality bricks were used for party walls and for the loadbearing piers behind the façade – those elements that were concealed but which, unfortunately, did most of the structural work. The good bricks used for the façade – often well laid and beautifully cut and rubbed for window arches or string courses – were mere skins, 4 inches thick and rarely bonded into the loadbearing work behind.

LIVING PATTERNS

Many terrace houses were occupied as lodgings from the day of their completion. This is not in itself surprising except that the plan form and construction of the London town house make it singularly unsuitable for multiple occupation. With its single front door, narrow hall, wooden stair, small landings and often flimsily constructed room partitions, it made an adequate home for a family but a bad lodging house. The speculative system hampered the development of an eighteenth-century building type suitable for multiple occupation to match the tenement blocks of Edinburgh or Paris. A block of flats would have needed stouter materials, sounder construction and, consequently, would have taken more time and more money to build – things that were anathema to the speculator.

As a single family home the typical Georgian terrace house worked well when the number of occupants was somewhere between 5 and 10. Nicholas Barbon, in his *Apology for the Builder* (1685), notes that the average City house then contained 8–11 people while Isaac Ware, in 1756, wrote that his 'common' London house would

OPPOSITE Elder Street, Spitalfields, dates from the 1720s and is one of the earliest surviving terraces in London. Today, these neat brick houses are admired for their well-proportioned elegance; but at the time they were built, it was their practicality much as their appearance that made them popular.

contain 'two or three people, with three or four servants'.

The manner of occupation is suggested by the plan form. There were several permutations of plan but by the early 1720s a standard form had evolved: one room in the front towards the street and one slightly smaller at the back which connected with a closet housed in a small rear wing. The staircase, typically of dog-leg form, rose in one of the rear corners of the house.

Slightly earlier houses were often of another form – with a large central stack which, with a central newel staircase, divided front room from back. Occasionally the staircases rose against the front façade to allow the best, largest room to be placed in the rear of the house away from street noise and commanding a view over gardens or countryside. Another common form is that found at 5–13 Queen Anne's Gate, Westminster, of 1770. Here the back and front rooms are divided by a closet and a centrally placed top-lit stair, with the chimney stack to each room placed centrally against the party wall.

Almost invariably after 1700 chimney breasts in London houses were in this position – against the party wall – although in humble houses, or in rear rooms, the stack could be placed in the angle of the wall. Here, if united with the angle stack of the house next door, it formed a useful buttress for the slender party wall or rear façade.

The typical three-room floor – large front room,

Houses in Bedford Square were favoured by the aristocracy when it was built in the late eighteenth century, hence this stylish entrance hall. The staircase in houses of the period was frequently at the rear.

medium rear room and small closet – was, in the early eighteenth century, probably conceived of as an apartment. If the house were divided into reasonably well-to-do lodgings, a floor could be occupied by one tenant; in more squalid tenements an entire family would be squeezed into one room. In houses in single occupation the three rooms of a floor would be occupied by a single member of the family, with a front drawing-room, rear bedroom and the closet serving as a cabinet for the reception of friends or for the more mundane function of a dressing-room.

Dining could take place wherever was convenient by merely opening a gate-leg table; the idea of a fixed dining table standing open in a room used exclusively for dining is of early nineteenth-century origin. Despite the flexibility offered by the gate-leg table, convenience suggested that dining should take place in a limited number of rooms. The kitchen was located in the basement so the ground-floor front would be most convenient for dining, though dining-rooms or dining parlours, when they are referred to in the eighteenth century, were just as likely to be located on the first floor. This was the most impressive floor in the house, with the highest ceilings and therefore the tallest windows.

The locations of other uses were established in a fairly rigid manner by the mid-eighteenth century. If the front basement room was the kitchen, the back room or rooms would be scullery, washroom or, in a large house, even accommodation for servants. With the dining-room in the ground-floor front room, the back room could be a parlour – a room for family life or conversation with friends or for business.

In a more crowded family house, both ground-floor rooms could be parlours with the front being a dining parlour – that is a dining-room doubling as a drawing-room. On the first floor would be the more formal drawing-room. The second and third floors were bedrooms, with children and servants on the top floor or garret.

SERVICES

Services in the terrace house were very limited until the end of the Georgian period. From the beginning of the eighteenth century piped water had been available in the better quarters of London, particularly in the newly developed West End. This came at certain hours on certain days of the week and usually arrived in the front basement room from an elm pipe in the street. The water was stored in a lead cistern from where it could be tapped for cooking or washing or pumped to higher levels of the house. Water was also available from public conduits, set in the street, or could be bought from carts.

Waste water would be discharged into sewers – a

The Vagaries of Fashion

Architectural taste, like most things, is subject to the whims of fashion, although buildings, by their nature, cannot be changed as quickly as clothes. The history of London's architectural styles is complicated by the time-lag between the introduction of the avant-garde and it becoming popular, by which time new ideas have been adopted by the arbiters of taste. These changes in fashion also affect districts. While Mayfair and Hampstead have remained constantly acceptable, the steady growth of London outwards has meant that other areas have gone up, then down, perhaps eventually to rise again. Mr Pooter's Holloway seemed seedy to the next generation; the Victorian respectability of Bayswater declined still further. Between the wars the respectable suburbs of Wimbledon seemed stuffy enough to sneer at; in the 1950s' Balham, 'gateway to the south', was funny, later to be replaced as a joke by Neasden, thanks to the magazine *Private Eye*.

Fashion must be distinguished from newness. The

Philip Hardwick's Euston Arch was built in 1838 and pulled down in 1962 despite an outcry from conservationists. In the 1950 edition of *The Face of London*, Harold Clunn called it 'an absurd-looking Doric archway which was built without reference to the courtyard into which it leads.'

Georgians wanted to live in Georgian houses because they were modern, smart and comfortable, leaving the poor to inhabit the old plastered and gabled houses that only began to seem picturesque in the late nineteenth century. The Victorians found Georgian terraces insufferably boring – 'hole in the wall' architecture – and wanted something more ornamental, leaving once smart districts to become seedy. Curiously, Georgian London did not start to be pulled down until the 1920s, when its virtues were again appreciated by architects and those of

advanced taste. Similarly, Victorian taste began to be laughed at from the moment the old Queen died: the Modern Movement condemned it utterly, but the worst destruction only really began in the 1950s. The Euston Arch, demolished in 1962, would have been preserved a decade later as Victorian architecture had by then returned to popular and intellectual respectability.

The tastes of the intelligentsia must be distinguished from general attitudes. The inter-war suburbs – 'by-pass variegated' and so on – were consistently ridiculed by the architectural establishment and by the avant-garde, yet the 'semi' or, better, the detached suburban house remained the English ideal. Nobody who had his own castle with a front and back garden would dream of living in a dirty old terraced house with the front door opening on to the street. This is still true today. Just as the young and upwardly mobile recolonized shabby late Georgian Islington in the 1960s, the indigenous inhabitants could not wait to get out to Romford.

Wanting to live in an old building is itself a matter of fashion as well as class: some modern Londoners regard a new house as irredeemably vulgar, no matter what it looks like. So Victorian terraces in, say, Herne Hill are respectable once again, while rising house prices and the needs of children are improving the desirability of even the semi-detached suburbs.

Everything comes back in the end. The cycles of fashion can be charted by the foundation of preservation bodies – the Society for the Protection of Ancient Buildings in 1877; the Georgian Group in 1938; the Victorian Society in 1958; the Thirties Society in 1979. And the styles come back for revival. The mid-Victorians liked the medieval, the late Victorians the seventeenth century, the Edwardian architects revived the Georgian and those of the 1920s the Regency. Today, after the trauma of the high rise and systems-built era, new housing looks almost neo-Victorian, with gables and polychromatic brickwork. Meanwhile, the avant-garde are reviving the early Modern Movement and the young are captivated by the 1950s. The wheel of fashion always turns full circle, but faster and faster.

Frontispiece from *Diary of a Nobody*, showing Mr Pooter's 'fashionable' home 'The Laurels', in Holloway.

feature included in most developments from the late seventeenth century onwards, though it was forbidden by law to discharge solid waste into the sewer. Intended mainly for street drainage and often designed with little or no natural current, it was only too easy for sewers to be blocked if made the receptacle of all types of household waste. Solid wastes were generally deposited in a cess pit, located in the yard or even beneath the home, which would be regularly, if not frequently, emptied by night-soil men.

Houses were lit, until the very late eighteenth century, by candles – commonly of tallow but also of beeswax. They were expensive, so light levels in the average Georgian houses were very low. A single candle (together with a coal fire) could be deemed sufficient to light a room in family use. Rooms not in use were usually unlit, candlesticks being carried from room to room.

By the end of the century Argand lamps burning colza oil were in common, if not general, use; they were expensive but a single Argand lamp had the power of ten candles. Gas was not introduced into the interior until well into the nineteenth century for fear of its fumes and explosive power. Heat came from coal throughout the Georgian period in London and was burnt in grates of ever-increasing efficiency.

The terrace house usually had very little garden. Even in late eighteenth-century developments such as that at 5–13 Queen Anne's Gate, or in the more modest Bloomsbury streets of the 1780s, houses were furnished with paved yards only a few feet long. These were functional rather than decorative and intended to contain the water closet (perhaps perched directly over the cess pit), water butt collecting rain from the roof, and storage bins for fuel.

Gardens, when provided, were usually formally planted, with much use made of gravel, but still containing the WC – now dressed up as a small temple at the far corner. Gardens seem to have been provided on a regular basis for the first time in London during the development of the Grosvenor estate in the 1720s. Here, the larger houses – such as those in Grosvenor Square – had generous, well-planted gardens. Apart from aristocratic West End developments, the only other houses regularly provided with large gardens were those on the very edge of London, such as Great Ormond Street, Bloomsbury, of the 1720s, or those suburban developments built along major roads that led through the fields out of London, such as Kensington Road or Kennington Road.

— VILLAS AND SEMI-DETACHED HOUSES: — THE END OF THE TERRACE

The 1790s were in many ways a watershed. Inflation – a consequence of the war with France – took hold in 1793 with a vengeance. For the first time in the eighteenth century, the speculative system had to contend with a new, threatening element. After 1793 prices rose dramatically during the building process, making credit tight, material increasingly expensive, wages unstable and house buyers cautious. This new element of uncertainty rocked the delicate financial balance of the speculative system and sent many builders and architects crashing to bankruptcy.

Among the long-term consequences were improved building efficiency, with an increased speed of construction and the appearance of large-scale developments masterminded by men who undertook the design, financing and construction of whole streets at a time.

OPPOSITE John Nash had planned that Regent's Park should be dotted with villas. This never came about, but in the 1820s he did complete Park Village. Just outside the park to its north-east, it is a unique group of individually designed stucco villas.

LEFT This contemporary print of Park Village East underlines the different designs of all the villas in the development – in contrast to the uniformity of Georgian terraces.

The control exercised by such men as James Burton in Bloomsbury in 1800 and, a little later, John Nash and Thomas Cubitt, meant that developments could go ahead more smoothly and more quickly than in the past.

There was another manifestation of this new concern for time. If the construction of a palace-fronted uniform terrace foundered half-way through, then the development could be a visual as well as financial disaster. If the streets were composed of villas, semi-detached houses, or houses linked by porches or colonnades (all favoured compositional devices after *c.*1795), then abridgement or delay of the initial plan could be accommodated.

Irregularly planned streets, in which the houses displayed movement and variety and were set among the ornament of nature, were calculated to appeal to the sensibility of the late eighteenth-century, with its liking for the picturesque. So, if the rapid London expansion of the 1720s is characterized by the terrace, that of the early nineteenth century is represented by the villa and the semi-detached house.

The moment of change, from the terrace to less formal compositions, is revealed accurately in the work of the architect and developer, Michael Searles. In 1789 he designed a long, uniform terrace in the Old Kent Road, Southwark (220–250 survive, much altered) in which central emphasis was achieved by the subtle use of window arcading and string courses. At roughly the same time (perhaps a little earlier), he designed a small group at Kennington Park Road, Lambeth (114–136),

consisting of tall semi-detached pairs united beneath a shared pediment and linked by single-storey entrance blocks. A trifle later, in *c.*1790, he was trying something similar for a crescent of houses in Gloucester Circus, Greenwich. In 1793, he designed the Paragon, Blackheath, as a series of tall semi-detached pairs of houses, linked by a single-storey colonnaded entrance block. To complete the spectrum of housing types, Searles built, in 1795, a freestanding, stucco villa for himself in the Old Kent Road (now no. 155).

By the 1820s it was usual to collect these different housing types together in a single development. This offered a choice of accommodation and, to the early nineteenth-century eye, created a pleasingly varied urban perspective. For example, Camberwell New Road and the adjacent streets, developed during the 1820s by a number of speculators on 99-year building leases, contain uniform terraces, semi-detached pairs and groups, villas and cottages. More interesting still is the Tredegar estate, off the Mile End Road, Bow, which was developed between 1822 and 1830 as a coherent, self-contained, urban unit catering for different classes of resident. The landlord was Sir Charles Morgan and the inspiration was clearly John Nash's mighty Regent's Park development. Nash combined palace-fronted terraces – for example Cumberland Terrace – with more humble terraces (Albany Street, 1820–5) and villa developments, notably the remarkable Park Villages West and East of 1824–8, made up of an eclectically

LEFT The suburban villas built alongside the main roads out of London in the early nineteenth century were impressive but never as grand as those closer to the centre. By 1932, when this picture was taken, this house on Brixton Hill was in commercial use.

OPPOSITE Tredegar Square was built between 1822 and 1830, just off the Mile End Road in Bow. These terraces, influenced by Nash, were designed for City merchants. Around the square are streets of more modest dwellings for artisans.

designed collection of freestanding cottages and villas.

INTERIORS

The interiors of villas and semi-detached houses were usually much the same as in the terrace house. Some, though, were a storey lower than the average terrace house (two and three instead of three and four storeys above ground level) and these would invariably have their main rooms – drawing-room and dining-room or parlour – at ground level, with main bedrooms on the first floor. This arrangement, though one of expediency, also reflected the early nineteenth-century country house and villa plan which placed main living rooms at ground level, near the garden and the attractions of nature, rather than up on the first floor.

The main contribution to the reorganization of internal planning was made by removing the entrance hall from the main body of the house and placing it in a separate, single-storey structure – as in the linked semis of Searles at Kennington Park Road and the Paragon, Blackheath. This not only allowed both back and front ground-floor rooms to occupy the full width of the main block but also permitted the entrance hall to enjoy special architectural effects like top lighting.

The location in London of these informal developments is revealing: all are to be found on what, in the early nineteenth century, was the edge of the city, or in semi-rural satellite towns or villages. They were places where land was available for low-density development and for generous planning, yet which were not too distant to make speculative development too great a risk. So, if the emergence of the Regency villa and semi-detached housing development was a product of a changing system of speculative building and a reflection of picturesque aesthetic tastes, it was also a result of improved public transport. The omnibus appeared in London in the late eighteenth century and regular services began in 1829. The wealthier population had both the desire and means to escape the cramped tenements of the old city quarters. The terrace, however – so economic of land use – remained the standard expression of central London house building until the appearance of the apartment block in the late nineteenth century.

VICTORIAN HOUSING FOR THE MASSES

At the death of Queen Victoria in 1901 the population of the area administered by the London County Council, as defined at its creation in 1889, was 4,536,000. This was a peak figure as central London was then at its most densely populated. At the beginning of the nineteenth century the population of the same area had been just under one million. It had nearly doubled by 1841. In the course of Victoria's reign, a further two and half million swelled the population of the largest city in the world, exacerbating the problems of housing, transport, sanitation, disease and overcrowding.

Most of the new housing required by this increase in population was supplied by speculative builders. As in the Georgian period, builders erected terraces of houses on land on the fringes of the built-up area. In essence, the Georgian terrace tradition continued right through the nineteenth century, the Victorian house differing from its predecessor only in external treatment.

One such house, and how it worked, is prettily described by George Grossmith in the opening sentences of his 1894 satire on middle-class life, *Diary of a Nobody*. His protagonist, Charles Pooter, announces:

'My dear wife Carrie and I have just been a week in our new house, "The Laurels", Bickfield Terrace, Holloway – a nice six-roomed residence, not counting basement, with a front breakfast-parlour. We have a little front garden; and there is a flight of ten steps up to the front door . . . intimate friends always come to the little side entrance, which saves the servant the trouble of going up to the front door, thereby taking her from her work. We have a nice little back garden which runs down to the railway.'

After the 1870s the basement was largely abandoned, partly because live-in servants were increasingly confined to the wealthiest class and partly because basements were thought to be unhealthy. Red brick began to replace yellow London stock. By the end of the century the typical London house was a two-storey, two-up, two-down terraced house with a small garden and a back extension – often for sanitary facilities – and the street front enlivened by projecting bay windows on one or both floors. The decoration of such modest dwellings became ever more fanciful, with stucco mouldings in sometimes quite elaborate designs, the use of contrasting bricks, multi-coloured tiles in the porches, stained glass on the front doors and other Gothic references. Inside, the ceilings of the main rooms were adorned with moulded plasterwork. The rooms were cluttered with

heavy furniture, often including an upright piano. They were heated by open coal fires and lit by gas, replaced by electricity from the 1890s.

Such houses, of which tens of thousands were built, were middle- and lower-middle-class residences. Pockets of cheaper working-class housing, found in the primarily middle-class suburbs – Hackney, Clapham, Walthamstow and so on – were to provide accommodation for the areas' tradesmen and artisans, but many of the more important builders, like Cubitt, would not build for the lower classes, because such speculative housing failed to bring in an adequate return. There were few variations on the single-family type of house. The back-to-back terrace hardly existed in London and only occasional experiments were made with cottage flats or 'half house flats' in terraces while there was in general no tradition of flat dwelling in England. Also, the new suburbs increasingly depended upon rapid mobility by train or by bus and working men could not afford the fares. Only the Great Eastern Railway took real advantage of the opportunity after 1860 to provide cheap workmen's fares and so encouraged the development of working-class suburbs in north-east London.

Inner suburbs evacuated by the middle classes were occupied by the working class and desperate overcrowding in what were, in essence, Georgian slums was further encouraged by official policies, or the lack of them. Town planning in Victorian London usually meant the elimination of notorious slums with little thought given to where the displaced inhabitants might live. Indeed, a principal argument advanced in favour of costly street improvements was that they removed insanitary and criminal areas. In the 1840s New Oxford Street wiped out the 'rookeries' of St Giles's; in the 1850s Victoria Street was aligned to drive through the slums around Tothill Street.

This process of slum clearance, which merely increased overcrowding in other poor areas, was accelerated by the construction of railways. Huge numbers of houses were demolished by the railway companies, particularly during the 1860s. The building of the Midland Railway into St Pancras alone rendered homeless some 10,000 people in Somers Town and Agar Town, while between 1853 and 1901 well over 76,000

OPPOSITE A late Victorian two-up, two-down terrace house in Beck Road, off Mare Street, Hackney. Basements were now out of fashion, the exterior was of patterned red and grey brick and there were decorative mouldings over the windows.

Public Health

People and their animals create waste, pollution and smells. Until the late nineteenth century, living in London was, quite simply, more dangerous than living in a small hamlet or village. The Bills of Mortality of the seventeenth and eighteenth centuries tell a grim tale of disease and premature death for many of its inhabitants. Overcrowding, smoke pollution, rotting refuse, horse dung, impure and intermittent water supplies, open drains and sewers and a sluggish Thames – these all contributed to what a modern visitor to Shakespeare's or Dr Johnson's or even Dickens's London would find most oppressive and overpowering: the stench. People complained, but only in Victorian times were sensibilities so affected that systematic campaigns to clean up the environment were initiated. As the public health reformer Edwin Chadwick (1800–90) wrote, 'All smell is, if it be intense, immediate acute disease.'

Mass transportation had made possible the Victorian urban sprawl. The increased domestic and industrial use of coal choked the atmosphere and more people meant new demands on water supply and more sewage. Although building regulations of one kind or another had existed since medieval times, alleys and courtyards were packed with dirty human beings and mews often housed people as well as livestock. More attention was paid to the quantity of water than its quality, but even its quantity was limited. The Thames, a major source of domestic water, also served as London's main sewer. The New River Company had supplied water to London from the north, in Hertfordshire, since the seventeenth century, and other rivers (described as 'stinking ditches'), such as the Tyburn and Fleet, were used. Private and public wells also supplied water and many streets and courtyards had standpipes where water was available for a few hours a day. Only a minority of houses had taps, and these operated intermittently. Consequently water-closets, although invented in the sixteenth century, were uncommon. Most privies were connected to private cesspits, often unemptied, whose contents regularly overflowed into the soil and even the houses. Such sewers as existed were several feet high and lined with brick or other porous material. They were cleaned occasionally by teams of men, horses and carts. Much night soil was simply collected in chamber pots and emptied into the pavements and street gutters. It was a paradise for rodents, whose fleas spread plague and typhus, but purgatory for human beings.

In these conditions, epidemics were common. Bubonic plague was the most important epidemic disease from the fourteenth to the seventeenth centuries. Although the Great Plague of 1665 was the last outbreak in London, epidemics of smallpox and typhus continued to occur in London in the eighteenth and nineteenth centuries. The appearance of cholera for the first time in 1832 finally galvanized a movement to prevent epidemic diseases. Edwin Chadwick (a lawyer, not a doctor) spearheaded the early public health movement. He had a passion for statistics and the figures he collected supported his contention that epidemics – 'filth diseases', he called them – were caused by dirt, overcrowding and

rotting matter carried through the atmosphere in the form of 'miasmata'. His solution was cleanliness: clean water pumped into homes under pressure for washing, cooking, drinking and general domestic use, as well as for taking away sewage in glazed, impervious pipes.

Chadwick's ideas, valuable if medically naive, dominated public health thinking in the 1830s and 1840s. The crucial role of sewage-contaminated water in the spread of cholera was demonstrated during the 1848 and 1854 epidemics by Dr John Snow (1813–58). He investigated a local outbreak around Broad Street (now Broadwick Street) in Soho and made a more systematic study of the way in which drinking unfiltered Thames water magnified the chances of dying from cholera. As if the Thames itself were crying out to be cleansed, the Great Stink of the hot, dry summer of 1858 produced a stench so powerful that Parliament had to take a recess.

By then, the Metropolitan Board of Works (created in 1855) had been charged with the responsibility of building a proper drainage and sewage system for London. The Board's chief engineer, Sir Joseph Bazalgette (1819–91), conceived and implemented a grand scheme which, completed in 1875, still serves as the basis of London's system. Rainwater and sewage

RIGHT Public baths were introduced into London in the 1840s, when epidemics and other scourges persuaded the Victorians to promote cleanliness. Among the first were the Metropolitan Baths in Shepherdess Walk, Hoxton, the subject of this painting by J. Borgnis.

LEFT The public disinfector was another Victorian weapon in the fight against epidemics.

were taken in conduits from both sides of the Thames to the edge of the river. Then the conduits flowed into large sewers running underneath the Thames Embankment from west to east, to be discharged into the North Sea (the sewage is now first sent into treatment plants). Intercepting sewers, eighty-three miles of them, had been built, capable of discharging 420 million gallons of waste and water each day. This volume was so much greater than the requirements of his day that his system still serves, although a century of use means that much of it will need to be replaced in the near future. The Embankment itself became a part of Bazalgette's scheme, which thus created above ground a thing of monumental beauty, with the added benefit that the Thames was contained within strict barriers. Visitors walking along the Embankment have no clues that it conceals the main arteries of London's sewage system.

While Bazalgette was concerned primarily with waste disposal, the quality of the water supply was also improved during Victorian times. The private water companies gradually (and sometimes reluctantly) introduced adequate filtration systems and constant water supplies became more common. The fight to nationalize the water companies was successful in 1902 after two decades of resistance from vested interests more concerned with profit than service. The water authorities are soon to return to the private sector, under government regulation.

Housing standards were improved through controls exerted through the Metropolitan Board of Works and, later, the London County Council, although landlords still found ways to erect shoddy building stock, and the continuing mushrooming of the population placed greater pressure on building sites. The atmosphere continued to suffer from industrial and domestic pollution, and the thick smogs of Dickens's day were even worse in the twentieth century: four thousand people died in the fog of December 1952. One outcome of this catastrophe was the Clean Air Act of 1956, which has resulted in the disappearance of the old pea-soup fogs, although lead levels and automobile exhaust fumes have presented new problems.

For all that, London is a far healthier place than it was a century ago. It still reaps benefits from the capital investments made by far-sighted Victorian reformers who recognized the value of pure air, clean water and decent housing in the preservation of health and the prevention of many diseases.

were displaced by railway building. Yet only in 1874 was any requirement imposed on the railway companies to re-house some of those displaced – and these statutory provisions were easily evaded. When Marylebone Station was built at the end of the 1890s, the 1750 people who lived on the site were not provided for.

Serious efforts to erase poor housing and overcrowding were made only when it was appreciated that there was a connection between disease and insanitary living conditions – and that cholera epidemics were not discriminatory in terms of income and class. Charles Booth's *Descriptive Map of London Poverty*, published in 1889, was a symptom of this growing awareness. A study of it provides evidence of when the problem began to be tackled. The areas of the map coloured blue or purple, where the worst poverty existed, are today often covered with working-class tenements. Before that period, experiments in providing better housing for the poor were carried out by independent philanthropic bodies.

In 1844, two years after the publication of Edwin Chadwick's *Report on the Sanitary Condition of the Labouring Population and on the means of Improvement,* the Society for Improving the Condition of the Labouring Classes was founded by a group which included the future Lord Shaftesbury, the great social reformer. In 1848, the society promoted the most important early experiment in providing good sanitary housing: the block of 'Model

Houses for Families' which still stands in Streatham Street off New Oxford Street. It is essentially a block of flats with open galleries overlooking a courtyard. The architect was Henry Roberts, designer of the neo-classical Fishmongers' Hall in the City, who gave the well-proportioned exterior of the building a restrained classical treatment.

Roberts was also the architect of the block of cottage flats that the society erected in Hyde Park for the Great

Exhibition of 1851. The design included a central staircase and open gallery so that the flats, on two floors, were divided by a well-ventilated space. The 'model cottages' attracted attention because they were paid for by Prince Albert and, when the Exhibition was over, they were re-erected in Kennington Park, where they remain occupied today.

Shaftesbury's society built little else. The serious efforts that were made in the following decades to re-house the poor were largely undertaken by philanthropic commercial societies – commercial because it was necessary to provide a dividend, however small, so that the good work could continue. There was the Metropolitan Association for Improving the Dwellings of the Industrious Classes and the Improved Industrial Dwellings Company, founded by Sydney Waterlow in 1863. Waterlow's company, which erected large numbers of standardized blocks with plans based on Roberts's, with open stair-wells and iron balconies, paid a steady five per cent dividend – hence the phrase 'five per cent philanthropy'.

There was also the Peabody Trust, founded by the American, George Peabody, in 1862. Its first block of tenements still stands in Commercial Street, Spitalfields. Designed by Henry Darbishire, it has shaped gables and a degree of classical detailing, but Darbishire's later buildings were remorselessly rectilinear blocks of grey brick in which only the doorcases to the communal staircases were given a degree of architectural treatment. Because the estates were strictly managed, Peabody tenants tended to do well for themselves and they were seldom amongst the poorest. To meet the real need for accommodation for 'the poorest class of self-supporting labourers', the East End Dwellings Company was founded in 1882 to build sanitary, well-ventilated but very basic blocks of tenements. Typical examples survive off Cromer Street in King's Cross, with galleries overlooking internal courtyards and a minimum of architectural treatment in red and yellow bricks given to the exteriors by the architects Davis & Emmanuel.

Nearly all the philanthropic housing blocks looked grim. Because worthy but unimaginative architects were working within very tight economic constraints, the poor may have been given solidity and convenience in such new housing, but never delight. By the 1890s such buildings were being decried. George Gissing wrote that they were 'barracks, in truth; housing for the army of industrialism ...'. One alternative was provided by the cottage estates erected by the Artisans', Labourers' and General Dwellings Company, founded in 1867. These were Shaftesbury Park, Battersea; Queen's Park, Kilburn; and Noel Park, Wood Green. All three consist of terraced houses occasionally enlivened by Gothic bays

and little spires, but the general impression is little different from an ordinary estate of terraced houses run up by a speculative builder.

Only after the Housing of the Working Classes Act in 1890 did local authorities begin to build housing themselves. The initiative was seized by the newly established London County Council, which had replaced the Board of Works and before the end of the century had undertaken two important housing schemes. One was the Boundary Street Estate in Shoreditch which replaced the notorious slum described by Arthur Morrison in *A Child of the Jago*; the other was the Millbank Estate behind the Tate Gallery, built on part of the site of Millbank Prison.

What is still conspicuous and impressive about the early work of the LCC's Housing of the Working Classes Branch, created in 1893, is the attempt to get away from the grim barrack-like appearance of earlier public housing. The blocks were still tenements, five storeys high, but were given a varied and well-detailed external appearance by the team of architects involved. These were young and idealistic disciples of Philip Webb and the Arts and Crafts movement and their designs reflect the sophistication of the late Victorian revival of a vernacular domestic architecture. Red brickwork, tall gables, white-painted sash windows and handsome porches give these estates a humane character that derives from the best middle-class country houses, instead of the grim style associated with working-class charitable housing.

Even so, by the end of Victoria's reign the LCC had scarcely begun to tackle the capital's appalling housing problems and the need to house the poorer members of the huge population in less crowded, and more sanitary conditions. While the more successful members of the working class might be in new terraced houses in the suburbs, or in clean and efficient tenement blocks, most of the poor were still crammed into the urban legacy of the Georgians.

Prince Albert commissioned the design of these model working-class flats for the Great Exhibition of 1851. Re-erected in Kennington Park, they are still lived in today.

The Poor and Homeless

Beggars in the street and people of all ages sleeping rough are present-day reminders that London, in common with many great cities, has acted as a magnet for those who believe it will provide chances denied them elsewhere. They have poured in from the countryside, from the provinces and from abroad, some escaping from famine, tragedy, persecution or disgrace. The city's attitude toward them has fluctuated between callous disregard and concerned philanthropy, but attempts to alleviate their plight have always fallen well short of success.

Plague and disaster, notably the Great Fire of 1666, brought a succession of misfortunes to its more vulnerable population in the Tudor and subsequent periods. Charitable schools and almshouses were set up – such as the Charterhouse in Clerkenwell, founded in 1611. Hospitals began as refuges rather than specifically as centres of medicine (see *Medicine*). Under the evolving Poor Laws various solutions for the plight of the poor were put forward. From the early nineteenth century they were obliged to enter workhouses, organized on a parochial basis, to obtain relief, but at the end of the century non-institutional 'outdoor relief' was introduced, so that the able-bodied poor were again back on the streets. The workhouse was a building which symbolized failure; its grim architecture reinforced the feeling that to be there was a cause for shame, rather than the result of accident or misfortune.

To some extent the poor were submerged, either within institutions or living in desperately overcrowded and insanitary conditions. Relief was charitable and sporadic at best. No one knew the scale of the problem, until the Victorians began to assess it more systematically.

With the coming of the railways, the development of London as an industrial and commercial centre led to a steep and constant rise in the population, inevitably many of them poor and without regular jobs. It has been estimated that the population of London doubled between 1841 and 1881.

Victorian philanthropists distinguished between those they saw as the deserving poor, merely the victims of circumstance, and those they regarded as unworthy of help – the idle, the drunk, the feckless. It was nothing new; in 1536 an Act recognized what it termed the 'impotent poor'.

One symptom of poverty in Victorian London was overcrowding. Families with six or eight children might be crowded in a single room in a slum 'court'. Often these were sublet by people almost as poor. The room was sometimes the place of work as well, for jobbing seamstresses and the like.

The East End saw the worst overcrowding, exacerbated by the docks as a port of entry and provider of casual employment. It was a place of desperate misery – no drains, sanitation or fresh drinking water. Cholera epidemics struck, over and over again. Yet the extent of poverty there was hidden from the comfortable denizens of the West End until, from the 1850s, accounts of the conditions in which their fellow-Londoners lived were produced. Some were moved, more were frightened. Revolutions in Europe were recalled with trepidation.

Publications such as Henry Mayhew's *London Labour and the London Poor* (1851–2, reprinted 1865) or John Hollingshead's *Ragged London in 1861* were appalling exposés; more followed. Mayhew's description of the Asylum for the Houseless Poor of London makes harrowing reading. It was opened as a shelter only in freezing conditions, 'a convocation of squalor and misery – of destitution, degradation and suffering, from all the corners of the earth'. The Asylum 'is at once the beggar's hotel, the tramp's town-house, the outcast's haven of refuge – the last dwelling, indeed, on the road to ruin'. Mayhew comments: 'It is hard for smug-faced respectability to acknowledge these dirt-caked, erring wretches as brothers ...'.

Hollingshead pointed out that areas of Westminster just behind the Abbey (mostly owned by the church) or

A family of six living in one room. Such conditions were all too common in Victorian London, where the building of houses and flats never kept up with the explosion in population.

Marylebone would tell the same tale as the East End or areas south of the Thames – 'a dead level of misery, crime, vice, dirt and rags'. These were the contemporary equivalents of harrowing television documentaries. The church, a major ground landlord in many pockets of poverty, was soon deeply embarrassed by the revelations about its property.

Attempts to legislate for relief, prompted by Select Committees and a Royal Commission in 1884, made scarcely any impact on the problem. The population was rising inexorably. There had been clearance for railways and no rebuilding. The small private landlords who owned most of the available housing had difficulty collecting rent, so the appalling slums fell into worse and worse repair. It was a vicious circle.

Such an enterprise, although widely known, did not begin to touch the real needs of most of the poor. Another idea was that of the settlements and missions run by university men, and soon women, who went to live in the East End and provide centres for education, entertainment and welfare work. An East End vicar, Canon Samuel Barnett, founded Toynbee Hall, on Commercial Street, in 1884. It still carries on its work.

In the last years of the nineteenth century chains of cheap lodging houses were established for single homeless men, the best known being the Rowton Houses, started by Lord Rowton in 1892. The first Rowton House, in Vauxhall, is the only survivor of the chain still serving its original purpose: the occupants of its 430 sought-after beds congregate in daytime in nearby

The Trinity almshouses in the Mile End Road were built in 1695 for retired sea captains and their widows by Trinity House, who operate lighthouses and lifeboats. This was an early charitable effort to relieve poverty. The chapel on the right of the picture (taken in 1910) stands between two parallel terraces of red-brick cottages.

Philanthropic 'model' schemes (see *Victorian housing for the masses*) did not begin to solve the problems faced by those who had casual work or worked seasonally, who had personal misfortune or had been dismissed from their employment. For this enormous hidden section of the iceberg, there was nothing. In 1864, with a sum of money provided by John Ruskin, the 26-year-old Octavia Hill set out not to build model blocks, but to improve the quality of life around the slum alleys. Starting in Marylebone, she worked with women volunteers, ostensibly rent collectors but also trained to offer help and advice. She set up clubs, provided entertainments and offered employment – for example repairing and redecorating her properties. By the beginning of this century she and her workers were looking after the poorest estates of the Church Commissioners, as well as many other properties all over London.

Vauxhall Park and surrounding streets. The Salvation Army, founded by William Booth in 1865, provides low-priced accommodation as well as soup kitchens.

The supply of low-cost housing has never caught up with the demand, and London local authorities are today forced to put people up in inadequate bed-and-breakfast accommodation.

George Orwell, in *Down and Out in Paris and London* (1933), gave a graphic description of life among the homeless in the late 1920s. Little has changed in sixty years, except that there are fewer institutional lodging houses, meaning that more people have to sleep rough. As in Orwell's day, men and women of all ages gather along the Embankment under the arches behind Charing Cross Station and round the South Bank, sleeping in boxes or wrapped in newspaper to keep out the cold – a few hundred yards from the West End's glittering shops and £100-a-night notels.

THE GROWTH OF THE SUBURBS

Despite constant attempts at deterrence by the authorities, London has expanded continuously since Elizabethan times, swallowing up outlying villages and creating the largest built-up area in the world. This process accelerated in the reign of Victoria, encouraged by both an influx of population and the advent of the railways, and reached a peak in the 1920s and 1930s, when huge areas of rural land were covered by low-density estates of detached or semi-detached houses. The peak year was 1934 when over 80,000 dwellings were built – 90 per cent of them by private speculative builders. In the two decades between 1918 and 1938 over 770,000 new houses were constructed – only a fifth of them by local authorities – to accommodate the 1.4 million people who moved to outer London, to the new suburbs. During the same period the population of central London fell by 400,000.

Horse-drawn and then motorized buses, trams and railways all facilitated and encouraged this suburban growth, although the relationship between railway building and suburban development was not always directly symbiotic. The Great Western out of Paddington and the London & North-Western out of Euston were only interested in mainline traffic, not suburban. As a result, London in the later nineteenth century did not expand as much to the north-west as in the other directions. This lopsidedness was eventually corrected by the influence of the trams and the expansion of the electric Underground system. Other railway companies depended on suburban commuter traffic, especially those south of the Thames. The electrification of the complex network of lines that was unified as the Southern Railway in 1923 encouraged extensive suburban growth in South London between the wars, while the extension of the Underground system – united under the London Passenger Transport Board in 1933 – achieved the same result in north London.

What chiefly assured the middle-class nature of suburban growth was the high level of fares. Hampstead Garden Suburb, planned in 1905 by Canon and Henrietta Barnett as an ideal, multi-class community, failed as a social experiment because no working man could afford to travel to work by the new electric Underground line from Golders Green. Working-class people tended to travel shorter distances by bus or tram. It was the extension of the electric tram system by the London County Council shortly before the First World War, that made viable the LCC's working-class 'cottage estates' at Tooting, Norbury, Tottenham and Acton.

THE IDEAL FAMILY HOME

The extraordinary fact about London, which seldom failed to impress foreign visitors, was that the residential areas consisted predominantly of single-family houses. This remained essentially true at least until the Second World War. London's builders were slow to evolve a more dense building type for multiple occupation even though, from the moment they were completed, many Georgian and Victorian terraced houses were subdivided. The family house – in a terrace before the First World War and detached afterwards – remained the middle-class ideal to which the speculative builders responded. London never had a tradition of flat dwelling – as Scottish cities did, for instance. The mansion flats

Wandsworth's growth as a suburb was hastened when tram lines were laid from central London in 1906, allowing cheap commuter transport.

OPPOSITE As the suburbs began to be built up in the early years of this century, nostalgia for the rural past fuelled the Old English revival. A rash of half-timbering broke out: this dream cottage in Ealing, West London, even has a half-timbered garage.

built in central London after the 1880s were initially intended for bachelors, or families who returned to the country at weekends. In the popular mind, flats were associated with working-class charitable housing and very few were built in the new suburbs.

Speculative builders were able to respond to the demand for single-family housing because there was no limit to the expansion of the built-up area other than the availability of transport. Low-density building was encouraged by the relative cheapness of land as well as the suburban 'garden city' ideal that emerged after the turn of the century. London was the reverse of most Continental cities in that its people did not wish to live in a smoky, dense, overcrowded environment if they could avoid it. The ideal was retreat, back to the country and the land – and, if the real country was not feasible, then a 'proper' house with a garden in a leafy suburb was an acceptable substitute. This ideal, first realized by Nash in Regent's Park, was encouraged by the railways, which

Bedford Park, between Acton and Chiswick, was partly designed by Norman Shaw and built between 1875 and 1881 as London's first garden suburb. It was an early example of the influence of the Arts and Crafts movement on English domestic architecture.

converted the City of London from a residential into an exclusively commercial district in a few decades. After the mid-nineteenth century the City businessman could commute from the semi-rural heights of Hampstead or Sydenham. In the twentieth century, with faster trains and motorways, he moved out considerably farther.

Architecturally, the suburbs have usually been conservative, with speculative builders adopting the architectural motifs fashionable with the avant-garde two or more decades earlier. The terraced house remained the standard building type until the early twentieth century, but it was given greater visual interest by the application of the bay window, the gable and a projecting porch. Brickwork could be enlivened by bands of colour and courses laid at an angle. After the 1880s red brick was favoured over yellow London stock. Only in the more affluent suburbs, like Hampstead or Norwood, were detached houses built in large numbers: these sometimes showed the impact of the Gothic revival, which had little influence on the conventional middle-class terrace.

By the end of the century, though, the vernacular motifs of the 'Old English' style and the Arts and Crafts movement were beginning to be adopted. One early example of this was Bedford Park, the suburb north of Turnham Green developed by Jonathan Carr after 1875. This was designed to appeal to couples with advanced tastes who were tired of the standard London terrace. Carr's architects were pioneers in the late Victorian 'vernacular revival': first Edward Godwin and then Norman Shaw, whose influence on the appearance of the suburb was paramount. Shaw and his followers designed both detached and terraced houses of red brick, which had the Dutch gables and white-painted classical wood details of the urban Queen Anne style combined with the half-timberwork and cottage motifs associated with his rural Old English style, evolved to replace the stiffness of secular Gothic.

Less urban, more countrified suburban developments were encouraged after the turn of the century by the garden city movement. The ideal of low-density new satellite towns, with residential areas strictly separated from industrial zones, was proposed in Ebenezer Howard's book of 1898, *Tomorrow: A Peaceful Path to Real Reform*. The first attempt to realize this ideal was made in the Hertfordshire town of Letchworth, north of London, after 1903. Soon after came Hampstead Garden Suburb, in the wake of the extension of the electric tube from Hampstead to Golders Green, which opened in 1907. The suburb had a picturesque, winding plan by Parker & Unwin and its buildings, with the exception of those in the centre by Lutyens, were in a semi-rural, cottagey style. Brentham, in Ealing, is a similar planned suburb. By 1914 the style of roughcast gables, leaded-

The Underground

The Underground railway system is the oldest and one of the most complex in the world. Its importance lies both in the effect it has had on the growth and development of London and in the quality of architecture and design associated with it.

The oldest part of the system is the former Metropolitan Railway from Paddington to Farringdon Street. Mostly a brick-lined cutting built by 'cut and cover' methods under Marylebone Road, it opened in 1863. This line became part of the Inner Circle which was eventually completed through the City in 1884. The same company constructed a long tentacle out into Buckinghamshire which, in the twentieth century, generated the suburban growth of 'Metroland'.

However, relief of central London's traffic congestion had to await the advent of electric traction. This came in 1890, with the City & South London Railway – the first electric Underground in the world – from Stockwell to King William Street, now part of the City branch of the Northern Line. This was followed by further 'tubes', steel-lined narrow tunnels burrowing through the London clay. The Central London Railway – the 'two-penny tube' – was opened in 1900. The Piccadilly, Bakerloo and Northern – unified as Underground Electric Railways of London by the Chicago tycoon Charles Yerkes – followed during the reign of Edward VII. Unification increased in 1933 with the creation of the London Passenger Transport Board. The tube lines were already being extended above ground beyond the built-up area, to Edgware and Cockfosters, where they encouraged suburban development. Further expansion followed, with new lines in Middlesex and Essex. By 1948 the Underground map of London was almost as it is today, apart from the more recent Victoria and Jubilee Lines. Few lines run far south of the Thames, for the Southern Railway was resolute in keeping out competition.

The first stations of real architectural interest are those designed by Leslie Green for the Yerkes lines. These standardized buildings were faced in ruby-red tiles and, below ground, were decorated with patterns of coloured tiles and details touched by *art nouveau*. Green's work has become characteristic of central London. The typical suburban Underground station is a product of the inter-war years; in the 1920s the architect Charles Holden was commissioned to design the new stations on the extension of the Northern Line to Morden. But Holden's finest work is in the Middlesex suburbs where he designed stations on the extensions of the Piccadilly Line

The Northern Line to Golders Green opened in 1907. This 1908 poster portrays the idyllic suburban life that the Underground could make possible.

in brick and concrete, in a manner strongly influenced by Continental modernism. Stations like Arnos Grove, Southgate, Turnpike Lane and Osterley are among the best examples of British architecture of the 1930s.

The handsome, sans-serif lettering in the 'bull's eye' symbol was commissioned as early as 1915 from Edward Johnston, and the stations were also enlivened with posters designed by first-class artists, notably E. McKnight Kauffer, many of which can be seen at the London Transport Museum in Covent Garden.

From the 1960s the Underground, under the wing of the Greater London Council, suffered from lack of investment, bad management and increasing overcrowding. When the GLC was abolished it was administered by a public corporation. A disastrous fire at King's Cross in 1987 prompted improvements and there are plans for new lines to relieve overcrowding.

light windows and touches of half-timber had also been taken up by the speculative builders.

BETWEEN THE WARS

The typical house of the inter-war years was detached or, to be slightly more economical, semi-detached. This change in the conventional practice of the speculative builder after the First World War was partly a result of the garden city movement and the ideal of the house in the country. The terrace became associated with the Victorian Age, with the dark, dirty, repressive past. The young middle-class couples, who suddenly found themselves able to buy a house for the first time, wanted something clean, modern, countrified and picturesque. Above all, it had to be their own, an individual house with a garden.

The typical suburban house of the inter-war years was built in red brick, often with the gable and parts of the walls covered in roughcast. The principal windows would be in projecting bays or even bows on two floors and the often decorative front door – perhaps with stained glass – would be approached through a brick arch. The gable would have barge-boards and might be embellished with a touch of half timber. Such designs were highly conservative, borrowing their motifs from progressive late Victorian domestic architecture; from the work of Norman Shaw and, above all, from the style of C. F. A. Voysey, who created a powerful image for house and home.

Caricatured by Osbert Lancaster as 'By-Pass Variegated' or 'Wimbledon Transitional', such houses were seldom the work of architects and, indeed, were universally despised by the architectural profession and press, which were also worried about suburban 'sprawl' and ribbon development along the new arterial roads. But this did not affect the popularity of these houses. The speculative builders simply found that more austere and tasteful designs did not sell as well, while the demand for 'ultra-modern' houses, with white walls and flat roofs, was almost non-existent in the ordinary middle-class suburbs. The only palpable influence of the Modern Movement was the use of horizontally proportioned metal windows with curved wrap-around corners on the projecting bays. Variations included the full-blooded essays in elaborately half-timbered 'stockbrokers' Tudor', usually found in the wealthy outer suburbs.

A TYPICAL OUTER SUBURB

Many outer suburbs conform to an immediately recognizable pattern. In the middle stands the remnant of the old village: some Georgian buildings, an old inn and an unrestored church, perhaps. The new centre is the wide High Street: long ranges of shops, some in Tudor or Georgian style. There is a large public house, either half-timbered or in the streamlined Georgian favoured for roadhouses. Until recently the most conspicuous building would have been the great brick bulk of the cinema with its flashy façade. Some suburban cinemas were of the 'atmospheric' sort, decorated on an exotic theme like the Spanish City (at Northfields); most, however, were jazzy, modernistic creations with which, in London, the American Art Deco style is most associated. A further gesture of modernity amidst the Tudor gables is the Underground station, perhaps designed by Charles Holden. The new church, a few streets away, would be a smooth essay in modernistic Gothic; a reinterpretation of Albi Cathedral in concrete and brick – like St Saviour's, Eltham; or a conspicuous tribute to the influence of German and Swedish modernism, like Holy Cross, Greenford – an extraordinary development of a timber Middlesex barn by Albert Richardson.

The suburbs of the 1920s and 1930s are now contained by the Green Belt. Suburban streets still end in fields where building suddenly stopped in 1939. Even as the twenty-first century draws near, the suburban house in its garden shows no sign of falling from favour as the conventional English ideal of a place to live.

LEFT These spacious villas in Hampstead Garden Suburb, begun in the years leading up to the First World War, radiate the calm and comfort that the garden suburbs were trying to foster.

OPPOSITE The GLC's Lambeth Walk Estate is a typical public project of the 1960s, with attempts made to relieve the tedium of the façade with chunky balconies and varying shaped windows. Out of the picture are three high-rise towers: the view was photographed from one of them.

PUBLIC HOUSING

At the beginning of the twentieth century, London at last had a metropolitan authority willing to undertake slum clearance schemes and build public housing. During the reign of Edward VII, the recently formed London County Council maintained the policy of replacing slum properties with the type of tenement

Acton. These estates have village-like plans and are similar in character to the idealistic private development at Hampstead Garden Suburb.

The LCC was not the only body building public housing. The East End Dwellings Company continued to erect its grim 'model' blocks until 1911. But a

The Bourne Estate, off Clerkenwell Road in Holborn, was one of the early LCC tenement blocks replacing former slums. Built in the first decade of this century, its plain lines represent a reaction against extravagant Victorian decoration.

blocks first built in the 1890s at Boundary Street and Millbank. Under the leadership of W. E. Riley, the LCC Architects' Department continued to design blocks of red-brick flats with a humane, domestic character deriving from late Victorian domestic architecture and the Arts and Crafts movement. Good examples are the Webber Row estate in Waterloo Road and the Caledonian Estate in Caledonian Road. The Bourne Estate in Holborn shows the contemporary classical influence beginning to change the direction of English architecture.

Slum clearance schemes in central London were not, however, regarded as the real answer to the over-crowded conditions of the capital. The influence of garden city theories, combined with the essentially anti-urban culture of the Arts and Crafts movement, en-couraged policies of moving working-class people to cleaner suburban locations, where the LCC built 'cottage estates' with groups of low-rise terraces designed in a careful vernacular manner. These were laid out at Totterdown Fields in Tooting, White Hart Lane in Tottenham, in Norbury and at Old Oak Common near

significant change had occurred: good architects were at long last becoming interested in housing and planning. This can be seen in the redevelopment of the Duchy of Cornwall estate in Kennington, where the architects appointed, Adshead and Ramsay, were in the vanguard of the classical revival. The new buildings were designed in the elegant style of the Regency but what was most remarkable about the estate was that the architects revived the Georgian square and terrace and that the development mostly consisted of two-storey houses on a modest, neighbourly scale. In many ways, this slum clearance scheme, completed immediately before the First World War, was among the most successful pieces of urban public housing carried out this century in London. Unfortunately, the lessons it provided were not well learnt.

In 1919 the first state subsidies for housing were introduced by the prime minister, David Lloyd George, who had campaigned for the election that year with the slogan 'Homes Fit for Heroes'. Under the Housing & Town Planning Act, some 35,000 new houses were built in London, largely by local authorities and the LCC until the subsidies began to dry up in 1923 and private developments came back into the ascendant. Most of the LCC's energies and money went into continuing the cottage estates begun before 1914 with groups of houses in a similar, if simplified, vernacular style. Examples include the Downham estate in south-east London, a complete garden suburb opened in 1925, and the Becontree estate at Dagenham, described at the time as the largest municipal housing estate in the world. A particularly sympathetic development is the cottage estate at Roehampton, opened in 1921, with its two-storey vernacular Georgian houses of soft pink brick with pantiled roofs.

Immediately after the First World War, high land values had discouraged the resumption of building in central London but after the 1929–31 slump the LCC began to concentrate on slum clearance schemes again. The typical LCC urban estate of the inter-war years consisted of formal blocks of flats of brick and concrete construction arranged around large courtyards or lawns. Examples can be found all over London. Access to flats was by long open concrete balconies but towards the street these estates presented elegant neo-Georgian façades with four or five storeys of repetitive sash windows and perhaps another storey in the pitched tiled roof, recessed above the brick elevations. Such a design was typical of most of the 30,000 flats built by the LCC between the wars, although towards the end of the 1930s they were sometimes given a slightly more modernistic treatment.

In terms of amenities, these flats were a great improvement on the conditions their residents formerly had to endure. They had indoor flush toilets, hot and cold running water and the latest kitchen appliances. Yet already some of the tenants were missing the neighbourliness and the street life that went with their old, dilapidated houses. In the terraces, neighbours were ever-present. You met them every time you left the house, you could look out of the window and see what they were doing. Flats encouraged a fortress mentality. If the planners thought it was simply a question of getting used to it, they were wrong. The hostility to flat-dwelling persisted and contributed to the failure of many later housing schemes.

UTOPIAN DREAMS

The Modern Movement, with its utopian social vision of transforming society through a new functional architecture, had little impact on public housing in London before the Second World War. Its most impressive achievement was Kensal House, a development of working-class flats promoted by the Gas, Light & Coke Co. as a social experiment and built on the site of a disused gasholder in 1936. Designed by a team of architects led by E. Maxwell Fry and built of reinforced concrete and steel, the development included community spaces and a school. Responding to the curves of the site, the light and airy flat-roofed buildings broke away from the standard block plan and the estate was in marked contrast to, say, the ranks of grim modernistic tenement blocks designed by John Burnet, Tait & Lorne in Amhurst Road, Hackney, at about the same time.

The whole nature of public housing in London was transformed by the Second World War. Not only was London's housing stock seriously diminished by bombing – the LCC alone suffered 89,000 homes damaged and 2500 totally destroyed out of a total of 98,000 – but the utopian, egalitarian spirit engendered by the war encouraged a belief in comprehensive redevelopment and sweeping away the past. The County of London Plan by Patrick Abercrombie envisaged both the rebuilding of entire working-class districts and the decanting of much of London's population to new 'satellite' towns – an idea which inspired the post-war new towns like Stevenage, Harlow and Crawley. Immediate action after the war was hindered by shortages of money and materials, but many homeless were housed in pre-fabricated bungalows – 'pre-fabs' – while new blocks of flats made more use of steel and concrete construction. Ironically many Londoners preferred the pre-fabs to the flats and new towns. They were on a human scale and preserved many elements of their old terraced streets. 'New town blues' became a familiar phenomenon, as exiled Londoners failed to adjust to being uprooted from their old communities.

The post-war triumph of the Modern Movement, with its belief in scientific planning and industrial methods, was confirmed by the results of two important competitions for housing schemes. One, for the Churchill Gardens estate in Pimlico held in 1946, was won by Powell & Moya with a design for a mixture of low and high horizontal blocks strongly influenced by pre-war Swedish and German modernism. The second, held in 1952, was for Golden Lane north of the City of London and was won by Chamberlin, Powell & Bon with a design including a sixteen-storey tower strongly influenced by the work of Le Corbusier. Other developments which represented the realization of pre-war Modern Movement ideas were the three estates in Finsbury designed by a team of architects led by Berthold Lubetkin: Holford Square, Spa Green and Priory Green.

The development with the most influence on the future course of public housing in London was the Alton Estate at Roehampton built by the LCC. On the Alton East Estate, opened in 1954, a mixed development

of flats and maisonettes, it was attempted to realize the vision of Le Corbusier with 'point blocks' surrounded with grass. At Alton West, opened in 1959, the tall point block was supplemented by the eleven-storey slab block, inspired by Le Corbusier's *Unité d'Habitation* near Marseilles. The reinforced concrete slab block, seldom in a parkland setting, became the standard local authority housing type in the 1960s and the social problems the design generated were soon compounded by the structural failings of prefabricated construction.

The Alton West estate in Roehampton, opened in 1959, pioneered the reinforced concrete slab block that became the standard material for new public housing in London in the 1960s.

A SOCIAL DISASTER

The housing experiments of the 1960s have left London with a huge stock of inadequate and socially disastrous council housing. A principal reason for building high and for ruthless standardization was the pressure put on local authorities by successive governments to use system building methods. Even so, it is hard to understand why local authorities and architects promoted high-rise blocks for so long when they remained more expensive to build than low-rise housing and when their unpopularity soon became apparent. Living high was only tolerable if the lifts functioned. Lobbies and walkways became centres of crime and the inadequate construction of the buildings themselves produced either condensation or huge heating bills. Many estates soon became neglected and vandalized. Some public housing, however, did not fall into the mechanistic Corbusian trap. The Holloway Estate, built by the Corporation of London in the 1960s to the designs of McMorran & Whitby, is a model of sanity, with low-rise brick buildings in a loose Georgian manner arranged around protected courtyards. But such conservative schemes never received accolades in the architectural journals.

The gas explosion at Ronan Point in 1968, which brought down much of the prefabricated structure of that tower block, effectively brought the high-rise era to an end. In fact, a different approach was already being explored in the Lillington Gardens estate in Westminster by Darbourne & Darke, the first phase of which opened that same year. Here, picturesquely irregular red brick flats with individual balconies are disposed around intimate gardens. This estate became a model for local authority housing estates in the 1970s, especially after Nicholas Taylor's book of 1973, *The Village in the City*, demonstrated that low-rise housing could house more people more satisfactorily than high-rise housing. The 1970s also saw a policy of rehabilitation rather than redevelopment by local authorities, while the 1980s has seen the demolition or major modification of many of the worst housing estates of the 1960s, as well as the virtual cessation of new council house building. Many of the better early twentieth-century council houses have been sold to their former tenants, resulting in the alteration of their considered architectural appearance by 'home improvement'.

HOMES OF THE FAMOUS

City dwellers are perpetually in motion. London residents move to keep up with fashion and their own changing fortunes. Tracing a notable citizen's odyssey from house to house therefore reveals much about both the person and the city. It can often be traced through the blue plaques placed on many houses and sites in London once occupied by well-known people – a scheme initiated by the Royal Society of Arts in 1867 and carried on since by the LCC, the GLC and English Heritage.

SAMUEL PEPYS, the seventeenth-century diarist and archetypal Londoner, was born in 1633 in the old City, then the main residential area. His father, a tailor, had a house in Salisbury Court, off Fleet Street. As a naval administrator he lived and worked at Seething Lane by Tower Hill, then moved to his grandest address in 1673 when, on being made Secretary of the Admiralty, he was entitled to an official residence in Cannon Row, at the heart of the political enclave of Westminster. After six weeks in the Tower, suspected of espionage, he moved in succession to two addresses in Buckingham Street, off the Strand, strategically sited between City and Court. When fashionable London turned against him he moved to a friend's house in Clapham – then a part of the countryside – where he died.

Nearly a century later SAMUEL JOHNSON spent most of his life near Fleet Street, as befitted a man of letters. His house at 17 Gough Square, where he worked on his dictionary, is open as a museum. His dictionary made him no money, so he moved to cheaper premises nearby, at Middle Temple Lane, then to a house in another courtyard off Fleet Street, now called Johnson's Court, though not named after him. In 1776 he moved to nearby Bolt Court, where he died in 1784.

CHARLES DICKENS, the son of a clerk, grew up at various unimposing addresses in north London, including Camden Town and Highgate. When he got a job in Fleet Street he took lodgings at Furnival's Inn in High Holborn, now the headquarters of the Prudential Assurance company. By 1837 his stories were gaining success and he could afford to move further from his low-life characters – to Bloomsbury and 48 Doughty Street, then a wide and elegant avenue with gates and porters at either end. (The house is open to visitors.) By 1839 he had fathered two daughters and the family moved to a larger house in Marylebone, facing Regent's Park, then back to Bloomsbury to a bigger house still in Tavistock Square.

The addresses of WILLIAM MAKEPEACE THACKERAY similarly speak of success. From 1846 to 1853 he lived quietly in Young Street, off Kensington High Street, then moved to 36 Onslow Square. With fashionable Kensington for inspiration, he wrote popular novels such as *Vanity Fair*, *Pendennis* and *Henry Esmond*. The profits funded the dream mansion that Frederick Herring built for him at 2 Palace Green, at the bottom of Kensington Palace Gardens, the smartest road in town. Sadly he was only to enjoy it for a year: he died in 1863 at the age of 52.

When GEORGE BERNARD SHAW arrived from Dublin in 1876, aged 20, he joined his mother and sister in a semi-detached house at 13 Victoria Grove (now Netherton Grove), an unfashionable cul-de-sac off Fulham Road. For a while he had rooms in Osnaburgh Street, off

The house in Bolt Court, off Fleet Street, where Dr Samuel Johnson lived for eight years before dying there in 1784. This nineteenth-century impression by Charles Tomkins shows a corpulent Dr Johnson about to return home.

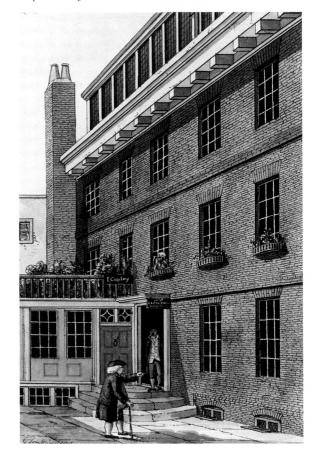

Euston Road, conveniently opposite an early meeting place of the Fabian Society. In 1887, the family moved into part of a white stucco house at 29 Fitzroy Square, a good literary address for a striving critic. In 1898, when his plays were becoming popular, he moved into a suitable flat in the theatre district, at 10 Adelphi Terrace, now demolished. (Other residents of the building included J.M.BARRIE and THOMAS HARDY.) In 1917, as well as their main house in Hertfordshire, the Shaws acquired a new London base at Whitehall Court, where H.G.WELLS had lived earlier. Shaw kept the flat until 1945, five years before his death.

VIRGINIA WOOLF lived at Shaw's old Fitzroy Square house from 1907 to 1911 – one of her several Bloomsbury addresses. Earlier she and her brother, Adrian Stephen, and sister, Vanessa Bell, had formed the nucleus of the 'Bloomsbury Set', centred on their house in Gordon Square. In 1915 Virginia and her husband Leonard Woolf moved to Hogarth House in Richmond, where they established the Hogarth Press. They returned to Bloomsbury in 1924.

GEORGE ORWELL achieved recognition but never material success and that is reflected in his London addresses. In the mid-1930s he lived above the bookshop where he worked in South End Road, Hampstead and in 1935 he shared a flat with two other writers at 50 Lawford Road in Kentish Town, before going to fight in the Spanish Civil War. During the Second World War he had several addresses. In 1940 he was at Dorset Chambers, Chagford Street, near Baker Street; in 1941 at Langford Court, Abbey Road, St John's Wood; in 1942 at 10 Mortimer Crescent in Kilburn. After the war he moved with his wife and adopted son to a flat at 27 Canonbury Square, then less fashionable than it was later to become. (The young EVELYN WAUGH had lived there twenty years earlier.) Orwell's wife died in 1945 and in 1947 he moved to the Scottish island of Jura.

ARTISTIC ENCLAVES

Artists and writers tend more than most to congregate in colonies. Hampstead has usually been able to muster a good cross-section of the intelligentsia. JOHN GALSWORTHY lived at Grove Lodge, Hampstead Grove; D.H.LAWRENCE at 1 Byron Villas, in the Vale of Health; and JOHN KEATS at Wentworth Place, now called Keats Grove, where his house is open to the public. Later SIGMUND FREUD came to 20 Maresfield Gardens when he fled from Nazi-dominated Vienna in 1938. He died a year later. The painter JOHN CONSTABLE liked Hampstead, too. Coming to London from Suffolk in 1817, aged 41, he and his wife Maria first lived in Bloomsbury but then moved to several Hampstead addresses before settling at 40 Well Walk. For the last five years of his life, after his wife had died, he lived above his studio at 76 Charlotte Street.

Constable was rare among successful painters in that he comparatively seldom turned his hand to portraits. Those who do, like to live near their patrons. In the eighteenth century Leicester Square was a much prized position, near the aristocracy who hovered around the Hanoverian court at St James's. JOSHUA REYNOLDS lived at 46 Leicester Square for thirty-two years, from 1760 to 1792. Here he made his reputation and fortune painting the leaders of society in his elegant salon, becoming the first President of the Royal Academy. WILLIAM HOGARTH lived at 30 Leicester Square from 1733 until

Keats House in Keats Grove, Hampstead, where the poet John Keats lived from December 1818 to September 1820, and where he wrote much of his finest work. Built in 1816 as a pair of semi-detached houses, it has been converted into a single unit and is open as a museum of the poet's short life.

The painter William Hogarth lived at 30 Leicester Square, in its south-east corner, from 1733 until 1764. By 1801, the date of this print, the house had become the Hotel de la Sablionère, possibly the first public restaurant in Soho.

his death in 1764, while he worked on his vicious and powerful series *The Rake's Progress*. (The Chiswick house was his country estate.) THOMAS GAINSBOROUGH lived even nearer the court at 82 Pall Mall, where he transformed duchesses and dukes into romantic figures on canvas. Marylebone was only slightly less lucrative for portraitists: before the doctors took over Harley Street in the 1840s, the Scottish painter ALLAN RAMSAY lived at number 67.

Young, struggling artists have always outnumbered established ones. One of them, VINCENT VAN GOGH, came to London in 1873, aged twenty. He took cheap rooms at 87 Hackford Road, Brixton and walked three miles every day to his job at a Covent Garden art gallery. One story is that he left after a year when the landlady made advances, being more interested in her daughter. He returned to France, but in 1876 moved back across the Channel briefly and stayed at 160 Twickenham Road. The Impressionist CAMILLE PISSARRO also sojourned for a while in South London, as his paintings of the Norwood area bear witness. His son LUCIEN, an artist too, lived at The Brook, Stamford Brook Road, from 1900 until his death in 1944.

The best-known enclave of artists had more humble beginnings. Cheyne Walk was a long, workaday riverside street in Chelsea, until development smartened it up and the new embankment road distanced it from the water. When in 1837 the moderately affluent Scottish historian and philosopher THOMAS CARLYLE came to live at 24 Cheyne Row, just behind Cheyne Walk, he wrote; 'Chelsea is unfashionable ... hence the numerous old houses in it, at once cheap and excellent!' It was soon to change.

Cheyne Walk is where JAMES ABBOTT MCNEIL WHISTLER lived in his early Chelsea days, including nos 92 and 96 in the 1860s. He called Chelsea 'The wonderful village' and lived at ten different addresses over the next forty-one years, until his death in 1903. The refined American made a huge impression on the modest local painter WALTER GREAVES, whose father was a ferryman and who lived at no. 104. Whistler thought the Greaves household 'a sort of Peggotty family' and told them: 'You are the pride of one end of the row and I am the pride of the other'. Greaves's end was later home to poet and historian HILAIRE BELLOC at no. 104 in 1900–5, to painter PHILIP WILSON STEER at no. 109 in 1898–1942 and to J.M.W. TURNER at no. 119 when, as an old man, he came here incognito, as Mr Booth, to watch storms over the river.

The end that Whistler claimed was by far the smarter one, with its glorious and grand Queen Anne and Georgian houses. In 1862 DANTE GABRIEL ROSSETTI moved into no. 16 with his friends ALGERNON SWINBURNE and GEORGE MEREDITH – and his zoo, complete with screeching parrots and armadillo. Chelsea was soon the centre of London's bohemian life. In Tite Street, AUGUSTUS JOHN's studio was at no. 33 and JOHN SINGER SARGENT's at no. 31, while Whistler was forced to leave after just a few months, financially crippled by the libel case against John Ruskin. OSCAR WILDE did little better at no. 16 (now 34), where he lived from his marriage in 1884 until his arrest in 1895 at the Cadogan Hotel, 21 Pont Street (where the actress LILLIE LANGTRY lived.)

In 1855, FREDERICK, LORD LEIGHTON made his reputation at the age of 25 where Queen Victoria bought his painting *Cimabue's Madonna*. A decade later he could build his

Leighton House in Holland Park Road was built in 1866 to the designs of its owner, the artist Lord Leighton (1830–96). Inside and outside it is packed with elaborate detailing in the Victorian taste. It is today an art gallery and museum.

exotic Italianate mansion at 12 Holland Park Road, then rural and leafy. The immediate area quickly became an enclave of wealthy aesthetes. Each could build, or live in, the house of their choice on virgin land. Philip Webb designed VAL PRINSEP's studio, next door to Leighton. WILLIAM HOLMAN HUNT, at the forefront of the Pre-Raphaelite movement, lived at 18 Melbury Road while another Victorian painter, GEORGE FREDERICK WATTS lived at no. 6. The Queen Anne Movement pioneer Norman Shaw designed no. 8, where MARCUS STONE lived and illustrated Dickens's novels.

PALACES OF POWER

Pragmatic rather than aesthetic motives dictate where politicians live. They like to be handy for Westminster and most aspire to the handiest address of all, 10 Downing Street (see *A centre of government*). Not all prime ministers, though, use it as their main London residence. HAROLD WILSON stayed at his home in Lord North Street when unexpectedly returned to office in 1974. BRENDAN BRACKEN was among other leading political figures to inhabit that elegant street. LORD PALMERSTON, twice Prime Minister in the 1850s, was born in style at 20 Queen Anne's Gate, overlooking St James's Park. Later he was at 4 Carlton Gardens and 94 Piccadilly, now the Naval and Military Club. WILLIAM GLADSTONE, too, liked the air of St James's. He lived at 11 Carlton House Terrace from 1856 to 1875, except while Prime Minister from 1868 to 1874. Then he moved to 73 Harley Street but darted back to Downing Street to be Prime Minister another three times. BENJAMIN DISRAELI's addresses tell a different story. Born at 22 Theobalds Road into a Jewish family, he was baptized in 1817, aged 13, and went on to become Prime Minister twice, ending his years at the grand Mayfair address of 19 Curzon Street.

A more recent former Prime Minister, EDWARD HEATH, used to live in Albany, the ultimate gentleman's address. The two blocks of chambers set back from Piccadilly have been home to GLADSTONE, MACAULAY, THOMAS BEECHAM, GRAHAM GREENE and, when they opened to women, EDITH EVANS. For residents, their greatest assets are peace and privacy, fiercely upheld by strict rules of entry: no estate agents, journalists, tradesmen, small children or animals, and nobody is allowed to run, whistle or take photographs in the corridors. It is the perfect bachelor address.

MUSICAL ADDRESSES

Patronage rather than privacy was what attracted GEORGE FRIDERIC HANDEL to London when his patron, the Elector of Hanover, became George I. Funded by a royal pension, 24 Brook Street, Mayfair, was his home for thirty years, until his death in 1759.

Other musicians and composers lived in less grand conditions. When MOZART's father was exhibiting his eight-year-old son for the second time in London, in 1764–5, he took rooms at the none-too-smart but economic 20 Frith Street, Soho, while advertising for Londoners to come and test his son 'by giving him anything to play at Sight, or any Music without Bass, which he will write upon the Spot'.

A century later, East End music hall was flourishing. Its queen was MARIE LLOYD, born in relative poverty at 49 Graham Road, Dalston. At the turn of the century it became briefly fashionable for music-hall stars to live around Brixton, Stockwell and Lambeth, in South London. The comedian DAN LENO lived at 56 Akerman Road, east of Brixton Road. CHARLIE CHAPLIN was born to a music-hall family in South London, at one time living with his father, his father's mistress and their child in two rooms at 287 Kennington Road. LILIAN BAYLIS and EMMA CONS, who founded the Old Vic music hall, lived near it at 6 Morton Place, and Miss Baylis also had a house at 27 Stockwell Park Road.

Many of London's residents who exercised the most profound long-term influence came to the city because it seemed more hospitable to unorthodox ideas than other European capitals. KARL MARX arrived in 1849 and died in London in 1883. From 1851 to 1856 he lived with his wife, maid and five children in two squalid rooms at 28 Dean Street, Soho, then 'one of the worst, therefore also the cheapest, quarters of London' – but handy for the reading room of the British Museum, where he wrote *Das Kapital*. Later he moved to two addresses in more salubrious Chalk Farm – 9 Grafton Terrace and 1 Maitland Park Road. Here he was closer to his comrade FRIEDRICH ENGELS, who lived from 1870 to 1894 on Primrose Hill, at 121 Regent's Park Road.

A PLACE TO WORK

THE GUILDS

A city provides many opportunities to make a living. As a trading centre, medieval London attracted merchants dealing in the main commodities of the time – foodstuffs, precious metals, clothing and wine. As a population centre, it required craftsmen and shopkeepers to serve its inhabitants' needs and wants. But the market for goods and services was limited and starvation was the potential price of failure to measure up to what today would be regarded as fair competition.

In this economic and social context, the trade guilds began to establish themselves in London and other cities in the late twelfth century. Their prime function was to control and protect their particular trade or calling.

and masses said for their souls. There were few other organized groups in the Middle Ages not directly answerable to the church or the court, which was why entry into them was so coveted and restricted. They were (and remain) the only citizens entitled to elect the Lord Mayor and sheriffs – who played an important role in governing the medieval city, although today their function is ceremonial. The power of the guilds grew, often enhanced by royal charters of incorporation and occasionally by Acts of Parliament. By the middle of the fourteenth century, according to some estimates, about a quarter of those working in the City were guild members.

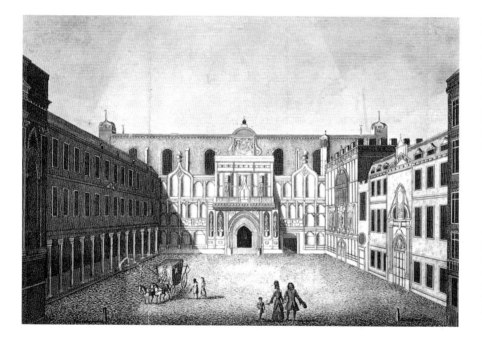

LEFT The Guildhall in 1720. Originally the headquarters of a single guild – possibly the Knighten Guild, primarily a religious organization – it became the centre of the City's government by virtue of its size and was rebuilt specifically for that purpose in 1411.

OPPOSITE The arms of the Clothworkers, topped by a sheep, their primary raw material. The guild, one of the twelve senior companies, was formed through a merger in 1528. Samuel Pepys was master of it in 1677–8.

They exercised strict supervision of the apprentice system, which was usually the only way of entering their 'misteries'. They enforced quality control and agitated for import restrictions to ward off competition. Occasionally they would take the law into their own hands: fights would break out between apprentices from different guilds, or between guild members and men from outside the city who threatened their markets.

This self-protective instinct vested the guilds with a strong sense of community. They became closely knit social institutions. They met to break bread and to worship together. They helped their sick and impoverished fellows and saw that their dead had a decent burial

With the Reformation the guilds became secularized. An expanding economy, together with legislation to protect artisans, meant that by the end of the eighteenth century their ancient legal functions, although technically extant, had fallen into disuse. Today the guilds flourish in the City, although comparatively few have anything to do with the trade they once embraced, but are simply social, charitable fraternities, similar to masonic lodges. Membership of them carries great prestige but seldom any more tangible benefit. There are 102, of which 98 can legitimately be called livery companies, having been granted the right to wear distinctive livery on ceremonial occasions. All liverymen automatically receive the Freedom of the City, originally simply a permit to work in it. (This is not the same as the Honorary Freedom of the City, an honour awarded sparingly to distinguished visitors and outstanding public servants.)

All the guilds used to have their own halls but today there are only 37 guild halls in the City – and most of these have been rebuilt or relocated following the Second World War and other depredations. The MERCHANT TAYLORS' hall has stood on the same site in Threadneedle Street since the fourteenth century but little of the post-Fire interior survived the Blitz. The APOTHECARIES' Hall in Blackfriars Lane contains much of its seventeenth-century structure, while the often rebuilt FISHMONGERS' Hall has the most prominent site, right alongside London Bridge. Companies that do not have their own hall customarily borrow one of the other companies' premises for social occasions.

The wealth and importance of a livery company does not depend on its size. For example the COACHMAKERS, who do not have a hall of their own, boast a livery (membership) of some 400, whereas the MERCERS, the senior of the twelve 'great' companies and exceedingly rich, have only 240 liverymen. (The Mercers are one of

THE CLOTHWORKERS'

the many companies that still do not admit women.)

A few companies still play a role in the professions that spawned them. The Society of APOTHECARIES, established in 1617, conducts examinations and awards diplomas, whose holders have the right to practise medicine. No notary public may practise in the City, or within a radius of three miles of it, without the imprimatur of the SCRIVENERS' company, which also holds annual examinations. The GOLDSMITHS' company, mentioned in records as far back as 1180, has the right to assay gold and silver plate and stamp it with the mark of a leopard's head. The company also assays new coinage at an annual ceremony known as the Trial of the Pyx, so

called because the mint sends the specimen coin to Goldsmiths' Hall in a sealed casket, or pyx, to be tested against trial plates.

A few companies are associated with schools, originally founded for the education of their members' sons and poor deserving pupils, now open to others on a fee-paying basis. Most date from Tudor times, including Merchant Taylors' (1561), Tonbridge (1553, governed by the Skinners' Company), Gresham's (1555, administered by the Fishmongers' Company) and Oundle (1556, but re-established in 1876 by the Grocers' Company). The Drapers' Company has a co-educational school and also a girls' school, while St Paul's schools for girls and boys are run by the Mercers' Company.

Over the centuries many guilds have been disbanded or absorbed into other companies: the Maltmen, Galochemakers and Virginal-makers are no more; on the other hand, in an effort to dispel criticism that the whole guild system is anachronistic, fourteen new companies have received a grant of livery from the Lord Mayor since the mid-1970s. Most of these are guilds of professional people such as the ACTUARIES and the ARBITRATORS, in which the livery consists of men and women who are qualified members of these professions.

Each guild is governed by a court of assistants presided over by a master and wardens. Although the customs in each company vary, in most of them officials of the court change annually. A candidate for election to a company must be approved by the court and then admitted in one of three ways: by apprenticeship, patrimony or redemption. If it is by apprenticeship, the candidate must have been bound apprentice to a liveryman for the customary number of years, usually seven. Today this is merely a formality but at the end of his apprenticeship the new member has the satisfaction of knowing that his admission 'fine' will not be too large. In the same way a smaller fine is usually extracted from someone admitted by patrimony, having been born to a liveryman. If neither of these qualifications applies, then entry can only be by redemption, that is payment.

Each guild has its coat of arms, designed for its exclusive use. Some of the earliest arms contain religious symbols but most depict items connected with their trade. They are devised and authorized by THE COLLEGE OF ARMS, an essential part of the livery companies' panoply of tradition. The college was given a charter by Richard III in 1484, but its function existed before that, because the grant of arms to the DRAPERS' company – the first known document allotting arms to an individual or a corporation – was made in 1439. Since the sixteenth century the college has occupied its present site in the western part of the City, on what is now Queen Victoria Street.

THE PORT OF LONDON

From the beginning the port was London. The first reference to Londinium, by Tacitus in AD 61, describes it as 'much frequented by a number of merchants and trading vessels'. In the eighth century the Venerable Bede wrote of London as 'the mart of many nations resorting to it by sea and land'. From there the port spread twenty miles downstream from the City on either side of the river, eventually with seven hundred acres of static water in enclosed docks, to become the biggest and busiest in the world. Since the 1950s it has dwindled for various reasons: failure to modernize after the damage of the Blitz, the end of the empire, labour troubles, competition from foreign ports, particularly Rotterdam, and especially the revolution in shipping and docking. Big modern container ships need deep-water berths and a quick turn around, without wasting time travelling up a congested tidal river. Today almost all the docking of the port of London is done at the modern container port at Tilbury, and the old docklands are being redeveloped in the most significant transformation of a part of London since the Great Fire.

The original port was in the Pool of London below London Bridge, where there were dry banks and deep water on either side, and the piers and tidal waterfall of the bridge stopped big ships sailing further upstream. The first docks were quays or hithes, cuts out of the river bank lined with stakes, where ships tied up and unloaded onto a wooden platform. Over the past ten years rescue archaeology has recovered many of these Roman and medieval quays, and recorded the early history of the port.

The Thames and its port and profits from customs were the property of the monarch, until at the end of the twelfth century Richard Coeur de Lion made them over to the powerful Mayor and Corporation of London for the vast sum of £20,000 to finance his crusades. Geoffrey Chaucer held the important post of controller of customs in the port of London. The growth of trade created the congestion, smuggling, robbery and corruption for which the port became notorious. Big ships anchored in the Pool and were unloaded by lighters, causing delay, restrictive practices and various kinds of theft for which the port developed an intricate specialized jargon. To control the anarchy a law was passed under Elizabeth I designating twenty 'legal quays' on the north bank between the Bridge and the Tower, through which all cargo was to be discharged and cleared by customs.

These legal quays were a profitable vested interest that resisted change, like many ancient institutions of the City of London. The first wet dock in London was built by the East India Company at Blackwall and was visited by Samuel Pepys, Secretary to the Navy, in 1661. Howland Great Wet Dock, named after a local landowner, was opened in 1696 at Rotherhithe and eventually merged into the Surrey Commercial Docks. But both these original docks were used for masting and fitting out rather than unloading vessels, and so did nothing to reduce the congestion and villainy of the legal quays. During the eighteenth century London became the greatest port in the world, but it was so crowded that a vessel had to wait a week downstream before there was a berth in the Pool, and a boat could not cross the Thames through the forest of shipping from the colonies.

Something had to give. In 1796 a Parliamentary Committee strongly condemned the inefficiency and corruption of the Port and from then on various schemes were proposed for building secure docks, some of them as fanciful as straightening the Thames from Greenwich in a channel and blocking off the redundant bends as docks.

The City Corporation was too attached to the profits from its legal quays to do anything itself, so it was left to private companies to build the London docks over the next century and introduce the industry that created much of the East End of London. The West India merchants, who were the biggest and most vulnerable single interest using the Port, opened the first in 1802 on the Isle of Dogs. The Act setting up the West India Dock set the pattern for future docks, built like fortresses and guarded by armed police:

> 'Such of the said Docks, as shall be used for unlading Ships, together with the Quays, Warehouses and other Buildings, shall be inclosed and surrounded by a strong brick or stone Wall, not less than 30 feet high, on all sides, leaving only proper spaces for the Cuts and Entrances into the Dock and proper Gateways through the Wall; and immediately without the Wall there shall be a Ditch, of the width of 12 feet, at least, to be always kept filled with water, 6 feet deep.'

Other docks followed: the London Dock at Wapping in 1805; the East India Dock on the Isle of Dogs in 1805;

OPPOSITE Construction paraphernalia at Canary Wharf on the Isle of Dogs symbolizes its rapid transformation from a working dockyard to a modern office and residential district.

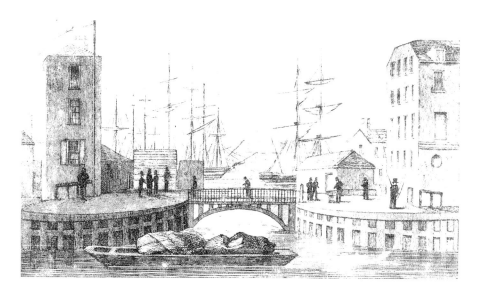

LEFT The Regent's Canal opened in 1820 to link the Grand Junction Canal at Paddington with Limehouse Dock, allowing freight to be taken by water from the docks to the Midlands.

BELOW This illustration from Mayhew's *London Labour and the London Poor* shows the chaotic scene as tea ships are unloaded in the East India Dock.

the Surrey Docks, the only one on the south bank, at Rotherhithe in 1807; St Katharine's Dock, evicting a large community and an ancient religious foundation, in 1828; West India South on the Isle of Dogs in 1829; the Royal Victoria Dock off Bugsby's Reach in 1855; the Millwall Dock on the Isle of Dogs in 1868; and the King George v Dock in 1921.

For convenience the docks specialized in different cargoes, the West India, for instance, dealing with rum and hardwood, Millwall with grain, Surrey with soft-wood, St Katharine with wool, sugar and rubber, and London with ivory, spices, coffee and cocoa. These docks were profitable and worked fairly well for a century. But labour troubles and cut-throat competition between the private dock companies led to the form-ation in 1909 of the Port of London Authority, which controls the tidal Thames and its docking from Tedding-ton to the Nore.

The complex business of loading and unloading cargoes of all sorts in cramped conditions on a strongly tidal river created specialists and dockland communities over the centuries. As well as changing the shape of London, the Port of London shaped the lives of those who lived by it. In the Middle Ages there were the watermen, lightermen and porters, making their living from the river and resistant to change. After the docks were built, there were new occupations: dockers or 'lumpers', coopers, dock police and stevedores, not employed by the dock companies and exercising a monopoly over the delicate business of loading vessels.

The number of dockers needed varied daily with the number and size of ships that had arrived in a dock. This produced the system in which casual labour was signed on at the dock gates daily at dawn, memorably described by Henry Mayhew, the campaigning journalist who

described *London Labour and the London Poor* in 1851. He opened the nation's eyes to the barbarous parade of outcasts and misfits hoping to be picked by the foremen and gangers:

'Dock work is precisely the office that every kind of man is fitted to perform and there we find every kind of man performing it. Those who are unable to live by the occupation to which they have been educated can obtain a living there without any previous training.'

The system survived into the 1960s. Jack Dash, the dockers' leader, described the scene outside the Royal Docks, by the Connaught pub where dockers went for a stiffener before signing on:

'Hundreds of men stream in through the gates, making their way to the various places for the general call-on, facing the firms' foremen and labour superintendents who will at exactly 7.45 am walk over to the waiting labour force and make their selection.'

The organization of labour in the London docks, labour disputes and the dock strike of 1889 were fires that helped to forge the British Labour movement. John Burns, a worker in a candle factory turned engineer who became the dockers' leader, a demagogue and the first socialist to become a cabinet minister, campaigned for 'the full round orb of the docker's tanner'. The dockers wanted sixpence an hour instead of fivepence and, at Tilbury, fourpence, as well as an end to the contract system of casual labour by which men were signed on or off at any time of day. Ben Tillett was another founding father of the Labour and union movement created by the upheavals in the London docks at the end of the nineteenth century. In the next generation Ernest Bevin, 'the dockers' KC', became a great foreign secretary and statesman.

The docks were as distinctive a part of modern London as London Bridge had been of medieval London. The East End, from the Tower to Tilbury, lived by the tideway and the exotic traffic that came there from all over the world. Communities of dockers, seamen and others who made their living from the London river had their terraced houses, pubs, shops and football clubs beside the docks where they worked.

There was Chinatown and the best Chinese food in London near the East India Dock, communities of lascars and Irish, all the races on whom the sun never set, foreign smells of spices and coffee and a cosmopolitan, dangerous atmosphere. Artists like Doré and writers like Mayhew and Dickens found rich material in Dockland:

> 'Captain Cuttle lived on the brink of a little canal near the India Docks where there was a swivel bridge, which opened now and then to let some wandering monster of a ship come roaming up the street like a stranded leviathan.'

There was poverty and hardship, crime and danger in Dockland; but it was not just Cockney sentimentality that also saw in it fraternity and the heart of London.

Today young City workers and property developers inhabit the riversides, where only twenty years ago dockers lumped bales and drank deep. The Port of London has moved downstream to Tilbury. The docks are being developed for other uses: a yachting marina and tourist pleasure ground at St Katharine, Fleet Street newspapers gone east to Wapping and the Isle of Dogs. The old warehouses, gentrified, are now expensive flats and offices. The life of Dockland has been transformed in a few years; but its extraordinary history and tradition will always be an important part of the story of London.

The docks in 1905. Coal barges are moored alongside steam boats with their elongated funnels. Three years later, an Act was passed which took London's docks out of private hands and placed them under the control of a government-appointed Port of London Authority.

MARKETS

For centuries the chief means of trade was markets. Old habits are not easily broken and throughout the capital markets thrive, both for everyday shopping and for more esoteric items. There are morning, lunchtime and all-day markets, markets on weekdays and Sundays, famous ones such as Petticoat Lane, wholesale and general markets, liberally sprinkled across the capital, each with its own character and clientele, reflecting the local neighbourhood, its people and their life style.

Despite the lure of modern stores and shopping centres, people still look for the satisfaction – or at least the illusion – of lower prices. They seek the thrill of the bargain, the deal with an independent trader, the repartee – rare at the supermarket till – and the sense of community. When town hall planners or developers propose to sweep a market into antiseptic tidiness and efficiency, popular protest swells.

Even wholesale markets touch an emotional chord. In the original COVENT GARDEN, traffic problems were appalling, with massive trucks as well as stacked crates and trolleys blocking streets and pavements. But Londoners still mourned the move in 1974 of the wholesale fruit, flower and vegetable market from the heart of the West End to Nine Elms, south of the river. For about 340 years, this former convent and market garden had provided a symbol of unconventional London, a market place surrounded by cafés, clubs, theatres, pubs open at peculiar hours, attracting rich and poor, the professor and the flower girl, and throbbing with life at all hours. Its replacement – a modern shopping precinct and an array of craft and antique stalls – is sanitized by comparison.

BILLINGSGATE has moved too. First officially recognized as a fish market in 1699, it was a welcome contrast to the world of the City office worker. Fishmongers, publicans, restaurateurs and buyers from hotels and department stores mingled in Lower Thames Street carrying boxes with their day's catch of cod, sprats, whiting, lobster or eels to a medley of vans. Now all have vanished into smart, hygienic premises in Docklands. The fish have been replaced by finance in the conversion of their historic market building to an international trading floor. The only remnant in the Billingsgate area is the annual fish harvest festival each October in the Church of St Mary at Hill, Eastcheap, where fish is displayed in alluring patterns (see *A London calendar*).

Cities live with constant change. Except for local street names – Bread, Milk, Goldsmith, Ironmonger –

London's original market in Cheapside has vanished. However, Smithfield and Leadenhall managed to survive, at least until the end of the 1980s. By 1174 there was a horse market on the 'smooth field', an area much used for archery and public executions, and this attracted farmers with livestock, driven in from the local countryside for slaughter and sale. The smooth field became SMITHFIELD, London's meat market. Different animals were corralled separately, the cattle often locked into rings or droves by their horns. The noise and smell were atrocious. In 1855 the live animals were removed to the CALEDONIAN MARKET in Islington but Smithfield retained its carcass-handling role and, with forthcoming refurbishments, is likely to stay.

LEADENHALL, London's most important medieval market, started with poultry and grain and was only saved from one proposal for conversion to a bourse, in 1534, by the prospect of famine and the need for continuing storage. Today, in a spectacular Victorian warren of glass and iron, it continues as a retail market with open-sided shops patronized chiefly by City workers. Its Christmas displays are famous, with richly feathered pheasants, colossal plucked turkeys, smoked salmon sides, whole honeyed hams, ripe Stilton cheeses and continental chocolates.

The spontaneous look of London's street markets conceals a history of strict regulation that persists today. In the Middle Ages, when there were comparatively few permanent shops, the rights to hold markets were so valuable that Edward III, wishing to gain the favour of City merchants, granted the Corporation an exclusive charter within a seven-mile radius. This gave the City control over BOROUGH MARKET, at the southern end of London Bridge, where fruit and vegetable growers from the south could bring their produce without having to tackle the traffic of the centre. This has a claim to be the oldest surviving market in London: it certainly existed in the thirteenth century, although it has since moved to a site slightly further from the bridge, near Southwark Cathedral, where the mid-Victorian market hall crouches awkwardly among the railway arches.

OPPOSITE A section of Brixton's large and bustling outdoor market in Electric Avenue, one of the first London streets to be lit by electricity. The stall at bottom left specializes in the fruit and vegetables used in Caribbean cooking.

A mile or so to the east, in Bermondsey, is the weekly CALEDONIAN MARKET, where antique dealers congregate before dawn every Friday to buy and sell priceless or worthless items – the art is to tell the difference. Traditionally, it is necessary to arrive very early to secure the real treasures, although much of the trade is between the dealers themselves. The market was originally held in the old cattle market off Caledonian Road, Islington, which did not handle livestock on Fridays. When that site was redeveloped in the 1960s, the market moved here, but kept its old name and its traditional market day.

While markets have adapted to modern planning demands as well as shopping tastes, PETTICOAT LANE, off

The Caledonian market in Islington was built as a cattle market, but on days when cattle were not being sold costermongers moved in selling bric-à-brac and old clothes. The market closed after the Second World War and today's Friday antiques market in Bermondsey is its successor.

Aldgate High Street, keeps something of its old character. According to local mythology, it is possible to 'lose' a watch in one of the market's ten streets and buy it back a few minutes later in another. The Lane's real name is Middlesex Street. It dates from at least 1540, when the area was known for its second-hand clothes stalls. Aldgate's and Whitechapel's Jewish tradition began as early as the thirteenth century, when the City banned Jews and they settled outside the walls. A later Jewish community was formed in the nineteenth century from European refugees, drawn by cheap housing. The market is on Sundays because Saturday is the Jewish sabbath.

Some four hundred and fifty stalls on and off the Lane sell clothes, leather goods, fruit, vegetables, jewellery and toys. Stalls and shops offer traditional East End and Jewish food – jellied eels, salt-beef sandwiches and bagels. Visitors spill into the Asian area around BRICK LANE, a few blocks east. Here are a further four hundred stalls with the accent on clothing and second-hand goods, especially as you move north towards Bethnal Green Road. Further north still, in COLUMBIA ROAD, symbols of urban deprivation yield to a street full of flowers, plants and people bearing aloft their spoils of good green things from the Sunday flower market – all that remains of a larger market set up by a Victorian philanthropist.

Columbia Road is one of the few specialist street markets to survive in London. Another appears fleetingly at lunchtime on weekdays in FARRINGDON ROAD, north of the underground station, where a handful of stalls remain from a once-thriving book market. Despite its shrunken size, bibliophiles find it worth the trip.

General markets have been more enduring. Every London neighbourhood has one within striking distance. Most of those listed in a 1936 book, *The Street Markets of London*, still exist. Among the most notable are Leather Lane (Holborn), Strutton Ground (Victoria), Brixton, North End Road (Fulham), Berwick Street (Soho), Northcote Road (Battersea), Rye Lane (Peckham), Tachbrook Street (Pimlico) and London's most authentic old-fashioned street market, East Street (Walworth).

The most varied is PORTOBELLO ROAD, Notting Hill. It has three distinct personalities. Best known is its southern stretch, where tourists throng at the weekend to buy knick-knacks and antiques – many of them bought by the stall owners in Bermondsey the day before. Because of its popularity with tourists, bureaux de change have sprouted among the stalls that sell early telephones, gramophones, worn brass light switches, jewellery, clockwork singing birds and rocking horses. Arcades lead back into shabby properties containing small booths let to individual dealers.

Further north the market changes character abruptly. Now come the food stalls, selling fruit and vegetables cheaper than in the shops and with a better selection of Caribbean produce – yams, sweet potatoes and mangoes – than in most other markets except Brixton. North again and it becomes recognizably part of North Kensington, one of London's less attractive districts. From a tented structure alongside the overhead motorway, stall-holders sell cheap, low-quality clothes, books, records and household goods, new and second-hand.

Street markets are by their nature open, concealing nothing. A walk of a few hundred yards along Portobello Road reveals much about contrasting aspects of contemporary London.

Street Traders

'There you are, my angel.' 'Thank you, my love.' The patter is all part of the personal service of the London street trader. The hours may be long, the weather cold, but the life is independent and the money good. It is a cash trade, with low overheads – about £20 a day for a regular pitch and in some markets an additional £5 for contractor-provided stalls. Prime pitches are often handed on from one generation to the next.

Prospects were less cheerful when Henry Mayhew wrote about the London street folk in his mid-nineteenth-century chronicle on *London Labour and the London Poor*. Barefoot children would buy a few penny-worth of watercress at Farringdon, for wetting at the Hatton Garden pump, bunching and selling on to the working class for just a few pennies more. A tray of oranges was another cheap way of making a little from a little. Flowers were more suspect; some were offering rather more than a bouquet of violets, using them as a cover-up for what Mayhew calls 'immoral purposes'.

Mayhew claimed that London had upwards of 40,000 street people. The majority were costermongers, a term originally used for apple sellers (from costard, a kind of apple) and later applied to all travelling shopkeepers. They had their own Cockney slang, often turning words back to front. Yenep meant a penny, top of reeb a pot of beer, a doogheno a good one (a good market).

Forced always to move on, they cried their wares: 'Strawberries ripe and cherries in the rise', 'Rushes green' (for floors), 'Small coals', 'Corns to pick', 'Old chairs to mend', 'Any old iron'. Street traders sold sparrows, larks and nightingales, roast chestnuts, hot eels, baked potatoes, muffins and ginger beer, writing ink and musical instruments – anything popular and portable.

'Duffers' sold fakes – imitation antiques, perfumes, and falsely painted birds. Their present-day descendants can be found working busy shopping streets, a lookout posted to watch for the police: their dubious bargains include imitation brand-named perfumery and watches. Slick men disgorge clockwork toys from suitcases to cash in on Christmas goodies before they are forced to move on.

More imaginative entrepreneurs have taken to nomadic selling of crafts and antiques. Foot soldiers of the bric-à-brac brigade, they move from Bermondsey on Friday to Portobello Road on Saturday, perhaps the Old Stables at Camden Lock on Sunday and Covent Garden on Monday. While the tinkling mobile van has tended to take over ice cream sales, the rag and bone man still sometimes rings his bell from horse and cart, or lorry, collecting junk, and unemployed youths go from door to door trying to interest householders in basic dusters, dishcloths and ironing-board covers. Fast food outlets have replaced the ham sandwich and mutton-pie sellers, but roast chestnuts can still be bought from glowing braziers in the busy streets of the West End.

Victorian street traders selling cough elixir (*above*) and apples (*right*). The word 'costermonger' originally meant apple seller, derived from the costard apple.

THE CENTRE OF GOVERNMENT

Early in the eleventh century the Danish rulers of England left Winchester to establish their Court in the Palace of Westminster, beside the existing Westminster Abbey. For five hundred years, until Henry VIII moved to nearby Whitehall Palace, England was ruled from that same small area. It embraced what Francis Bacon described in 1597 as the four pillars of Government: religion, justice, counsel and treasure. Since the Norman Conquest the City of London has been designated for trade, Westminster for national administration. A possible reason for this duality, unusual in medieval European countries, was that by distancing himself from the city, the King would have a greater chance of escaping any insurrection. The relationship between the monarch and the City is unique to England. Even William the Conqueror permitted the City a degree of autonomy in return for its cooperation and the sovereign is still technically not permitted to enter the City without the permission of its Lord Mayor.

The United Kingdom is a constitutional monarchy. The will of the people is represented by the House of Commons, whose members have all been elected by the public and must present themselves for subsequent re-election at least every five years. Traditional Parliamentary rituals foster the myth that power still emanates from the monarch, via the House of Lords and the House of Commons, advised by the Crown's civil servants. In effect, almost the reverse is the case, with a small Cabinet of ministers, under the chairmanship of the prime minister, playing the executive role in managing the nation's affairs, often strongly influenced by the Civil Service. All measures must, however, be approved by both Houses of Parliament before they receive the monarch's assent and become Acts of Parliament.

––––––– MONARCHY AND DEMOCRACY –––––––
Shakespeare said a king was hedged by divinity and it took a civil war to persuade the Stuart monarchs that by the seventeenth century they had no divine right to rule. Charles I remained unconvinced: he went to the scaffold declaring that 'a subject and a sovereign are clean different things'. After the Restoration the monarch's powers and pretensions were severely qualified but in 1707 Queen Anne was still able to refuse the royal assent to an Act of Parliament. From George II onwards the Crown's power gradually diminished until today its real function is to represent the unity of the British people and act as a figurehead for the Commonwealth. The

nineteenth-century constitutional authority Walter Bagehot wrote that a constitutional monarch had three rights: to be consulted, to encourage and to warn. A new role imposed on royalty in the last quarter of the twentieth century (as at some earlier periods) has been as the subject of disrespectful gossip in the popular press. Some fear that this assault on its dignity could damage the institution and negate its symbolic role.

The reformer John Bright spoke of England as the 'mother of parliaments'. Some form of consultative body has played a part in government since 1272, when Henry III assembled the Great Council in the recently completed Chapter House of Westminster Abbey. After the death of Edward I separate houses were established for peers and commoners. The peers have always been accommodated within the Palace of Westminster. The Commons were less fortunate, during the fourteenth century sitting in either the Chapter House or refectory of Westminster Abbey. A move to the Palace of Westminster was at last made, but which chamber was provided depended on availability. Eventually, following the secularization of all private chapels in 1547, the young Edward VI presented the Commons with St Stephen's Chapel, where they sat until the devastating fire of 1834. The present Palace of Westminster was then constructed: the first purpose-built headquarters for Parliament. Spread over eleven acres, it comprises more than a thousand rooms laid out around courtyards. Gothic detailing and romantic towers disguise the basic symmetry of the building's plan, which when constructed, was entirely functional, although it is today far from being an efficient office building.

Halfway along the corridor that links the two Houses is the Central Lobby, in which Lords and Commons discuss parliamentary business informally amongst themselves and, by appointment, with members of the public and their constituents.

Public galleries of both Houses may be entered during parliamentary sessions, either by arrangement with a member of the Commons or Lords as applicable or by queueing on the day. Overseas visitors obtain tickets from their embassy. Visitors to either public gallery are also permitted to see the interior of Westminster Hall.

OPPOSITE The lobby of the House of Commons is where all citizens have the right to go to seek a meeting with their Member of Parliament. It is also the high point of Augustus Pugin's majestic Gothic detailing in the Palace of Westminster.

THE HOUSE OF LORDS

William the Conqueror replaced most English earls with Norman barons and the House of Lords derives from their function as royal advisors. It is still known as the Upper House, a status emphasized each autumn when the Sovereign opens Parliament from the throne, which remains permanently in the Lords' chamber. The Commons are then summoned to join them and the speech outlining the administration's plans for the coming year is read by the Monarch, although written by the Government.

Members of the Upper House are not elected. They comprise the Lords Spiritual – 26 archbishops and senior bishops of the Church of England – and the Lords Temporal – all English peers and 16 representative Scottish peers, plus the Lords of Appeal (known as the Law Lords, who form the highest court in the land). Members of the royal family who have peerages are entitled to speak in the Lords and sometimes do. Peers are paid an allowance for each day they appear in the House, but only a small proportion of those entitled to take part in the proceedings do so regularly.

Life peerages were introduced in 1958 to dilute the hereditary nature of the House. They are awarded to eminent people nominated by leaders of all parties, often former members of the House of Commons. Their titles are not passed on to their descendants. Discussions in the Lords, as in the Commons, are on a party basis, although there is a fairly large corps of so-called cross-benchers, who declare no party allegiance. The Lords no longer have the power to delay finance bills and they may postpone other Government measures for only thirteen months. The primary function of the Upper House is to provide a forum for fuller discussion of Bills in detail and an opportunity for revision. The Lord Chancellor, the head of the judiciary, presides over the House, traditionally seated on the Woolsack, a large bag of wool in a red cover.

THE HOUSE OF COMMONS

Members of the Lower House are elected to represent geographical constituencies by adults over the age of 18. The last barrier to full adult suffrage was lifted in 1928, when women were given the vote on the same basis as men. General elections must take place at least every five years, except in times of emergency such as war. The Prime Minister can advise the monarch to dissolve Parliament and call a general election at any time within the five-year term.

Since the beginning of British democracy, members of the House have generally been split into two main parties, although their names and natures have changed. For most of this century the two largest parties have

been Conservative and Labour. The Conservatives derive directly from the old Tory party of landowners, while Labour was created in 1906 to represent trade unionists. Labour quickly rose to dominate left-of-centre politics, eclipsing the Liberals, now merged into the Democrats, the third largest party.

As the parties have changed, so has the nature of the MPs who represent them. Until the twentieth century being an MP was not considered a full-time job. Most members were gentlemen of leisure who used the House of Commons as an exclusive club. The arrival of working-class representatives signalled the start of the change and today the Commons is filled with ambitious men and (still comparatively few) women who have chosen to make politics a career. On both sides of the House, today's MPs are for the most part articulate and better educated than most of the voters they are supposed to represent – in no sense a cross-section of society. The established procedures of the House encourage confrontational politics and personal invective that many, hearing it on the radio, find irrelevant and infantile. Winston Churchill said in 1947: 'No one pretends that democracy is perfect or all-wise. Indeed, it has been said that democracy is the worst form of government except all those other forms that have been tried from time to time.'

As the job has become more professional, the MPs have been allowed the help of secretaries and researchers. But the accommodation in and around Westminster is never sufficient to give them comfortable working conditions, despite the acquisition of MPs' office suites in new and converted buildings in the vicinity. The Commons chamber of 1847, destroyed by bombs in 1941, was rebuilt almost identically and reopened in 1951. It was not enlarged to take account of the growing number of MPs as the population expanded. This means that there are not enough seats for all 650 members. When vital debates are taking place some have to sit on the steps or stand at the back – but except on such rare occasions the House is sparsely attended. MPs find they can do their job more effectively by dealing with constituency or other political business in their offices. But they can seldom stray too far from the Chamber in case they are required to vote in divisions, the system by which the House arrives at decisions. Voting in divisions, with rare exceptions, is along party lines.

Government and Opposition MPs face each other in tiered rows of seats separated by the length of two swords – a reminder of less phlegmatic times. Ministers and the Opposition 'Shadow Cabinet' occupy the front benches. No monarch has been allowed to enter the Commons since 1642, when Charles I stormed in, wanting to arrest five members. The Speaker, who

Demonstrations and parades have been an integral part of British political life for more than two centuries. In Victorian times people would take to the streets agitating for social and economic reform. Most demonstrations were peaceful but this 1887 sketch shows police clashing with a crowd outside the Palace of Westminster.

oversees the business of the Commons, declined to answer the King's questions, firmly establishing his office as serving the Commons rather than the Crown. The Speaker is chosen from among the elected members of the House and, once installed, is expected to ignore his former party affiliation.

Most MPs, except those representing seats in or near London, have two homes – one in the constituency and one near Westminster. They spend the weekend in the constituency and stay in London during the week. When a division is called they have ten minutes to vote, so a house or flat within a short distance of the House is desirable, preferably one close enough to be wired directly into the division bell. Mansion blocks south of Victoria Street are packed with MPs and a few have strayed across the river into Waterloo and Kennington.

── THE CABINET AND PRIME MINISTER ──

Under the Prime Minister's leadership, the Cabinet, of around twenty members, is effectively the government of the nation and only rarely are its recommendations rejected by Parliament. Historically, the Cabinet evolved in the seventeenth century when the king began to hold discussions with groups of ministers outside his Privy Council. Its members are personally selected by the Prime Minister. They may sit in either House but, except in unusual circumstances, all will belong to the majority party. Most are in charge of the major departments of

state, but a 'minister without portfolio' is sometimes added to the team. Meetings are held in the ground floor Cabinet Room at the rear of 10 Downing Street. During Second World War air raids Winston Churchill held Cabinet meetings in a bomb-proof subterranean room below the government offices that are approached from Clive's steps – now open to the public as a museum.

Like all ministers of state, the Prime Minister is formally appointed by the sovereign but, except in rare cases of coalition government, is the leader of the party that possesses a working majority in the House of Commons. He or she is the most powerful single person in the nation's political life.

The Prime Minister oversees Government policy and selects all ministers. Other tasks include advising the sovereign on the appointment of bishops and recommending candidates for honours. When Parliament is in session, the Prime Minister has to answer general questions in the House of Commons on Tuesday and Thursday afternoons – often the dramatic centrepieces of the political week.

Prime Ministers have lived and worked at 10 Downing Street since George II presented the building for their use in 1731. Robert Walpole, Britain's first Prime Minister, occupied the house shortly after his appointment. No. 10 is linked internally with no. 11, the Chancellor of the Exchequer's residence, and no. 12, the ground floor of which serves as the office of the Government Chief Whip.

─────── THE CIVIL SERVICE ───────

The equivalent of civil servants existed before the Norman Conquest, to collect property taxes imposed by the king. By the mid-seventeenth century, according to Samuel Pepys – who worked for many years at the Admiralty – the Civil Service had already assumed an important role, but it was in the late eighteenth and nineteenth centuries, with the rapid growth of the Empire, that its great expansion took place. Many administrators were appointed to oversee the management of the subject lands and to service the occupying forces. Fortunately, land for developing the buildings to accommodate them almost immediately became available, adjacent to Parliament on the site of the old Whitehall Palace, much of which had become derelict due to the departure of the king and the major fire that followed. In a relatively short time the old buildings were demolished, apart from the Banqueting House, and the administrative buildings of Whitehall eventually took their place.

Although Empire has been replaced by Commonwealth, with a subsequent reduction in servicing requirements, the twentieth-century introduction of public welfare, combined with new forms of taxation and licensing, once more led to the expansion of the Civil Service. Under the direction of their departmental ministers, civil servants are ultimately responsible to the Crown. None are elected but, at higher levels, they must pass entrance examinations. Members of the service are not in theory affected by change of government and are supposed to be non-political but the most senior civil servants, closest to the Prime Minister and the Cabinet, are sometimes changed by a new administration.

Because they continue to hold office as ministers come and go, civil servants can exert a powerful influence on policy-making. They must first persuade their ministers to argue for a particular policy in Cabinet and then, using their own Whitehall network, persuade officials in other ministries to talk *their* ministers round. Many vital political initiatives, therefore, are hatched between civil servants at discreet lunches in Pall Mall clubs or during earnest strolls by the lake in St James's Park. The power of the administrator can scarcely be overestimated. Alexander Pope recognized it when he wrote:

'For forms of government let fools contest,
Whate'er is best administer'd is best.'

LOBBYING

The Central Lobby of the Palace of Westminster has given its name to a verb, 'to lobby', meaning to seek to exert influence on a legislator or someone else with the power to take an important decision. Today, the most significant lobbying goes on elsewhere: a constituent who goes to the lobby to meet his or her MP will often meet only a secretary, who will pass the message on. Professional lobbyists, usually called 'parliamentary consultants', operate less publicly, many from small but expensive offices in the immediate vicinity of Parliament. They are engaged by commercial or professional interests to promote favourable views on matters that affect their businesses. Lobbyists entertain MPs and civil servants to lunches, dinners or drinks and organize all-party groups and committees in the Palace of Westminster, where leading businessmen can tell their stories to MPs.

Lobby correspondents are journalists working for national or large regional newspapers, agencies and broadcasting organizations, who are accredited to Parliament, exercising the hard-won right of the press to report its affairs (see *The press*). Nowadays they do not often beard MPs in the lobbies themselves, more often in the bars or tea room, or in the small meeting room reserved for them at the top of the building. Discussions generally take place 'on lobby terms', which means that the reporter will not disclose the source of any information or insight. Over the years politicians have learned to use the press. Ministers, civil servants and Opposition

leaders hold regular formal briefing sessions to explain and excuse their actions.

DIPLOMACY

London is host to one of the world's largest colonies of overseas diplomats. Embassies, consulates and high commissions (for Commonwealth countries) cluster in Belgravia and Kensington, with outposts such as Portland Place and Mayfair, where the huge United States Embassy in Grosvenor Square is a magnet for others. The former Dominions of Canada, Australia, South Africa, New Zealand and India – as well as Zimbabwe and Uganda – have drifted a little further east, to Trafalgar Square and the Strand.

Apart from making formal contacts with ministers and businessmen, and representing their countries on state occasions, diplomats do a large amount of their work at numerous receptions at each other's embassies, celebrating national events, official visits or changes among their personnel. Like lobbyists, they enthusiastically take advantage of London's expensive restaurants for entertaining MPs, civil servants and journalists, to promote their countries' interests and reputation.

LONDON'S GOVERNMENT

The Metropolitan Board of Works, established in 1855, was the first local authority for London as a whole. It was succeeded by the London County Council and the Greater London Council. Since the GLC's abolition in 1986 there has been no central authority for London. The capital and its hinterland are divided into thirty-two boroughs, each with its locally elected authority to run municipal services. Members of these authorities are part-time and unpaid, but they are serviced by bands of paid officials. Meetings of the borough councils are held in local town halls, often Edwardian buildings of some splendour that symbolized the aspirations of local authorities in the early twentieth century. In those days councillors were usually worthy local citizens, independent of political parties but with a reputation for probity and sound judgment. Today council elections are fought on a party basis and councillors are often fledgling politicians whose true ambitions lie at Westminster. At the same time the duties of the councils have become more onerous and complex, especially in the area of public housing. The combination of these two factors has caused a decline in the reputation of London's town halls as repositories of common sense and efficiency. The City has its own unorthodox form of government.

OPPOSITE Pevsner described the triple-towered Department of the Environment building on Marsham Street as 'an honest and ruthlessly utilitarian statement'. Figures silhouetted in windows show that the work of government continues round the clock.

THE BUSINESS OF MONEY

In the grand courtroom of the Bank of England is a working wind dial installed in 1805. The directors consulted it during their meetings to discover when strong easterly winds were blowing up the Thames, to bring the East India Company's bullion ships into port. Finance, trade and shipping have always been intricately linked. Until a few decades ago the City of London's pre-eminence as a world financial centre derived almost entirely from its position as the capital of a great trading nation whose empire spanned the globe. Sterling, backed by gold, was the main trading currency in the nineteenth century and accounted for a quarter of world trade even in 1939.

When the empire faded and Britain emerged economically crippled from two world wars, the City should perhaps have begun a genteel decline. Instead it developed at enormous speed between the 1960s and late 1980s, because of a happy combination of accident, skill, language and geographical position.

A splendid example of the resurgence of the City – and of continuity with the past – stands right at the heart of the financial district, opposite the Bank of England. It is the ROYAL EXCHANGE, constructed in 1844, the third on the same site. The original was founded in 1569 by Sir Thomas Gresham, merchant and financial adviser to Elizabeth I. Gresham wanted to imitate the great bourse in Antwerp and his building housed a general market place, the precursor of the stock exchange and other modern markets. The building fell out of use as a market place and in 1928 much of it was taken over by an insurance company. But in 1982 the old trading hall sprang back into action as the most colourful and noisiest market floor in the City, the LONDON INTERNATIONAL FINANCIAL FUTURES EXCHANGE, where traders speculate in currency to hedge against the effect of fluctuating exchange rates on their international deals. After more than half a century the Royal Exchange has gone back to its roots.

The futures market is the latest of several new ventures that have revived the fortunes of the City since the early 1960s, causing a growth in its international standing rather than the decline some expected. The most important are the euromarkets, dealing internationally in bank loans, bonds and shares issued in many different currencies, especially dollars. There are no trading floors: business is conducted discreetly by telephone in hundreds of glass-walled office suites. The markets grew to their present size largely as a side effect of United States banking controls, including a legal block on the issue of securities by American domestic banks.

By the 1960s industry and governments worldwide were hungry for capital. What more natural than that Americans should gravitate towards a less tightly regulated centre, English-speaking, with a large reservoir of financially skilled people? Add to that a sophisticated banking system already in place and a geographical position half way between the Asian and North Amer-

The Bank Parlour of the Bank of England was, like nearly all of John Soane's stately eighteenth-century interiors, heavily modified in the 1920s and 1930s by Herbert Baker in the interests of a more efficient use of space. This print shows how the Parlour looked in the mid-nineteenth century.

Edward Jarman's Royal Exchange of 1667–71 replaced the Elizabethan Exchange destroyed in the Great Fire. It was in turn burned to the ground in 1838. In 1781, the date of this print, it was still surrounded by residential accommodation.

ican time zones so that it can trade while one is getting ready to sleep and the other is waking up. London soon became the largest single source of freely available borrowing in the world, attracting the offices of more than four hundred and fifty foreign banks.

THE BANK OF ENGLAND

A central though silent role in all this was played by the Bank of England, the City's power centre, but at the same time something of an enigma. Its contribution to the success of the new money markets was simply to do nothing, not to interfere, not to insist on the level of regulation that had prevented such markets from being formed in New York. In this the Old Lady of Threadneedle Street, as the bank is known, was showing the pragmatic, some would say buccaneering side of her character – a contrast to her popular image as a fussy guardian of financial rectitude.

That same devil-may-care attitude sometimes has less happy results. In the 1920s and 1930s a complete reconstruction of the interior of the bank wiped out the elaborate courtyards and passages designed by Sir John Soane when he put up the present building in 1788. Pevsner called it 'the worst individual loss suffered by London architecture in the first half of the twentieth century'.

Soane's windowless curtain wall, calculated to deter demonstrators and potential intruders, is the most distinctive feature of the Bank's exterior, a symbol of solidity and financial probity. The bank had been founded in 1694, to raise a loan of £1.2 million for William III's campaign against the French. It has since

been the government's bank and in the eighteenth century was given a virtual monopoly over the issue of English banknotes. (Minting coins is traditionally the prerogative of the Crown, but the Bank regulates their issue.) Despite these strong links with government, the Bank of England remained privately owned until it was nationalized in 1946 and became a direct instrument of government fiscal control and regulation.

THE STOCK EXCHANGE

The business of buying and selling stocks in joint stock companies grew up in the seventeenth century, conducted at the Royal Exchange or nearby coffee houses. At the end of the century came the first legislation to license brokers and prevent the corrupt manipulation of prices. The bursting of the South Sea Bubble in 1720 – the first stock market crash – led to a greater degree of control and organization. Brokers now met to do business first in Jonathan's Coffee House, then in the first purpose-built stock exchange in Threadneedle Street. In 1801 it moved to its present site in Throgmorton Street. Business expanded in the nineteenth and twentieth centuries, when stocks and shares became a major vehicle for investment.

The latest Stock Exchange building was constructed in 1972, but as the stockbrokers settled into their new premises it became increasingly apparent that the modernity of the building was in stark contrast to the

OVERLEAF Men and women in their twenties can make big money fast if they keep their nerve during noisy, hectic trading on the floor of one of the specialized exchanges in the City – here the London Metal Exchange.

antiquated regulations of their profession. The exchange was a backwater of restrictive practices, a gentlemen's club where firms could be owned only by members, whose conduct was governed by the motto: 'My word is my bond'. The central problem was that, under this traditional private ownership, the brokers could not get access to sufficient capital at a time of huge expansion in international share trading. The Bank of England foresaw that without reform the exchange would lose business to both the London-based euromarkets and other financial centres.

In 1983 the government decided to force reform on the exchange, resulting in the 'Big Bang' of October 1986. Brokers were initially opposed, but in the end accepted more radical reform than many expected. Most firms were bought by banks, which pumped in capital. The name was changed to the International Stock Exchange. The traditionally frantic trading floor, one of the sights of the City, was abandoned in favour of electronic trading over screens in new concrete and glass office complexes throughout the City. London is the only major market in the world to have made a complete break from its trading floor, deserted now except for a few specialized options traders.

The banks that now owned the old firms hired staff at such a rate that salaries soared. The new brokers got a bad press, depicted as champagne-swilling, Porsche-driving arrivistes. They bought apartments and houses in Docklands and other convenient areas, provoking a boom in property prices. The vintage champagne stopped flowing abruptly in October 1987, when stock markets crashed and business dwindled. The following years saw thousands of redundancies, hundreds of millions of pounds of losses among the dealing firms and a new realism about salaries. But the revolution, however painful, succeeded in keeping London among the big three markets in shares alongside Tokyo and New York.

MONEY MARKETS

One of the City's oldest skills is trading money, particularly sterling bills of exchange – in effect post-dated cheques used to finance banking and commerce. The traditional top-hatted bill broker still visits the Bank of England – but the quaintness conceals another revolution in the money markets: back at the office, he is likely to be dealing in bonds or other sterling debt at a computerized terminal.

These domestic markets are common to all financial centres. What boosted London's money markets was the end of floating exchange rates in 1971 – which encouraged more people to buy and sell currencies. Eight years later British exchange controls were abolished. As a result a huge international market in currencies and bank deposits has grown in London. Having survived a period of over-rapid growth and exploding salaries a decade earlier than the stock market, today the money markets are more level-headed, and daily turnover averages $90 billion, as much as New York and Tokyo combined.

BANKING AND INSURANCE

The money market dealing rooms scattered around the City provide the financial infrastructure for Britain's own banking system. The five biggest British banks all have their headquarters in London, though only Barclays, whose antecedents are seventeenth-century, is in LOMBARD STREET, the traditional centre of banking. National Westminster has a huge modern tower nearby.

The City is also home to many merchant banks, which advise on bids and deals, manage investments and trade bonds and shares. Corporate financiers in merchant banks regard themselves as the cream of the City, but in the late 1980s scandals sullied their reputation.

London is also one of the world's leading insurance centres, host to over eight hundred companies as well as to the Lloyd's market (see *Lloyd's of London*).

COMMODITIES

The City has been leader of the international gold market for many years, helped by the historic connections with gold mining areas, especially South Africa, and by the Bank of England's expertise in storing and moving bullion. The London gold fixing is still a pricing benchmark throughout the world.

Less well known are the commodity exchanges, which tend to be in the eastern part of the City, near the former docks. Like Lloyd's, the commodity markets grew from seventeenth-century coffee houses and most have been based for centuries in the area of Mark Lane and Mincing Lane near the Tower of London.

In 1987 the old London Commodity Exchange, renamed the LONDON FUTURES AND OPTIONS EXCHANGE (or London Fox), moved a few hundred yards to a new building near St Katharine's Dock. Its main business is soft commodities such as sugar and cocoa. Hard commodities are traded at the LONDON METAL EXCHANGE.

Finally, goods must be moved. The BALTIC EXCHANGE in St Mary Axe, centre of the shipping industry, is the only international marketplace in the world where ships are hired for cargoes and cargoes found for ships. Air freight is included nowadays too. The exchange, in a 1903 building, is named after the eighteenth-century coffee house which specialized in trade with the Baltic.

Lloyd's of London

The world's largest insurance market takes its name from Edward Lloyd's coffee house in the City, where from the seventeenth century shipowners would meet wealthy merchants and negotiate insurance cover for their ships. Because no one merchant would want to carry all the risk of a ship himself, brokers set themselves up as intermediaries, arranging groups of underwriters to spread the risk.

The balancing of risk with reward was and remains a sophisticated form of gambling. By the middle of the eighteenth century the more upright brokers and underwriters were becoming increasingly dismayed at the low class of person being attracted to Lloyd's to share in the spoils, giving it the atmosphere, in today's terms, of a high street betting shop. So in 1769 they decamped to what they called the New Lloyd's Coffee House and drew up rules to put the insurance business on a sound footing.

Soon *Lloyd's List* was established to supply the reliable news of shipping movements that the brokers needed. In 1774 they moved away from the coffee house circuit to the Royal Exchange, where they soon began to take on other kinds of risk. In parallel with London's rise as the financial centre of the world, it became the global insurance capital as well. Lloyd's reputation was strengthened when, after the San Francisco earthquake of 1906, it promptly paid claims of $45 million, when some American insurers demurred.

Over the years Lloyd's moved to ever larger headquarters and from 1986 it has occupied Richard Rogers's controversial post-modernist building in Leadenhall Street. One traditional feature that has been retained there is the Lutine Bell, recovered in 1859 from a French frigate that had sunk with a cargo of gold sixty years earlier. The Bell is sounded to mark significant events – two rings for good news and one for the opposite, such as the 1912 sinking of the *Titanic* and Hurricane Betsy in 1965, which cost Lloyd's £125 million. Not all claims involve natural disasters. One of the worst losses was $400 million on a complex claim from the computer industry involving cancelled leasing contracts.

Risks are covered by underwriters on behalf of syndicates made up of thousands of 'names'. These are rich men and women willing to pledge their wealth to cover insurance, in return – most of the time – for a healthy reward in the form of premium income. The cosmopolitan names include royalty, entrepreneurs and celebrities from the worlds of sport and show business.

Even today, more than two hundred years after the first attempt to regulate Lloyd's, the insurance market is occasionally rocked by financial scandal. During the 1980s the rules governing the market were overhauled twice to re-establish its reputation for integrity. The insurers have also to be on the lookout for sharp practice from their clients. In 1979 Lloyd's refused to pay an $80 million claim on the sinking of an oil tanker, when it was proved that the crew had made sandwiches and packed suitcases in advance of the ship going down!

Lloyd's headquarters in Leadenhall Street is the City's most notable high-tech building, completed in 1986. The architect was Richard Rogers, who designed the Pompidou Centre in Paris, also notable for its exterior pipes and utilities.

CRAFTS OLD AND NEW

Craftsmen have always been attracted to the capital where the spending power of the inhabitants is augmented by that of visitors from the country and abroad. For the most skilled and the best connected, patronage from royalty and nobility, the state and the church, can provide the most lucrative commissions. Evidence of the skills of Roman and medieval craftsmen can be seen in the Museum of London. From the twelfth century the guilds required young people to spend many years in an apprenticeship learning from qualified craftsmen.

Today such a time-scale is unattractive and many crafts are neglected in consequence. The 1980s have witnessed the closure of a parchment and vellum works in Brentford and a firm of cart-makers in Covent Garden. However, the breed of artist–craftsman, typified by William Morris and his co-workers, survives in this new environment, encouraged by the opening of such ventures as the Rotherhithe, Clerkenwell and Cannon Workshops. Today's craftsmen and women who sell their wares in the weekend markets are the modern counterparts of the traditional craftsmen who once worked in London.

WOODWORKING TRADES

London's most diversified craft, woodworking, encompasses everything from cabinet to coffin making. Fashionable Georgian furniture-making was originally located in the West End but from about 1830 woodworkers making lower quality goods became established in the East End. The West End remained a centre of that quality trade typified by Heals (established 1810) and Waring & Gillow (first established in Lancaster in 1731).

The East End furnished the suburban villas of the new middle classes and later the terraced homes of artisans. With these markets the numbers employed grew rapidly. At its peak in about 1930, some 15,000 workers were employed in the trade in Shoreditch alone. They often worked individually, from small, cramped workshops in alleys and courts, requiring little capital outlay. From 1881–6 the extensive Jewish immigration coincided with the creation of a new work pattern, including subdivision of jobs and sub-contracting to specialist firms. The trade divided into various skills – cabinet making, fancy work, chair making, upholstery, turning, carving and french polishing. During the 1930s there was a shift to more spacious factories in northern suburbs such as Enfield and Tottenham, leaving the East End trade to decline. Today the craft in London consists of many small firms, often cooperatives, operating from traditional premises around Hackney. About two thousand people are employed making reproduction furniture with a few designer–craftsmen.

Combining the skills of the furniture and musical instrument trades, piano-making became established in Camden and Lambeth. The craft experienced a boom when upright pianos became popular after the 1851 Great Exhibition. Broadwoods (established 1771), makers of the first grand pianos, now operates from an industrial estate in Acton. Boosey & Hawkes makes a variety of brass instruments at its Edgware works. Makers of most types of musical instruments, from concertinas to French horns, are found somewhere in London.

In 1891 some 3600 coopers made vast numbers of barrels, casks and vats for trades from brewing to pickling, as well as for use in manufacturing industries throughout London. Today, with mass production, the demand is limited – although a cooper at Young's Brewery in Wandsworth still makes barrels.

TEXTILE TRADES

Before the Industrial Revolution spinning, weaving and dyeing of wool were Britain's main craft industry: finer

LEFT In the nineteenth century Tottenham Court Road became the centre of the quality furniture trade. In 1897 Maple's – which still has a showroom there – were advertising a suite of a settee and eight ornate chairs for £18 10s.

OPPOSITE The hand moulding of glass is one of the crafts being revived in the Covent Garden area. This workshop is in Long Acre.

materials were imported. From 1619 tapestries were made in Mortlake but the factory closed in 1703 following the gradual desertion of the Flemish weavers to new workshops in Soho; these lasted until about 1800. Following the revocation of the Edict of Nantes in 1685 Huguenot craftsmen were encouraged to settle in London. The fine Queen Anne houses with roof-top weaving garrets in Fournier Street, Spitalfields, are evidence of the successful silk weaving enterprise they established. Silk weaving was gradually mechanized: the first factory to use Jacquard looms opened in Streatham in 1820 and has been restored as part of a supermarket complex. But, unable to withstand competition from the Midlands, the north and overseas, it did not last long. By 1900 only a few old men were still weaving and all had stopped by 1939, although narrow fabric handloom weaving continued in Dalston until 1981. In south London, the river Wandle allowed the Huguenots to develop crafts requiring water power and clean air such as calico bleaching and fabric printing. The Liberty Print works at Merton, with its colour house (1742) and a still workable waterwheel (1885), is preserved, but nothing remains of the nearby premises where the William Morris firm made tapestries and printed fabrics from 1881 to 1940. Hand-block fabric printing is still practised at David Evans (established 1800) in south-east London.

GLASS-MAKING

Glass-making began in 1567 with the establishment of a crystal glasshouse at Aldgate by Venetian migrants. There were twenty-four glasshouses by 1696 but only three glass-makers survived into the present century. With the closure in 1980 of Whitefriars Glass, originally sited off Fleet Street but from 1922 in Harrow, that long history ended. The products of the London glass-works ranged from fine cut-glass to bottles and window glass. Some glass-using trades still thrive, such as glass bending in Stratford, and a few glass-blowing workshops, including one at Rotherhithe. The making of stained-glass, once a major London craft, is being revived.

METAL WORKING

Blacksmiths were once common in the engineering firms of Docklands, repairing equipment and making small items. Today they have vanished, but elsewhere a few blacksmiths are still to be found in their forges, chiefly to bend wrought iron into gates and security grilles. Non-ferrous metalwork, using copper and bronze, was once an important London craft. The coppersmith has almost gone but in Wapping pewter is still cast in eighteenth-century moulds and turned by hand into mugs and tankards. Since 1570, church bells have been cast in

Whitechapel, whose bell foundry, one of only two in Britain, has occupied its present premises since 1738.

Among the earliest craftsmen were those working in the noble metals, gold and silver. To their chagrin, the arrival of the Huguenots after 1685 set new standards of excellence in London silver manufacture which reached a peak in the Georgian era. The high value of the objects necessitated a guarantee of quality and since 1300 all gold and silver objects have been assayed by the Goldsmiths' Company and hallmarked, with a coded year of manufacture. To be near Goldsmiths' Hall, the smiths worked and lived in Hatton Garden and other parts of Clerkenwell. Today this is still the centre of the jewellery trade, although silver-wire items are made by craftsmen in many London street markets and gold and silver wire is drawn in Southwark. Coins were minted first in the Tower and from 1810 to 1975 at the Royal Mint opposite, but now they are all minted in Llantrisant, South Wales. By 1800 the finer skills of clock and watch making were one of the leading London crafts. Also centred on Clerkenwell, the industry gradually evolved from individually made items to mass production. Faced with Swiss and then Japanese competition, only a few skilled craftsmen survive. Similar changes have also reduced the number of scientific and medical instrument makers in the area.

This inscribed gilt cup and cover was made in London at the end of the fifteenth century. It was presented to the Armourers and Brasiers' Company in 1548.

The Rag Trade

In the earlier years of this century a gentleman was in no doubt where he should buy his clothes. He went to Savile Row for made-to-measure suits, to Jermyn Street to be measured for shirts, and to St James's Street for hand-made shoes and hats. The retail clothing trade is much changed since then; but it is still possible to visit the same shops and buy – at a price – the same goods.

Savile Row, the home of bespoke tailoring, like other traditional quarters of London, is under threat from rising rents. Recent changes in planning regulations have made it easy for landlords to convert light

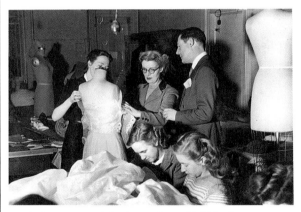

Hardy Amies (to the left), dressmaker to HM The Queen, typifies traditional, classically English, *haute couture*. It is in stark contrast to this scene (right) from Mayhew's *London Labour and the London Poor*, which shows the seedy side of the rag-trade: cheap fabrics and poor workmanship sold in down-at-heel shops to the poor.

industrial premises to more profitable offices. Tailors with workrooms on their premises face the prospect of paying higher rents or moving elsewhere. Meanwhile, the street is still home to several well-known gentlemen's and a few ladies' tailors, including Hardy Amies, who has designed clothes for the Queen.

Modern designers in London present their collections to buyers and the fashion press twice a year at the London Fashion Collections, held in Olympia in March and September. Jasper Conran, Anthony Price, Katharine Hamnett, Jean Muir and Betty Jackson are leading names in British fashion. Those who aspire to emulate them study design at some of London's art schools or at the School of Fashion in Oxford Street.

The wholesale clothing trade in London is concentrated in a small area behind Oxford Street, in and around Great Portland Street and Great Titchfield

Street. The garments offered here, however, are as likely to be made overseas as in Britain. Only vestiges remain in modern London of the sweatshops that used to supply the capital's tailors and ready-made clothes shops. In the nineteenth century, clothes were often made by out-workers based either at home or in workshops set up in whatever space could be found for them: basements, attics and back rooms. Because the work was poorly paid and required neither special training nor expensive equipment, it tended to be done by those most in need: women with no other source of income, and immigrants.

The sewing machine revolutionized the rag trade, but chiefly in ways that benefited the employers rather than the employed. It made possible the production of cheap,

ready-to-wear items that the masses could buy 'off the peg', rather than being kitted out from old-clothes stalls. The sweatshop worker was saved a great deal of hand sewing: a machine could complete between 1000 and 2000 stitches a minute, thirty times as many as a hand worker. But wages for sweated female labour fell in real terms during the last half of the nineteenth century.

There were sweatshops all over London, but particularly in the East End and Spitalfields, which had been colonized by Huguenot silk weavers in the late seventeenth century. By the Victorian era, what had once been prosperous Georgian merchants' houses had been colonized by poor Jewish immigrants and had degenerated into overcrowded workshops. Today in Spitalfields, side by side with smartly renovated buildings, sweatshops filled with Asian workers are a modern version, a sharp reminder of the past.

MADE IN LONDON:
MANUFACTURING INDUSTRIES

London does not *appear* industrial – there are no satanic mills, mines or furnaces – yet it is Britain's greatest manufacturing centre. Over the years geography, climate and the City have forced industry eastward along the river, following the prevailing wind. Manufacturing plants were established just outside the City boundaries, in places such as Hackney and Southwark, then further out with each passing decade. The nineteenth-century development of docks and railways meant that bulk products could be brought conveniently into the eastern areas. In 1843 the writer George Dodd noted that Southwark was 'as distinguishable for its tall chimneys and smoke as London is for its church spires'. Evidence of such extensive industry is today more elusive, although in some areas the terraces of cramped houses built for factory workers – artisans' dwellings – have lasted longer than the factories themselves.

BUILDING MATERIALS

Lacking suitable building stone, London's very structure was formed from its earth. The stock brick of Georgian and Victorian terraces was burnt from local clays extended with local rubbish. Temporary brickfields opened on speculative property developments while permanent brickyards existed in the suburbs, those at Enfield and Croydon surviving to the mid-1970s. Cement, too, had to be formed on site. Coade stone, an artificial architectural ornamentation in earthenware, was produced at Eleanor Coade's Lambeth manufactory, from 1769 to about 1840. The South Bank Lion, outside County Hall, is made from it. Structural members such as roof trusses and columns were also originally made from local timber but after the seventeenth century oak and deal were imported from the Baltic. As cast iron replaced wood, London firms found it increasingly difficult to compete with provincial foundries.

FOOD AND DRINK

As a major port handling raw foodstuffs from around the world, and with a heavily concentrated population, London has always had a large and varied food

OPPOSITE Clothing manufacture is a labour-intensive business, which is why it has often attracted recent immigrants looking for work. This kind of crowded workroom is still common in the East End: this one is in Shoreditch.

manufacturing industry. Grain was milled at water mills and tide mills along the Thames. Two tide mills survive at Bromley-by-Bow, and windmills at Brixton and Wimbledon. Steam milling was attempted from 1786 at Albion Mills, Southwark, but the process only became established from the 1880s when it was used at Millwall Docks to mill imported wheat. Bakeries, domestic and large-scale, survive. Biscuits – Jacobs and Peek Frean in Southwark – and confectionery were other London products.

For liquid refreshment there were numerous breweries, many producing a characteristic London porter. Rationalization in the 1970s reduced those in the central area to Trumans in Brick Lane, Youngs in Wandsworth and Fullers in Chiswick. Old breweries have been converted into apartments (Courages in Southwark) and entertainment suites (Whitbreads in Chiswell Street). The hop trade has left decorated warehouses and the fine Hop Exchange (1866) in Southwark, now offices. Vinegar brewing continues near Tower Bridge. Distilleries, particularly for gin, centred on Clerkenwell and Lambeth. Companies such as Rawlings of Camberwell, established in about 1810, provided non-alcoholic drinks including mineral water, fruit squashes and sarsaparilla.

ENGINEERING INDUSTRIES

As the seat of government, London attracted the industries of warfare. Cannon were cast at the Tower from about 1350, while smaller weapons of war were made at Moorfields. In 1515 Henry VIII recruited German craftsmen to make armour at the Royal Greenwich workshops, but this and the related armoury at Lewisham were closed in about 1640. An ordnance depot opened at Woolwich in 1671, and in 1805 this became the Royal Arsenal. A superb range of buildings from 1696 to the late nineteenth century, part of London's largest industrial complex, survive within the compound.

Until the end of the eighteenth century Britain had relied on private manufacturers, often foreign, for its small arms, but in 1807 the Government repurchased the old Lewisham armoury for a gun works. Nine years later most production transferred to Enfield Lock, which afforded better water power and communications. This new works, the Royal Small Arms factory, became

Henry VIII made Deptford into a shipyard for the British fleet. This painting by Daniel Maclise (1806–70) portrays Peter the Great visiting the dockyard in 1688.

OPPOSITE Brewing is one of London's oldest industries. Records show that there has been a brewery on the site of Fuller's in Chiswick at least since the Elizabethan era. The venue has not changed but the process has: today the industry is highly mechanized.

famous for the Lee-Enfield rifle. Its rival, the London Small Arms Company (established 1865), was in Gunmakers Lane, E3. Gunpowder was made at remote sites including Balham, Hounslow Heath, Bedfont and Waltham Abbey – the last acquired by the state in 1795 but, like the RSA at Enfield, now being redeveloped.

Henry VIII was also the father of British shipbuilding, at least as far as warships are concerned. In 1513 he established dockyards at Deptford and Woolwich. Hundreds of men-o'-war and, later, iron-clad battleships were built on the Thames before changes in naval architecture, calling for deep-water yards, forced their closure in 1869. At Deptford the master shipbuilder's house (1708) and two giant iron-framed ship sheds (1847–8) survive in a paper importer's premises, while some of the Woolwich buildings were incorporated in a housing development.

These government establishments prompted the growth of related firms, particularly in shipbuilding, They were also a training ground for many enterprising engineers. Henry Maudslay, apprenticed at the Arsenal, went on in 1795 to found, in Well Street in the West End, the pre-eminent mechanical engineering firm of the Industrial Revolution – Maudslay, Sons and Field. They produced machine tools and steam engines for waterworks, factories and ships – and incidentally trained the next generation of engineers including James Nasmyth and Joseph Whitworth. (A beam engine survives at Kew Steam Museum while the site of their later works in Lambeth is commemorated in the entrance to Lambeth North underground station.)

Until the Victorian era the distinctions between millwrights, coppersmiths and engineers were vague.

Among the earliest was Thomas Savery, who produced a forerunner of the steam engine from works near St Bride's in Fleet Street in 1698. Harrison & Waylett were casting steam cylinders in Southwark by 1730. Around 1800 Joseph Bramah, at his Pimlico works, developed hydraulic presses, while Bryan Donkin in Bermondsey perfected both paper-making machinery and food canning. From the 1830s Penns in Greenwich, Rennies in Blackfriars and Simpsons in Pimlico started to supply engines and boilers for London's public utilities and shipyards, and later diversified. The largest engineering firm was the Thames Ironworks & Shipbuilding Company, (established in 1856) on Bow Creek. It had civil and electrical engineering, motor-car and shipbuilding departments, but closed in 1912 after building HMS *Thunderer*, the last Thames-launched warship.

London foundries cast everything from locomotives to bridges and machine tools, but domestic and architectural items predominated. Street furniture provides clues to lost firms; the products of St Pancras Ironworks (for instance, pavement lights) and Haywoods (coal-hole covers) can be seen in most English towns. Others, such as Dewers (founders of the City dragons) and Youngs (who cast the Embankment lamp standards), raised casting to an art.

—— CHEMICAL AND LEATHER TRADES ——
With its low-lying land and many water-courses, Bermondsey became home to the smells of leather manufacture. Fellmongering (dealing in skins) lasted here until 1972 and many works and warehouses, the Leather Market (1833) and the elaborate Leather Exchange (1878) survive off Bermondsey Street. To their west

The Potteries

London was an important centre for the production of pottery and porcelain for nearly four hundred years, from the establishment of a tin-glazed earthenware (Delftware) pottery in Aldgate in 1571 to the closure in 1956 of the Doulton factory on Albert Embankment, just south of Lambeth Palace. London Delftware, Chelsea and Bow porcelain and the Doulton wares are today collectors' items.

Slipware tiles and vessels, in the natural brown or red colour of the clay, were made in London throughout the Middle Ages, probably by small-scale artisans, but the secret of making white porcelain, perfected by the Chinese in the ninth century, eluded Europeans for a further nine hundred years. In the sixteenth century Dutch potters began making earthenware vessels glazed with a tin solution that provided a near-white base for

Apothecaries' Company; and large dishes (chargers) bearing portraits of royalty and the aristocracy or flower designs, especially tulips. In 1672 a pottery was established at Fulham, making salt-glazed stoneware, tougher than Delftware, therefore popular for bottles and jugs. The last vestiges of the factory, in New King's Road, were not demolished until the 1970s.

Many of the designs on seventeenth-century London pottery derived from those on Chinese porcelain, but with earthenware it was never possible to duplicate porcelain's delicacy. By the mid-eighteenth century a technique had been discovered for making soft-paste porcelain, a kind of pseudo-porcelain that shared many characteristics with the Chinese original. A factory was established at Lawrence Street in CHELSEA in 1745 and for forty years produced some of the most decorative English china. In addition to crockery and vases with finer decoration than that used on Delftware, the factory became known for its figurines – small, subtly painted statuettes. Another important factory was opened at the

ABOVE A Chelsea punch bowl of 1770 with views of Chelsea and Battersea.
LEFT John Doulton opened his Lambeth pottery in 1815. By 1879, the date of this engraving, it had become noted for sanitary as well as decorative wares. The company left London in 1956 but one of its former buildings still stands on the corner of Lambeth High Street and Black Prince Road.

decoration in blue and other colours. In 1571 two potters from Antwerp began to produce the new wares in Aldgate and they came to be known as Delftware, after the pottery at Delft in Holland.

Early in the seventeenth century the Aldgate potters moved to Southwark, by the Thames. This was more convenient because they had to ship clay from Norfolk and Kent, London clay being unsuitable for tin-glazing. Later in the century they moved to less crowded Lambeth, where a number of potteries were established near the riverside between the present-day Lambeth and Vauxhall bridges. Characteristic London pieces include wine bottles, often dated; bulbous drug jars used by pharmacists; pill slabs with the coat of arms of the

same time in BOW, making more robust and practical dishes but also many figurines, some copied from the Dresden wares made at Meissen in Saxony.

In 1815, John Doulton opened a Lambeth pottery and by the end of the nineteenth century the company's name had become associated with vases and bowls in flamboyant patterns and colours, as well as with its ubiquitous stoneware sanitary ware for private bathrooms and public lavatories – catching the tide of the Victorian drive towards hygiene. All Doulton's production was switched to the Potteries in 1956 but one of the factory buildings survived the subsequent demolition: on the corner of Black Prince Road and Lambeth High Street, it is recognizable by its quaint tiles and reliefs.

gathered the poisonous lead-smelting trades characterized by tall chimneys and shot towers – one of them incorporated into the Festival of Britain site in 1951. Today a solitary shot tower remains in Tottenham.

An area east of the City became an early centre of the equally noxious chemical industry. The earliest firms exploited inorganic chemistry. The Deptford beds of copperas (an iron salt used in ink and black dyes) were described in 1678. The manufacture of paint and pigment was also long established: Bergers started in Shadwell in 1760. Surviving firms include Ilfords, makers of photographic materials, established in 1879; and Bryant & Mays, the matchmakers, set up in London in 1841. Another group derives from processing vegetable matter for dyestuffs, essences and medicines. Allen & Hanbury, founded in 1715, now part of the Glaxo group, and May & Baker, established in Battersea in 1834, are still active in the chemical and drugs industries but have their laboratories in the surburbs.

The introduction in 1812 of lighting by gas, distilled from coal, led to a search for uses for the coal-tar by-product and the development of the tar-distilling industry. London's most significant contribution was the discovery in 1856 by Henry Perkins of Shadwell of the first synthetic dyestuffs derived from coal tar. Commerical production of his mauve dye started in Greenford in 1857 and within six months was being used to dye silk in Bethnal Green. North Sea gas completely transformed the industry. The gasworks, including the giants at Beckton and East Greenwich, closed, leaving only groups of gasholders, notably Fulham (1830, 1871), St Pancras (1861–83), Bromley-by-Bow (1870s) and those at Kennington, by the Oval.

Rubber and gutta-percha processing were based in the East End and Hackney Wick became the centre of the early plastic industry when the British Xylonite Works opened in 1864. Artifical silk (viscose rayon yarn) was discovered by Cross & Bevan in 1892 and manufactured in the mews at Kew Gardens station from 1894. Carless, Capel & Leonard of Hackney Wick, oil distillers since 1859, became in the 1890s the first British producer of petrol – a name they coined.

VEHICLE MANUFACTURE

Carriage building began in London in the sixteenth century and by 1750 was centred on Covent Garden. Firms executed individual orders for clients rather than building speculatively. With the arrival of the motor age, firms like Hoopers and Mulliners built car bodies on separate chassis, developing a grandiose style for the rich clients who were then the only people who could afford motor cars. Many of the best-known makes originated in London but soon moved elsewhere when growing demand meant that they needed more space. Vauxhall Motors began as the Vauxhall Ironworks in Wandsworth Road, Vauxhall. Cars were produced there from 1902, but four years later the company moved to Luton, Bedfordshire, where it remains today. Talbot, later Sunbeam–Talbot, began life in North Kennington. Ford at Dagenham is the only car manufacturer left in the London area.

The manufacture of larger vehicles similarly began in the capital. Scammell, makers of trucks, was established in Spitalfields in 1850, while AEC and Park Royal buses were first built on London's fringes. Short Brothers started in 1906 as balloon makers in railway arches in Battersea and began to build aircraft there in 1909, but soon found the space too cramped. In north London, especially around Hendon, was a thriving aircraft components industry. When these engineering companies moved away they took their skilled artisans with them, leaving the old factory sites and the housing around them to degenerate into slums.

OTHER INDUSTRIES

Fleet Street (see *The press*) was only the most visible element of London's printing trade. With the nineteenth-century mechanization of printing, every district had its jobbing printers but the larger firms, including Waterlows, congregated around Finsbury and Clerkenwell with an outpost in Southwark. Support trades were established nearby including Figgins, the largest printing-press makers and typefounders in Britain. Today the photocopying shop is replacing the jobbing printer and, with the development of computer typesetting, the largest printers are now outside London, accelerating a trend started before 1900.

In 1889 Ferranti opened the world's first high-voltage power station at Deptford and London entered the electrical age and following the First World War demand for electricity increased rapidly. Heavy electrical engineering was dominated by Ferranti and Siemens, with works in Greenwich. New industries developed using mass production techniques and often employing women. They made domestic goods such as vacuum cleaners, radios and car components. These relatively clean industries built innovative modern factories along the arterial roads, most spectacular of which is the Art Deco Hoover's on Western Avenue.

The electronic revolution of the 1980s has accelerated the changeover in London from manufacturing to service industries. Manufacturers find themselves unable to compete for labour and space. Small-scale new industries occupy science parks, sometimes in Victorian factory conversions, or are returning east to high-technology units in rebuilt Docklands.

LAWYERS AND COURTS

The traditional heart of legal London lies in a compact area barely a half-mile square, no part of it more than fifteen minutes' walk from any other. The east–west axis is bounded by two great courts of law – the Royal Courts of Justice in the Strand and the Old Bailey. Gray's Inn forms its northern outpost; the Temple, which wanders down to the Embankment, its southern boundary. It is bisected by busy Fleet Street, once synonymous with the national press. That small patch contains two-thirds of all the practising barristers in England and Wales; hundreds of solicitors' firms; the most famous criminal court-house in the world; the most important appeal courts in the land; the headquarters of the two branches of the legal profession; and a complex infrastructure of shops, offices and services dedicated to serving the law and its trappings. Some 13,000 people are employed here in the business of law, and about 16,000 elsewhere in London.

THE LAWYERS

English lawyers are of two kinds. Solicitors work in their offices, seeing clients, drawing up documents and dealing mainly with the legal aspects of divorces, wills, house-buying, and acting for defendants on criminal charges. Barristers are, in theory, the experts in a particular field of the law or in advocacy, the art of arguing cases in court. They are called in – 'instructed' or 'briefed' – by solicitors to take on the specialist work. But these strict divisions are under threat. At present, for instance, only barristers can plead a case before the higher courts and only barristers can become senior judges. Soon both these privileges are to be watered down. Solicitors, of whom there are more than 50,000 in England and Wales – nearly a third of them in London – work in ordinary offices, wear ordinary clothes, and speak in more or less intelligible English. Barristers are at the glamorous end of the legal profession: they wear the horse-hair wigs and long black gowns, work in delightful surroundings, participate in ancient rites and customs and often communicate in a jargon few outsiders can understand.

At the hub of legal London are the four Inns of Court, clusters of elegant, mainly eighteenth- and nineteenth-century buildings, courtyards and gardens where London's 4000 barristers ply their ancient trade. The Inns – Inner Temple, Middle Temple, Lincoln's and Gray's – have largely managed to fight off the ravages of modernization. Protected by the planning laws and the determined conservatism of their own officials, they are, on the outside at least, much as they were a century ago.

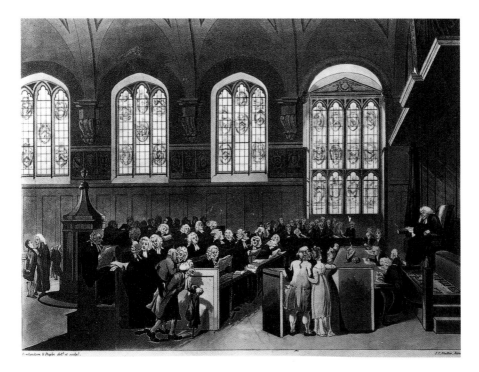

LEFT In 1808, the Court of Chancery sat in the fifteenth-century hall at Lincoln's Inn. Now it is part of the nearby Law Courts but Lincoln's Inn barristers still specialize in Chancery cases involving commercial and company law.

OPPOSITE The gilded figure of Justice wielding sword and scales, by the Victorian sculptor F.W. Pomeroy, rises above the Central Criminal Court at Old Bailey, turning her back on the City's modern office buildings.

The Criminal Underworld

During the eighteenth and part of the nineteenth century no city had so varied and so sophisticated a range of criminals as London. Today London crime is a shadow of its former self, far down the world league table, with few of the colourful characters and activities that gave it its reputation.

Records of criminal London go back to medieval times. There are references dating from the thirteenth century to those who 'broke open many houses belonging to other persons and carried such goods as were there to be found'. Out of incidents like that grew the network of watchmen, beadles and constables – citizens charged with the duty of keeping the peace in their area. They did so with little success, and were often as dishonest as the criminals they were supposed to suppress.

In the seventeenth century the respectable citizens of London started to suffer seriously from what would now be called organized crime. The growing prosperity of the city was accompanied by a growth in villainy at all levels, from petty theft to professional murder. Criminal

areas developed, filled with 'flash houses' populated by thieves and their business associates, where young homeless boys could learn their trade – precursors of Fagin's school for thieves so vividly described by Dickens in *Oliver Twist*. Fleet Street and its immediate neighbourhood was one such area. Later Seven Dials and St Giles – where New Oxford Street is now – became the centre of criminal activity.

Crime and criminals were highly specialized and hierarchical, with a bewildering array of professional descriptions. Henry Mayhew, the chronicler of London's streets in the mid-nineteenth century, lists hundreds of criminal occupations. Terms like mobsmen, shofulmen, ringers, mouchers and skittle-sharps all had specific meanings. 'Buzzers' were pickpockets, but they were subdivided into 'stock-buzzers' – who picked handkerchiefs – and 'tail-buzzers', who were more interested in snuff-boxes and pocket-books. The thieves, burglars, footpads, fences, forgers and other representatives of the criminal classes mingled with beggars, down-and-outs and prostitutes – many of them girls barely in their teens – in the smelly, unlit, rat-infested alleyways of criminal London.

The penalty for many categories of crime was death by hanging and thousands of petty and serious offenders took their last journey from Newgate Prison (near the site of today's Old Bailey) to the gallows at Tyburn, where Marble Arch now stands. Yet it was not the police who captured the criminals. London up to the early nineteenth century was still without a police force. Crime-fighting was left to the haphazard efforts of inefficient watchmen and constables – and, in the eighteenth century, to a new class of private entrepreneur, the thief-taker. The greatest of them, Jonathan Wild, was a former robber with a comprehensive network of informants. His substantial earnings came both from the rewards on offer from the authorities and from helping himself to a cut of the booty he recovered from the thieves he handed over. Wild ended up taking the same route to the gallows that he had marked out for so many others, and the role of thief-taker faded out.

Then came the Bow Street Runners, but it was not until 1829 that the Home Secretary, Sir Robert Peel, managed to get a Bill through Parliament creating the Metropolitan Police – now better known as Scotland Yard. The idea had first been proposed nearly a half-century before but had been blocked by the City of London, jealous of its independence and demanding to

Mayfair has always been a magnet for prostitutes and their potential clients, as shown in this print dated 1786. Today the lady's successors, equally well turned out, patrol the streets of Shepherd's Market, only a few hundred yards away.

RIGHT In the 1880s Jack the Ripper, the East End murderer, caught the national imagination and provided dramatic material for the cheap illustrated press. He was never identified but was probably Montague Druitt, a young barrister who drowned in the Thames after the Ripper's last murder.

BELOW This 1832 cartoon, with its dreadful and morbid pun, portrays Robert Peel's new police force, authorized by Act of Parliament three years earlier.

remain in charge of its own policing. Its continued objections to a London-wide police force meant that the 1829 Act did not apply to the square mile; to this day the City has a separate and anomalous force, distinctive in its red and white checked caps and epaulettes.

The arrival of a disciplined police force did not immediately result in a diminution of crime, but the nineteenth century was also an era of social reform. Some of the slums were cleared and gradually, through this and other factors, the worst excesses of criminal London were removed. Yet organized crime has made its mark at various times over the last century. Some of it has been the responsibility of specific national groupings – like the Maltese gangs that controlled prostitution and crime in Soho in the 1950s, and the more recent Mafia drug connections. Other criminal organizations have been more straightforwardly territorial – the Kray

brothers in the East End and the Richardson gang in South London in the late 1950s and 1960s.

But it is mainly the individual criminal, the killer especially, who has captured public attention. London has had its fair share of gruesome murderers. Most of the infamous homicidal addresses, though, have been transformed and sometimes the very street names changed to hide ghastly memories. Notting Hill's 10 Rillington Place, where John Christie killed a succession of women, is now disguised as Ruston Mews; and 39 Hilldrop Crescent, Tufnell Park, under whose floorboards Dr Crippen buried the wife he had killed, is now part of a council estate. Some of the streets around Whitechapel, where London's most famous killer of all, Jack the Ripper, perpetrated his atrocities, are still there – and can be visited by guided tour – but their clammy and sinister Victorian atmosphere has long given way to a succession of untidy developments. (It is now widely accepted that the evidence of the Ripper's identity points to Montague Druitt, a young barrister. His body was fished out of the Thames shortly after the last Ripper killing in 1888.) Not all has been lost. The Blind Beggar pub, where East End gang leader Ronnie Kray blasted an underworld colleague through the head, is still there; so is the Magdala pub in Hampstead, outside which Ruth Ellis, the last woman to be hanged for murder in England, shot her unfaithful lover.

It is difficult today to pinpoint criminal areas of London. Lawlessness is more fragmented now, like the city itself. Wherever there is money, there are criminals – even if some sophisticated City fraudsters may be harder to spot than the Artful Dodger himself.

THE INNS

The Inns of Court, which date back to the fourteenth century or perhaps before, were originally, as their name suggests, eating and lodging places for students of the law. There are references to more than thirty different inns over the centuries, each with its own purpose and character. The four that remain still offer living accommodation and food, but only a few privileged judges and senior barristers have rooms at the Inns, snapped up when they were available decades ago, at controlled rents. Even fewer live in the Inns permanently; most use them only during the working week.

Eating, though, is still taken seriously. Each of the Inns has an imposing, high-ceilinged, oak-beamed, panelled hall, resplendent with coats of arms and painted portraits. At lunch time it serves as the works canteen, with simple self-service food consumed at long refectory tables. The evening meal is more formal, with the judges and barristers joined by a gaggle of young law students reading for the bar. No one can be 'called to the bar' – allowed to practise – without having eaten twenty-four dinners. The requirement goes back centuries. In theory, turning up for the dinners is supposed to allow the young barrister-to-be an opportunity to mix with his or her qualified elders and to absorb the customs and traditions of the bar – such as never shaking hands with a fellow barrister, and the directions in which wine and port are passed around the table.

Barristers' offices, called 'chambers', are still organized along nineteenth-century lines. Clerks arrange business for the perhaps fifteen or twenty barristers in their chambers, each of whom is technically self-employed. Until a barrister is established, he (most are still men) may not be in sufficient demand to earn a decent living, which is why the profession has traditionally been dominated by the middle and upper classes. The explosion of legal aid in the 1950s and 1960s improved the lot of the newly qualified and encouraged a wider spread of recruitment, although recent restrictions on legal aid have again put the squeeze on. The clerks, on the other hand, who had no need of formal qualifications, could until recently earn substantial sums; they received up to ten per cent of all their barristers' fees, which in successful chambers might mean take-home pay of £50,000 a year or more. Those golden days are ending, though: today most clerks are on fixed salaries, or a combination of salary and a small commission.

Barristers are not supposed to discuss fees directly with the solicitors who instruct them – indeed, their charges are still regarded, legally, as voluntary honorariums. There is a flap at the back of barristers' gowns into which, in bygone days, solicitors used to slip their payment. Walking into a typical set of chambers in one of the inns for the first time, the visitor half expects to step into another Dickensian scene. The reality is less charming: the majority of chambers have long abandoned the quill pen for the word-processor and the calf-bound ledger for computerized print-outs.

The four inns fulfil identical functions but are deeply conscious of their separate histories, attractions, foibles and traditions. According to an old rhyme, one chooses 'Gray's Inn for walks/Lincoln's Inn for a wall/Inner Temple for a garden/And the Middle for a hall'. The last two lines are still true. The Inner Temple's lawns and gardens, meandering down to the Embankment, are the best kept and most striking; the Middle Temple's hall the most splendidly opulent, crowned by a magnificent interior roof supported by Elizabethan hammer beams. But the walks of Gray's Inn – a reference to a time when its gardens were a rendezvous for smart society – have mostly gone. Lincoln's Inn today boasts the most impressive library, an old hall originally built in 1489 and a seventeenth-century chapel, much of it rebuilt, but still with its original pillars. The Temple, too, has its church, its origins in the twelfth century, when it was the site for the religious order of the Knights Templars (hence, still, 'the Temple'). Over the centuries the different inns have attracted different kinds of students and barristers but distinctions are fewer now – although Lincoln's has kept its separate identity as the inn for barristers at the Chancery bar, and its members have the curious and unique privilege, conferred more than three hundred years ago by Charles II after a dinner there, of being allowed to stay seated during the loyal toast to the monarch.

If the heart of legal London is that small area around the inns of court, the last few years have seen its head move east, into the City itself. The large solicitors' firms in the City earn, in total, a far greater income than the bar. Lawyers' incomes are not made public, but estimates put the accumulated earnings of London barristers at around £150 million a year. In contrast, the City of London law firms combined would reach an income of £1000 million. The few dozen sizeable firms in the City (out of nine thousand countrywide) monopolize much of the remunerative commercial and financial legal work for both English and, increasingly, international clients. The largest firm, Clifford Chance, has two hundred partners, and there are another half-dozen with more than one hundred. Compare that with the majority of solicitors' firms, which have at most four partners.

London has nearly fifteen thousand solicitors. Apart from the City, there are concentrations in the West End and in Holborn, but the remainder are scattered around the high streets of the capital. The headquarters of their professional body, the Law Society, is at 113 Chancery

Lane, in the heart of the legal enclave, but few of the capital's solicitors venture there.

THE COURTS

The Royal Courts of Justice – usually just called the LAW COURTS – is an imposing Victorian Gothic edifice where the Strand meets Fleet Street. It accommodates all but one of the country's highest courts: only the House of Lords, the highest in the land, is absent. The more prolific appeal courts are there, with their twenty-seven judges hearing nearly ten thousand appeals a year, on both civil and criminal matters. The eighty or so judges of the High Court also operate there, dealing with the most serious civil issues. The High Court itself is divided into three. The Queen's Bench division mainly handles claims for damages for personal injury arising from accidents, and disputes over money owing. The Family Division attempts to resolve sensitive legal issues affecting the breakdown of marriages and the plight of children. The Chancery Division, the target of Charles Dickens's savage pen in *Bleak House*, handles commercial and contract cases and now provides a rather speedier and fairer service than its predecessor more than a century ago.

The Law Courts do not include London's criminal courts. Criminal trials take place in the ninety-four Crown courts all over England and Wales. The senior of them all, is the prosaically named Central Criminal Court, far better known as the OLD BAILEY, after the short street where it is situated. Some of the most notorious murderers of the century have stood in the dock of Number One Court, many to hear the solemn words of the death sentence passed on them before the abolition of the death penalty in 1965.

There are ten other Crown courts scattered around London, as well as nearly thirty county courts (for minor civil cases) and fifty magistrates' courts, which handle minor criminal cases – some ninety-seven per cent of all criminal cases. The magistrates' court at BOW STREET is redolent with history. One of its first paid magistrates was Henry Fielding, the author of *Tom Jones*. He was succeeded by his brother, the blind John Fielding, who started the Bow Street Runners, the capital's first policemen and predecessors of today's Metropolitan Police. Bow Street is still the most important magistrates' court in the country. It is there that demands for extradition are decided. In the West End, the MARLBOROUGH STREET court is notable for the variety and occasional celebrity of its customers. One day may see a foreign princess in the dock, charged with shoplifting; the next a famous pop star accused of brawling outside a local night spot.

At the other end of the legal spectrum is the HOUSE OF LORDS, the highest appeal court in the United Kingdom, manned by ten law lords. They sit, in panels of five, in a committee room of the House of Lords at Westminster. The shock to the first-time visitor is that these judges, the most eminent in the land, are the least bedecked and majestic. No wigs, no gowns – just five elderly gentlemen in dark suits. It is typical of a legal system famous for its panoply that, at its highest level, it reverts to mundane simplicity.

Street's Law Courts soon after they were opened by Queen Victoria in 1882. The view is much the same today. Temple Bar, which stood on the site of the griffin statue, had been removed four years earlier to ease traffic problems.

THE PRESS

At the end of the 1980s London, for the first time since the start of the eighteenth century, had no definable newspaper district. The *Daily Courant*, the city's first daily paper, began publication from an office near Ludgate Circus in 1702, since when the newspaper industry had never strayed far from FLEET STREET, the artery linking the centre of government at Westminster with the City. Yet since the mid-1980s, when the deadlock with the unions over the introduction of new technology was finally broken, the great Fleet Street

All Englishmen delight in News
In London there's enough to chuse
Of morning papers near a Ream
Fill'd with every kind of theme
At Noon there's such a duced Clatter
Strangers must wonder what's the matter
And Een that day the Lord hath blest
Is now no more a day of rest

Forth from the Prefs the Papers fly
Each greedy reader to supply
Of battles fought, and numbers slain.
Of Towns besieg'd and prisoners ta'en.
Engagements both by Sea and Land
Ecche from Aldgate to the Strand
Hail! happy land, sure none's so blest
With News to comfort every breast

Published as the Act directs 30 Dec.r 1780 by W. Richardson No 68 high Holborn.

This poem was published by W. Richardson in 1780, a satire on the number of newspapers published in London – although none of today's papers was in existence then.

papers have scattered east to Wapping and the Isle of Dogs, west to Kensington and south to Battersea. Their old Dickensian offices and press rooms have been pulled down, to be replaced by tall towers housing extensions of the financial district.

EARLY TIMES

A number of factors conspired to make Fleet Street the centre of the newspaper industry for nearly three hundred years. In 1500 Wynkyn de Worde, a former associate of William Caxton, had established his printing works near St Bride's church by the Fleet river. Other printers followed. The legal profession was among the best customers for the printed word and the location was conveniently close to the inns of court. In 1712 a heavy duty was imposed on newspapers by a nervous government, anxious to increase their price so as to limit circulation to the wealthy and reduce the opportunity of spreading seditious ideas among the masses. The papers had to be taken physically to the Government Stamp Office to be stamped. In the 1770s the Stamp Office moved from Lincoln's Inn to the newly reconstructed Somerset House, at the Fleet Street end of the Strand. In 1820 W.H.Smith, the company that distributed newspapers outside the capital, moved its centre of operations to a building almost next door to Somerset House.

Because most of the main population centres could be reached by stage coaches within a day, the London papers quickly established a national market. With few exceptions, they deterred the growth of strong regional rivals so that, unlike those of most other countries, Britain's great provincial cities have never spawned papers to rival the influence of those published in the capital. The coaches on which the London papers were loaded for their journeys left from St Martin's Le Grand, just east of Fleet Street by St Paul's Cathedral (and today the headquarters of the Post Office). Fleet Street was at the centre of all these strategic locations.

Circulation of the earliest papers was minimal. In 1711 the total sale of all daily papers was a mere 7500, about half accounted for by Addison and Steele's *Spectator* (short-lived as a daily but still with us as a lively weekly). New titles appeared throughout the century and disappeared as rapidly. They were hampered by a ban on reporters in Parliament. Accounts of Parliamentary business were gained at second hand by writers talking to people who had been inside the chamber. In 1771, after a campaign by the reformer John Wilkes, the restriction on direct reporting was lifted, but not until 1803 were reporters allowed to sit in the gallery of the House. In 1828 the historian Lord Macaulay described the Parliamentary press gallery as 'the fourth estate of the realm' (see *The centre of government*).

The first paper with true staying power was launched in 1785 as *The Daily Universal Register*, a name changed three years later to *The Times*. John Walter started it at Printing House Square, just east of Fleet Street, primarily to promote a new printing process; but the paper outlasted the technology. It won a reputation for speed and accuracy in reporting – rare characteristics among its rivals, which were largely political pamphlets. It brought London the first reports of the French Revolution and was the first paper to set up an embryo foreign service by sending a correspondent to Paris. It scooped its rivals on the Battle of Trafalgar and later sent William Howard Russell to the Crimea as Britain's first war correspondent: his accounts of the incompetence of the leadership provoked an outcry and subsequent reforms.

The introduction of steam printing in 1814, and the appointments of first Thomas Barnes and then John Delane as editors, made *The Times* the dominant paper during the first half of the nineteenth century, with a reputation for revealing confidential government information. At its peak it commanded 80 per cent of all daily newspaper circulation. When President Lincoln welcomed Russell to Washington before the Civil War, he described *The Times* as one of the greatest powers in the world – 'in fact I don't know anything which has much more power, except perhaps the Mississippi'.

The stamp duty, which was the same for all papers

principally been aimed. Stories about crime, scandal and other sensations – hitherto restricted to the cheap weekly journals – found their way into the daily press. A tradition of newspaper stunts was begun; the *Telegraph* co-sponsored Stanley's trip to Africa to find Livingstone. In 1870 the Elementary Education Act enlarged the literate working class and the potential market for still racier and more succinct journalism. First to exploit it was Alfred Harmsworth, later Lord Northcliffe, who started a chain of successful weekly journals. In 1894, he bought the failing *Evening News* and, using the populist techniques he had been refining on his weekly papers, he increased the circulation dramatically. Two years later launched the *Daily Mail*, selling for only a halfpenny – half the price of its competitors. Within two years its circulation was half a million copies a day.

Northcliffe went on to establish the *Daily Mirror* and in 1908 to buy *The Times*, which he owned for fourteen years. He left *The Times* much as it was editorially, although he strengthened its commercial base, but with the other two papers he pioneered techniques that are the basis of today's popular journalism – sensationalism, gossip, circulation-building promotional stunts and

The composing room of the Temple Printing Office in Bouverie Street, off Fleet Street. The invention of the Linotype machine in the 1880s ended the need for hand setting letter by letter, but after that there was no real change in printing technology for a hundred years.

regardless of size or circulation, protected the position of *The Times* by making it prohibitively expensive to launch competition. The abolition of the duty in 1855 signalled the start of a price war. In 1858 the *Daily Telegraph* appeared as a twopenny paper (compared with *The Times* at fivepence) and soon brought its price down to a penny. Within a few years it became the first to achieve a six-figure circulation.

THE MASS MARKET

With higher sales came attempts to appeal to readers other than the ruling élite at which *The Times* had

competitions. By the time he died in 1922 the *Mail*'s circulation stood at 1¾ million.

Competition for its market increased in the inter-war years, especially from Lord Beaverbrook and his *Daily Express*. In 1930 a new competitor appeared, the *Daily Herald*, launched to provide a platform for the trade union movement and quickly locating a seven-figure market. It was the first newspaper to sell two million copies a day, largely through starting a giveaway war – free books, free insurance – in which its competitors were forced to participate.

The *Express* overtook the *Herald* in 1937 by investing

more in its overseas and domestic news services than had been customary in the popular market. It remained dominant until outstripped after the Second World War by the tabloid *Daily Mirror* (no longer part of the Harmsworth empire) which, by pioneering the use of large headlines and pictures, reached a circulation of more than five million in the 1950s. Even this, however, was exceeded by some Sunday papers, notably the *News of the World* whose unvarying diet of sex and scandal took it to a sale of eight million copies a week soon after the war. In the mid-1950s television became a rival advertising medium, but circulations and revenue remained buoyant.

The arrival of the Australian press magnate Rupert Murdoch in Fleet Street in 1969 heralded the next great changes in the newspaper industry. He bought first the *News of the World* and then *The Sun*, a failing paper that had grown from the ashes of the *Daily Herald*. By a greater emphasis on sex, including printing regular pictures of semi-naked women on page three and franker revelations of the private lives of the famous, it climbed to overtake the *Mirror* in the mid-1970s as the most popular daily paper. Soon all the mass- and middle-market daily papers switched to tabloid format, leaving only *The Times*, *Telegraph*, *Guardian* and *Financial Times* with the traditional broadsheet page size.

TECHNOLOGICAL CHANGE

Murdoch was responsible for the revolution in production techniques that led to the exodus from Fleet Street in the 1980s. For years the technology had existed for journalists to type directly into machines that would send their words straight to the page. The closely knit print unions had resisted its introduction because of the threat to jobs – and they had the power to stop the production of any daily paper simply by downing tools at the critical moment. To prevent such disruption, newspaper owners allowed the unions to control entry into the industry. To be 'in the print' was to hold a privileged position in the skilled working class. Printers traditionally lived in London's eastern and south-eastern suburbs and their well-paid jobs would often be handed down from father to son. The proprietors would also turn a blind eye to the 'Spanish customs' – small-scale fiddles by which print workers were paid for work they had not done. No wonder they would not budge.

Murdoch outflanked the unions by building a new plant in Wapping, east of Tower Bridge, in the 1970s, installing modern equipment and secretly arranging to staff it with technicians who were not members of the print unions. At two days' notice he shifted production of his four papers – he now owned *The Times* and *Sunday Times* as well – to Wapping. Another national paper, *The Independent*, was launched successfully a few months later, with no printing capacity of its own.

The unions accepted defeat and agreed terms with the other papers for introducing labour-saving machinery. Now on a firmer financial footing, the papers built new publishing headquarters away from Fleet Street's congestion and high overheads. The last holdout was the *Daily Mirror*, owned by the millionaire Robert Maxwell, who was considering the future of the 1950s' skyscraper on the corner of Holborn and Fetter Lane.

MAGAZINES

Thousands of weekly and monthly journals coexist with the daily press. The initial effect of the competition from television was to damage general-interest magazines – *Picture Post*, *Lilliput* and *Illustrated* closed down – but specialist magazines flourish, especially those aimed at women. Most form part of large magazine groups, the largest of them IPC (or the International Publishing Corporation), which publishes scores of titles from its headquarters on Stamford Street, south of the river. Although these magazines are often typeset and printed outside London, their editorial staffs have to stay in the capital to keep up with what is going on.

In the 1960s Sunday newspapers began inserting free magazines to accommodate lucrative colour advertising and in the 1980s some daily papers began to do the same with their Saturday editions. Faced with this explosion of reading matter, literary and political magazines were having a hard time. The historic *Spectator* changed hands severals times while *New Statesman* and *New Society* were forced to merge in 1988 to keep going. *Punch* repeatedly changed editors in a bid to halt its slide and so did *The Listener*. *The Illustrated London News*, once a popular weekly, became a monthly, then a quarterly. That historic title was an early victim of new technology. It made its reputation by getting artists to do rapid sketches of the events of the week and never truly recovered from the invention of the camera.

Newspapers, magazines, television, radio and the advertising industry are lumped together as 'the media' and as such are a significant component of central London's work force. They cross-fertilize: the papers and magazines write a lot about television and its stars, while television and radio incessantly quote from the press. The advertising agents are important clients for all of them. They meet each other at social and commercial functions and are part of a thriving sub-culture that is immensely influential in shaping the tastes and style of the city.

OPPOSITE Public interest in the doings of celebrities is reflected in the popular press and fed by a large fraternity of photographers (the *paparazzi*), here snapping a member of the royal family.

MEDICINE: ITS TEACHING AND PRACTICE

Doctors have always been interested in the business side of their endeavours, and London's size and wealth attracted medical men to it. In earlier times, however, neither the institutions nor the personnel of medicine were as prominent as today, and most illness was coped with through self-medication, household remedies and family or neighbourhood networks. Even the numerous hospitals of medieval London were more concerned with the succour of religion than the healing arts *per se*. Most of them disappeared when the monasteries were dissolved in the 1530s, but Henry VIII and Edward VI did leave four hospitals to the City Fathers. Of these, St Bartholomew's Hospital (Bart's) in Smithfield (founded

*c.*1123) was the oldest and is the only one retaining its original site, though largely rebuilt from the eighteenth century. It and St Thomas's Hospital, originally in Southwark, acquired more explicitly medical functions. St Mary Bethlehem (Bethlem, 'Bedlam') became a place for 'distracted' or lunatic patients and Christ's Hospital evolved from an orphanage into a public school.

Except for temporary accommodation sometimes commandeered during plague crises, these were all the hospitals Londoners had during the rapid population expansion of the seventeenth century. This meant that most patients and even many doctors would never have come into contact with a hospital. Indeed, many of the poor would never have been treated by a medical man, though midwives with dubious training (but often much experience) would usually have delivered their babies.

The boundaries between 'regular' medical men and quacks were vague. Nor, it has to be said, were the patient's chances of cure likely to be better with the one than with the other. The medics of course thought otherwise. There were three orders of regular medical practitioners whose origins, education and functions were diverse. At the top of the heap were the physicians, educated at university and believing they carried the torch of medicine as one of the learned professions. In fact, the medical faculties at the only English universities

ABOVE The old St Thomas's Hospital, built in the early eighteenth century, was demolished in 1859 to make way for London Bridge Station. The hospital moved to a new site by Westminster Bridge.

RIGHT This photograph was taken in 1925, five years before the Bethlehem Royal Hospital, for the mentally ill, moved from St George's Fields, Lambeth, to new premises in Surrey. The wings were demolished and the central block is now the Imperial War Museum.

– Oxford and Cambridge – were sleepy and many physicians owed their social positions to their classical learning. One exception, William Harvey (1578–1657), physician at Bart's and discoverer of the circulation of the blood, had an inquiring mind but a rather ordinary medical practice.

In 1518 Henry VIII granted the physicians their own institution (the Royal College of Physicians of London), with powers to regulate the practice of 'physick' in London and seven miles around. Despite its collegiate status, the College was traditionally concerned more with guarding physicians' privileges and income than in furthering knowledge or improving standards of care. Physicians from Oxford or Cambridge were eligible for Fellowship in the College (FRCP); those with Scottish or Continental degrees generally had to content themselves with becoming Licentiates (LRCP). The physicians catered mostly for the well-to-do, advising and prescribing for their clients. Appointment at Court or to one of the aristocratic households did wonders for the reputation and pocketbook. The College's modern building, in Regent's Park, is one of Sir Denys Lasdun's best.

By contrast, surgeons were doers, not talkers. Rooted in the medieval guild tradition, they trained by apprenticeships and until 1745 were part of the Barber–Surgeons Company. Shaving, trimming beards and letting blood were equally within their ken, though surgeons would also lance boils, pull teeth, remove superficial wens and tumours, treat skin and venereal diseases with salves and ointments, and – rarely – perform what we call surgery. Major operations included cutting for bladder stones, amputating limbs and attempting to repair strangulated hernias. Mortality rates were high, infection common and the control of pain minimal. Pain placed a premium on speed and bleeding was controlled by cautery. The thorax and abdomen could not be opened without almost certain death for the unfortunate victim.

No wonder it was a slightly disreputable business. Nevertheless, in the eighteenth century, men like William Cheselden (1688–1752), Percivall Pott (1714–88) and (above all) John Hunter (1728–93) raised the status of surgery through their operative skills and their anatomical and scientific expertise. The surgeons separated from the barbers in 1745 and became the Royal College of Surgeons in 1800. Their building in Lincoln's Inn Fields was damaged in the Second World War, but has been restored.

Surgeons were craftsmen: apothecaries were tradesmen who made their living selling medicines and often other commodities. Formerly associated with the grocers, pepperers and spicers, the apothecaries got their own company, the Society of Apothecaries, in 1617;

The trade card of Richard Siddall, a chemist in Panton Street, Haymarket, provides both a romantic and a heroic view of the art of medicine in the eighteenth century. He offers elixirs for asthma, gout and rheumatism.

Apothecaries Hall, near Blackfriars Bridge, is a fine late seventeenth-century building. Officially, apothecaries were supposed mostly to compound and dispense the prescriptions written by the physicians. In reality, physicians were too scarce and expensive to be available for everyone, so apothecaries were the medical men of first (and last) call for many. The apothecaries' collective reputation was helped when many of them stayed in London during the plague year of 1665, after most physicians had fled to the safer countryside. After a legal battle with the physicians in the early eighteenth century, apothecaries won the right to dispense medicines directly. As the 'poor man's physician', they were the prototype of the modern general practitioner.

Enhanced public concern with health during the eighteenth century benefited medics, who increased in numbers, wealth and status. Middle- and upper-class people would be treated and nursed in their homes, whereas the 'worthy poor' – artisans, servants, journeymen – were often catered for within the vigorous 'voluntary' hospital movement. Five new general hospitals (Westminster, Guy's, St George's, Middlesex, London) were opened between 1719 and 1745. Guy's was endowed by the wealthy printer and publisher,

Thomas Guy (1645–1724), but the others were supported by the voluntary contributions of worthy citizens who thereby became governors and could recommend patients for admission. Physicians and surgeons were eager for appointments at the hospitals, even though these paid no salary, since this gave them a reputation as charitable individuals, let them rub shoulders with the élite governors (who might become their paying patients) and helped them earn money from pupils' fees. Surgeons were particularly keen, as hospitals gave their pupils and apprentices opportunities to practise on the poor before offering their skills on the open market. A wealthy man might pay a hundred guineas or more for relief from the exquisite pain of a bladder stone. From the mid-eighteenth century, a number of specialist hospitals – lying-in, lock (for venereal disease), smallpox, fever and psychiatric – began catering for patients excluded admission to the general hospitals which would not treat such conditions for a mixture of medical and moral motives. Charitable dispensaries sprang up to see out-patients. As a last resort, medical care was available via the Poor Law, by doctors appointed by the Poor Law guardians.

This enormous growth of hospital patients made London an attractive place for young students to gain clinical experience. 'Walking the wards' became common during the eighteenth century, and private anatomy schools offered the chance for students to learn anatomy through dissection. Most successful of these was the Great Windmill Street School of William Hunter (1718–83), which survived in Soho until the 1830s. Hunter's brother John offered surgical teaching at his home in Leicester Square and at St George's Hospital, where he was surgeon. Spurred by the success of the private schools, medical and surgical staff at the hospitals began to offer lectures and formal clinical teaching. The 1815 Apothecaries Act required any would-be apothecary in England and Wales to present certificates for courses in a number of scientific and clinical subjects, thereby further heightening demand for formal education. By the 1830s, the hospital medical schools had squeezed out the private ones and, following the foundation of the University of London in 1826, students from them could present themselves for London medical degrees (MB and MD). Since then about half the doctors in Britain have had at least some of their training in London.

A second wave of general hospitals (Charing Cross, University College, King's College, Royal Free, St Mary's), dates from the early and mid-nineteenth century. Specialist hospitals for children and for diseases of the chest, eyes, ears, skin and gastro-intestinal tract further consolidated the hospital orientation of élite

doctors. As London spread, hospitals followed, though never quite so rapidly, since benefactors and consultant doctors preferred the more prestigious sites in the centre, closer to their private consulting rooms – from mid-century often located in Harley, Wimpole and Wigmore Streets. The East End was never as well provisioned with hospitals, though, ironically, fashionable West-End dwellers would routinely have been treated at home through most of Victoria's reign.

Standards of hospital hygiene and nursing went up, but so did costs, and most charitable medical institutions had difficulty making ends meet. One solution was partially to centralize fund-raising, through the King Edward's Hospital Fund. Another was to attract the wealthy to hospitals as paying patients, a task made easier with the coming of antiseptic surgery, pioneered by Joseph Lister (1827–1912), who was a student at University College Hospital and later Professor of Surgery at King's College Hospital. Other attractions were the development of complicated diagnostic and therapeutic procedures involving x-rays and specialist nursing. Private wings were built on more luxurious lines than the larger, open wards which characterized earlier hospitals. Florence Nightingale (1820–1910) favoured the pavilion design for wards, with large floor-to-ceiling windows for ventilation. These can still be seen at St Thomas's, which moved to Lambeth in the 1860s to make way for London Bridge Railway Station. Still on the original site, an old operating theatre, dating from 1821 and now restored as a medical museum, survives in the roof of the Southwark Cathedral Chapter House, St Thomas's Street.

The voluntary hospitals were nationalized in 1948, when the National Health Service came into being. For the first time, consultant physicians and surgeons (along with other hospital specialists such as paediatricians, gynaecologists, anaesthetists and radiologists) were paid for their hospital work with all patients, not simply the rich ones. General practitioners, who worked outside the hospitals, were paid capitation fees for each patient on their register. Many hospital consultants preferred to engage in some private practice as well, using the private wings of the NHS hospitals (many now dispersed out of central London) as well as newly-built private establishments such as the London Clinic and the Wellington Hospital. Wealthy foreign patients and the increased popularity of health insurance fund the private sector, although most Londoners rely on the NHS.

OPPOSITE The Royal College of Physicians was formed in 1518, primarily to protect the privileges of its members. Since then it has become a professional body of high repute. Its modern headquarters in Regent's Park was designed by Denys Lasdun and opened in 1964.

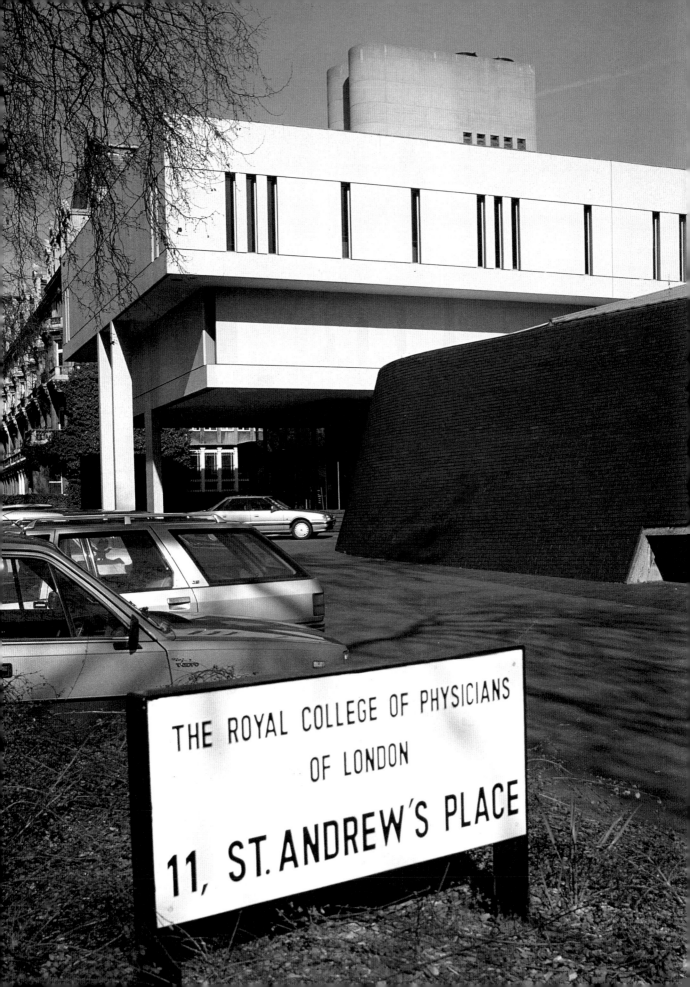

A Centre of Learning

When scholars from the Sorbonne in Paris came to England to establish its first university in 1167, they pointedly avoided London, with its noise, its distractions, its political and religious intrigues, settling instead for the seclusion of Oxford. And when, forty-two years later, a dissatisfied group of them set up a rival learning centre, they too avoided the capital and headed out to Cambridge.

As a thriving port, and a centre of commerce and government, London was a pragmatic city of doers rather than thinkers. Even the monastic tradition of study was lost following Henry VIII's Dissolution of the abbeys and monasteries in the 1530s.

A century or so later, when the Renaissance sparked

lectures to members in the early days and became the Society's president. Other notable presidents have included Samuel Pepys, Isaac Newton, Joseph Banks, Thomas Huxley, Joseph Lister and Ernest Rutherford. The society presents awards for scientific research and has helped organize several exploratory expeditions.

In the century following the Royal Society's creation, curiosity about the natural world increased. In 1788 the first specialist scientific society outside the Royal Society was created when James Smith, a young botanist, bought the collections of the Swedish naturalist, Carl Linnaeus. With two others, he formed the LINNEAN SOCIETY to promote the study of natural history. Under its roof in Burlington House in 1858 Charles Darwin and

LEFT Burlington House in Piccadilly was bought by the Government in 1854 for the use of the Royal Academy of Arts and several other learned institutions. This Piccadilly frontage was completed in 1873.

OPPOSITE King's College in the Strand was founded in 1828 by the bishops of the Church of England, as a rival to University College, which they believed to be irreligious. In 1908 it became part of London University. This photograph was taken in 1928.

interest in the sciences and arts, the capital began to acquire its first learned societies. This was scholarship with a bias towards the practical. The ROYAL SOCIETY, the oldest scientific body in the world, originated in Oxford as a group of scholars who met to discuss science and philosophy, disciplines which in the seventeenth century appeared to be interdependent. The group moved to London, where the Society was formally established in 1666. London was where the influential and the powerful were based – men like Christopher Wren, who gave

Alfred Russell Wallace first outlined the theories of evolution that were to shake the foundations of Victorian Christianity and alter the course of natural history studies. Today the Linnean Society's library contains a magnificent collection of early works on natural history.

At Burlington House the Linnean rubs shoulders with many other learned societies: the Royal Astronomical Society, the Society of Antiquaries, the Royal Society of Chemistry and the Geological Society are all based there. Most date from the early years of the nineteenth century, when each new scientific and geographical discovery whetted the early Victorian thirst for still more knowledge.

The best-known occupant of Burlington House is the Royal Academy of Arts (see *Museums and Galleries*). The RA sticks to its brief by concerning itself only with the fine arts. The ROYAL SOCIETY OF ARTS, on the other hand, takes what seems at first a perverse interest in other matters. This is because it began life in 1754 as the Society for the Encouragement of Arts, Manufactures and Commerce: in that era there was less of a gulf between the arts and the other two spheres than there is today.

The RSA had a hand in organizing the Great Exhibition of 1851 and the Festival of Britain one hundred years later: both were by and large successful attempts to blend art with industry. It held the first-ever formal art exhibition in 1760. On the scientific side it has awarded its Albert Medal (Prince Albert was one of its

presidents) to such as Marie Curie and Alexander Fleming. It has occupied its home in John Adam Street ever since the house was built as part of the Adelphi complex in 1774.

Another recipient of the Albert Medal was Michael Faraday, a chemist and natural philosopher more usually associated with the ROYAL INSTITUTION. Faraday was employed there as assistant to the director of the laboratory, Humphry Davy, in 1812, thirteen years after the Institution had been founded to further the teaching

of the practical application of science. Faraday went on to make major discoveries in electricity in the Institution's building in Albemarle Street, where his Christmas lectures were extremely popular. On retirement he was given a grace-and-favour home in Hampton Court.

Among the many other learned societies in London are the ROYAL COLLEGE OF PHYSICIANS, a venerable society founded in 1518 (see *Medicine: its teaching and practice*); the BRITISH ACADEMY, granted its royal charter in 1902 after a number of scholars decided there should be the equivalent of the Royal Society for humanities and the social sciences; and the ROYAL GEOGRAPHICAL SOCIETY, founded in 1830, which has sponsored expeditions led by explorers such as Richard Burton, David Livingstone and Robert Scott.

UNIVERSITIES

By comparison with such as these, the University of London is a relatively recent addition to the city's academic community. Indeed, had it not been for the fact that Oxford and Cambridge did not admit Dissenters, London might have had to wait even longer for a university of its own. As it was, its first university opened in Bloomsbury in 1826, becoming known as University College, or 'that godless institution in Gower Street', as its detractors called it. Anglicans established King's College three years later as a rival.

The University of London itself was created in 1836 to set examinations and grant degrees to students from both colleges and is an umbrella name covering a number of colleges which are now part of it.

It is therefore individual colleges that have developed reputations rather than the university itself. The LONDON SCHOOL OF ECONOMICS AND POLITICAL SCIENCE (LSE), founded in 1895 on the instigation of Sidney Webb with money left by the Fabian, Henry Hunt Hutchinson, is one of these. Members of its staff have included the economists Harold Laski and Friedrich von Hayek. Several of its former students have become prominent politicians in many countries, especially in the Third World. Its reputation as a hotbed of socialism is less pronounced today than earlier in the century.

Other celebrated institutions within the University include IMPERIAL COLLEGE, formed out of three separate colleges in 1907 and having a worldwide reputation for technological education, and the COURTAULD INSTITUTE, endowed by the textile baron Samuel Courtauld earlier this century, highly respected in the fields of art and architecture history. THE SCHOOL OF ORIENTAL AND AFRICAN STUDIES (SOAS) was founded in the imperial era to educate those expecting to work in the Far East and Africa.

The University of London was granted a new charter in 1858 which allowed external students to sit its examinations, and this resulted in the rapid expansion of what was to become another well-known college within the University. BIRKBECK COLLEGE, as it is now called, started life in 1824 as the London Mechanics' Institution. This was the first college in the country to offer education to people outside their working day. It was renamed the Birkbeck Literary and Scientific Institution in 1866, in recognition of one of its founders, the physician Dr George Birkbeck. It became part of the University in 1920.

In 1878 the University of London opened its examinations to women and, in the following years, admitted two women's colleges to its organization. The first, BEDFORD COLLEGE, had been founded in 1849 by Mrs Elizabeth Jesser Reid and named after its site in Bedford Square. The second, ROYAL HOLLOWAY COLLEGE, was opened by Queen Victoria in 1886. Both had become co-educational by the time they merged in the 1980s and moved to Malet Street and Egham in Surrey.

At the same time as colleges for the full-time education of students were evolving in the nineteenth century, part-time adult education – as at Birkbeck – was also becoming more widely available. Demand for universal suffrage was growing and the need for widespread education became apparent, not only at school level but for those who had to earn their living during the day.

Early attempts at adult education were often heavily linked with religious movements. Quintin Hogg's Youth's Christian Institute, founded in 1882, was a later example of this. Starting at the same time as the City and Guilds Institute (see *The guilds*), while the City and Guilds concentrated on part-time technical courses, Hogg's 'polytechnic' developed into an institution offering full-time courses in practical and commercial education: the Polytechnic of Regent Street.

Since merging with the Holborn College of Law, Language and Commerce, it has been renamed the POLYTECHNIC OF CENTRAL LONDON, but its connection with the Hogg family was reinforced in 1971 when Lord Hailsham, grandson of the founder, opened its new buildings.

London's youngest university is BRUNEL UNIVERSITY at Uxbridge. Founded in Acton in 1957 as a college of advanced technology and engineering, named after the father of Victorian engineering, it quickly outgrew its site and moved out to the suburbs a few years later, shortly after achieving the enhanced status of university.

SCHOOLS OF ART AND MUSIC

The ROYAL ACADEMY was founded in 1768 as a school of art as well as a centre for its exhibition. For nearly a century it was London's only significant training school for artists, although there were a number of small private establishments. ST MARTIN'S SCHOOL OF ART, now on the edge of Soho in Charing Cross Road, was among the earliest major schools, founded in the middle of the nineteenth century. What is now the ROYAL COLLEGE OF ART had begun in 1837 as a school of design and 'practical art' to serve the emerging industries of the Victorian age. Run by a succession of government departments, it became fashionable in the 1950s and 1960s: David Hockney is its most notable alumnus from those years.

At the end of the nineteenth century the Royal Academy schools gained a reputation for conservatism, for being unwilling to encourage and accommodate modern styles of painting. The torch of the new movements was taken up by more recent arrivals such as the SLADE SCHOOL OF FINE ART, opened as part of University College in 1871 and named after Felix Slade, an art collector, who endowed it. For many years it enjoyed the highest reputation of the London schools, numbering among its pupils Walter Sickert, Augustus John and Stanley Spencer. Its location in Bloomsbury contributed to the artistic and literary flavour of the district in the early years of this century.

Among the newer schools, the most fashionable is CHELSEA SCHOOL OF ART, which has existed independently only since 1965: before that it was part of Chelsea College, later Chelsea Polytechnic. Its popularity is due not only to the excellence of its teaching but also to its location. Chelsea has long been even more popular with artists than Bloomsbury and since the 1960s King's Road has acted as a magnet to students.

Two schools that opened in the same year – 1896 – bear witness to the late Victorian interest in crafts. The CENTRAL SCHOOL OF ART AND DESIGN (originally the Central School of Arts and Crafts) was established by the London County Council and the CAMBERWELL SCHOOL OF ARTS AND CRAFTS by private philanthropy. Both have made important contributions to modern British design and craftsmanship.

The performing arts have schools of equal renown, notably the ROYAL ACADEMY OF DRAMATIC ART (RADA), founded by the actor-manager Sir Herbert Beerbohm Tree in 1904 and still occupying the Gower Street building it moved into later that year. Many of the

OPPOSITE The Linnean Society is named after the pioneering eighteenth-century Swedish botanist and fosters study in that field. Its well-maintained premises, including the valuable research library, are in an extension of Burlington House, fronting Piccadilly, erected between 1868 and 1873.

biggest names on the stages of London and New York, as well as in the cinema, have trained at RADA, and competition for places there is always intense. Other well-respected drama schools include the CENTRAL SCHOOL OF SPEECH AND DRAMA, now in Hampstead, established by Elsie Fogerty in 1906. The ROYAL BALLET SCHOOL has two centres, one in Richmond Park for students under 16 and an upper school in Kensington. Founded in 1931 by Dame Ninette de Valois, it has produced generations of top-class dancers, many of whom are taken into the Royal Ballet company.

The ROYAL ACADEMY OF MUSIC is England's oldest music school, founded in 1823 as a boarding school for boys wanting a musical education. After thirty years it became a non-residential centre for advanced musical training. In 1864 the ROYAL COLLEGE OF ORGANISTS was established and twenty years later the ROYAL COLLEGE OF MUSIC.

The existence of all these specialized training centres in or around the middle of London, alongside the universities and colleges and the numerous language schools for foreign students, fosters a young, eager atmosphere in many central areas. They are part of the mix that has kept the city vibrant and changing, resisting stagnation and decay.

A characteristic Victorian board school, in red brick with high ceilings, large windows and a Dutch-style roof, at Primrose Hill.

─────── EDUCATING CHILDREN ───────

The Victorian red-brick elementary school, with its expanses of window and oversized gables, is a distinctive feature of London's landscape. The explosion of school building at that time was the product of the 1870 Education Act. Before that education was on a voluntary basis, provided chiefly by religious organizations and charity schools. The Act did not abolish denominational schools but filled the gaps they had left. This was done through the creation of local school boards and the institutions became known as board schools. London's fast-spreading suburbs were ill-served by voluntary schools so there was plenty of demand for new ones under the terms of the Act. Though some have cramped and dingy playgrounds, many are still in use today.

Until the inter-war period, only a small proportion of London children went on from elementary to special secondary or grammar schools. After 1944, children aged eleven to fifteen (now sixteen) were assured of secondary education. In inner London, comprehensive schools for children of all abilities were favoured above grammar schools for the academic and secondary modern or technical schools for the rest. Although some of these schools are today still housed in the old premises of their predecessors, many are now in large, modern, purpose-designed buildings. London's most renowned is HOLLAND PARK COMPREHENSIVE, built between 1956

and 1958 on Campden Hill, above Kensington High Street. It is a predominantly middle-class area and the school became – and remains – fashionable, particularly with liberal and left-wing intellectuals.

London's best known schools serve the wealthy minority of its population – the private, fee-paying establishments inaccurately known as public schools. Formerly only for boys, most now admit girls, albeit in restricted numbers. There used to be more London public schools than there are now, but several moved out, seeking room to expand. Between 1872 and 1935 the city lost three of its most famous. CHARTERHOUSE, established in 1611 in an old Carthusian monastery (see *Clerkenwell*), was the first to go when it moved to Godalming in Surrey. It was followed by Christ's Hospital, founded by King Edward VI, which left Newgate Street for Horsham in Sussex in 1902. Merchant Taylors' School remained in Charterhouse Square until the 1930s, when a new home was found for it in Northwood, Middlesex.

The four important public schools remaining in London were all in existence by the early seventeenth century. WESTMINSTER was already educating clerks attached to the Abbey in the early Middle Ages. ST

PAUL's was founded in 1509 by the dean of St Paul's Cathedral, but now occupies modern buildings beside the Thames at Barnes. It has an influential sister organization, ST PAUL'S GIRLS SCHOOL, located in Hammersmith. Winston Churchill's old school, HARROW, was established in 1572 by a local farmer. DULWICH College started life in 1619, endowed by a wealthy actor, Edward Alleyn, for the education of poor boys; former pupils include the writers P. G. Wodehouse and Raymond Chandler.

LIBRARIES

While schools were improving during the nineteenth century, the idea of the lending library was also developing to supply the demand created by growing literacy. By 1900 London had more than thirty library authorities, entitled to raise local rates in order to open public libraries.

In earlier centuries, libraries were to be found only in religious foundations, in one or two learned institutions, or attached to cathedrals or universities. Not until the eighteenth century and the establishment of the British Museum Library did this begin to change. Now called the BRITISH LIBRARY, it began in the 1750s as a 'museum of books' amassed through the donation of various private libraries. Today it receives copies by right of every book published in Britain and, although now independent of the Museum, it retains (for the time being) its famous domed reading room providing an incomparable reference library for students and researchers. Expanding as it does by two miles of bookshelves each year, it is due to move shortly to new premises near St Pancras station. Among its satellite institutions is a newspaper library in Colindale, north London.

The provision of books to the educated public had increased in the eighteenth and early nineteenth centuries when circulating libraries took advantage of public interest in the reading of novels. Church and philanthropic libraries increased in number and mechanics' institutes kept small numbers of books for the improvement of their members' minds.

Private subscription libraries were popular with the middle classes. Most of them vanished in the mid-twentieth century because of the excellence of the free libraries, but London still possesses a fine example in the LONDON LIBRARY. This lending library, founded in 1841 by a group of men who included Thomas Carlyle and John Stuart Mill, aimed to provide for its members 'good books in all departments of knowledge' and does so to this day, in a building in St James's Square, built to its requirements in the 1890s. One of its advantages is that most of the books are on open shelves, and can be borrowed for fairly long periods.

The provision of public libraries on a national scale was made possible by the Public Libraries Act of 1850, but the decision of a borough to raise rates for such a purpose was voluntary. In London response from local authorities was so poor that, for thirty years after the Act, the parishes of St Margaret and St John in Westminster provided the only rate-aided library in the entire city. Matters improved in 1872 when the GUILDHALL LIBRARY, also an excellent source of information on London, became a public reference library. Wandsworth opened the second rate-aided lending

This drawing of the British Museum Library reading room was published in the *Illustrated London News* in 1857, just after it was opened on the site of the old museum courtyard.

library in 1885 and others followed quickly, encouraged by the generosity of benefactors such as the publisher John Passmore Edwards, the sugar tycoon Sir Henry Tate (founder of the Tate Gallery) and the Scottish-American steel magnate, Andrew Carnegie. They were so popular that the library at Bethnal Green, in the East End, was established in the underground station air-raid shelter during the Blitz of 1940.

Today there are eighty-four public libraries in inner London, including the large WESTMINSTER CENTRAL REFERENCE LIBRARY near Leicester Square. Reference facilities are boosted by unique sources outside the system such as the library of the Royal Institute of British Architects in Portland Place, and the genealogical records at Somerset House and St Catherine's House, Kingsway.

A CITY OF SHOPKEEPERS

London grew up as an international trading centre. The Romans imported their wine from Italy, glass from Germany, dried fruit from Palestine and olive oil from Spain. Soon ships were landing cargoes of silks and spices from the East, while producers from all over the country brought their goods to London, whose cosmopolitan citizens paid the best prices. In addition to the markets, street traders such as cutlers had portable shops, stalls hung with goods that they pushed from place to place.

Medieval London's biggest shopping mall was CHEAPSIDE. Goods were still sold from stalls, but with time the shops behind became increasingly permanent and prosperous. Specialist craftsmen lived, worked and kept shops in nearby lanes whose names persist as reminders of their earlier occupants (see *The City*). Cheapside maintained its reputation for centuries, despite the exodus west of its affluent clients. In the 1720s one visitor found it 'a very spacious street, well inhabited by goldsmiths, linen drapers, haberdashers and other great dealers'. Until the nineteenth century it still rivalled the West End.

The goldsmiths were also well-placed in LOMBARD STREET, named after Italian financiers and even today hung with banking signs. This is where the goldsmith John Spink set up in 1666; but his descendants moved west to St James's to stay near their wealthy clients.

VICTUALS FOR THE COURT

As London grew, there were not only wealthy merchants and their wives to serve. The king's increasingly flamboyant court needed goods, too. Down the Strand, east of what is now Charing Cross station, NEW EXCHANGE, built in 1608, became the rival shopping centre to Royal Exchange in the City. James I opened it and its two floors became a favourite of the nobility for their 'rich shops of drapers and mercers filled with goods of every kind'. Quality shops did well. Thomas Twining, tea supplier to Queen Anne, set up shop at 216 Strand in 1706 and has not moved since. Arthur Ackerman had made enough money from the sale of his prints by 1810 to light his shop by the latest extravagant method, gas, before moving west with his clients.

When the court moved to St James's Palace, after the Whitehall fire of 1698, streets were created dedicated to serving high society's every whim. Clubs and coffee houses were soon interspersed with new clusters of fashionable shops. Some survive today, with their quaint shopfronts and their high standards of goods and service. At the bottom of ST JAMES'S STREET, hard by the palace, wine merchants Berry Brothers and Rudd succeeded the grocer William Pickering who set up in 1703. They retain their fine panelled interior – as do Lock & Co., who have been fitting smart heads with top hats, bowlers and polo caps since Robert Davis followed his clients here from the City in 1676. JERMYN STREET was the court's most exclusive shopping lane; although no original house stands, its atmosphere is still as select as its specialist and long-established institutions. A Spaniard from Minorca, Juan Famenias Floris, judged the courtesans' taste right when he started the perfumers Floris in 1730; and a cheesemonger from Suffolk founded Paxton and Whitfield in 1740. The interiors of both are redolent of the past.

BY APPOINTMENT

Many of the shopkeepers of St James's proudly display the arms of one or more members of the royal family, topping it with the words 'By appointment to . . .'. These royal warrants are awarded to those who supply the households of the Queen, the Queen Mother, the Duke of Edinburgh or the Prince of Wales. 'By appointment' is not only a sought-after honour; it increases sales, for the holder may advertise the privilege by displaying the royal coat of arms in the shop and printing it on the product and even the carrier bag. The system began in the Middle Ages and could be applied to any sort of personal service. Henry VIII had Anne Harris as his 'King's laundresse'; George III had a 'mole taker', 'card maker' and 'rat catcher' by appointment.

Today there are some eight hundred royal warrant holders, with a concentration in high society's traditional spending haunts, St James's and Mayfair. Liberty's are 'silk merchants to HM The Queen Mother'; Stanley Gibbons Ltd are 'philatelists to HM The Queen'; and Wilkinson Sword Ltd are 'sword cutlers' to the Queen and the Duke of Edinburgh, although to most people they are suppliers of razor blades. A few boast all four royal coats of arms, among them Harrods.

OPPOSITE Burlington Arcade was covered over in 1819 by Lord George Cavendish, reputedly to stop people throwing rubbish (in the form of discarded shells from oysters sold by a street-trader nearby) over the walls of his Burlington House next door. It quickly became a fashionable shopping centre and remains so.

SHOPS FOR THE WEALTHY

As smart residential London expanded north from St James's, new opportunities arose for shopkeepers. Since the building boom of the 1720s, Mayfair has been one of London's most expensive shopping areas. PICCADILLY is even named to commemorate a shopkeeper, Robert Baker, who built his mansion here with profits from selling stiff collars known as 'pickadils' to fashion-conscious courtiers. John Hatchard opened his book-shop here in 1797, soon so cosy that Gladstone would come to peruse new books beside the fire and the Duke of Wellington would ride down on horseback from Apsley House. London's grandest grocer's shop is here, Fortnum & Mason. It was founded in 1707 by William Fortnum, a footman to Queen Anne who learnt the

Liberty's, established in Regent Street in 1875, developed piecemeal until it was rebuilt in its present eclectic style in 1926. This photograph shows the Regent Street frontage in 1913.

courtiers' tastes and left to set up a shop to satisfy them. Such was its success that his partner built Mason's Yard, behind, to handle deliveries. Off both sides of Piccadilly run a number of shopping arcades where people can window-shop even in inclement weather. Burlington Arcade, guarded by uniformed beadles, is the largest and most stylish, dating from 1815. Mayfair is the centre of the art world, with dealers lurking in every corner (see *The art business*). It is also the centre of extravagant shopping. In BOND STREET the long Victorian windows of Asprey's display anything from a gold letter opener to a bejewelled tie-pin.

GREAT STORES

OXFORD STREET, with smart Marylebone above and Mayfair below, began to develop into a major shopping

street in the eighteenth century when it was also known for its entertainment halls and its gruesome but popular parades of convicts on their way to a hanging at Tyburn. Drapers, furniture shops and shoemakers lined the street, then slowly gave way to department stores, an idea adopted from America. Indeed, the most famous, Selfridges, was conceived and built by a Chicago retail millionaire, Gordon Selfridge, begun in 1907 and not completed until 1928. The steel-framed building dec-orated with stately Ionic columns, designed by the Chicago architect Daniel Burnham with R.F.Atkinson, is a temple to Edwardian affluence, although it was among the last of the great stores to arrive in Oxford Street. John Lewis, D.H.Evans, Peter Robinson, Mar-shall and Snelgrove and Debenham and Freebody were all established earlier. Many survive, although their ownership has changed and their style of trading is now geared to the breakneck pace of the 1990s rather than the more leisurely early years of the century.

Where Selfridge literally broke new ground was in siting his store west of Oxford Street's junction with Marylebone Lane. Until then, 'Ladies' Mile' ended abruptly here but Selfridge foresaw the day when the shopping section would stretch all the way to Marble Arch. In 1930 Marks and Spencer, then Britain's leading drapery chain, confirmed his hunch when it opened its largest store one block west of Selfridge's. Its second Oxford Street store opened in 1937, east of Oxford Circus.

REGENT STREET is a cut above Oxford Street in terms of style. Almost as soon as Nash built it between 1817 and 1823, it began to accommodate the kind of shops in which the fashionable wanted to be seen. Liberty's is the most celebrated. Opened by Arthur Liberty in 1875 for the import of silks from Asia, it expanded to give its name to a range of printed fabrics and a style of decoration that epitomized the Arts and Crafts move-ment. The present eclectic building, echoing elements of British architecture of the last five hundred years, dates from 1925. Other famous Regent Street names are Dickins and Jones, Hamley's, Jaeger, Burberry's, Aus-tin Reed and Aquascutum – the last four representing the heavyweight tradition of classical English tailoring. Garrard, jewellers to the sovereign since their appoint-ment by Queen Victoria in 1843, boasts a sumptuous interior and its own goldsmiths working on site.

The rise of KNIGHTSBRIDGE had a double impetus: the royal move to Buckingham Palace and the Great Exhibition of 1851. Just before the exhibition, a tea merchant named Henry Charles Harrod opened a small grocery shop opposite Knightsbridge village and green. Trade boomed during the exhibition and with expan-sion, coupled with immaculate service, the institution

The Art Business

London likes to regard itself as the senior city so far as antiques are concerned. This is justifiable, for it has probably retained a greater range and a greater quality of art objects than anywhere else. This becomes evident in June when – overlapping with Ascot, the second cricket test match at Lord's, and Wimbledon – the art and antiques world dusts itself down, shoots its collective cuffs, lacquers its nails and parades up Park Lane to the Grosvenor House Antiques Fair. For ten days the Grosvenor House Hotel resembles an off-shoot of the Victoria & Albert Museum, the Louvre or the Boston Museum of Fine Arts. It seems as if half the contents of Britain's stately homes is on show and for sale.

The London art and antiques trade is structured like a pyramid. The firms at the top of it operate on an international scale. An efficient bush telegraph system tells these senior dealers when an important painting or object is to come on the market or, better still, a major collection to be broken up because its owner has died or is acquiring other interests. They will seek to negotiate the sale themselves but nowadays the most valuable works are customarily auctioned at one of the major houses (see *The auction houses*). This is the chief reason why most of the top art dealers are grouped around the big auction houses in Bond Street and St James's. They contact likely clients and if there is interest they will go to the sale and bid on their behalf. Naturally they take a commission for this, often a substantial one. Added to the commission the auction houses take from the vendor, and the premium they charge the buyer, it makes the arts and antiques business one of the most labour-intensive and commission-padded undertakings in the capital. The dealers maintain that what they are selling is their expertise. In a business where fakes and forgeries abound, their knowledge can prevent costly mistakes – although the record shows that they are by no means infallible.

The most venerable of the Old Master galleries is Agnew's, in Old Bond Street, not far from Colnaghi's (originally an Italian firework manufacturer) and the Leger Galleries, specializing in British art. The big Impressionist galleries – Wildenstein, Lefevre and David Messum – are in the same area, as are the jeweller's Asprey and Co., who have been in Bond Street since 1830. Contemporary art centres on Cork Street, where leading galleries include Leslie Waddington, Nicola Jacobs and Kasmin.

Away from these haunts of the well-heeled, and forming the wide base of the trade's pyramid, are shops and markets where prices are at a more accessible level, although mark-ups are still high – sometimes more than 100 per cent. These are the dealers who get up in the small hours of Friday morning and repair to Bermondsey, where they buy and sell between themselves, pushing up the price each time before the item finally reaches a member of the public. Many of the goods traded here end up in antiques shops in the United States or Japan, where British items are much in demand. Or they can turn up in Kensington Church Street, a place to forage for good antiques of most kinds, including furniture – or at another Church Street, off Edgware Road in Marylebone, a smaller centre but with a number of good shops. Knightsbridge and South Kensington have specialists in porcelain and the decorative arts.

Colnaghi's was once a firm of Italian firework manufacturers but is now one of London's most reputable art galleries, specializing in costly Old Masters. Its Old Bond Street premises have the elegance of an aristocratic drawing room.

Camden Passage in Islington mixes traditional antiques with modern 'collectibles': postcards, old toys and cameras, clothes and uniforms, buttons and medals, Victorian and Edwardian knick-knacks.

Portobello Road is the most renowned centre for decorative items, jewellery and Victoriana, but nowadays the genuine antiques are in danger of being overwhelmed by worthless souvenir items and memorabilia. For book hunters, Charing Cross Road is not the bountiful feast it was, but a few shops hold out there. The remains of the Farringdon Road book market operates at lunchtime on weekdays (see *Markets*). Many second-hand bookshops also sell prints and maps: there are a handful in Cecil Court, off Charing Cross Road, and several in Bloomsbury.

was born. Its 230 departments are spread over 20 acres and are manned by 4000 staff.

Harrods is unique, but by the 1980s it appeared that the all-embracing department store was losing its appeal. Many held out in the West End, although there were even casualties here: Marshall and Snelgrove, Swan and Edgar, Peter Robinson, Gorringes and Gamages were among the historic names that disappeared from the 1950s on. It was away from the centre, however, that the carnage was worst. In Kensington High Street only Barkers remains. Pontings and Derry and Toms have both gone, as has John Barnes in Finchley Road and Bon Marché in Brixton. The most poignant loss of all was Whiteley's in Queensway, Bayswater, founded by the man who can claim to have invented the department store. William Whiteley began as a draper but by the 1870s was selling a seemingly inexhaustible range of goods and called himself 'the universal provider'. But the rambling store closed in 1981 and its 1911 building has become a shopping centre made up of individual retail units.

The change was symbolic, for what drove out the big stores were chains of small, strongly themed shops that sprouted in the West End as well as in suburban high streets. The success of fashion boutiques in King's Road and Carnaby Street in the 1960s persuaded entrepreneurs that most people – not only the stylish young – preferred shopping on a human scale rather than in the colossal, impersonal super-stores. Before long no self-respecting high street lacked its Top Shop or Next, its Mothercare, its Laura Ashley; and before much longer these names found their way to Oxford and Regent Streets as well.

In the 1980s specialization became narrower still, with the launch of chains of successful limited-range mini-shops such as Tie Rack and Sock Shop. Debenhams split its Oxford Street store into a galleria of specialist units. New commercial developments began to incorporate malls lined with the smaller shops that were now the fashion, as in the entrance to Bond Street and Charing Cross underground stations and the Trocadero and London Pavilion sites at Piccadilly Circus. Formerly quiet alleys in the Oxford Street area, notably St Christopher's Place, have taken on a new lease of life as their once shabby buildings are converted into smart new branches of Monsoon and Principles.

The London clientèle has changed, too. The tradition of going 'up West' for shopping declined as the most desirable chains established branches in suburban high streets and shopping centres. The West End now caters increasingly for overseas visitors, or office workers shopping in their lunch break.

Central London continues to hold an edge over the suburban competition in specialist retailing, where the sheer quantity and variety of stock held is paramount. The serious book buyer must still go to Charing Cross Road, or to Hatchard's or Dillons, while nobody stocks more maps than Stanford's of Long Acre. The Virgin, Tower and HMV record emporia are unmatched elsewhere. The seeker after hi-fi and other electronics can browse along Tottenham Court Road, where most of the former furniture shops, except Heal's and Maple's, have given way to this newer trade. Buttons and bows adorn the garment district around the southern end of Great Portland Street. Keen cooks, seeking the perfect implements to construct their perfect dishes, still make the pilgrimage to Soho, to shop for pans and crocks.

A PLACE TO ENJOY

THEATRE

The fact that there have been public theatres in London since 1576 and that some theatre sites can claim a very long continuous tradition – Drury Lane from 1663, Her Majesty's from 1704, Covent Garden from 1731 – leads many to suppose that the capital's present wealth of theatre buildings must include examples from all periods. In fact, among London's 70-plus theatres, nothing is visible earlier than 1812 and very little earlier than 1880. Although Drury Lane, the Haymarket and the Lyceum are pre-Victorian in external appearance, only Drury Lane retains some Georgian interiors. The earliest surviving complete working theatre is the Royal Opera House (Theatre Royal, Covent Garden) of 1858.

The historical reasons for this dearth of earlier buildings are complex, but one is of particular significance. London's theatres were from the beginning commercial ventures. With few exceptions, theatre architects were largely concerned with squeezing the

This frontage of the Theatre Royal, Drury Lane, was designed by Robert and James Adam in 1775 and built on to Wren's earlier theatre. The present Theatre Royal dates from 1812.

greatest possible theatrical advantage out of the smallest usable patch of ground. Unlike their Continental counterparts, they were rarely given an island site at a focal point in the city or commissioned to create a permanent monument to a powerful private or municipal patron. In periods of booming demand theatres were often built to low standards of construction, with scant regard for safety. Until the late nineteenth century they were regarded as short-lived structures which would, in the ordinary course of events, eventually perish by fire.

In this climate the total reconstruction of a profitable theatre on more fashionable lines, or to a larger capacity, would always be readily undertaken, whilst a theatre which did not pay would be cheerfully cleared away. Towards the end of the nineteenth century an official crackdown on provision for fire safety accelerated obsolescence. These factors, plus the demands of a growing population, combined to produce a surge of theatre building between 1880 and 1914. Most of London's theatres and variety palaces belong to this period.

The physical record may be incomplete, but the London theatre of today owes much of its strength to historical continuity over more than three hundred years. Its extraordinary variety of presentation, wealth of talent and concentration of technical expertise could hardly be sustained in the heart of the capital if it had not established itself there long ago. Its foothold is, nevertheless, precarious. In property terms, few theatre buildings are now worth more than a fraction of the development value of the land they stand upon. If demolished, their replacements would be perfunctory elements of larger developments. The future of London's theatreland depends on its holding its historic ground in a literal sense.

THEATRES IN THE FIELDS

The first public theatres were established outside the City walls (and beyond the reach of its authority) in the late sixteenth century. Companies of professional players were previously limited to performing either in the halls of noble patrons or, when seeking a public audience, on temporary stages in a variety of inn yards or bull- and bear-baiting arenas. In such locations it was not always easy to accommodate all who wished to attend, or to control the cash takings.

In 1576 James Burbage, a carpenter and actor whose company held a royal patent, created the first specially

This is a seventeenth-century drawing of Shakespeare's Globe Theatre on Bankside, Southwark. The stage was open to the elements but much of the seating area was sheltered. Drawings of this period are not necessarily reliable in detail, and this one probably shows the theatre as taller than it actually was.

designed building for the public performance of plays, the Theatre, in the Liberty of Holywell to the north of the City. A year later the Curtain was built nearby and in 1600 the Fortune, outside Cripplegate. Between 1587 and 1614 a group of playhouses, the Rose, the Swan, the Globe (which was the Theatre, dismantled and re-erected) and the Hope, appeared on Bankside in Southwark – possibly the most important concentration of theatres at any time in any land.

These unroofed playhouses were polygonal, with tiers of seated galleries around a yard for standing spectators. The audiences at their afternoon performances saw the flowering of the English drama. Accomplished actors such as Richard Burbage (son of James) created the great dramatic roles of Marlowe and Shakespeare. In 1989 the discovery of remains of the Rose provided the first hard evidence of the Elizabethan playhouses. There are plans to build a working recreation of Shakespeare's Globe on Bankside.

INDOOR THEATRES

Purpose-built or permanently adapted indoor theatres had begun to appear at about the same time as the playhouses in the fields, but they were private establishments and at first used only by companies of boy players. Court theatricals usually took place in the great halls of the palaces (such as Hampton Court) but Inigo Jones designed a new Cockpit-in-Court for the drama in

Whitehall Palace in 1629. His still extant Banqueting House of 1622, also in Whitehall, made provision for the specialized needs of the Court masque. Masques designed by Jones introduced Italian traditions of proscenium staging with elaborate scenic mechanics, contrasting with the open-stage techniques of the public playhouses.

All the theatres were shut down in 1642 after the start of the Civil War. Although the period of closure was less than twenty years and actors like Lowin – who had been instructed by Shakespeare himself – survived to pass their knowledge on to Restoration players, the unroofed playhouses were never to reopen. All that now remains from the pre-Commonwealth period are the Banqueting House and those halls which were commonly used by players, including Middle Temple.

THE PATENT HOUSES

Royal patents granted by Charles II to the acting companies of Davenant (the King's Men) and Killigrew (the Duke's Men) made their two playhouses the only public places in which spoken drama could legally be presented. Inheritors of the patents guarded their rights jealously and this led to constant challenges and evasions by the so-called 'minor' theatres which came to be built in subsequent years.

The Restoration playhouses were adapted to the Italian fashion for painted, changeable scenes and introduced women actors for the first time (female parts had previously been played by boys). Actresses like Anne Bracegirdle and Anne Oldfield were important to the success of the 'Comedies of Manners', some of which, combining wit, bawdiness and artificial morality, still please modern audiences.

During the eighteenth century the playhouse developed into a form peculiar to England, combining the scenic stage of Italian and French tradition with a deep forestage, bringing the actor out between the box tiers of the auditorium and into close contact with the audience. A move away from artificiality, in both content and performance style, was signalled by John Gay's immensely popular *Beggar's Opera* (1728) which satirized the absurdities of conventional opera by telling a lowlife story (a 'Newgate Pastoral') with street songs and traditional airs.

When David Garrick made his London début in 1741 at Goodman's Fields, his natural style displaced the mannerisms of the older school of actors. One of the greatest of English actors, his range extended from Shakespearian tragedy to farce. He spent the greater part of his working life at Drury Lane, where he made many reforms to stage lighting and scenery and – in defiance of firmly established tradition – banished spectators from the stage.

Garrick's Drury Lane was an intimate house in which his style could flourish. After his death the new romantic spirit fostered a taste for scenic spectacle. This, and the desire of managements to pack in ever larger audiences, led to the rebuilding with massively increased capacities of both the patent houses, Drury Lane and Covent Garden, between 1792 and 1812. The acting styles of John Philip Kemble and Sarah Siddons had to fill these vast spaces, which were 'henceforward theatres for spectators rather than playhouses for hearers' (Richard Cumberland, 1806). Their grand neo-classical manner was succeeded by the fiery genius of Edmund Kean who, in a short, wild life, transformed the way in which many classic roles were viewed and played.

THE 'MINOR' THEATRES

The public taste for theatrical entertainment ensured that the legal monopoly of the two patent houses did not long go unchallenged. The 'minor' theatres, operating at first outside the law, multiplied. One of the earliest, the Haymarket (1720) did, in 1766, receive a patent permitting summer operation, as did the Lyceum (opened 1809). Most, however, including Sadler's Wells (1753), the Surrey and the Adelphi (1806), the Olympic (1813), the Royal Coburg (the present Old Vic, 1818) and the Grecian Saloon (1830), achieved only fragile legality by the grant of a 'burletta' licence, which meant that all their productions had to be balletic or interspersed with music. The resulting curious mixtures, with spectacular scenery, mechanical effects (including those made possible by the new gaslight and focusable limelight), equestrian displays and solo songs 'in character', did little for the development of drama. They did, however, produce generations of extremely popular and versatile performers like Mme Vestris and Little Robson, who were as much at home on the musical stage as in the drama houses.

By 1850 London had twenty-five theatres, by this time operating freely under a new system of licensing. The main cluster was around Covent Garden and Drury Lane, extending along the Strand – the first appearance of a 'Theatreland' in the modern sense. There were other groups, notably on the South Bank (the (Old) Victoria, the Surrey and Astley's Amphitheatre) and the East End (the Royalty, the Pavilion and the Garrick).

The fact of legal existence made little difference to the fare on offer at the more popular theatres, which presented operettas, farces, pantomimes, burlesques, extravaganzas, travesties, melodramas and 'amazing effects and transformations' as enthusiastically as their predecessors. Theatre became a mighty and profitable industry, but lost much of its appeal to discriminating audiences.

A DRAMATIC REVIVAL

Although the drawing power of the theatre continued to depend on idolized performers, a revival of interest in the drama as such began to be felt, with writers like Tom Taylor and T. W. Robertson introducing a note of realism and an awareness of social issues. In their different ways, the wit of Oscar Wilde and the comic operas of Gilbert and Sullivan helped give new brilliance to the London theatre scene. The fashion for 'well-made plays', by such writers as Henry Arthur Jones and Arthur Wing Pinero, prepared the way for the more challenging works of Ibsen and Shaw.

The period of revival sparked a theatre-building boom and this, with a number of major structural changes in central London, led to the centre of gravity of Theatreland moving westward. The cutting of Charing Cross Road and Shaftesbury Avenue in 1887, together with the formation of Piccadilly Circus, produced new central sites on which a number of theatres were built – the old Shaftesbury (demolished), the Lyric, the Royal English Opera House (Palace Theatre), the Duke of York's, Wyndham's, the New (now the Albery), the Apollo, the Globe, the Queen's, and the Prince's (now called the Shaftesbury). The cutting of Aldwych and Kingsway in 1903 depleted the older Theatreland group by the loss of the Gaiety, the Olympic, the Opera Comique and the old Globe, but a new Gaiety (since demolished) and the Aldwych and Strand theatres rose at once on neighbouring sites.

A giant among actor-managers of the later Victorian period was the first stage knight, Sir Henry Irving. His management of the Lyceum from 1878 to 1902, with Ellen Terry as his leading lady, took that former minor theatre to a pinnacle of fame. The reign of the actor-managers – George Alexander, Harley Granville Barker, Charles Wyndham, Herbert Beerbohm Tree – continued until the First World War when, amongst other influences, the challenge of the cinema began to be felt. During and after the war big theatre and music hall syndicates competed with the movies by putting on musical plays, farces and revues. In the midst of the cinema building boom, and with many theatres being converted to film projection, a surprising little flurry of theatre building occurred in central London between 1924 and 1931. The Fortune, Piccadilly, Duchess, London Casino (Prince Edward), Cambridge, Phoenix, Whitehall and the reconstruction of the Adelphi and the Savoy all belong to this time.

OPPOSITE Denys Lasdun's concrete National Theatre, completed in 1976, is criticized by people used to the stucco Edwardian opulence of traditional London theatre architecture. Yet inside it works supremely well, with up to 2500 patrons of its three theatres mingling in foyers with bookshops, restaurant and bars.

Music Halls

The music hall came into existence, flourished and passed away in less than three generations. A dwindling minority of people now living can have personal recollections of even its final agonies, and yet the idea of music hall seems deeply ingrained. Present-day comedians are still commended as being 'in the music-hall tradition'. London is never without an entertainment styled 'music hall' and one of the most consistently popular regular television shows in recent years was a music-hall pastiche.

This robust entertainment had several essential ingredients. One was variety: a succession of individual 'turns' – solo singers, duettists, choristers, dancers, conjurers, illusionists, acrobats, strong men, quick-change artistes, monologists, eccentrics – all without formal or dramatic links between the separate programme items. Vocal music was the mainstay of the programme. Most of the other acts also required music, even if only as a background. The singers nearly always appeared 'in character'. The most memorable songs and visual images of the music hall are those which were created by and for the comic character singers.

Audiences joined in the choruses with gusto. They also had to be responsive to rapid changes of mood,

Billy Bennett (1887–1942), one of the last comedians in the true music-hall tradition. The character he created, billed as 'Almost a Gentleman', with hobnailed boots, soiled dress suit, fruity voice and grossly uncultured outlook, was grotesque and yet utterly convincing. He specialized in wildly nonsensical monologues and parodies.

from outrageous comedy to pathos. An affectionate relationship was built up between the best performers and their audiences.

All the ingredients which combined to make music hall were already present in seventeenth- and eighteenth-century London. Tavern music houses, travelling theatre booths, miscellaneous entertainers, posturers and rope dancers at Bartholomew Fair, ballad and comic singers in the pleasure gardens and concert rooms, and the interludes of dance and song between burlettas and musical plays at minor theatres contributed to the mix.

The first music halls were attached to public houses. Drink and song have always enjoyed a good working relationship and a great many taverns had (some still have) singing rooms in which patrons entertained themselves with part-singing or were called in turn to sing a solo ballad or comic song by a chairman appointed from their number. Some enterprising publicans formalized this kind of 'harmonic meeting' by paying (always with food and drink and occasionally in cash) the most accomplished local semi-professional singers to take part. Since the object was to sell more liquor, the chairman then became an important servant of the house, introducing the performers and exhorting the patrons to fill their glasses.

By the 1840s a number of pubs and tavern pleasure gardens throughout London had well-appointed, often purpose-built, concert rooms or 'long rooms' which were, in effect, proto-music halls. Although the form of the chairman-led harmonic meeting was still observed in most places, the principal performers were really professional entertainers. Solo character singers were the growing attraction. Some were shared with the minor theatres but others had no employment other than 'room singing'.

A few ambitious publicans had taken another course, building saloon theatres for the hybrid musical dramas which were all that the law would then permit. Some houses (for example, the Earl of Effingham in White-chapel) had both a saloon theatre *and* a large concert room.

The final catalyst was a new law in 1843, which freed the minor theatres (see *Theatre*) but removed drinking from their auditoriums. The concert rooms, however, could still be licensed, for musical entertainment only, as part of the pub. The advantage the embryo halls then enjoyed in being able to sell liquor during the performance led to a rapid development of this branch of the entertainment industry, accompanied by a building boom which culminated in the appearance of a number of giant 'grand music halls', much bigger than their parent pubs. Of these early drinking halls only Wilton's in Stepney now remains to be seen, in altered condition.

The Canterbury Hall in Lambeth, built by Charles Morton in 1854–7, was bigger and presented a more ambitious programme than any of its predecessors. It is often called the first music hall and it was certainly of outstanding importance. Morton adopted the style and the best of the entertainers of the classier Covent Garden supper rooms and transferred them to Lambeth Marsh.

The Canterbury, like all halls of this period, had brilliant gas lighting, an open platform stage and rows of dining tables between which waiters weaved, serving food and liquor. At the head table, below the stage, sat the chairman (usually an accomplished singer) with gavel and tilting mirror giving him a view of the performance. At the back and sides of the hall, men and women stood drinking at the mahogany-fronted bars, free to come and go and meet their friends as they would in a pub. On stage, the resident singers wore evening dress for their performance.

The character singers of the old concert rooms were succeeded by the first generation of true music-hall artistes. Mrs Caulfield at the Canterbury was one of the first of the 'serio-comic' female singers whose art reached a peak of perfection in Jenny Hill, 'The Vital Spark'.

By the end of the century the pub-style music halls had been totally replaced by gorgeous variety palaces, nearly indistinguishable in appearance from contemporary drama houses. They had proscenium-arched stages and fixed seats in raked rows. They also lowered their house lights during the performance. The sparkling chandeliers, the stentorian chairmen, the open bars and the waiters had all gone, but the artistes on the stage continued and developed the robust performance tradition of the classic halls.

The transformation came about for a number of reasons. Music hall had become big business, with syndicates, circuits and magnates like Oswald Stoll and Edward Moss looking for family audiences to fill not only their new suburban variety palaces but also their giant West End Coliseums and Hippodromes. Ever stricter safety controls forced the rebuilding of many old halls and the near-prohibitionist tendency of a powerful faction in the London County Council forced drink out of the auditorium and very nearly out of the building. The licensing processes were dominated by arguments over temperance and morality. While celebrated battles were fought over the notorious promenade at the Empire, Leicester Square and the unspeakably naughty implications of Marie Lloyd's song, 'I've asked Johnnie Jones, so I know now', at the Oxford, the smaller pub halls were being finally forced out of existence.

Despite the demolition orgy of the 1950s and 1960s,

The Oxford, on the corner of Oxford Street and Tottenham Court Road, was one of the most popular of the West End music halls from its opening in 1861 until 1917, when it became a theatre.

some of London's finest variety palaces remain, including Golders Green Hippodrome (now a TV theatre), the Victoria Palace, the London Coliseum (the biggest of them all and now the home of the English National Opera) and Hackney Empire. The last-named returned triumphantly to its proper use in 1987, after years as a bingo house.

It is the artistes of the variety palace era who are particularly remembered today and some of them, fortunately, have left excellent sound recordings and, in a few cases, filmed records of their work. The voices of the most popular – Dan Leno's patter at the 'Tower of London', Marie Lloyd's 'A Little of What You Fancy', Gus Elen's 'The 'ouses in Between', Charles Coborn's 'Two Lovely Black Eyes', and many others – can still be heard today.

The rapid decline of the music halls after about 1920 is usually attributed to the growing popularity of the movies and the appearance of the lavish super cinemas. Television dealt a crushing blow to the variety stage, but it would be premature to announce its death. Some fine modern performers in London's folk clubs and cabaret – and at the reopened Hackney Empire – would have been perfectly at home in the halls.

The Alhambra was a music hall from 1860 until 1912, when it became a home for revues, musicals and straight plays. It was demolished in 1936 and replaced by the Odeon, Leicester Square.

The greatest danger for the London theatre came in the two decades after the end of the Second World War. As theatre-going showed signs of holding its own, at least in central London, a new threat appeared in television. The advantages of being entertained at home seemed irresistible. Theatres began to be closed and demolished. The earliest and most extensive losses occurred in the suburbs (about thirty-five in twenty years), but pressure was soon felt in central London. The Stoll, the Scala and the Gaiety fell to the redevelopers and it seemed that planning policies would lack the strength to prevent the destruction of the greater part of London's theatrical inheritance. Super cinemas, previously seen as the main threat to the theatres, proved no less vulnerable to the tide of commercial redevelopment.

Fortunately, the protection of older theatres as historic buildings was extended after 1971 and the Theatres Trust Act of 1976 strengthened the safeguards further. More Theatres opened or reopened in London in the following ten years than were closed. Amongst the most remarkable recent revivals have been the Playhouse and Hackney Empire, both reopened in 1987 after long years of darkness.

A NATIONAL THEATRE

David Garrick's idea of a National Theatre was canvassed continuously for two hundred years before the building became a reality and opened on the South Bank in 1976. A National Theatre Company had been housed in the Old Vic since 1963, but in the minds of many the former Old Vic company had been effectively standing in as the National Theatre for many years before that.

As the Royal Coburg, presenting sensational melodramas, the Old Vic was one of London's leading popular theatres. It served for a short time as a music hall before 1879, when it came into the hands of Emma Cons, a social reformer and teetotaller. She opened it as a temperance coffee music hall and founded an adult education college (now Morley College) in part of the building. Her aim was to provide the working and lower middle classes with first-class entertainment and educational facilities including concerts, recitals and staged scenes from Shakespeare.

Her niece, Lilian Baylis, who became manager in 1897, dedicated her life to the presentation of Shakespeare, opera and ballet at the Vic and at Sadler's Wells (acquired in 1931). The cast lists for Old Vic productions during and since the Baylis years amount to a roll call of the British theatre. In the 1980s a Canadian entrepreneur, Ed Mirvish, restored it to its 1871 appearance.

The National itself, designed by Denys Lasdun, contains three theatres: the Olivier, the Lyttelton and the Cottesloe, respectively open-stage, proscenium and adaptable courtyard spaces. Revivals, new and foreign plays are staged in repertory. In 1989 the National Theatre was renamed the Royal National Theatre.

THEATRE-GOING TODAY

The establishment of new theatres just outside the walls of the old City (the Barbican and Pit) and the presence of the National group (and soon, perhaps, a new Globe) on the South Bank, carry echoes of the distant past. Beyond West End Theatreland, which now wraps itself around the old market area of Covent Garden, there are many outliers like the Mayfair (in a hotel building off Piccadilly), the Mermaid (City), the Royal Court (Chelsea), the Apollo Victoria, the Victoria Palace and the London Palladium. Theatres of distinction in the outer suburban

OPPOSITE Visitors outside the half-price ticket booth in Leicester Square select from the wide variety of theatrical attractions that the West End and the fringe theatres have to offer.

ring include those at Richmond, Greenwich and Wimbledon, and the Bush, the Tricycle and the Lyric, Hammersmith.

The choice of entertainment offered is almost endless: visitors can see premières and revivals, blockbuster musicals, one-person shows, intimate plays with music, classic drama of all kinds and periods, new writing, light comedy, alternative comedy, traditional music hall, improvisation, opera and ballet. The venues vary from superb Victorian and Edwardian proscenium houses like the elegant Wyndham's and the London Coliseum (built as an immense variety palace and now the home of the English National Opera), to Art Deco jewels like the Whitehall, modern wonders like the New London, and no-frills studios like the Donmar Warehouse, the urban equivalent of a theatre fit-up in a barn.

Great national companies based in subsidized houses stand alongside (and sometimes in mutually beneficial relationship with) a commercial structure where the owners and lessees of the theatres let and sublet down a chain that leads eventually to the risk-taking production companies.

Tourism and business entertainment help keep London theatre buoyant and justify the risk of investment in large-cast, technically sophisticated productions. Yet for those who know the ground well there is particular pleasure in going to places off the beaten track. The Royal Court, which saw the first London productions of a number of Shaw plays and premièred the works of Osborne, Wesker and Simpson in the 1950s and 1960s, is not far from the centre. Stratford Theatre Royal, former home of Joan Littlewood's Theatre Workshop and still producing lively work, is easy to reach on the Central Line. The London fringe includes theatres with a deserved national reputation, like the Young Vic (yards from its elderly neighbour), the Almeida in Islington and the Half Moon in the East End. Stimulating work can also be seen in some of London's innumerable pub theatres, harking back to the very earliest traditions of the galleried inns.

Built as a variety theatre in 1904, the Coliseum in St Martin's Lane was the first in England to have a revolving stage. Now the home of the English National Opera, it is London's largest theatre and its Edwardian interior survives largely unaltered.

MUSIC

No other city supports the number of symphony orchestras or the range of specialist musical groups that can be found in London. The BBC Symphony Orchestra, the London Symphony, the London Philharmonic, the Philharmonia and the Royal Philharmonic are all of world class, as indeed are the two opera house orchestras and many of the smaller ensembles.

A PUBLIC AND PRIVATE PAST

London's development as a centre of music dates back to the Norman Conquest. The choral grammar school attached to St Paul's Cathedral already existed in the eleventh century. The city's great churches such as St Paul's and Westminster Abbey laid then a tradition which their choirs still maintain. In particular the frequent presence of the Chapel Royal, a group of church musicians who attended the sovereign to provide choristers for services at the various royal palaces, secured London's place at the centre of British musical life. Since the twelfth century its members and music-masters have included many of the most distinguished British composers.

As the capital, London was also in the vanguard of the development of secular music through the ceremonial and military bands which accompanied the court. The earliest professional bands were formed by the 'waits' – watchmen appointed in the thirteenth century to guard the gates. They were issued with reed instruments for signalling purposes and played music for civic functions and, later, dancing.

William the Conqueror's minstrel, the harpist Taille-fer, died (singing, it is said) at the battle of Senlac. Thereafter the number of royal minstrels increased steadily so that the royal household of the Middle Ages included many musicians. In 1628 Charles I officially grouped them into the King's Band of Music which, by the time of Queen Victoria, had grown into the monarch's personal symphony orchestra.

But the court was never the sole source of patronage. By the mid-fourteenth century there were enough minstrels working regularly in London to form a guild. Nonetheless, early musical entertainment was largely an amateur affair. The Inns of Court played an important part, organizing masques and revels. Henry VIII was himself an amateur composer. Unaccompanied choral music flourished under the Tudors when groups met in homes and taverns to sing madrigals. Some working-class London pubs maintain the musical tradition,

The third Covent Garden Opera House, which stands today, was designed by E.M. Barry in 1858, after Smirke's 1809 building had burned down.

encouraging singsongs and solos helped along by piano accompaniment, although in most pubs the music is more likely to be made by a juke-box.

It was inevitable, when theatres opened, that singing should take to the stage. Shakespeare had to write songs into his plays to accommodate the public taste for incidental music. In recent years, a spate of hugely successful musicals has augmented the box-office earnings of London's theatres, attracting a new and wider audience.

OPERA'S BEGINNINGS

Performances of opera began in the seventeenth century, at first in English but later, to be fashionable, in Italian. It was as a composer of Italian operas that Handel first came to London where, under the patronage of the Hanoverians, he followed a successful and influential career for half a century. Many of his operas and oratorios received their first performance at the OPERA HOUSE in Covent Garden, though the original building there was funded by the success of *The Beggar's Opera* (written in English by John Gay) in 1728.

Through a glorious though chequered career the Royal Opera at Covent Garden has remained London's principal centre for international opera. Plans are now in hand to extend and improve the present theatre, built in 1858 and already the third to have occupied the site. Thanks to the initiative of the social reformer Lilian Baylis, who wanted London's poor to hear grand opera in a language they could understand, the Royal Opera has an energetic rival in the English National Opera, a descendant of the Sadler's Wells Opera which Baylis established in the 1930s. It is now based at the COLISEUM in St Martin's Lane and performs an excitingly broad repertoire of opera and operetta, including newly commissioned works, all in English.

In the last decades of the nineteenth century the partnership of the impresario Richard D'Oyly Carte with the librettist W. S. Gilbert and composer Sir Arthur Sullivan gave London a world-famous repertoire of comic operettas. Like Handel's oratorios these are constantly revived in amateur and professional performance and the D'Oyly Carte Opera Company has been newly reconstituted to perpetuate their popularity.

CONCERT LIFE

There had been music rooms in taverns since Tudor times, but London's public concerts properly began in 1672, when a former violinist in the King's Band, John Banister, opened his house for a season. The next venue was a coal merchant's warehouse in Clerkenwell, where a weekly series ran for thirty-six years. The first large concert-room, Hickford's, opened in the Haymarket in 1714.

An offshoot of concerts in the halls and opera in the theatres was summer music in the parks. Vocalists and musicians earned their off-season living in more than thirty pleasure gardens of which Marylebone, Vauxhall and Ranelagh were the most famous (see *The pleasure gardens*). From the eighteenth century, leading composers visited or settled in London to compose for its rich and appreciative audiences. They included Handel, J. C. Bach, Mozart, Haydn, Chopin, Mendelssohn, Verdi and Wagner.

By the nineteenth century regular concerts known as the Monday and Saturday 'Pops' drew capacity audiences for performances of chamber music by the world's greatest artists. Orchestral promenade concerts started in 1838 with cheap admission for those willing to stand. The 'Proms' became London's most distinctive annual musical event and the world's greatest music festival through the work of the conductor, Sir Henry Wood, whose series, begun in 1895, takes place in the Royal Albert Hall and is now sponsored by the BBC.

During the Second World War London's concert halls were closed, and some destroyed, but the capital's musical tradition was defiantly maintained by the pianist Dame Myra Hess, who instituted a daily programme of lunchtime recitals in the National Gallery. Lunchtime concerts continue in many of London's churches and former churches such as ST JOHN'S, Smith Square; ST MARTIN-IN-THE-FIELDS and ST JAMES'S, Piccadilly. Since the war the construction of two major concert halls has greatly improved the quality of London's musical life. The Royal Festival Hall was opened for the 1951 Festival of Britain, and the Barbican Centre, now the home of the London Symphony Orchestra, was completed in 1982.

With the advent of recording and popular music in the present century, London's musical activity became all the more vigorous and vital. DENMARK STREET (off Charing Cross Road), where the music publishers were concentrated, became famous as London's 'Tin Pan Alley' and ARCHER STREET in Soho was thronged each day with musicians seeking session work with jazz bands and dance orchestras.

London's historic musical tradition is constantly being enriched. There are festivals of contemporary and experimental music, notably at the ALMEIDA THEATRE in Islington. Immigrants have introduced new musical experiences. From bars, restaurants, clubs and community centres come the sounds of Caribbean reggae, steel bands, calypso or rap, Indian ragas, Chinese pop from Hong Kong, Irish jigs and folk songs, or African tribal music. American and indigenous jazz has a permanent centre at RONNIE SCOTT's club in Soho, and the latest of international pop is at the 100 CLUB or the MARQUEE. Audiences of tens of thousands crowd the outdoor stadium at Wembley for established pop and rock stars.

Some London music can be enjoyed at little or no cost. There are free performances in the parks in summer and in the foyers of concert hall complexes throughout the year. Even the streets and underground can provide musical entertainment in the form of buskers, musical descendants of the vagabond minstrels and organ-grinders of earlier centuries.

LEFT The Royal Albert Hall was opened in 1870 and has since been among London's premier concert halls, despite imperfect acoustics. The series of promenade concerts established by Sir Henry Wood takes place here every summer. On the left is the Albert Memorial, completed in 1876.

OPPOSITE A musical interlude in a busy working day. Many churches have lunchtime concerts: this is St Olave's in Hart Street in the City.

PARKS AND GARDENS

Londoners have been able to enjoy their largest central park from the early seventeenth century. That was when Hyde Park – a royal deer park enclosed by Henry VIII and at that time still in the countryside – was opened to the public. Other royal parks, from early on, were used for occasional public festivities. It was not until the nineteenth century, when the metropolis had expanded over so much open land, that forceful campaigns developed to preserve more green breathing spaces for its overcrowded citizens. New public parks were created and existing common land safeguarded (see *Heaths and commons*). Private estates threatened by expanding suburban development were gradually acquired or handed over for public use. Londoners now have access to a wealth of parks and gardens, their variety illustrating the changing ways in which such open space has been used and developed over the centuries.

—— THE SEVENTEENTH CENTURY ——

The largest and most ancient parks are the hunting enclosures near the sites of the royal palaces of Greenwich and Richmond. At RICHMOND, enclosed in 1637, deer still wander among several hundred ancient oak trees. GREENWICH PARK is of medieval origin but modified by later landscaping: one can still trace the late seventeenth-century avenues which run from near Inigo Jones's Queen's House to the crown of the hill and the Royal Observatory. The best place to appreciate the fashion for French-inspired formal landscaping is HAMPTON COURT. Here Charles II laid out a long canal to the east of the palace, flanked by radiating double avenues. William III added the magnificent chestnut and lime avenues to the north, which stretch for nearly a mile into Bushy Park. At the time their grandiose scale must have appeared a striking contrast to the tight, enclosed Tudor gardens to the south, embellished with heraldic figures and overlooked by mount and banqueting house, which we now know only from drawings.

Early formal gardens that lay close to great mansions rarely survive, but at HAM HOUSE, near Richmond, there is an authentic re-creation of the seventeenth-century layout, restored in 1975–6, and at KEW a formal garden in seventeenth-century style has been laid out to complement the seventeenth-century brick merchant's house that later became known as Kew Palace. During the Anglo-Dutch reign of William and Mary the fashion for extensive formal gardens was at its height. The wilderness and maze designed by George London and Henry

Wise as part of their improvements at Hampton Court are still popular with visitors; at Kensington Palace, although the gardens have been much simplified, survivals from their time are the Broad Walk and Round Pond, later to become the haunt of Kensington nannies.

The seventeenth-century passion for gardening was matched by a growing interest in botany. A precious survival is the CHELSEA PHYSIC GARDEN, established by the Thames in 1673 by the Worshipful Company of Apothecaries for the purpose of studying medicinal plants. Its original geometric layout is partially preserved and the garden is still a centre of plant research. It was at this time too that exotic plants began to be brought to England. The two Tradescants, royal gardeners (commemorated in the museum of garden history at St Mary, Lambeth) were among the leaders in this movement. So too were several Bishops of London: the grounds of their former palace at Fulham, although much replanted, maintain a tradition of exotic trees and shrubs.

—— THE EIGHTEENTH CENTURY ——

During the eighteenth century the fashion for formal layouts gave way to more irregular, 'picturesque' planning. One of the most instructive examples of the transition is the small park around Lord Burlington's Palladian villa at CHISWICK in west London. Neglected after it became a public park in 1929, its recent restoration is designed to demonstrate the stages of its development: the early formal radiating avenues where tall yew hedges enclose vistas of classical monuments; the wilderness garden added after 1727, and – novelty of the 1730s – the natural-looking river with 'ruined' cascade at one end. Garden buildings had an important role at this time, increasingly used as elements in creating 'picturesque' compositions reminiscent of Claude's painted Italian landscapes. Most were classical, but there were more exotic contributions too, such as William Chambers's remarkable Chinese pagoda of 1761, one of a series of buildings at Kew put up for Princess Augusta when the gardens there were in royal ownership.

The new fashion for curving expanses of water is seen on the grandest scale in HYDE PARK, where the majestic Serpentine, central London's largest boating and bathing lake, was formed in 1730 by damming the River Westbourne, as part of the new landscaping extending east from Kensington Gardens. This had significant effects on the public use of Hyde Park, for the enlarged

water isolated the driving enclosure known as the ring in the north part of the park, where it had been the custom for society to parade in their coaches. Riders gravitated south to the old royal drive to Kensington Palace known as Rotten Row (perhaps from *route du roi*), still a fashionable place for riding.

By 1800 nearly all the formal parks shown on Rocque's mid-eighteenth-century maps had been replaced by the sweeping lawns and informally grouped trees popularized by Capability Brown and Humphry Repton. At KENWOOD, the seat of Lord Mansfield adjoining Hampstead Heath, the grass runs down from the house to a lake where a white sham bridge provides a delightful eyecatcher for the visitor to the summer concerts. Danson Park at Bexley, Osterley Park in west London and Grovelands in Southgate are three further examples where fine late eighteenth-century mansions can still be enjoyed in original landscaped settings, preserved as public parks as twentieth-century suburbia expanded around them.

THE NINETEENTH CENTURY

The vision of the grand house within a private park lay behind John Nash's plan for his new suburb of REGENT'S PARK, laid out from 1811. Here the park was at first railed off from the drives and intended solely for the residents of the palace-like terraces and select villas. In contrast, the more urban scheme which Nash devised at the other end of his Regent Street development included the remodelling of ST JAMES'S PARK for use by the general public. Originally forming the grounds of St James's Palace (together with Green Park to the north), the park

had for long been used for special public occasions. (Indeed it had not recovered from the peace celebrations of 1814, when the gaslights and fireworks set fire to the festive pagoda erected on the bridge over the canal.) Nash's scheme of 1828 retained the late seventeenth-century Mall, but laid out the area to its south in the manner favoured by Repton, with curving walks and a winding lake. It became a model for public parks to follow. Enlivened by its ornamental water fowl, already a feature in the nineteenth century, it remains one of central London's most charming small landscapes. At lunch time on fine summer weekdays the grass is covered with sunbathing office workers.

The move to create completely new parks for public use began with a parliamentary report of 1833, the first of several to stress the need for open space near populous towns. No immediate action was forthcoming, but in 1845 VICTORIA PARK was opened in the East End, in 1852 KENNINGTON COMMON was enclosed and landscaped, and 1858 saw the completion of BATTERSEA PARK, transforming an unappealing swampy area by raising the ground level with earth excavated from the docks. Victoria Park, which once drew crowds of East Enders to its famous flower displays, is now sadly neglected, its horizons confined by tower blocks, although its large romantic lake is still attractive. Battersea is a more mature design whose final form owes much to the landscape gardening skills of the parks superintendent John Gibson. As well as a sizeable lake surrounded by dense planting, Gibson created a sheltered sub-tropical garden, rocks and cascades, happily refurbished as part of a restoration programme inaugurated by the GLC and

The Pleasure Garden

Vauxhall, Marylebone, Ranelagh and Cremorne were the most famous (at times notorious) of more than sixty pleasure gardens created in and around London over two centuries following the Restoration. Set in what were, in their time, rural suburbs within walking (or boat tripping) distance from the heart of the City, they brought to a paying public the kinds of ornamental grounds, shaded walks and alfresco concerts previously enjoyed only by the wealthy.

Some were based on mineral springs with supposedly medicinal qualities (for example Bagnigge and Sadler's Wells, Islington and Bermondsey Spas and Dog and Duck Gardens). Many small resorts, like Highbury Barn, Jenny's Whim and the Yorkshire Stingo, started life as tea gardens attached to public houses. Cuper's Garden in Southwark was one of the earliest, opening in the mid-seventeenth century and closing in 1760. From the Restoration to the early Georgian period this and other pleasure gardens were precisely what the name suggests – tranquil ornamental grounds with relatively few buildings. Later eighteenth-century gardens offered a range of diversions with ambitious catering arrangements and elaborate buildings, often including a 'long room' or 'great room' for use in inclement weather. The Victorians shifted the emphasis firmly from rural peace to pleasure, in competition with the emerging music halls.

In its extraordinarily long life, from about 1660 to 1859, VAUXHALL, on the Thames at Lambeth, went through the complete cycle of change, offering every kind of popular public entertainment from oratorio to balloon ascents.

Samuel Pepys and John Evelyn both visited New Spring Garden, as it was called, in the early 1660s. It was then a place for a summer evening's stroll, laid out with formal avenues and arbours. A few years later, open-air music was introduced. The only substantial building seems to have been the proprietor's house. Until the 1750s the normal approach was by water. Admission was at first free, but Vauxhall's wine, beer, transparently sliced meats, cheesecakes and syllabubs were notoriously expensive.

From the beginning, dark walks leading out of lamplit alleys made Vauxhall a place for flirtation, assignation and intrigue. By 1728, when Jonathan Tyers took over, it was one of London's most celebrated public attractions. Tyers made extensive improvements, adding a great rotunda, a saloon, an 'orchestra' with an organ, rows of pretty supper boxes, ornamental ruins, a cascade and thousands of lamps. Instrumental evening concerts given from six to nine o'clock became the staple entertainment.

Masquerades patronized by Frederick, Prince of Wales, ensured the success of the new régime. In 1737 Tyers commissioned Roubiliac's statue of Handel (now in the Victoria & Albert Museum) to grace the entrance. Twelve years later a rehearsal of the *Royal Fireworks* music attracted an audience of twelve thousand. Vocal concerts were added to the nightly attractions in 1745 and for the next hundred years the

Marylebone Gardens occupied the site of what are now Devonshire Street and Beaumont Street, at the north end of Marylebone High Street. Opened in 1650, they closed in 1776. This view depicts the scene in the mid-eighteenth century.

best singers from the opera houses and theatres performed there.

Later improvements included a supper room, covered walks and scenic illusions. Fireworks were introduced at the end of the eighteenth century. The music of Vauxhall was by the 1820s only the main element in a variety programme which included wirewalkers (Madame Saqui in 1816), jugglers, sword swallowers and equestrians. Gas light was introduced in 1846, by which time some of music hall's first stars – Jack Sharp, W. G. Ross, Sam Cowell – gave performances there.

Vauxhall closed in 1859: no longer a leafy garden, it had fallen from its position as a fashionable resort and was disliked by local residents, who complained that it was noisy and attracted disreputable characters.

The sociable Pepys also visited MARYLEBONE GARDENS, and declared it 'a pretty place'. Situated at the north end of the present Marylebone High Street, it had a bowling green, gravel walks and topiary hedges. It enjoyed a much shorter life than Vauxhall, closing in 1776, but established an outstanding reputation for its music, presenting vocal and instrumental concerts, burlettas and operas.

RANELAGH, in Chelsea, was opened in 1742 when John Lacy, patentee of Drury Lane's Theatre Royal, acquired the old Ranelagh House and its grounds. From the outset an attempt was made to outbid Vauxhall by solving the pleasure garden's perennial problem of a short season, frequently spoilt by inclement weather. A giant rotunda was built, one hundred and fifty feet in diameter, with its ceiling supported at the centre by a splendid structure containing an immense fireplace. There were fifty-two boxes around the circumference and a platform for orchestra and organ. Promenading in the rotunda was the main appeal of Ranelagh, which aimed to attract fashionable society, presenting the first performances of many of Handel's works. Mozart, aged eight, played the harpsichord and the organ there in 1764. The concerts ended in 1803 and the gardens were sold, but part of the ground is still open as a park.

CREMORNE, also in Chelsea, was the last great pleasure garden. It became a popular resort in the 1840s, brilliantly illuminated, with exotic architecture, grottoes, bowers, a bowling saloon, theatre, banqueting hall and dancing platform. It never aspired to musical excellence, but provided first-rate dance music, ballets, circuses and aeronautical feats. Cremorne was renowned for its well-dressed society prostitutes, who never solicited custom. After a rowdy decline it closed in 1877. Lots Road Power Station now covers the site.

With the closure of Cremorne, Highbury Barn (1871), the Surrey Zoological Gardens, Kennington (1877), St

At Ranelagh, seen here in a painting by Canaletto, John Lacy built an indoor, all-weather pleasure garden. The fanciful arched column in the middle supports the roof and also serves as a fireplace.

Helena Gardens, Rotherhithe (1877) and the Royal Pavilion, North Woolwich (1890), the pleasure gardens faded away. After 1900 Londoners could still take a steamboat or excursion train to Rosherville (Gravesend), but new pleasures were taking over.

When the 1851 Exhibition building, the Crystal Palace, moved to Sydenham in 1854, it became a great leisure centre, complete with theatre, concert hall and ornamental grounds. Its popularity killed off the neighbouring Beulah Spa (opened 1831). Crystal Palace burned down in 1936. Subsequent exhibitions (including White City, 1908 and Wembley, 1924) had a holiday atmosphere and some offered spectacular shows, but only the Festival of Britain, in 1951, attempted a sincerely flattering twentieth-century re-creation of the Vauxhall spirit.

The Emmet Railway, Tree Walk, funfair and indoor and outdoor theatres in Battersea Park delighted millions. Curiously, the giant leisure centre in the former Battersea Power Station (which looks to American rather than local precedents) is within sight of the few remaining relics of the Festival Pleasure Gardens, its riverside location inviting memories of Vauxhall and Ranelagh.

continued after 1986 by Wandsworth Council.

The smaller SOUTHWARK and FINSBURY PARKS, both laid out by Alexander McKenzie and opened in 1867, repeated the formula of lake, gravelled drive, smaller winding paths, and a variety of planting within a small compass. These first parks were funded with public money, but new parks were also a favourite subject for the Victorian philanthropists. Sydney Waterlow's gift of his romantically planted estate on the slopes of Highgate Hill, as 'a garden for the gardenless', now WATERLOW PARK, is still a delightful place. Gifts of sculpture, monuments and drinking fountains (the last especially favoured by the Temperance Movement) were frequent. Baroness Burdett Coutts presented a vast Gothic drinking fountain, now unused, to embellish Victoria Park. Public parks were seen as places for instruction and education as well as enjoyment – although more recreational aspects were not neglected: bandstands and refreshment pavilions enticed the Sunday stroller, while 'gymnasia' (the dangerous play equipment deplored by later generations) were provided for children.

The small but attractive VICTORIA EMBANKMENT GARDENS of 1870, another McKenzie design, was from the 1880s particularly favoured for memorials – but these are on a modest scale compared with the monumental shrine to Prince Albert in KENSINGTON GARDENS, designed by Gilbert Scott and completed in 1872. It incorporates nearly two hundred large sculptured figures, an intense expression of noble Victorian aspirations. Despite its size, its filigree silhouette seen from across the park is surprisingly delicate.

Apart from the settings for such monuments, public parks were rarely given expensive architectural layouts. Exceptions are the formal terraces built to complement the CRYSTAL PALACE when it was moved to a new park at

Sydenham in 1852. They survive in part, as do the lifesize prehistoric monsters that embellish the lake, the remains of a grand scheme of educational landscaping. There are also formal Italianate balustrades and fountains of around 1860 at the head of the Serpentine.

Later nineteenth-century parks saw a return to formality, with horticulture reigning supreme. The craze for formal borders (200,000 plants were bedded out annually at Victoria Park) inevitably has given way to less labour-intensive schemes, although a good survival from this period is the densely planted garden created by J.J. Sexby, LCC Superintendent of Parks, within the old kitchen gardens of BROCKWELL PARK, a landscaped estate near Brixton, acquired for public use in 1892. Another former private estate, HOLLAND PARK, also retains some nineteenth-century formal gardens. It was acquired for public enjoyment in 1952.

The most remarkable demonstration of the Victorian interest in plants is the development of the ROYAL BOTANIC GARDENS at Kew. The botanic collection begun in the private gardens of Princess Augusta became a state concern in 1841; the grounds, enlarged from eleven to seventy-six acres under the first director, William Hooker, were newly landscaped and planted, and an ambitious building programme planned. Burton and Turner's splendid curvaceous palm house, recently restored, was completed in 1848, their temperate house, or winter garden, in 1862 (enlarged 1898). Conservatories and plant houses were essential adjuncts for gardens specializing in tender or exotic plants; notable precursors of Kew are the camellia house of 1813 at Chiswick Park and the conservatory of 1830 at the Duke of Northumberland's SYON PARK (a garden whose botanical traditions go back to the sixteenth century). The latter, designed by Charles Fowler, has an early example of the steeply curved dome used later for the palm house at Kew. The best surviving private Victorian winter gardens on a grand scale are those of the 1890s at AVERY HILL, Woolwich, built for Colonel North, who made a fortune from nitrate. They are now open to the public.

THE TWENTIETH CENTURY

As sedate Victorian Sunday walks gave way to bicycling (Battersea Park was a favourite place for this) and then to other organized sports, preoccupation with recreational facilities took precedence over landscape design. Urged on by the National Playing Fields Association, founded in 1927, local authorities laid out games pitches and swimming pools in older parks, but their attendant functional buildings rarely enhanced the landscape. Formal flower beds were simplified, although rose gardens, whose upkeep required less labour, remained popular; a fine example is the one planted in 1932 in the Inner Circle of Regent's Park.

Post-Second World War plans for London were generous in their open space provision, but it has taken many years even for the partial realization of BURGESS PARK in Camberwell and MILE END PARK in Stepney. From the 1960s local authorities began to create more practical small local parks catering for young children; likewise in the metropolitan parks the GLC introduced imaginatively landscaped play areas (there are good examples in Alexandra and Victoria Parks) in place of bleak tubular steel equipment set on bare asphalt. Meanwhile, a growing concern with ecology has encouraged interest in natural landscape, demonstrated in CAMLEY STREET NATURE PARK, north of King's Cross.

Syon House, London home of the Earls then Dukes of Northumberland in 1788. Robert Adam and Capability Brown were hired to improve the house and grounds in the 1760s although Adam never finished his work.

OVERLEAF As well as its large showpiece parks, London has a number of smaller open spaces much valued by local residents. This is Springfield Park in Clapton, north-east of the City, overlooking the River Lea.

MUSEUMS AND GALLERIES

Rome is the greatest *living* museum and the Louvre in Paris the biggest single institution under one roof. Prague, Berlin and Madrid all had national galleries before London. But London is unique for the variety of its collections, their depth, their range, their richness.

Most of its museums were founded between 1750 and the beginning of the First World War, 1914. Several factors coincided in those years to generate the great collections that made London a treasure house. The first was the appetite for exploration. Although this was shared with the other European maritime powers, the love of travel was especially intense in Britain, no doubt because it is an island. By the early eighteenth century much of the most dangerous exploration had been accomplished, the horizons of the world fully mapped. It became the fashion for educated gentlemen to make the Grand Tour, to complete the refinements of a man of taste by a first-hand acquaintance with the classical antiquities of Rome, Istanbul, Greece and Egypt. Returning to their estates in Britain, gentlemen brought back large numbers of sculptures, paintings and antiquities with which to furnish their own houses. This tradition continued well into the nineteenth and even the twentieth centuries.

By the end of the eighteenth century appreciation of fine paintings was becoming fashionable at court. This coincided with the great flowering of British arts: the age of Reynolds, Constable, Romney, Lawrence, Blake; the watercolourists Cox, Cotman and Cozens; and, the greatest of them all, Joseph Mallord William Turner. With the arrival of the nineteenth century, the British were becoming rich in classical antiquities and the fine arts, and increasingly knowledgeable about them. To that wealth was suddenly added the arts of France, Holland and parts of Germany and Spain, for the French Revolution and the Napoleonic wars heralded widespread plunder across Europe. Much of the booty ended up in Britain, as *ancien régime* families fled with whatever treasures they could carry. London became a centre of the art market, a position it has held ever since (see *The art business*).

Thus when Victoria came to the throne, Britain was already lavishly endowed with the arts of western Europe. During her reign other influences came into play. The most important was the Industrial Revolution, which had begun earlier but was now consolidated by the development of railways and canals. The industrial and decorative arts – pottery, textiles, silver, furniture – were developed to a high standard, as better massproducing machinery was invented and a rising middle class was able to afford decorative objects. For the first time in Britain art was owned by people of more modest means as well as the rich. The power that the Industrial Revolution brought to Britain helped create the Empire. Now artefacts were brought back from the East, especially India and Persia. Textiles, ivories, jewels and Indian miniatures were added to London's stock of exquisite objects.

— THE FOUR GREAT TREASURE HOUSES —

The British Museum, or BM as it is familiarly called, is the senior institution in the arts in Britain (see *below*), followed by the National Gallery, the Victoria & Albert Museum and the Tate Gallery, in that order.

This might seem unfair to the V & A, whose collections are more extensive than those of the NATIONAL GALLERY – 70,000 objects in the V & A's ceramics department alone, as compared with only 2000 pictures in the National. But paintings still move us in a way that textiles, silver or Japanese lacquer do not, and the quality of pictures at the National is prodigious. Here is almost every Western artist of note at the top of his (seldom her) form. Hans Holbein's *Christina of Denmark, Duchess of Milan*, is for some the most beautiful portrait in the world. She was sixteen when Holbein painted her and already a widow. Henry VIII was considering her as his bride and Holbein was despatched to Brussels to take a likeness. Nearby is Veronese's *Family of Darius before Alexander* – quite different, a huge, sumptuous canvas from sixteenth-century Venice in which everyone is caught up in an invisible wave sweeping across the picture. The gallery has a dozen and a half Titians, as many Rembrandts, Leonardo da Vinci's *Virgin of the Rocks*, Velazquez's *Rokeby Venus* and a *Sunflowers* by Van Gogh, one of the same series from which another sold for £22¾ million when it was auctioned in 1986.

The gallery had not so much a difficult birth as a reluctant one. A number of prominent figures in the late eighteenth century tried to persuade the governments of the day to start an institution to match the Prado in Madrid or the Rijksmuseum in Amsterdam. The governments repeatedly refused, even turning down offers of collections with which to found the gallery. It was eventually established in 1824 after the Government, under pressure from King George IV among others, agreed to accept, on behalf of the nation, a collection of

thirty-eight paintings put together by John Julius Angerstein. A slightly mysterious figure of Russian extraction, he was rumoured to have been an illegitimate offspring of a member of the Russian royal family. His fortune was based on clever dealing in the City. Parties at his rooms in Pall Mall, where all his paintings were hung, were attended by the prime ministers of the day. His offer to the nation, when it came, was too good to refuse. Those Pall Mall rooms served as the temporary home of the Gallery until William Wilkins's long, low building in Trafalgar Square was completed in 1838.

Throughout the nineteenth century many of the gallery's acquisitions were by bequest, although one of the early directors, Charles Eastlake, made a name for himself by picking up a large number of bargains in Italy. In 1897 many of its British works were transferred to the Tate. The gallery's best-known director in recent years was Kenneth Clark, who much later became a public celebrity through his television series, *Civilisation*. He was director of the gallery throughout the Second World War, when the pictures were evacuated to Wales. While there they were cleaned, and the transformed, gleaming canvases alarmed traditionalists when they were returned to London in the late 1940s.

The VICTORIA & ALBERT MUSEUM acquired its present name in 1909, when Aston Webb's fluid building in Cromwell Road was completed. Formerly the South Kensington Museum, it contains countless treasures. It is the home of the national sculpture collection, in many ways its most remarkable, though also its most poorly displayed section. In general sculpture is less highly valued today than paintings, but at the V & A it is easy to see what so excited the British collectors of the

nineteenth century: white marble figures, black tombs, red warriors, green saints, make it an overcrowded stone jungle, but a fertile one.

Much of the V & A is organized differently from most other museums, not by subject but by material. The main holdings are grouped according to whether they are textile, ceramics, metalwork or stone. This is the unique insight the V & A offers: a chance to see how the use of a material varied around the world at different ages, and so to gain an understanding of the artistic impulse that can be obtained almost nowhere else.

The impulse for the museum itself stemmed from the Great Exhibition of 1851 which sparked enormous interest in applied art – the application of artistic principles to industrial products. The Exhibition was a huge success and made a profit of £186,000. The money was used to buy a site in South Kensington where the V & A now stands, along with the Science Museum, the Geological Museum, the Natural History Museum and the Royal Colleges of Art and Music. In 1852 the Museum of Manufactures was opened at Marlborough House, St James's, moving to the Kensington site in 1857, when it became known as the Museum of Ornamental Art. It was enlarged piecemeal and intended to demonstrate new techniques of building and ornamentation, as well as to display beautiful objects, hence the elaborate terracotta of the quadrangle and the colourful ceramics.

The foundation stone of the new front blocks was laid

OPPOSITE One of London's most popular museums, the V & A is devoted to design and applied arts. The full inscription above the entrance, adapted by the architect Aston Webb from an aphorism of Sir Joshua Reynolds, reads: 'The excellence of every art must consist in the complete accomplishment of its purpose.'

RIGHT In 1787 the Royal Academy, founded nineteen years earlier, held the first of its annual exhibitions in Somerset House. Frugal use of space meant that up to 700 paintings could be displayed, although in conditions that would appal modern exhibition designers.

in 1899 by Queen Victoria, in almost the last official act of her reign. The museum opened ten years later. Its exhaustive collection of furniture, textiles, porcelain, clothing and the decorative arts has always been immensely popular, although the introduction of a voluntary admission charge in the 1980s caused attendances to fall. Two of the V & A's outposts are the Theatre Museum in Covent Garden and the Bethnal Green Museum, with its bewitching Victorian dolls, dolls' houses and other playthings.

The fourth of the treasure houses, the TATE GALLERY on Millbank, is the official home of two distinct national collections – British art since Tudor times and modern art (essentially from the beginning of the twentieth century) from all over the world. It is an illogical and sometimes uneasy mix. On the one hand are Hogarth, Gainsborough, Reynolds, Romney, Constable, Blake, Whistler and the Pre-Raphaelites. This is an impressive collection, but many visitors all but ignore it in favour of the more spectacular rooms containing seminal works from the twentieth century by such as Picasso, Dali, Braque, Matisse, Bacon, Rothko and Hockney. They hang incongruously in the high-ceilinged galleries of Sidney Smith's late Victorian (1897) neo-classical building, funded by Sir Henry Tate, the sugar magnate and philanthropist (see *The makers of London*).

Next door is the Clore Gallery, a self-contained annexe named after the financier Charles Clore, who underwrote it. Designed by James Stirling, it opened in 1987 to house the hundreds of Turner's paintings that the artist bequeathed to the nation. He left specific instructions in his will about how his pictures should hang – in what relation to one another and even the colour of the walls. Controversy still rumbles on as to whether the gallery fulfils the terms of the bequest but, in spite of this, it remains a breathtaking memorial to one of the greatest British artists.

Apart from its permanent collections, the Tate accommodates many of the large special exhibitions mounted in London. The National Gallery holds very few and the V & A abandoned big shows in the early 1980s (its new director says she wants to revive them). This leaves the Tate, the Hayward Gallery (part of the South Bank complex) and the ROYAL ACADEMY OF ARTS as the main centres for temporary exhibitions. The Academy, founded in 1768 and now at Burlington House, Piccadilly (see *Great houses and palaces*) has a small but choice permanent collection of its own, notably a Michelangelo tondo. It is best known for its annual summer exhibition, for which established and struggling artists alike submit their latest work. The pictures and sculptures, most of them for sale, are variable in quality but to have one accepted by the Academicians is an enormous boost to a young artist. For most of the rest of the year the Academy's rooms are filled with visiting exhibitions, often so popular that the queue, snaking round the eighteenth-century courtyard, has become one of the more familiar sights of London.

SMALLER COLLECTIONS

The smallest of London's national galleries is the NATIONAL PORTRAIT GALLERY, tucked in behind the National Gallery with its entrance across the road from St Martin-in-the-Fields. Most of the important national figures, from Richard II to Margaret Thatcher, are depicted here, not always in a flattering likeness. There

The British Museum

It has been criticized for its overawing size, the sometimes random nature of its collections and the acquisitive philosophy that motivates it. Yet the appeal of the British Museum is apparent from the fact that more than three million people visit it each year, making it by far the most popular institution of its kind. It invests an entire area of London with a scholarly flavour, surrounded by publishers and bookshops, map and print galleries and the editorial offices of small magazines and academic journals.

Its foundations were laid by Act of Parliament, but four men made it possible: Robert Cotton, Robert Harley (first Earl of Oxford, second creation), Hans Sloane and Denis Diderot. The first three owned the collections on which it was based: respectively, medieval manuscripts; books, charters and rolls; botanical and zoological specimens. A public lottery raised £100,000 so that all three could be bought, then housed together. Diderot was among the French *encyclopédistes* who, in the mid-eighteenth century, made the case for a central museum where knowledge could be organized under one roof. For the first century of its existence the British Museum was the only great institution conforming to their precepts and even now has only one serious rival –

the Smithsonian Institution in Washington DC.

To save money the early trustees decided to convert an existing building. Buckingham House – later Buckingham Palace – was rejected because the £30,000 asked was thought excessive. The solution was Montagu House, Bloomsbury. The museum opened there in 1759 but for the first fifty years the public had only limited access. The early museum was strong on natural history – stuffed animals greeted the visitor in the main hall – and originally it was organized in just three departments. The collections expanded greatly in the later part of the eighteenth century, especially in the wake of the Napoleonic wars, when the Hamilton, Townley and Egyptian collections were acquired, soon to be followed by the Elgin marbles. These were removed from Athens in controversial circumstances by Lord Elgin and bought for the nation, for £35,000, in 1815. The fervent campaign by the Greek Government for their return has raised fundamental questions about the right of modern nations to hang on to the proceeds of imperialist adventures. The museum has adamantly refused to accede to the Greek request, because if the principle were conceded the entire basis of its existence would be called into question.

The books, bronzes and drawings of Richard Payne Knight were incorporated in 1824 at much the same time as George IV 'gave' the royal library to the museum (although, in fact, the king was secretly paid £180,000

LEFT This gallery tucked away in the basement of the museum houses the collection of mainly Roman sculpture put together by Charles Townley in the second part of the eighteenth century. The central standing figure is the young Bacchus, sculpted in marble, *c.* AD 150–200.

RIGHT The Rosetta Stone, found in the Nile Delta in 1799, is one of the most popular exhibits in the museum. The inscription in three forms (hieroglyphics, demotic and Greek) enabled scholars to decipher hieroglyphic script for the first time.

via the Admiralty). The museum was now outgrowing itself and a new building called for. The architect selected, Robert Smirke, was a fervent neo-classicist who had toured Europe looking at buildings. He had been pipped by Nash on the commission to revamp Buckingham Palace and by Soane on the Law Courts. The BM was his triumph. His original plans were approved in 1823, revised for reasons of economy in 1833 and not really finished until 1852. The Natural History collection was transferred to its present purpose-built museum in South Kensington in 1881.

The British Museum today has nine curatorial departments, of which one, ethnography, is housed away from Bloomsbury at the Museum of Mankind in Burlington Gardens. The British Library, commonly thought to be part of the museum, has been a separate institution since 1973, although, confusingly, it continues to occupy a large part of the site, including the magnificent domed reading room where Karl Marx wrote *Das Kapital*. The Library is due to move to new premises at St Pancras from the early 1990s, releasing space to the bulging museum.

The museum's possessions are unique in a wide range of scholarship. The collection of coins is a numismatist's dream: kept in row upon row of carved mahogany boxes are examples of every coin ever minted in England and Scotland, and the most representative collection of world coinage. The Egyptian antiquities, rivalled only

by the Metropolitan Museum in New York, comprise 70,000 objects, most notably the Rosetta Stone, a piece of black basalt rock dating from 196 BC. This played a vital part in the deciphering of hieroglyphics, crucial to reading ancient Egyptian texts. The allied holdings of the department of Western Asiatic Antiquities provide an insight into the lives of the peoples of Sumeria, Babylon, Assyria, ancient Persia and Palestine.

The Greek and Roman section contains objects dating from 3000 BC to the later Roman Empire. It includes a huge amount of monumental sculpture and the collection of vases assembled by Sir William Hamilton when he was ambassador in Naples. Their decoration reveals much about the lifestyle of the Greeks, including details of costume, food and furnishings. Upstairs, in the galleries of the department of Medieval and Later Antiquities, is the remarkable Sutton Hoo ship burial. Evidence of man's earliest existence is chronicled in the department of Prehistoric and Romano-British Antiquities, which also has a fine Celtic collection (including Lindow man – the body in the bog) and a magnificent corpus of material from Roman Britain.

The prints and drawings department is home to millions of items dating from the fourteenth century and contains Michelangelo's *Virgin and Child*, Botticelli's *Abundance*, Rubens's portrait of his first wife and Goya's haunting red and brown drawing of the Duke of Wellington. Too numerous and too delicate to be on permanent display, the works can be consulted in the print room by arrangement.

The oriental collections cover most of Asia and a time span from the neolithic period to the present day. Its most outstanding fields are Chinese and Japanese decorative arts, oriental painting and graphic illustration, Islamic ceramics and religious art including sculpture.

Space in the museum is at a premium and the problem will be only partially relieved when the Library moves to St Pancras as the ethnography department will then move in to fill much of the space. The British Museum today is like an iceberg: not quite six-sevenths is hidden and a great deal goes on behind the scenes. There is an enormous stone-conservation laboratory in the basement of the front elevation; a massive research laboratory on the east side employing twenty-four full-time scientists (where broken jars and other treasures are painstakingly reassembled); and a large shed just inside the tradesmen's entrance on the north side, given over entirely to the care of delicate clay cuneiform tablets. This is the oldest known form of writing and is one of the innumerable fields where the museum can claim the finest collection in the world.

are death masks of Keats and Shelley, Turner's hands from the life, self-portraits of many leading artists, early photographs and enormous compositions recording great moments of Parliament.

Three privately formed collections in London stand out. The pre-eminence of the WALLACE COLLECTION in Manchester Square is evident from the influence it has exerted on other collectors down the ages. The finest single collection of eighteenth-century French painting, furniture, porcelain and *objets d'art*, it was built up over many years by successive generations of the Seymour-Conway family, marquesses of Hertford. The fourth marquess bequeathed it to Richard Wallace, to the disappointment of his family, but the bequest survived two law suits. The Seymours were a distinguished family, whose ambassador members had built up the collection while abroad, especially in France. Many French believed that the collection rightfully belonged in their country, but Wallace left it to his widow (herself French), on whose death it became the greatest gift ever left by one person to the state.

The objects are beautiful enough in themselves – Gobelins tapestries, pictures by Watteau, Boucher and Fragonard, busts by Houdon, ormolu clocks and commodes by Cressent and Oppenordt, *torchères, boiseries, girandoles* – it sounds like France before the Terror. But the main appeal of the Wallace Collection is that it tries hard to be, not a museum, but the private house it was when Lady Wallace died: the bronzes are on the tables, where they always were, alongside the flowers; the Avignon clock, a seething mass of fighting bronze figures, is on a marble mantelshelf. Less domestic – but popular with young visitors – is the large collection of armour. The Wallace has also been instrumental in the creation of other great collections. It inspired the American industrialist Henry Frick to form his own collection – of pictures, tapestries, bronzes and enamels – in New York. Andrew Mellon, chief benefactor of the National Gallery in Washington DC, similarly conceived his passion for collecting after he saw the Wallace.

The marquesses of Hertford amassed an eclectic range of art; Samuel Courtauld collected only Impressionist and modern paintings. The COURTAULD COLLECTION, now at Somerset House in the Strand (and augmented by the further, munificent bequest of Count Antoine Seilern), is more remarkable today than when it was assembled.

Courtauld bought his pictures, with money derived from the Courtauld fabric and chemical company, when Cézanne, Pissarro, Sisley, Renoir, Van Gogh and Monet were not recognized as the major artists they have since become. The Courtauld is not simply about beauty: it is about what dealers and auctioneers call the 'eye', the ability to spot where taste is going in art, to discern quality even when it is unfashionable and when the name of the painter is no guide to intrinsic worth. Courtauld undoubtedly had an eye and it is fitting that Britain's foremost institute of art history should be named after him.

Smaller collections of great interest and quality include the QUEEN'S GALLERY at the back of Buckingham Palace. Here are displayed masterpieces from the Royal Collection of paintings, drawings, miniatures, porcelain, furniture, clocks, etc. SIR JOHN SOANE'S MUSEUM at 13 Lincoln's Inn Fields was created by the architect in the early nineteenth century to house both himself and his fine collection of drawings, paintings, sculpture and *objets d'art*. The result – left intact, unlike his design for the Bank of England – is a superbly idiosyncratic monument to Soane's genius. His intention was to express 'the poetry of architecture', and the house abounds in mirrors, *trompe l'oeil*, domed ceilings, narrow passages, sculptures in every nook, niche and cranny. There is a crypt, a catacomb, even a mummy of Pharaoh Seti I, and books galore. The GEFFRYE MUSEUM, a row of eighteenth-century almhouses in Shoreditch, contains furniture and furnishings, and some vivid reconstructions of period rooms.

HISTORY AND SCIENCE

London's main historical museum is the MUSEUM OF LONDON, opened in its present premises in 1975 as part of the Barbican development. This provides a comprehensive and intriguing account of the development of the capital from Roman times, using modern museum techniques of lighting and tableaux to make its scholarship accessible. It has an active archaeological department which takes part in digs on central sites as they are cleared for redevelopment. Less scholarly – but immensely popular with visitors – is MADAME TUSSAUD'S in Marylebone Road, a miniature National Portrait Gallery in wax. Its founder came to London from post-revolutionary France in 1802 and established a travelling exhibition of thirty-five wax figures. It now contains hundreds of realistic models of people from history as well as current celebrities. Its Chamber of Horrors graphically depicts some of the most ghoulish murders on record – a theme treated in greater detail in the LONDON DUNGEON, near London Bridge Station, where customers willingly pay to be terrified.

Military history is spread over several museums. The TOWER OF LONDON (see *The Thames*) contains not just the

OPPOSITE Just looking. The social side of the art world at a Mayfair gallery's exhibition opening.

The Auction Houses

The great British auction houses – alphabetically, Bonham's, Christie's, Phillips and Sotheby's – are household names these days, with seven-figure sale totals almost as common as fake Salvador Dalis. The houses themselves are tolerably ancient – Sotheby's started in 1744, Christie's in 1766 – but their pre-eminence is recent, certainly post-Second World War, and their international fame really stems from the reign at Sotheby's in the 1960s and 1970s of Peter Wilson.

Throughout the nineteenth century the auction houses were mainly trade outlets, though they had not

Pugin and Rowlandson's portrayal of Christie's auction room in 1808, then in Pall Mall, a few yards from its present headquarters in King Street.

begun that way. Auctions are reputed to have begun with *sub hasta* (under the spear) sales on the field of battle, when Roman legionaries would auction off the spoils of war. Their first – and most colourful – phase of social acceptability occurred in the late eighteenth century when the original James Christie established his rooms in Pall Mall. Christie was an elegant man, a close friend of the likes of Garrick, Reynolds and James Boswell. For a time the 'upper ten thousand', as high society in London was called in Victorian times, hob-nobbed in Christie's rooms. At private views the chief flunkey was

brought in from the Opera House at Covent Garden. These formal affairs (Lord Chesterfield arrived in 'full livery', meaning he was accompanied by footmen) were social occasions of the grandest kind but there were no printed invitations: those not recognized by the Covent Garden flunkey, who knew everyone who was anyone, were not admitted.

The pre-eminence of London in the art world stems from the French Revolution and the Napoleonic wars. Until that time, mainland Europeans – especially the Italians, Germans and French – believed that the British were constitutionally incapable of appreciating Old Masters. Certainly, the British taste had previously been for British art – and contemporary British art at that. But, when the *anciens régimes* of Europe found themselves under threat, they realized that their most portable wealth was their art. Between 1795 and 1825 innumerable collections found their way to London. Christie benefited, as did the older London dealers, Agnew and Colnaghi (see *The art business*).

As a result the great British country houses amassed unrivalled collections of art. Then, at the end of the nineteenth century, cheaper corn in the American midwest caused the break-up of many great estates – a process which continues to this day. The beneficiaries of this next wave of movement in the trade were again Christies's, Agnew, Colnaghi and, by now, Knoedler; Sotheby's in this period was mainly an auctioneer of books, and it was not until after the Second World war that the firm broadened its range.

Now, the big sale rooms are huge businesses, with annual turnovers of hundreds of millions of pounds. They have offices in Amsterdam, Geneva, Hong Kong, Tokyo – and in New York, which has already surpassed London in the money spent on Impressionist and contemporary art and jewellery. Geneva also rivals London in jewellery and Hong Kong is now the centre for oriental art. London, however, still offers the greatest diversity of sales, objects and people. Peter Wilson expanded the role of the auction houses flamboyantly. Now their social pre-eminence is underlined by the fact that it is customary for them to appoint their chairmen from the ranks of the peerage.

The rivalry between the two major firms reached its peak in 1987–8 over two great Van Goghs. Christie's had the first, *Sunflowers*, in London. It made £22¾ million. Sotheby's had to beat that – and did. *Irises* sold in New York for £31 million. Many people cannot distinguish one house from another but the trade can, and the old aphorism is still held to be true: Christie's are gentlemen trying to be autioneers; Sotheby's are auctioneers trying to be gentlemen.

crown jewels but also a fine collection of medieval and Tudor armaments. The IMPERIAL WAR MUSEUM occupies the truncated Bethlem Royal Hospital, the former lunatic asylum in St George's Fields, Lambeth. Huge mortar guns stand to attention at the entrance to an exhibition of military equipment – the early fighter planes are especially popular – as well as some moving examples of wartime art and literature, including Henry Moore's notable drawings of people sleeping in the underground during the Blitz.

The NATIONAL MARITIME MUSEUM has the added attraction of a fine building, occupying Inigo Jones's Queen's House in Greenwich and the wings added in the early nineteenth century (see *Great houses and palaces*). Models and paintings of ships abound, along with reconstructions of Cook's and Drake's voyages of

The SCIENCE MUSEUM's collection was originally housed in the V & A but moved into its own building, across Exhibition Road, in 1913. The increased pace of scientific discovery has forced it to expand constantly to keep up – space exploration now occupies a substantial area – and in 1976 the Wellcome Museum of the History of Medicine moved here. Many visitors still derive most enjoyment from the examples of Victorian technology – the massive engines, aeroplanes, motor cars, trains and buses. In the basement a selection of games for children, illustrating basic principles of physics and electricity, is always busy.

Backing on to the Science Museum, with its entrance in Cromwell Road, the NATURAL HISTORY MUSEUM was opened in 1881 to house collections hived off from the British Museum, including the unfailingly popular

The South Kensington Museum was opened in 1857 in the aftermath of the Great Exhibition six years earlier, as a showcase for the emerging discipline of industrial design. It was housed in temporary buildings known derisively as the 'Brompton Boilers', on land now occupied by the Victoria & Albert Museum.

exploration, and re-creations of British naval engagements from the defeat of the Armada to the Battle of the River Plate. The cruiser HMS *Belfast* has been converted into a small museum of the Royal Navy, moored on the south bank of the Thames between Tower and London Bridges. The NATIONAL ARMY MUSEUM, opened next to Chelsea's Royal Hospital in 1971, has the advantage of purpose-built premises to recall Britain's military past and present. There are more weapons at the Royal Artillery Museum at Woolwich, while the Royal Air Force has its own museum at Hendon Aerodrome.

The most important scientific museums are grouped with the V & A in the part of South Kensington earmarked for the purpose after the 1851 Exhibition.

dinosaurs. The terracotta building, with its overawing neo-Gothic entrance hall, is by Alfred Waterhouse. The newest and smallest of South Kensington's four shop windows of scholarship is the GEOLOGICAL MUSEUM, just south of the Science Museum, built in 1935. This has fewer attractions for non-specialists, although some of its crystal and mineral formations are spectacular.

Numerous small museums in London cater for more specialized interests. There are few fields of knowledge that do not have some kind of permanent display to lure enthusiasts to the capital: museums of transport, postal history, garden history, musical instruments, broadcasting, films, photography, astronomy, sport – the variety is as rich as the city itself.

INNS AND PUBS

The capital was once much more endowed with pubs than it is today, and there are fewer now than there were a generation ago. Former pubs – now banks, shops, offices, or restaurants – may be spotted by the observant.

The old larger inns were associated with transport by coach and horse: they often had balustraded galleries around yards with stables and various rooms, but they became redundant when the railways arrived, living on only in the pages of Dickens and on Christmas cards. An example of this large inn type is the George at Southwark, heavily restored but recognizable today as a survivor of a once common pattern of coaching inn.

Pubs before 1830 were not often distinguished architecturally and many taverns looked rather like ordinary dwellings, identified by the hanging signs or other devices. Most were cosy dark places, like the Cock in Fleet Street with its rows of snugs, settles and large fireplace. Perhaps the nearest example of an old tavern is the Cheshire Cheese in Wine Office Court, Fleet Street, although the bar is a later addition. The series of small rooms, fireplaces and wooden seats was usual. Great changes occurred after 1830 when duty on beer was abolished in an attempt to wean the lower orders off gin. Freed from the control of the licensing justices, a great many beer-shops opened. Beer was perceived as wholesome, while gin was regarded as deadly and responsible for a crime wave. The problem was that duty on spirits had been greatly reduced to encourage free trade, with the result that drunkenness increased and crime with it.

As with nearly every attempt at reformist legislation, a new, unforeseen phenomenon occurred. Establishments licensed to sell alcoholic drinks of all sorts – not just beer – were embellished to make them smarter and more enticing than beer-shops. The fronts acquired pilasters, columns, entablatures, large plate-glass windows, costly gas fittings and elaborate lettering, while interiors sported decorated spirit-barrels, bar-counters, mirrors and much ornament. Barmaids added to the glittering attractions, and gaslight illuminated rich, vulgar and showy rooms for the sale of drink.

These gaudy gold-encrusted temples became known as gin-palaces and were the result of legislation to *reduce* the consumption of gin rather than the cause of the dram-drinking epidemic. Gaslight became widely and cheaply available in the 1830s and it was possible to manufacture plate glass in large sheets at economic rates: big windows and enormous plate-glass mirrors through which gaslit interiors would be seen or reflected became a feature of public houses for the next few generations.

From the 1830s dates the bar for the dispensing of drink to all parts of the establishment across counters. Formerly drinks had been served to customers at tables.

LEFT The Swan with Two Necks in Lad Lane (now part of Gresham Street) was one of the City's most important coaching inns from the seventeenth to the nineteenth centuries. There were many such galleried inns around courtyards but the only partially surviving example is the George in Southwark.

OPPOSITE In the 1880s and 1890s the pubs tried to win a higher class of client by using elaborate interior decoration, including mirrors and highly polished wood. At the Salisbury in St Martin's Lane the style is in keeping with the theatre district.

Soon bars became features of all pubs, with spirit dispensers, beer-engines to draw liquids up from the cellars, and ornate gantries behind for the display of bottles and barrels. Later bar-counters were planned on a horseshoe pattern, as islands or, more often, peninsulas, reaching into the main floor areas, so that the next step was to subdivide the space into various rooms by means of wooden screens, enabling different social groups to meet in relative privacy. It is clear from drawings and cartoons of the 1830s that all sorts would frequent pubs, including women and children, and this was the case until the 1850s. Few 'respectable' women used London pubs by then, but the subdivision of larger areas by screens to create private and saloon bars signalled an attempt to win back a clientèle that had deserted the tavern for other establishments.

A higher standard of finish, comfort and privacy, and interiors with etched glass, mirrors, French-polished surfaces, lavish fireplaces and good-quality furniture made pubs attractive to professional men and to women during the 1880s and 1890s. The most spectacular examples were on the corners of streets: The Salisbury, St Martin's Lane, is a good specimen. The Red Lion, Duke of York Street, St James's, although small, seems bigger by virtue of its mirrors and etched glass, while the Princess Louise, High Holborn, demonstrates how glazed tiles and hard surfaces (both easily cleaned) could enliven pubs. A complex Arts and Crafts interior survives in the sumptuous Black Friar, Queen Victoria Street, designed by H. Fuller Clark and Henry Poole in 1905. Such design cannot be provided cheaply, and by the 1890s pubs were changing hands at inflated prices. The crash duly came, many publicans were bankrupted and the brewers acquired a majority of pubs.

Historically, London pubs were open from the early hours to after midnight, but morning closing on Sundays was introduced in 1839. The long weekday hours, however, ensured that pubs were patronized fully as social centres. Pressure to curtail licensing hours increased in our own century, usually from the Liberal camp (the Conservatives were traditionally the 'drinkers' party'). Drastically reduced hours were brought in during the First World War, supposedly to keep the factories busy in the afternoons, but probably more to do with a perceived need to stiffen national moral fibre. Restrictions continued until 1988 when legislation permitted longer hours, but such liberalization is unlikely to bring customers back on a Victorian scale. Many pubs have closed or have been changed into 'theme' pubs, wine bars and American-style cocktail bars. Repeated campaigns against drinking and driving have also played their part, as has the rival attraction of television – even when TV sets were installed in the bars.

Many pubs suffered modernization during the 1950s and 1960s. The abolition of distinctions between public and lounge or saloon bars stemmed from the egalitarianism of the same period. A growing patronage of pubs by women from the early 1960s led brewers to discard a tough, masculine character, put down carpets and establish a more suburban image for their pubs.

The boring similarity of so many pubs and beers produced a reaction: from the 1970s real ale made a comeback and attempts were made to re-create Victorian pubs, the real thing having been wrecked. This revival was counter-balanced by an invasion of juke-boxes, one-armed bandits and electronic games in an attempt to attract young people, while taste in beer, under American and Australian influence, had swung to lager.

Until the 1830s, pubs had no bars, but customers were served at their tables by waiters. The Cheshire Cheese of Fleet Street, depicted here, is one of the few London pubs to have kept its old arrangement of small rooms and wooden seats, although today's customers have to serve themselves from the bar.

FAIRS

Bartholomew Fair was originally a cloth fair, but by the eighteenth century, when this drawing was made, it had become a riot of sideshows and attractions. It was suppressed in 1855 on public order grounds.

The modern fair, with its rides, hamburger vans and prize stalls, has deep historical roots. Fairs were established in England before the Conquest, commonly at places where pilgrims congregated. They fulfilled a practical function. Weekly markets met most ordinary needs of the community; town fairs were annual markets for larger scale trading, attracting travelling merchants who set up shop for three or four days in a tented village. Stall tolls brought in revenue to the city or religious house exercising control through 'Courts of Pie Powder' – the name said to derive from the French *pieds poudreux*, meaning dusty feet.

Some of London's extinct fairs had thirteenth-century or earlier charters. Charlton Hornfair, an ancient fair abolished in 1873, maintained almost to the end a strong legendary tradition in its St Luke's Day procession, in which people wore horned head dresses; it also had its own song.

Amongst the oldest established fairs still taking place in Greater London are those at Pinner (1336), Mitcham (1732 or earlier) and Barnet, but few fairs now occupy early sites. These tend to be commemorated in names like Mayfair (which had a fair from the late seventeenth to early nineteenth century) and Fairfield, as at Charlton and Croydon.

The ancient fairs were no sooner established than they began to acquire hangers-on. Tumblers, jugglers, posturers, merry-andrews, freaks, mountebanks, swordfighters, bear leaders and morris dancers thronged the old metropolitan fairs, like Bartholomew, Magdalen, Southwark and the May Fair. Most of the fairs we see today were established much later and they, in their turn, are now completely dominated by the big 'rides' which began to proliferate in the nineteenth century. They are, nonetheless, the direct descendants of these earlier open-air entertainments.

BARTHOLOMEW FAIR, in the City itself (the site is now covered by Smithfield meat market), illustrates this progress. It was the prince of all London fairs. Its charter was granted to the Priory of St Bartholomew in 1133 and it continued for more than seven hundred years. Although it was England's principal cloth fair (the street

LEFT A copy of a Hogarth engraving of Southwark Fair made in 1733. The scenes of mayhem are possibly exaggerated but suggest the anarchy and licentiousness of the occasion.

OPPOSITE Every February thousands of Chinese – and many more onlookers – parade through Soho in a colourful procession to mark the Chinese New Year.

on the north side of the church is still so called), Bartholomew Fair was very soon accompanied by an uncontrolled assemblage of entertainers. The founder, Rahere, had been court jester and an accomplished juggler before taking holy orders, and is said to have performed at the fair himself.

By the seventeenth century, when the City Corporation took control, the three days of Bartholomew Fair had become one of the great popular events in the London calendar and Ben Jonson set his most boisterous play there. As well as the usual fire-eaters, rope dancers and comedians, the fair was famous for its sideshows, menageries and theatre booths, culminating in Richardson's Great Booth which, from 1796, toured the major fairs with astonishing feats of dramatic abridgement, permitting Shakespeare's *Richard III* to be performed twenty times in seven hours.

The disorder created by having a huge fair and cattle market in the very heart of London was regularly attacked in the press (with *Punch* in the forefront) in the 1840s and 1850s. Finally, the City Corporation, which had already in 1763 suppressed another great medieval fair (Southwark, founded in 1402), brought Bartholomew Fair to an end in 1855.

What distinguishes the fair (and its cousin, the travelling circus) from other forms of outdoor entertainment is that it appears for only brief periods in the year. A train of wagons arrives, the ground is marked out, the showmen set up their apparatus and a field or common is transformed into a colourful and noisy fairground. A

few days later, every trace, apart from a pattern of wear in the turf, has gone. The showmen have moved on to their next 'mop', feast or fair.

Historically, FROST FAIRS were the most impermanent type of all, since they could only take place on rare occasions, when the slow-flowing Thames above the narrow arches of old London Bridge froze over. They were, however, very big and went on for not just the few days of the charter fairs but as long as the strength of the ice would permit. Memorable frosts occurred in the winters of 1564–5, 1608 (when 'booths and standings' were first recorded), 1683–4, 1715–16, 1739–40, 1788–9 and 1813–14. With the demolition of the old bridge in 1831 and the embanking of the river forty years later, the conditions for frost fairs ceased to occur.

Although fairground stalls and rides must move from place to place, their proprietors, who are mostly born to the trade and live with their families in handsomely furnished wagons, are rarely Romany gypsies or 'travellers' and they are regarded differently (not always to their advantage) in the eyes of the law. Most follow their individual but almost unvarying circuits, coming together in different groupings at different places. Each family spends several months of each year 'wintering' on a semi-permanent site, sometimes singly but more often in groups. The winter site is regarded as a home base, where essential maintenance can be carried out. The shortage of such sites acceptable to planning authorities and local residents is a major problem today for the modern show family, especially in and around London.

Carnivals

London's best-known carnival takes place each August Bank Holiday weekend (the bank holiday is the last Monday in the month) in the Notting Hill area of Kensington. Streets are closed to traffic, visitors from all over the capital mingle with local residents and there is a grand procession of floats. The NOTTING HILL CARNIVAL has grown enormously since it began in 1966. Based on Trinidadian pre-Lenten festivals, it was the idea of West Indians who had come to Britain immediately after the Second World War. From the start it included the calypso and jazz of West Indian steel bandsmen. Occasionally it has been marred by violence and crime and has been the subject of complaints by residents, but it is usually well-run and peaceful.

For the most part, Londoners are too phlegmatic for carnivals to play an important role in the life of the capital. Yet over the years there have been many informal celebrations on its streets marking an annual occasion, or as a spontaneous reaction to some important event. On the night of 18 May 1900, when news arrived of the relief of Mafeking, during the Boer War in South Africa, there were announcements in theatres, music halls and restaurants. Crowds of all classes poured into Piccadilly Circus to sing, dance and celebrate victory. The Oxford and Cambridge Boat Race was also once marked by annual revelry in the Circus, though it now passes with little general festivity. New Year's Eve is customarily celebrated noisily in Trafalgar Square, but it was once marked on the steps of St Paul's Cathedral. On 31 December 1882, according to the diaries of the then verger, Robert Green, people were attracted by the chiming of the new bell, Great Paul, and this, he claimed,

'was the origin of the multitude of Scotsmen and others who now assemble on that occasion'. By the end of the century, however, the occasion had lost its Scottish character and the steps had been railed off from the public.

Plenty of other occasions give rise to celebrations: election nights, the Football Association Cup Final and royal weddings. In 1977 there were street parties all over London to mark the Queen's Silver Jubilee. The Berkeley Square Ball spills out on to the streets of Mayfair each July and the Chelsea Arts Ball had a reputation as a wild carnival until it was held for the last time in 1959.

The conclusions of the two World Wars have prompted some of London's greatest street celebrations. VE (Victory in Europe) Day in 1945 was marked by huge gatherings and on Armistice Day 1918 *The Illustrated London News* reported that 'London broke into a spontaneous outburst of joy ... [and] soon became the scene of an improvised carnival'.

The Notting Hill Carnival, held every August since 1966, is the most important annual festivity for London's black population, especially those from the Caribbean.

Queen Victoria's Diamond Jubilee procession passes Waterloo Place and the Athenaeum Club, 1897. Royal anniversaries provide some of the best excuses for mass celebrations in the capital – more recently Queen Elizabeth's Silver Jubilee in 1977.

Showmen throughout history have been reluctantly tolerated by authority and shunned as pariahs by a section of society which regarded them as lawless, dangerous and encouraging rowdiness and immorality. Many fairs (including May Fair) were closed down in the eighteenth and nineteenth centuries for that reason and attempts to squeeze fairground showmen off the road and out of existence have been numerous. The Metropolitan Fairs Act of 1868, for example, made it unlawful to hold a fair in London on a site where no fair had been held during the previous seven years. Three years later, the Fairs Act declared that 'fairs are unnecessary, are the cause of grievous immorality and are very injurious to the inhabitants of the towns where they are held'. Shortly afterwards Charlton Hornfair, Blackheath and Clapham Common Fairs were terminated. But the universal popularity of the 'fun of the fair' continues to ensure their survival against all the odds.

Hampstead Heath and Blackheath illustrate the resilience of the fair in modern times. Both were popular Cockney Bank Holiday resorts in the nineteenth century, with outdoor sports and donkey rides (a paved ride can still be seen outside the main Blackheath gates of Greenwich Park). Both came to the fore *after* the passing of the Fairs Act. An earlier Blackheath Fair, which had taken over the role of the suppressed Greenwich Fair in 1857, was itself abolished under the Act's powers, but crept back into existence in the 'porridge pots' (gravel diggings) on the Heath. Fairs well beyond the suburbs in places like Epping Forest attracted hordes of tripping Londoners in the last century and the annual 'Going to the Derby' exodus to Epsom was always as much for the fun of the fair as it was for the horse races.

Within the wall of living wagons and generators which surround a modern fairground, the amusements mainly take the form of stalls, shies, sideshows and rides. Lines of stalls house shooting galleries, darts boards, and coin and ball-rolling games. Free-standing round stalls offer hoop-la and mechanical games of chance. All the stalls are decorated with huge cuddly animals and other showy prizes (rarely disturbed) and small gifts (frequently won). Some stalls for children guarantee a modest prize every time. The true Aunt Sally is now rare, but coconut shies are always found, as are varied tests of skill and strength. Amongst the sideshows, portable theatres are now extinct and wrestling and boxing booths are rarely seen in London; but giant rats, creatures from outer space and gorgeously decorated Haunted Houses and Houses of Fun are common. On the fringes the tents and caravans of fortune tellers (the only fairground people proclaiming themselves as gypsies) belong to an ancient tradition.

Some of the rides also have a long pedigree. Swing-

The Sunday bird fair in Whitechapel was popular with Londoners at the turn of the century.

boats and simple forms of big wheel and slide can be seen in early Victorian pictures of the fair. Today's helter-skelters and chairoplanes have changed very little over the last sixty years. Hand-operated children's round-abouts of the primitive 'dobbie' type, are not completely unknown today, but the great platform roundabouts with fantastically carved 'gallopers' and ostriches and gleaming twisty metalwork – some of them now treasured antiques – are the centre and symbol of every fair. Their magnificent Gavioli and Marenghi organs, originally blown by showmen's huge steam engines, still give the fair its characteristic music – powerful enough to be heard alongside the blasting pop music on the dodgems' public address system.

Every year, new hair-raising super-speed rides are added to the Galloping Steeds, Noah's Arks, Whips and Waltzers. Whether new or old, the best stalls, sideshows and rides share an architectural and decorative tradition of extraordinary energy, which seems to have ingredients of oriental imagery and Central European rococo decoration combined with modern pulp comic graphics. The tradition is carried on today by such artists as Fred Fowle, whose work was exhibited at Whitechapel Art Gallery in 1977.

The most enduring characteristic of the modern fair, however carefully controlled, contained, policed and subjected to safety checks, is that it retains that sense of misrule and enjoyable danger which has always been its main attraction.

CEREMONIES

An American television commentator, describing to his home audience the wedding procession of the Duke and Duchess of York, said: 'The British pull off ceremonial the way the army of Israel pulls off commando raids.' If he was talking about the faultless execution of the show-business side of constitutional monarchy, he had a point. The British, after all, have had plenty of time to practise.

One day every autumn, when the leaves of the London planes are falling to a crunchy carpet on the pavement, the city's normally chaotic traffic suffers an additional paralysing thrombosis for a couple of hours while the Sovereign conducts the most important single function of the ceremonial year: the STATE OPENING OF PARLIAMENT.

The procession is grand and never varies; a thick army manual lays down its directions in the most minute detail. Leading the parade is a coach bearing, unaccompanied by its wearer, the Imperial State Crown, made for Queen Victoria's coronation in 1838. Apart from the coronation, opening Parliament is the only time the monarch wears a crown; not surprising, as the world's most valuable hat weighs three tiring pounds.

The head of state rides in the Australian State Coach, given to the Queen in 1988 to mark that country's bicentennial. It is accompanied by 109 troopers and seven officers of the Household Cavalry; their ceremonial uniform includes a polished steel breastplate, the only item of armour surviving in the British army. (When not on parade they are real soldiers; two troops were in action with light armoured vehicles in the 1982 Falklands campaign.)

Bringing up the rear are two farriers, each carrying an axe with a sharp pointed handle. The point is to kill any lame horse and the axe is to chop off its hooves as evidence that they have not sold the beast to some passing horse trader. The squeamish can rest assured that the axes are never used; they are just part of the hocus-pocus of military tradition.

The procession moves from the gates of Buckingham Palace down the wide boulevard of The Mall and cuts off the Trafalgar Square corner by crossing the parade ground of Horse Guards and emerging into Whitehall through Horse Guards Arch. This is because the arch is a remnant of Whitehall Palace, once the home of the Sovereign. Another old bit of hocus-pocus – but the arch, although for long a public walkway, is still guarded daily by two mounted sentries.

When the procession arrives at the Sovereign's Entrance to the Palace of Westminster, under the great square Victoria Tower at the opposite end from Big Ben, the charade of constitutional monarchy really takes wing. The Sovereign dons the crown, mounts the throne in the House of Lords (its members there by privileged birthright or appointment and not by elec-

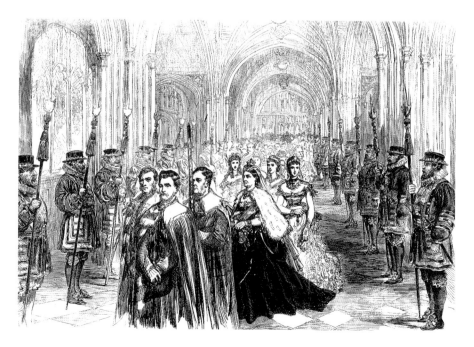

LEFT Queen Victoria in procession to the peers' chamber in the Palace of Westminster to open Parliament in 1876. Towards the end of her reign she abandoned the ceremony but her son Edward VII revived it.

OPPOSITE The Lord Mayor's Show, more strictly a parade, is one of the capital's most ancient ceremonies. It dates from the fourteenth century and still draws crowds of onlookers to the City on the second Saturday in November.

tion) and summons the elected rabble of the lower House of Commons, the real politicians, to come and hear her.

The speech is written by the Government and the monarch might not necessarily agree with it (see *The centre of Government*). The Queen once even had to read a few lines proposing the abolition of the hereditary Upper House, of which she is the titular head.

ROYALTY ON SHOW

The State Opening is a ceremony dating from 1681, created in the aftermath of the Civil War. It was abandoned by Queen Victoria, revived by her son Edward VII and suspended during the Second World War. Its underlying purpose is to summon Parliament to meet its Sovereign and to remind each that one is not supposed to function without the other. It is the major formal ceremony of the royal year and one of the very few at which the role of the constitutional monarch is played out in public. There is no public admission to the State Opening itself, although it is today shown live and in full on television. Almost all the rest of the Sovereign's public appearances are, strictly speaking, social events. Reigning is a business conducted largely behind closed doors.

Among the exceptions are STATE VISITS, usually two or three a year, when foreign heads of state are frequently accorded a carriage drive through London. Increasingly, the reception of such dignitaries has been taking place at Windsor Castle, to avoid bringing the capital's traffic to a dead stop. Foreign potentates have to be in the megastar class to attract more than a passing glance from Londoners made blasé by their own first-division monarchy. Pope John Paul II drew huge crowds, but not even President Reagan could attract more than a handful as he cruised by in his smoked-glass Cadillac during a brief stopover in 1988.

The monarch is head of the armed forces and every year they celebrate his or her birthday at a splendid drill and marching display on Horse Guards Parade, TROOPING THE COLOUR. The ceremony originates from the practice of military commanders parading the regimental flag before their men so that they would recognize it as a rallying point in the heat of battle. Turning it into a public show in honour of the Sovereign dates only from Queen Victoria's time. She liked that sort of thing.

Yet Victoria very nearly killed off royal ceremonial altogether. After the death of her beloved Prince Albert in 1861, she withdrew from public life and from London to such an extent that there was a noticeable stirring of republicanism in Britain, fed by her eldest son's rakish lifestyle among the fleshpots of the capital. She was

persuaded back into the public eye for celebrations to mark her own Golden Jubilee in 1887 and such was the popularity of the processions, parades and street parties that royal ceremonial has never really looked back since. It is largely tolerated because it is not a demonstration of power on the streets, but rather a reminder that the crown represents the continuity of the nation far beyond the life of governments.

The coronation of George VI in Westminster Abbey in May 1937. He had become King after the controversial abdication of his brother, Edward VIII, who was never formally crowned. The pomp and grandeur of the ceremony helped restore respect for the monarchy after the undignified dispute that led to the abdication, underlining a principal function of traditional ceremonies.

The appeal of the royal family this century has been very much as a *family* and as such its family occasions have become public spectacles. ROYAL WEDDINGS used to be private affairs, but not any more; hundreds of thousands watch them on the street, and 500 million more around the world view them on television.

Walter Bagehot, the nineteenth-century commentator on the English constitution, appreciated their appeal. 'A princely marriage', he wrote, 'is the brilliant edition of a universal fact and as such it rivets mankind.' A desire for spectacle, ceremony and celebration in the aftermath of the First World War – not to mention an exceptionally large guest list – created the first royal wedding-as-spectacle in 1919, when Victoria's granddaughter Princess Patricia of Connaught wed in Westminster Abbey and rode through the streets with her bridegroom Alexander Ramsay.

The very great royal occasions of state happen only once or twice in a lifetime. The CORONATION of every English crowned head since William the Conqueror in 1066 has taken place in Westminster Abbey, attended by immense spectacle. The solemnity of a STATE FUNERAL, in which the body of the deceased monarch lies in state in

a gilded coach accompanied by bands and floats. He no longer presents himself to the Sovereign, but to senior judges at the Royal Courts of Justice in the Strand.

The Lord Mayor, usually someone who works in the City but may live in the outer suburbs, carries heavy civic and social responsibility. For visiting heads of state to dine with him at the Guildhall is second only to an invitation to dine at Buckingham Palace. In ceremonial

LEFT The funeral procession in 1827 of Frederick, Duke of York, the second son of George III. The artist, Joseph Nash, might have exaggerated the size of the crowd, but it indicates the level of public appetite for state ceremonial, even on solemn occasions.

BELOW Design for the float of the Fishmonger's Company for the Lord Mayor's Show in 1616.

Westminster Hall and is then borne for burial at Windsor, is equally awesome.

CITY FUNCTIONS

The royal family does not have a monopoly on London's ceremonial. True royal ceremony is infrequent and often not half as old as it looks. In many ways much more genuinely historic are the public appearances of the Lord Mayor of London. The City has a long and continuous history; its first mayor, Henry Fitzalwin, was elected in 1192 and it has never been without one since. A condition of its charter, granted in 1215, was that each newly elected mayor should present himself to his Sovereign to swear loyalty and therein lies the origin of the LORD MAYOR'S SHOW.

From the earliest times the Lord Mayor travelled with a large and colourful retinue, partly to show himself to the citizens of London, but equally to demonstrate to the king the power and wealth of the principal city in the land. For a time he travelled part of the way from his official residence at Mansion House to Westminster by barge on the Thames, but today the annual procession is entirely through City streets. The Lord Mayor travels in

terms, his standing can rival that of the monarch. When the Sovereign visits the Square Mile, it is tradition that the royal procession halts at its boundary to ask the Lord Mayor's permission to enter.

Much of the mayoral year is attended by ceremonial. On the day of the Lord Mayor's election in late

September he (or she – women are eligible for election) and all the City dignitaries attend a church service in St Lawrence Jewry, a tradition begun by Lord Mayor Richard Whittington in 1406. Thereafter he attends the election itself in Guildhall, where the council members are presented with nosegays, a reminder that medieval London was a foul and stinking place. The present-day election is not altogether democratic: the post goes, for a year, to the most senior alderman who has not yet had his turn at England's grandest municipal office.

MILITARY DISPLAY

Every morning the military conduct the CHANGING OF THE GUARD at Buckingham Palace and have done so since Queen Victoria chose the palace as her official residence in 1837. The Guard is also changed daily at the other royal palaces of St James's, Horse Guards and the Tower of London, and at Windsor Castle, but in all cases with less ritual.

GUN SALUTES are fired in Hyde Park and at the Tower of London on major royal anniversaries or for a visiting head of state. A better spectacle is BEATING RETREAT, conducted on several evenings in early summer at Horse Guards Parade, when the élite troops of the Household Division show off their bands and their marching skills. The ancient practice has nothing to do with retreat from battle, but is a survival of the old custom of signalling the retreat of day and the onset of night.

Old ceremonies die hard and sometimes they even retain a token purpose. In 1605 Guy Fawkes and his fellow conspirators attempted to assassinate King James I by placing barrels of gunpowder in the cellars of Westminster. Today, before the opening of each new annual session of Parliament, the cellars are still searched by members of the Yeomen of the Guard, the oldest royal bodyguard in the world, carrying lanterns. The pattern has not changed, except for one thing: the cellars are now double-searched by anti-terrorist squad detectives with sniffer dogs.

And still, every night, as they have done for seven hundred years, the Yeomen of the Guard go through the same ritual of locking the main gates of the Tower of London in the CEREMONY OF THE KEYS, assuring one another that 'all's well'. Fortunately these retired regular soldiers have the support of sophisticated electronic security systems – but there is no colour, no spectacle, no sense of history, no *fun*, in a burglar alarm.

OPPOSITE One of the lesser-known ceremonies: every Easter and Whit Sunday, and the Sunday before Christmas, the yeoman warders of the Tower of London, in their historic uniforms, parade in the Tower courtyard before and after the church service.

The first royal wedding performed as a public spectacle was that of Princess Patricia, a grand-daughter of Queen Victoria, to Commander (later Admiral) Alexander Ramsay in February 1919.

A LONDON CALENDAR

January

Opening of the Old Bailey: (early January) Lord Mayor of London and his retinue in procession from Mansion House to the opening session of England's premier criminal court.

International Boat Show: (early January) All the latest 'state of the art' yachts, pleasure craft and sailing equipment on display in the largest show of its kind in Europe. Everything – and more – for the boating enthusiast.

Charles I Commemoration: (last Sunday) Service and wreath-laying by costumed royalists at the site of their hero's 1649 execution in Whitehall.

February

Chinese New Year: (Sunday nearest new lunar calendar) All-day firecrackers, dragons, riotous noise and colour in Soho's Chinatown, centred on Gerrard Street.

Clowns' Service: (first Sunday) Annual homage to original clown Joseph Grimaldi (died 1837) at Holy Trinity Church, Dalston, E8, with congregation in costume and a free show afterwards.

Pancake Day: (Shrove Tuesday) Last frivolity before Lent, with pancake races in Lincoln's Inn Fields and Covent Garden, open to all.

March

Spring Equinox: (on or near 21st) White-robed Druids gather at noon on Tower Hill for pre-Christian ritual of sowing symbolic seeds.

Oxford and Cambridge Boat Race: (Saturday late March, occasionally April) Since 1845 eight grunting hunks and a tiny coxswain from each of England's two premier universities have done yearly battle over four miles of the Thames from Putney to Mortlake.

April

London Marathon: (Sunday late April, occasionally May) A cast of thousands running, stumbling, hopping, crawling from Greenwich to Westminster Bridge. Always heavily oversubscribed. The fit take under three hours, but no disgrace befalls those who take all day.

May

Football Association Cup Final: (Saturday early May) Showpiece and summit of the English soccer season, at Wembley. A Royal always on hand to present the cup. Packed, well-behaved, but wild rejoicing among victors' supporters permeates to late-night central London.

Chelsea Flower Show: (four days late May) Biggest and best of its kind in the world, held since 1913 in the grounds of Wren's Royal Hospital. Up to four hundred exhibitors, some building entire gardens.

Beating Retreat: (late May, sometimes early June) Immaculate precision military square-bashing, to music and occasionally under floodlights, on three successive evenings on Horse Guards Parade.

Royal Academy Summer Exhibition: (until August) Burlington House, Piccadilly, shows a copious collection of new paintings, submitted in thousands by the famous and obscure and selected on the whim of a distinguished panel.

June

The Derby: (first Wednesday) The monarch does not gamble. Tens of thousands of her subjects do, when they join the Royal family on Epsom Downs to witness the premier event of the flat racing season, run here since 1780. Funfair on the Downs; champagne in the stand.

Trooping the Colour: (second Saturday) On the official Royal birthday the monarch goes to Horse Guards to review troops of the Household Division in a spectacular marching and drill display, and afterwards appears on the Buckingham Palace balcony to watch a fly-past.

Royal Ascot: (third week, Tuesday–Friday) The Royal family, in residence at Windsor Castle, arrives at nearby Ascot races daily in open carriages. A social meet at which hats and *haute couture* are of equal account with horses.

Wimbledon: (late June) Two weeks of the world's finest grass-court tennis, when tickets are more prized than rubies and the price of strawberries annually sets new records.

Cricket at Lord's: (various dates) Usually the Second Test match, and in July the Benson and Hedges final. In good weather a capacity crowd whatever the present state of the English game. Middlesex county ground since 1814 with original turf from an earlier pitch of 1787.

July

Henley Royal Regatta: (first week July) The oarsman's Ascot. Major international rowing and social event founded 1839. Champagne on the riverside, races on the water.

Royal Tournament: (for 2½ weeks mid-July) Two and a half hour action-packed military variety show, from musical cavalry rides to field gun races, all under cover at Earls Court. Royal family members frequently take the salute.

August

London Riding Horse Parade: (first Sunday) Open-to-all dressage contest in Hyde Park, held annually at Rotten Row since 1938. A merit rosette is the thrill of many a young pony-rider's life.

Notting Hill Carnival: (Sunday–Monday, August Bank Holiday) London's large Caribbean community hangs loose in the streets of Notting Hill area. Floats, processions, outdoor discos, steel bands, costume dances, ethnic food stalls, until well into the night.

September

Last Night of the Proms: (late Saturday) High-spirited audience in party mood, traditionally echoed by conductor, at programme of well-loved and well-worn nationalistic English favourites as grand finale to summer concert season at Albert Hall. Tickets by stoic queuing weeks before.

Election of Lord Mayor: (late September) Annual tradition in present form since 1546, when newly elected figurehead of the City of London rides through his Square Mile in a state coach to the accompaniment of the City's bells.

Royal National Rose Society Show: Held at the Horticultural Hall, Westminster. After Chelsea, London's finest annual display of enviably perfect gardening.

October

Costermongers' Harvest Festival: (first Sunday) Cockney street traders arrayed in intricate patterns of pearl buttons celebrate traditional autumn thanksgiving service at St Martin-in-the-Fields, Trafalgar Square.

Punch and Judy Festival: (usually first Sunday, sometimes late September) Dozens of Mr Punches from throughout Europe beating daylights out of their wives and dogs in the piazza at Covent Garden.

Harvest of the Sea Thanksgiving: (second Sunday) Mountains of fresh fish (afterwards distributed to hostels for homeless) in the vestry of St Mary-at-Hill, Eastcheap, for annual fishmongers' thanksgiving attended by Lord Mayor and Aldermen of London in full insignia.

Trafalgar Day Parade: (Sunday nearest 21 October) March and wreath-laying at the Cenotaph, Whitehall, in honour of Nelson's 1805 victory and of all lost in action at sea.

State Opening of Parliament: (late October or early November) Highlight of the monarch's ceremonial year. State procession from Buckingham Palace to Westminster (with the monarch and the Imperial State Crown in separate carriages) where the Sovereign reads the speech written by the Government on planned legislation for coming year.

November

Veteran Car Run: (first Sunday) Three hundred spotless museum pieces, all pre-1906, commemorate abolition of man with red flag (who had to precede all motors until 1896) by spluttering from Hyde Park Corner to Brighton. Under three hours for the fifty-three miles frequently achieved.

Remembrance Sunday: (Sunday nearest 11th) Royal family and political leaders lay wreaths at the Cenotaph, Whitehall, shortly after 11 am, the hour the guns of the First World War fell silent.

Lord Mayor's Show: (second Saturday) Huge procession of carnival floats follows the new Lord Mayor in his gilded coach through the streets of the City from Mansion House to the Royal Courts of Justice, Strand, where he swears allegiance to the crown, represented by senior judges.

Christmas Lights: Celebrities switch on lavish, crowd-pulling, traffic-gumming illuminations in main shopping parades of Oxford Street and Regent Street in mid-November, when stores have already been Christmas trading for weeks.

December

Christmas Tree: From mid-December, carols every evening beneath the Trafalgar Square tree, presented since 1947 by the City of Oslo in gratitude for wartime help to Norway.

New Year's Eve: Informal and unabashed frolics in Trafalgar Square, but fountains now boarded up to prevent former popular custom of fully-clothed bathing. Gatherings also in Parliament Square to hear Big Ben's full midnight chime.

The Makers of London

SIR PATRICK ABERCROMBIE (1879–1957) shaped post-war London with two plans for restructuring the region. An architect–planner and academic with sympathy for garden-city ideals, Abercrombie was appointed in 1941 to prepare a report on inner London. The County of London Plan was followed by his Greater London Plan. These recommended dispersing population and industry so as to achieve lower densities in the centre. They led to the belt of New Towns round London, the accelerated loss of industry from the centre, and the comprehensive replanning – in a way Abercrombie himself would largely have disliked – of parts of inner London.

ROBERT ADAM (1728–92) and his brother JAMES ADAM (1732–94) were the most active and fashionable architects of their day. Scottish-born, they captivated London with their

clever planning and delicate 'Etruscan' decoration. An early work was the screen in front of the Admiralty, Whitehall. Their main surviving West End houses are Chandos House, Chandos Street; 20 and 33 St James's Square; and Home House, Portman Square. The brothers were nearly ruined by their Adelphi speculation of 1768–72, consisting of two terraces raised above the river on top of vaults.

NICHOLAS BARBON (c. 1640–98) was a key figure in the development of speculative building in London. Son of a Puritan zealot, he was educated in Holland. He took advantage of conditions after the Great Fire to become London's first major developer, versed in every wile of law, finance and shoddy building. Essex Street, Strand, on the site of a Tudor mansion, was an early speculation. There followed Buckingham Street and Villiers Street nearby, and much building in Holborn, notably Red Lion Square. A few Barbon houses survive in Bedford Row and Great Ormond Street. He left immense debts and a legacy of dubious development practices.

SIR CHARLES BARRY (1795–1860) deserves gratitude as the architect of the world's most memorable and pleasurable public building, the Palace of Westminster (alias the Houses of Parliament). Gothic it may be, like one or two of Barry's Islington churches, but it was in the Italian palazzo manner that Sir Charles was most at home – the style of his Travellers' Club and Reform Club in Pall Mall, of Bridgewater House behind St James's Palace and his three houses in Kensington Palace Gardens. The Houses of Parliament owe their clarity of arrangement and their discipline to Barry, but the beauty of their detail to his collaborator Augustus Pugin.

GEORGE BASEVI (1794–1845) designed some of the capital's smartest developments in the architectural tradition set by Regent's Park. Belgrave Square, built from 1825 on land leased by Thomas Cubitt from the Grosvenors, is the best known. Basevi designed its all-stucco terraces with their cavernously proportioned houses, but not the mansions in the corners. Friendlier are his compositions in Brompton, centred upon Alexander Square, the prettily stuccoed Pelham Crescent and Egerton Crescent and the more explicitly Victorian Thurloe Square. He was killed by a fall at Ely Cathedral.

SIR JOSEPH BAZALGETTE (1819–91) masterminded the Victorian cleansing of London. Chief engineer successively to the Metropolitan Commission of Sewers and the Metropolitan Board of Works, Bazalgette brought forward comprehensive plans for London's main drainage in 1856. Parliament approved them in 1858, and Bazalgette proceeded with his grand plan for four great lines of 'intercepting sewers' out to pumping stations in the far East End. Its completion in 1875 marked a turning point in the health of the capital. Bazalgette also constructed embankments on both sides of the river and built the present bridges at Battersea and Putney.

ISAMBARD KINGDOM BRUNEL (1806–59) was the more celebrated son and successor of SIR MARC ISAMBARD BRUNEL (1769–1849), the French-born engineer. Father and son collaborated on the world's first under-river tunnel from Rotherhithe to Wapping. It was started in 1825, finished after herculean effort in 1843 and is now incorporated in the Metropolitan Line river crossing there. Brunel junior built the short-lived Hungerford Suspension Bridge (1841–5), but is best known for his railway and steamship work. The graceful iron roofs of Paddington station (1850–4), designed with Matthew Digby Wyatt, are his enduring monument in London.

DECIMUS BURTON (1800–81) was the tenth son of James Burton, the biggest London builder before Thomas Cubitt. Burton senior built tracts of Bloomsbury and St Pancras. The son acquired large architectural responsibilities through his father's friendship with John Nash, designing Cornwall and Clarence Terraces, the Colosseum, the original parts of the zoo and a handful of villas (all at Regent's Park), the Athenaeum Club in Waterloo Place, the screens at Hyde Park Corner and the great arch which looks down Constitution Hill. All these were built before Burton was thirty. In later life he departed from the Grecian fervour of these early works.

SIR WILLIAM CHAMBERS (1723–96) shares the honours with Robert Adam as London's foremost mid-Georgian architect, but his buildings, always suave and scholarly, have been depleted by demolition. Gower House, Whitehall, with its superb staircase (a

Chambers speciality), was destroyed a century ago; Melbourne House, Piccadilly, has been converted into part of the Albany; but Manresa House survives at outlying Roehampton amidst an ocean of public housing, as do several of Chambers' garden buildings at Kew, above all the soaring pagoda. His reputation rests on Somerset House, the first great complex of government offices.

SIR HENRY COLE (1808–82) was the founding father of institutional 'South Kensington'. An advocate of the unity of arts, sciences and manufactures, Cole was involved in the Great Exhibition of 1851. He pressed for its profits to be spent on establishing a Department of Science and Art at South Kensington, of which he took charge. From 1855 until 1873 Cole oversaw the development of institutions and collections in the area, putting his vigorous stamp on the whole style of South Kensington. One of the buildings of the Victoria & Albert Museum is named after him.

THOMAS CUBITT (1788–1855) was the pre-eminent speculative builder between 1825 and his death. Starting with small enterprises in Highbury and Stoke Newington, Cubitt entered a larger league when he agreed in the 1820s to build Tavistock and Gordon Squares on the Bedfords' Bloomsbury Estate, and embarked simultaneously on sectors of Belgravia and most of Pimlico on Grosvenor and Lowndes land. Cubitt's success depended on sound finance, social respectability and

reputable building practice. He had model building works by the Thames in Pimlico and employed a prolific staff of architects, lawyers and craftsmen. He was a benevolent autocrat whose firm fragmented after his death.

GEORGE DANCE THE OLDER (1695–1768) and GEORGE DANCE THE YOUNGER (1741–1825) were successively architect–surveyors to the City Corporation. Extant buildings by Dance senior include the Mansion House, with its grand Egyptian Hall, and St Botolph's, Aldgate. His son, a more sophisticated architect, designed several planning schemes on the fringes of the City, including the road layouts south of Blackfriars Bridge. With Sir Robert Taylor he drafted the seminal London Building Act of 1774. His most celebrated building was Newgate Prison, replaced in 1902 by the Old Bailey. The interior of All Hallows, London Wall, conveys something of the younger Dance's abilities; the south front of the Guildhall is also his, but is not typical.

TERRY FARRELL (b. 1938) is a Post-Modern stylist of London office buildings. His speciality is the recasting of old buildings to give them added value and a certain panache. The TV-am building at Camden Town, ornamented with breakfast egg cups along the back, put Farrell's name on the map. In 1989 he was busy with one vast office building on top of Charing Cross station, another over London Wall, and a scheme to reclothe the brutalist buildings of the South Bank arts complex in a glitzy, marketable skin.

HENRY FIELDING (1707–54), the author of *Tom Jones*, spent the last years of his life as a Westminster magistrate. Appalled by the rising level of thefts and burglaries and the hoplessness of the poor law, he propagandized for reform. He died before achieving anything practical, but his work was taken up by his half-brother SIR JOHN FIELDING (d. 1780), who pressed from the bench for legal and charitable innovation and instituted the Bow Street Runners, predecessors of the Metropolitan Police.

SIR THOMAS GRESHAM (1520–79) was the wealthier son of a wealthy merchant adventurer trading from the sign of the Grasshopper, Lombard Street. Personal business and royal agencies took Gresham on frequent trading missions to Antwerp, where he became versed in the vital economic activities of the bourse or exchange. In 1565 he offered to build an exchange on the Flemish

model. It was finished in 1568 and formally opened by Elizabeth I in 1571. It contributed to London's mercantile development and also functioned as a shopping centre.

HENRY CHARLES HARROD (1800–85) and CHARLES DIGBY HARROD (1841–1905) founded the world-famous centre of conspicuous consumption on Brompton Road which still bears their name. The business started in the mid-nineteenth century as a small grocer's and tea-dealer's; other departments were added from the 1870s. Harrods

made spectacular progress after becoming a limited company in 1889 under the management of (Sir) Richard Burbidge (1847–1917), who enlarged and rebuilt the store from 1894 and fended off the challenge of Selfridges and other competitors. Harrods' pre-eminence among London department stores has not been challenged since the First World War.

NICHOLAS HAWKSMOOR (*c.* 1661–1736) passed most of his life in the shadow of his architectural mentor, Sir Christopher Wren, but ranks as an equally remarkable architect in his own right. Under Wren he worked on Chelsea Hospital, several City churches and St Paul's Cathedral and, with greater freedom, at the Royal Naval Hospital, Greenwich. Hawksmoor's independent reputation rests on the six full-blooded Baroque churches he built in the years after 1711. Though most have been damaged and altered, they display a talent for drama and compression unequalled in British architecture. Christ Church, Spitalfields, now restored to its former glory, is the best of them. Among the others are St George's, Bloomsbury, St Lukes, Old Street and St Mary Woolnoth.

OCTAVIA HILL (1838–1912) was a pioneer of housing improvement and management. Influenced by the sanitary reform movement and the social vision of John Ruskin, she began in 1865 managing a small court of poor houses in Marylebone. Gradually her scope extended until she was supervising and improving large swathes of working-class property, notably for the Ecclesiastical Commissioners. She also contributed to the movement for securing open space in inner London. In part through her influence, many small pockets of space or 'urban lungs' were created in the East End and south London, and in the north Parliament Hill was added to Hampstead Heath.

CHARLES HOLDEN (1875–1960) was one of the few Arts-and-Crafts architects at home with London building forms. An early work is Zimbabwe House off the Strand, whose statues by Epstein were mutilated on grounds of their obscenity. Holden's masterpiece is the London Transport headquarters above St James's Park Underground Station, with reliefs by Eric Gill. He went on to design a brace of superb Underground stations, notably at the ends of the Piccadilly Line, and helped create a unified image for London Transport. His Bloomsbury buildings for the University of London are less appealing, though Senate House possesses grandeur and dignity.

HENRY HOLLAND (1745–1806) has had bad luck with his London buildings. The front of Dover House, Whitehall, Brooks's Club in St James's and the chambers of Albany are the only conspicuous reminders of his Francophile elegance. Yet Holland was a major London architect and developer. His big scheme was Hans Town, projected on Lord Cadogan's land around Sloane Street. He also designed the short-lived Carlton House with its pretty screen towards Pall Mall for the future George IV, built the first Battersea Bridge, reconstructed Drury Lane Theatre for Sheridan and altered Covent Garden Theatre.

SIR HORACE JONES (1819–87) was the City's architect and surveyor from 1864 until his death. Carrying on the work of rehousing London's markets from his predecessor Bunning, Jones rebuilt Billingsgate fish market and raised the handsome iron structures of the central meat market at Smithfield and the Leadenhall poultry market. Jones's last big job was the conception of Tower Bridge. Though his original design was revised, the bizarre and very English amalgamation of industrial function with picturesque appearance was his idea.

INIGO JONES (1573–1652) raised architectural horizons through the example of a handful of buildings. The first English professional architect to study in Italy, he transformed expectations with three uncompromisingly classical buildings for James I – the Queen's House at Greenwich, the Queen's Chapel at St James's Palace, and the Banqueting House, Whitehall. All three have survived, as has the form though not the exact substance of Jones's equally revolutionary venture in town-planning, Covent Garden piazza with St Paul's church on one side. This was the original of the London square.

SIR EDWIN LUTYENS (1869–1944), supreme stylist among twentieth-century British architects, graduated from country houses to a large London practice. His first major urban building was the neo-Georgian *Country Life* office in Tavistock Street, Covent Garden. Two fine churches in the centre of Hampstead Garden Suburb followed. The swagger of his Britannic House, Finsbury Circus and Midland Bank, Poultry, showed banker's classicism at its best. As a consultant, Lutyens designed façades for several of the American-sized blocks in Park Lane and for the 'chequerboard flats' in Page Street, Vincent Square.

HERBERT MORRISON, LORD MORRISON OF LAMBETH (1888–1965) was London's commanding twentieth-century politician. He made his early reputation

in Hackney. Morrison led the London Labour Party to victory in the county council election of 1933. His blend of clean but disciplined 'boss' politics and his stress on the delivery of services kept Labour in power on the LCC for over thirty years. Morrison himself moved into national politics when the Second World War came. London Transport was largely his creation. He also had much to do with the Festival of Britain, created on the South Bank site which had been acquired during his years of power at the LCC.

SIR HUGH MYDDLETON (1560–1631), a Welsh-born goldsmith, master-minded the New River, which brought ample fresh water to London from the unpolluted Amwell and Chadwell springs in Hertfordshire. The scheme was subsidized by James I in return for a half-share in the profits. Complete by 1620, the New River transformed London's water supply without recourse to complex pumping. Myddleton Square, close to the New River Head in Clerkenwell, commemorates the goldsmith's name.

JOHN NASH (1752–1835) did more than anyone to make London distinctive. Full of ideas and easy-going, his eye for architectural scenery made him the perfect architect–developer. Regent's Park and Regent Street, Carlton House Terrace, the Strand and the rebuilding of Buckingham Palace gave Nash opportunities no other London architect has had. He siezed them superbly, delegating particular frontages to others but controlling the overall conception. His stucco architecture is sometimes said to be slapdash, but at its best, as at Park Crescent, it can be exquisite.

GEORGE PEABODY (1795–1869), an American businessman and banker, lived in London for the last twenty-five years of his life. He used his fortune charitably, above all to endow London with money to be spent on working-class housing. The first Peabody Dwellings were built during his lifetime in Spitalfields. In the twenty years after his death, the Peabody Trust built solid, sensible but dour tenement buildings for the respectable artisan in many parts of London. Its role was largely superseded by municipal housing, but the Trust still owns, manages and builds housing on a modest scale.

SIR GEORGE GILBERT SCOTT (1811–78) was primarily a church architect. London has several Scott churches, pre-eminently St Giles, Camberwell and St Mary Abbots, Kensington. They seem modest compared with his two major buildings in central London. For the Foreign Office in Whitehall, he was forced by Lord Palmerston to change from his beloved Gothic to Italian Classic, and made a good fist of it. He had his Gothic revenge with the Midland Hotel, St Pancras, where rational construction and planning vie with extreme picturesqueness of outline and ornamentation. SIR GILES GILBERT SCOTT (1880–1960), his grandson, designed Waterloo Bridge and the façades of the Battersea Power Station and the Bankside Power Station, Southwark.

RICHARD SEIFERT (b. 1910) was the shrewdest London architect of offices and hotels during the 1960s and 1970s. His meticulous grasp of planning law and his negotiating skills endeared him to property tycoons, but the slick, sometimes strident nature of his firm's buildings made them a target of abuse. In the early 1970s he had six offices with 280 staff and a turnover of £50 million, figures then unprecedented for a British architect. Centre Point next to Tottenham Court Road Underground Station, the National Westminster Tower (London's tallest building) and the Forum and Royal Garden Hotels in Kensington are among Seifert's forceful statements. A sweeter, earlier Seifert is represented by the Woolworth Building, Marylebone Road.

GORDON SELFRIDGE (1858–1947) gave up a partnership in the Marshall Field retailing empire in Chicago to set up his own department store in London. Selfridges was the one such store to be started from scratch, rather than evolve by degrees. It was built over a twenty-year period from 1906 in a grand, American–classical style complete with roof garden. Though Selfridges never fulfilled its founder's ambition of overtaking Harrods, it set an example of scale and style. Beset with financial worries, Selfridge lived extravagantly till his death.

THE SEVENTH EARL OF SHAFTESBURY (1801–85) was the greatest of Victorian evangelical philanthropists. The treatment of lunatics and the

employment of child labour were his early preoccupations. Appalled by poverty and the danger of revolution, he turned his attention in the 1840s to London's housing conditions. He procured an Act in 1851 for regulating lodging houses and encouraged house-building for artisans, such as the Shaftesbury Park Estate, Battersea. The statue of Eros by Alfred Gilbert at Piccadilly Circus commemorates his life and work; officially it is the Shaftesbury Memorial, at the end of Shaftesbury Avenue.

RICHARD NORMAN SHAW (1831–1912) designed ebullient, witty and influential buildings in various styles between 1870 and 1910. Individualistic houses were his speciality: 'Queen Anne' studio houses for painters in Kensington and Hampstead, houses for brokers, bankers and collectors in Queen's Gate, Cadogan Square and Chelsea Embankment, and the intricate Lowther Lodge on Kensington Gore, overshadowed by Shaw's own Albert Hall Mansions. He also designed key elements of the middle-class suburb of Bedford Park, Chiswick. Shaw's later buildings tend towards classicism and weight, beginning with New Scotland Yard, the former police headquarters on the Embankment, leading to his ponderous designs for rebuilding the Regent Street Quadrant, finished in a plainer manner after his death.

SIR HANS SLOANE (1660–1753), physician, naturalist and antiquary, was for many years Secretary to the Royal Society. In 1712 he purchased the manor of Chelsea, where he improved the Physick Garden which survives on the Embankment. Under the terms of his will, Sloane's collection of curios was purchased for the nation and became the kernel of the British

Museum. Outstanding among these were the natural history specimens, now at South Kensington. His daughter Elizabeth married into the Cadogan family, which continues to own a large proportion of Sloane's original property in Chelsea.

SIR ROBERT SMIRKE (1781–1867) is best known as the architect of the British Museum, where his King's Library is an apartment of grandeur and technical virtuosity. He was responsible also for a variety of other public buildings in the Greek taste of the early nineteenth century. Among these were the second Covent Garden Theatre; the General Post Office, St Martin-le-Grand; and the largest and grimmest of London's prisons, the Millbank Penitentiary on the present Tate Gallery site. He also designed what is now Canada House, Trafalgar Square, formerly the Royal College of Physicians, and the fine church of St Mary, Wyndham Place, St Marylebone.

SIR JOHN SOANE (1753–1837) was an obsessive, productive architect of profound originality. His eccentricity and collecting mania can be savoured in the rambling house–museum he left in Lincoln's Inn Fields, one of the outstanding attractions of London. Accessible suburban buildings by Soane include Dulwich College Art Gallery and Pitshanger Manor, Ealing, now a library. The grander works on which Soane's reputation rests have mostly gone. Foremost among them were the cavernous, toplit interiors of the Bank of England, though his blank screen wall round the building survives and one of his offices has recently been reconstructed.

JOHN STOW (c. 1525–1605) was a merchant tailor of modest means turned antiquary and historian. He wrote abstracts and chronicles of English history, but is chiefly famous for his *Survey of London*. First published in 1598, it is the most graphic account of sixteenth-century London. The *Survey* is London's first proper history book and has been through numerous editions and revisions, such as 'Strype's Stow' of 1720. The historian's monument can be seen in his own church of St Andrew Undershaft; aptly, he is shown reading.

GEORGE EDMUND STREET (1824–81) was the most obsessively productive church architect of the Gothic Revival. London possesses three churches of the first rank by Street: St James the Less, off Vauxhall Bridge Road, St John the Divine, Kennington; and St Mary Magdalene, off Harrow Road. His main London building is secular, though it hardly looks it – the Royal Courts of Justice at the entrance to the City from the Strand. This huge complex went through so many changes of brief, size and even site that it wore its workaholic architect to death.

SIR HENRY TATE (1819–99), patentee of the sugar cube, spent some of his large Liverpool sugar-refining fortune in furnishing London with district public libraries. So also did two contemporaries of equal wealth and zeal for public enlightenment, the Cornish-born newspaper owner Passmore Edwards and the Scottish–American steel magnate Andrew Carnegie. Tate is best remembered of the three because he supplied the wherewithal, the initial collection and the eventual name for the National Gallery of British Art, built on the site of Millbank Prison in 1896–9.

ALFRED WATERHOUSE (1830–1905), most robust and productive of Victorian architects, set his uncompromising mark on several British cities. His London buildings include two nonconformist churches with distinctive plans, the oval King's Weighhouse Church in Mayfair and octagonal Lyndhurst Road Church, Belsize Park, and the National Liberal Club overlooking the Thames. Two gigantic Waterhouse buildings overawe the Londoner: the Prudential Assurance headquarters in High Holborn, in ruddy-red brick and terracotta, and the Natural History Museum, South Kensington, a colourful, turreted essay in Romanesque style, and the first British building to be wholly faced in terracotta.

SIR ASTON WEBB (1849–1930) enjoyed a large architectural practice around the turn of the century and specialized in public building. In a capable Beaux-Arts style he refronted Buckingham Palace, raised the Queen Victoria Memorial and built Admiralty Arch at the other end of the Mall. Less suave are his front blocks of the Victoria & Albert Museum, though the entrance hall is fine. Among his lesser works the French Protestant Church in

Soho Square, a massive grain silo at Deptford and his own charming house in Ladbroke Grove testify to his versatility.

HUGH LUPUS GROSVENOR, FIRST DUKE OF WESTMINSTER (1825–99), can stand as a model of the enlightened Victorian landowner. He succeeded his father as owner of the Grosvenor estates in 1869. An enthusiast for 'improvements', the Duke caused swathes of Mayfair to be rebuilt in the red brick which was his favourite material, employing a variety of architects and styles. Mount Street, Duke Street and Green Street testify to his policies. Philanthropic and serious by temperament he also erected model working-class tenements behind Oxford Street.

WILLIAM WHITELEY (1831–1907), a Yorkshire-born draper, founded London's first proper department store. Whiteley opened his original drapery in Westbourne Grove, Bayswater, in 1863. Meeting quick success, he added different departments all along the street and round the corner in Queensway. Whiteley's business philosophy was epitomized in the slogan 'The Universal Provider'. There were Whiteley depositories, laundries and stabling at West Kensington, and Whiteley farms for fresh produce at Hanworth. Shop assistants lived in dormitories in streets behind Westbourne Grove. Harrods and other stores founded their methods on Whiteley's example. He was shot dead in his office by a man claiming to be his son in January 1907. Shortly afterwards, the store was rebuilt in Queensway: the building survives but the business does not.

RICHARD WHITTINGTON (d. 1423) was London's first great private benefactor. A wealthy City merchant with overseas trading interests, three times Lord Mayor and creditor successively to Richard II, Henry IV and V, Whittington died a childless widower. By then he had already given Leadenhall to the City Corporation, added to St Thomas's Hospital and reconstructed a church. His executors rebuilt Newgate Prison, added a gateway to St Bartholomew's Hospital, helped pay for the new Guildhall, founded a college and almshouse, and erected a vast public latrine near the Thames. In return, posterity endowed Whittington with an impoverished

boyhood, a fictitious cat and an enduring place in London legend.

SIR CHRISTOPHER WREN (1632–1723), scientist and self-taught architect, has a unique place in London's history. Though his plan for reconstructing the City after the Great Fire was rejected, he was entrusted with rebuilding almost every City church as well as the Monument and St Paul's Cathedral. The fifty-two churches, of which twenty-five survive substantially, were not his unaided work, but their plans and their varied towers and steeples emanated largely from his office. As Crown Surveyor, the indefatigable Wren also built ranges at Hampton Court, Kensington Palace and Greenwich Hospital and the whole of the Royal Hospital at Chelsea – the trimmest of his buildings and a gentlemanly contrast to the thundering grandeur of St Paul's.

HENRY YEVELE (c. 1320–1400), 'the Wren of the fourteenth century', was the outstanding royal mason–architect of the early Perpendicular Gothic period. He worked for the Black Prince at his Kennington palace in the 1350s, then went on to add to or alter many major London churches, above all Old St Paul's and the west end of Westminster Abbey, where the tombs of Richard II and probably of Edward III are his work. As part of his work at the Palace of Westminster, Yevele in old age designed the present Westminster Hall, London's unrivalled masterpiece of secular medieval architecture.

CHARLES TYSON YERKES (1837–1905) was an American entrepreneur. Falling foul of the law in Philadelphia, he moved to Chicago, where he manipulated electric traction schemes to personal profit. When Chicago in turn became too hot to hold him in 1900 Yerkes moved to London, where plans for deep-level tubes were maturing. By force of personality and banking connections, Yerkes put together the combine which constructed the core of the Piccadilly and Bakerloo Lines and large sections of the Northern Line. He died before the lines were complete, but his Underground Electric Railways Company of London became the nucleus around which London Transport was formed in 1933. Yerkes is commemorated in a trilogy of novels by Theodore Dreiser.

Glossary of Place Names

In the City many streets are named after the commodities that used to be sold or the services performed there (e.g. Milk, Bread, Threadneedle). Others are named after the gates in the old City wall. On former private estates, especially in the West End, they commemorate their erstwhile owners or their properties elsewhere (Portman, Harley, Grosvenor). Elsewhere, monarchs and saints are popular; witness the number of King and Queen Streets in the London gazetteer. Below is an explanation of the names of some of the capital's localities:

ADELPHI: Greek for 'brothers'. The Adam brothers coined it for their development between the Strand and the river, now mostly demolished.

ALDWYCH: Danish for 'old settlement', from pre-Norman times. The present crescent dates from only this century but one of the streets destroyed to make way for it was called Wych Street.

BARBICAN: An outer fortification to the City wall.

BLOOMSBURY: 'Bury' in Old English means a large house or farm. Hence also Finsbury, Lothbury, Brondesbury.

CHARING CROSS: 'Charing' may derive from an Old English word meaning a turn in the road. The original cross was the last of those that Edward I had erected in memory of his wife Eleanor in 1290.

CHEAPSIDE: 'Cheap' is Old English for market, which this was in medieval times.

CHELSEA: Perhaps 'chalk wharf' in Old English.

CORNHILL: Probably not where corn was sold but, long ago, where it was grown.

DULWICH: The suffix 'which' means village or meadow, hence also Greenwich and Woolwich. 'Dul' could mean dill, the herb.

ELEPHANT AND CASTLE: Named after a large tavern, possibly a corruption of 'the Infanta of Castile'.

FULHAM: 'Ham' means home or settlement, probably of a man named Fulla. Hence also Balham, Eltham.

HACKNEY: 'ey' endings could derive from words meaning a river (in this case the Lea) or a group of islands. Hence also Putney and Stepney.

HAMPSTEAD: A former Saxon homestead.

HIGHGATE: A toll gate on the top of the hill.

HAYMARKET: London's main hay market from the seventeenth to the early nineteenth centuries.

ISLINGTON: Perhaps from 'isen', a spring containing iron, or from Gislandune (hill of Gisla). The suffix 'ton' usually denotes a settlement, hence Kennington, Kensington, Paddington.

KING'S CROSS: The site of a former police station with a statue of George IV on top of it.

KNIGHTSBRIDGE: A bridge over the Westbourne river where two knights may or may not have fought a duel.

LAMBETH: Lamb's hythe (harbour).

LOMBARD STREET: Italian merchants settled here in the twelfth century.

MARYLEBONE: The fourteenth-century parish of St Mary-by-the-bourne (the Tyburn river).

OXFORD STREET: Probably not because it was the road to Oxford (or it would have been Oxford Road) but because the land was owned from the eighteenth century by the Earl of Oxford.

PICCADILLY: From pickadils (various spellings) – fancy collars fashionable in the seventeenth century. Robert Baker, who sold them, owned land here.

PIMLICO: Maybe from Ben Pimlico's Ale, sold at a tavern near what is now Victoria Station.

REGENT STREET: Cut between 1813 and 1819, during the Regency.

ROTHERHITHE: A hythe (harbour) from either *redhra* – a mariner in Saxon – or *rother*, an ox.

SHOREDITCH: Once Scoredich, perhaps a ditch belonging to Score.

SOHO: Said to be a hunting cry – this was once hunting country.

SPITALFIELDS: The fields near St Mary Spital, an early hospital.

STOCKWELL: The well by the wood.

STRAND: Originally the road that followed the river bank.

VAUXHALL: Where Falkes de Breauté built his hall in the thirteenth century, thus Falkes' hall.

VICTORIA: The station was named after the street, which had been named after the Queen.

WANDSWORTH: Village by the River Wandle.

WAPPING: After a Saxon chief called Weppa.

WATERLOO: The uncompleted Strand Bridge had its name changed in 1816 to celebrate Wellington's victory. The bridge gave its name to the station at its southern landfall, then to the locality surrounding it.

WHITECHAPEL: A thirteenth-century white chapel.

Further Reading

Many thousands of books have been published on London and its different aspects, so it is inevitable that a list of suggested further reading of this kind will be personal and subjective. As far as possible we have tried to include titles that are readily available, if not in book shops then in public libraries, and the list here has been compiled following the suggestions of the contributors to this volume. Some of the titles have appeared in many editions and we have not attempted to list all these here. After the general works, the list follows the pattern of the structure of the book so that, for instance, a title on London's underground is to be found under *A Place to Live*.

General

Survey of London, 42 vols, LCC and GLC, 1900–86

NIKOLAUS PEVSNER AND BRIDGET CHERRY, *London*: 1. *The Cities of London and Westminster*, 3rd ed., 1973; 2. *South*, 1983; 3. *North West*, 1990; 4. *North and North East*, 1990, Penguin, 'The Buildings of England'

FELIX BARKER AND PETER JACKSON, *London: 2000 Years of a City and its People*, Cassell, 1974; Papermac, 1983

HAROLD CLUNN, *The Face of London*, Spring Books, 1970

W. R. DALZELL, *The Shell Guide to the History of London*, Michael Joseph, 1981

CHRISTOPHER HIBBERT, *London: a Biography of a City*, Penguin, 1986

IAN NAIRN, *Nairn's London*, Penguin, 1966

V. S. PRITCHETT, *London Perceived*, Hogarth Press, 1962

STEEN EILER RASMUSSEN, *London, the Unique City*, MIT, 1974

BEN WEINREB AND CHRISTOPHER HIBBERT (eds), *The London Encyclopaedia*, Macmillan 1983; Papermac, 1987

Guide books

ANDREW EAMES (ed.), *London*, Apa 'Insight Cityguide', 1988

YLVA FRENCH, *Blue Guide London*, Black, 13th ed., 1988

MARIANNE MEHLING (ed.), London, Phaidon 'Cultural Guide', 1988

LOUISE NICHOLSON, *London: Louise Nicholson's Definitive Guide*, Bodley Head, 1987

DAVID PIPER, *The Companion Guide to London*, Collins, 6th ed., 1977

ANN SAUNDERS, *The Art and Architecture of London: An illustrated guide*, Phaidon, 2nd ed., 1988

The Growth of London

WILLIAM PAGE (ed.), *London*, 'Victoria History of the Counties of England', vol. 1, Constable, 1909 (reprinted Dawsons, 1974)

PETER MARSDEN, *Roman London*, Thames & Hudson, 1980

SIR WALTER BESANT, *Early London: Prehistoric, Roman, Saxon and Norman*, Black, 1908

CHRISTOPHER N. L. BROOKE AND GILLIAN KEIR, *London 800–1216: The Shaping of a City*, Secker & Warburg, 1975

A. L. BEIER AND ROGER FINLAY (eds), *London 1500–1700: The Making of the Metropolis*, Longman, 1986

SIR WALTER BESANT, *London in the Time of the Tudors*, Black, 1904

COLIN AMERY, *Wren's London*, Lennard, 1986

W. G. BELL, *The Great Fire of London in 1666*, Bodley Head, revised ed., 1951

NORMAN G. BRETT-JAMES, *The Growth of Stuart London*, London and Middlesex Archaeological Society/Allen & Unwin, 1945

GEORGE RUDÉ, *Hanoverian London 1714–1808*, Secker & Warburg, 1971.

JOHN SUMMERSON, *Georgian London*, 1945; Barrie & Jenkins, revised ed., 1988

E. BERESFORD CHANCELLOR, *Life in Regency and Early Victorian Times: An Account of the Days of Brummell and D'Orsay 1800 to 1850*, Batsford, 1926

JAMES LAVER, *The Age of Illusion: Manners and Morals 1750–1848*, Weidenfeld & Nicolson, 1972

DONALD J. OLSEN, *The Growth of Victorian London*, Batsford, 1976.

FRANCIS SHEPPARD, *London 1808–70: The Infernal Wen*, Secker & Warburg, 1971

GRAHAM NORTON, *London before the Blitz 1906–40: From the Coming of the Motor-Car to the Outbreak of War*, Macdonald, 1970

STEVE HUMPHRIES AND JOHN TAYLOR, *The Making of Modern London 1945–85*, Sidgwick & Jackson, 1986

JOHN SCHOFIELD, *The Building of London*, Colonnade, 1984

GAVIN STAMP, *The Changing Metropolis*, Viking, 1984

The Areas of London

PETER H. CHAPLIN, *The Thames: From Source to Tideway*, Whittet, 1982

PHILIP HOWARD, *London's River*, Hamish Hamilton, 1975

ERIC DE MARÉ, *London's River: The Story of a City*, Bodley Head, 1964

Stephen Croad, *London's Bridges*, Royal Commission on Historical Monuments, 1983

W. M. CLARKE, *The City in the World Economy*, Institute of Economic Affairs, 1965

RACHEL HARTLEY, *No Mean City: A Guide to the Economic City of London*, Queen Anne Press, 1967

JOHN PLENDER AND PAUL WALLACE, *The Square Mile: A Guide to the New City of London*, Century, 1985

CHRISTOPHER HIBBERT AND TESSA STREET, *London's Churches*, Macdonald, 1988

W. MACQUEEN POPE, *Goodbye Piccadilly*, Michael Joseph, 1960

CAROL KENNEDY, *Mayfair: A Social History*, Hutchinson, 1986

JOAN GLASHEEN, *St James's, London*, Phillimore, 1987

WENDY ARNOLD, *The Historic Hotels of London: A Select Guide*, Thames & Hudson, 1986

ANNABEL WALKER AND PETER JACKSON, *Kensington and Chelsea*, Murray, 1987.

JOHN BETJEMAN (photographs by John Gay), *London's Historic Railway Stations*, Murray, 1972

A. A. JACKSON, *London's Termini*, David & Charles, 1969

MARTYN DENNEY, *London's Waterways*, Batsford, 1977

HERBERT SPENCER, *London's Canal: The History of the Regent's Canal*, Lund Humphries, 1976

M. C. BORER, *Hampstead and Highgate: The Story of Two Hilltop Villages*, W. H. Allen, 1976

CONRAD BAILEY, *Harrap's Guide to Famous London Graves*, Harrap, 1975

HARVEY HACKMAN, *Wates's Book of London Churchyards: A Guide to the Old Churchyards and Burial-grounds of the City and Central London*, Collins, 1981

ALAN PALMER, *The East End: Four Centuries of London Life*, Murray, 1989

ALAN FARMER, *Hampstead Heath*, Historical Publications, 1984

A Place to Live

DAVID PEARCE, *London's Mansions: The Palatial Houses of the Nobility*, Batsford, 1986

R. DUTTON, *London Homes*, Allen Wingate, 1952

SIMON JENKINS, *Landlords to London: The Story of a Capital and Its Growth*, Constable, 1975

ANDREW BYRNE, *London's Georgian Houses*, Georgian Press, 1986

S. C. RAMSEY AND J. D. M. HARVEY, *Small Georgian Houses and Their Details 1750–1820*, Architectural Press, 1972

A. L. COX-JOHNSON, *The Regent's Park Villas*, Bedford College, 1981

HENRY MAYHEW, *London Labour and the London Poor*, 1851, 1861 (condensed and ed., Peter Quennell as *Mayhew's London*, Bracken Books, 1984)

J. N. TARN, *Five per cent Philanthropy*, Cambridge University Press, 1973

G. STEDMAN-JONES, *Outcast London*, Oxford University Press, 1971

A. M. EDWARDS, *The Design of Suburbia: A Critical Study in Environmental History*, Pembridge Press, 1981

ALAN A. JACKSON, *London's Local Railways*, David and Charles, 1978

H. F. HOWSON, *London's Underground*, Ian Allen, 6th ed., 1986

SUSAN BEATTIE, *A Revolution in London Housing: LCC Housing Architects and Their Work 1893–1914*, Architectural Press, 1980

KATY CARTER, *London and the Famous: An Historical Guide to Fifty Famous People and their London Homes*, Muller, 1982

CAROLINE DACRES, *The Blue Plaque Guide to London*, MacMillan, 1981

A Place to Work

JENNIFER LANG, *Pride without Prejudice: The Story of London's Guilds and Livery Companies*, Perpetua Press, 1975

Port of London Authority, *The Port of London: The Capital Port*, Port of London Authority, 1978.

JOHN PUDNEY, *London's Docks*, Thames & Hudson, 1975

ALEC FORSHAW AND THEO BERGSTRÖM, *The Markets of London: A complete guide with maps and photographs*, Penguin, revised ed., 1989

O. J. T. Englefield, *Whitehall and Westminster: Government Informs Parliament – The Changing Scene*, Longman, 1985

Antony Brown, *Hazard Unlimited: The Story of Lloyd's of London*, Peter Davies, 2nd ed., 1978.

Hermann Burrows, *A History of the Rag Trade*, Maclaren, 1956

J. A. Schmiechen, *Sweated Industries and Sweated Labor: The London Clothing Trades 1860–1914*, Croom Helm, 1984

P. G. Hall, *The Industries of London since 1861*, Hutchinson 'University Library', 1962

Sir Robert Megarry, *Inns Ancient and Modern: A Topographical and Historical Introduction to the Inns of Court, Inns of Chancery and Serjeants' Inns*, Selden Society, 1972

Henry Mayhew, *London's Underworld*, 1862 (ed. by Peter Quennell, Bracken Books, 1983)

Susie Barson and Andrew Saint, *A Farewell to Fleet Street*, English Heritage, 1988

Vivian Brodzky (ed.), *Fleet Street: The Inside Story of Journalism*, Macdonald, 1966

Geoffrey Rivett, *The Development of the London Hospital System 1823–1982*, King Edward's Hospital Fund for London, 1986

T. L. Jarman, *Landmarks in the History of Education: English Education as Part of European Tradition*, Cresset, 1951.

J. S. Maclure, *One Hundred Years of London Education*, Allen Lane, 1970

Dorothy Davis, *A History of Shopping*, Routledge, 1966

W. Hamish Fraser, *The Coming of the Mass Market 1850–1914*, Macmillan, 1981

Jeremy Cooper, *The Complete Guide to London's Antique Street Markets*, Thames & Hudson, 1974

A Place to Enjoy

R. Bergan, *The Great Theatres of London*, Admiral, 1987

Diana Howard, *London Theatres and Music Halls 1850–1950*, Library Association, 1970

Wilfrid Mellers, *Harmonious Meeting: A Study of the Relationship between English Music, Poetry and Theatre, c.1600–1900*, Dobson, 1965

A. R. Warwick, *A Noise of Music*, Queen Anne Press, 1968

The Hon Mrs Evelyn Cecil, *London Parks and Gardens*, Constable, 1907

Nathan Cole, 'Royal Parks and Gardens of London, Their History and Mode of Embellishment', *Journal of Horticulture*, 1877

J. J. Sexby, *The Municipal Parks, Gardens and Open Spaces of London*, Stock, 1898

Warwick Wroth, *London Pleasure Gardens of the Eighteenth Century*, 1896; reprinted, Macmillan, 1979

Malcolm Rogers, *Museums and Galleries of London*, Black, 'Blue Guide', 2nd ed., 1986

L. T. Stanley, *The Old Inns of London*, Batsford, 1957

Ian Starsmore, *English Fairs*, Thames & Hudson, 1975

Henry Morley, *Memoirs of Bartholomew Fair*, Routledge, 1988

M. K. K. Brown, *Ritual of Royalty: The Ceremony and Pageantry of Britain's Monarchy*, Sidgwick & Jackson, 1983

Thomas Girtin, *The Lord Mayor of London*, Oxford University Press, 1948.

Index

Contributors

PETER BARBER has been deputy map librarian in the British Library since 1987: previously he was a curator in the department of manuscripts. He belongs to historical and topographical societies in north London and wrote *The Old Streets of Highgate*.

MARCEL BERLINS, a former practising lawyer, was for many years legal correspondent of *The Times*. He has been editor of *Law Magazine* and written books on legal matters. Now a freelance journalist and broadcaster, he presents *Law in Action* on Radio 4.

STELLA BINGHAM has written for a number of newspapers and magazines including *The Observer*, *Daily Mirror*, *Homes and Gardens* and *Today*. Latterly she has specialized in writing about property.

JOHN BROOKE LITTLE is Norroy and Ulster King of Arms, responsible at the College of Arms for the issue of coats of arms in Northern England and Ulster. He is chairman of the Heraldry Society, which he founded, and has written numerous books, including *An Heraldic Alphabet* and *Beasts in Heraldry*.

WILLIAM BYNUM is Reader in the History of Medicine at University College, London, and head of the academic unit at the Wellcome Institute for the History of Medicine. He has written widely on the history of psychiatry, clinical medicine and the medical sciences.

BRIDGET CHERRY is an architectural historian and editor of the Penguin Buildings of England series founded by Sir Nikolaus Pevsner. They co-authored *London 2 South* and she is working on two volumes covering the north London suburbs. She is a member of the London Advisory Committee of English Heritage.

DAN CRUICKSHANK is features editor of *The Architects' Journal* and an assistant editor on *Architectural Review*. His particular interest is Georgian architecture and among his recent books is *A Guide to the Georgian Buildings of Britain and Ireland*.

Prof. JAMES STEVENS CURL is an architectural historian, author of many articles and books, including *A Celebration of Death* and *The Egyptian Revival*. He is Director of the Historical Architecture Research Unit at the School of Architecture, Leicester.

GILLIAN DARLEY is an architectural writer, photographer and journalist. Author of *Villages of Vision* and co-author of *Dictionary of Ornament*, she is preparing a biography of Octavia Hill.

JOHN EARL has been director of the Theatres Trust since 1986, after 30 years of preservation work with LCC and GLC Historic Buildings Division. He has written widely on the history of theatres and music halls and was co-author of *The Canterbury Hall and Theatre of Varieties*.

ALAN HAMILTON has been a writer on *The Times* since 1970, in recent years specializing in the royal family and public ceremonies. His six books include *Essential Edinburgh*, *The Royal 100* and *The Real Charles*.

JUDY HILLMAN is a specialist in urban affairs and author of the Royal Fine Art Commission 1989 report, *A New Look for London*. For some years a planning specialist on national newspapers, she has written and edited books on planning in London and on Covent Garden.

PHILIP HOWARD has worked on *The Times* for 20 years, mostly as Literary Editor. Among his many books are several collections of his popular columns on English usage, and he is the author of *London's River*.

CAROL KENNEDY is a journalist and author, whose books include *Mayfair: A Social History*. She has also written about antiques, entrepreneurs and business history. She is deputy editor of *Director*, the journal of the Institute of Directors.

OLGA LEAPMAN works for an international scientific organization based in Marylebone. She collaborated closely with her husband Michael on the prize-winning *Companion Guide to New York*.

ELIZABETH LONGFORD's books include *Victoria RI*, *Wellington* and *Elizabeth R*. A Vice-President of the Royal Society of Literature and the London Library, she has been a trustee of the National Portrait Gallery and on the advisory committees of the Victoria & Albert Museum and the British Library.

LOUISE NICHOLSON worked for Christie's, the auctioneers, before becoming a freelance contributor to several national papers. Her book *London: Louise Nicholson's Definitive Guide* won the annual award from the London Tourist Board for the best book about the capital.

DAVID PEARCE, a former practising architect, now writes about architecture. He has edited specialist journals and worked for conservation societies. His books include *London's Mansions* and *Conservation Today*.

DAVID PERRETT is a medical research biochemist with many scientific publications to his credit. His enthusiasm for Britain's industrial heritage has gained him office in local and national societies studying industrial archaeology and the history of engineering.

CHRISTOPER PICK is a writer specializing in travel, history and heritage, with a particular interest in the history of London. His books include *Children's Guide to London*, *The Railway Route Book* and *Exploring Rural England and Wales*.

PETER RODGERS has been City Editor of *The Guardian* since 1984. A Cambridge physics graduate, he has spent most of his career writing for quality national papers about industry, finance and energy, including a spell on the *Sunday Times*.

ANDREW SAINT is a historian in the London division of the Historic Buildings and Monuments Commission (English Heritage). His books include *Richard Norman Shaw, The Image of the Architect* and *Towards a Social Architecture*.

GAVIN STAMP is an architectural historian and journalist, contributing mainly to *The Independent* and *The Spectator*. He is chairman of the Thirties Society. His books include *The Great Perspectivists* and *The Changing Metropolis*.

CHRISTOPHER TURNER is author of the 'Step by Step' series of guide books. His *London Step by Step* won the London Tourist Board award as the guide book of the year. He has previously been an advertising copywriter and a hotel manager.

ANNABEL WALKER is a freelance writer specializing in social, architectural and landscape history. She contributes to a range of publications including *The Times* and *The Sunday Times*. She is the author of *Kensington and Chelsea – a Social and Architectural History* and *England from the Air*.

PETER WATSON writes about the art world for *The Observer* and *The Spectator* and has worked for *The Times* and *The Sunday Times*. In 1982, disguising himself as an art dealer, he exposed a gang smuggling stolen Old Master paintings. The resulting book, *The Caravaggio Conspiracy*, won an award from the Crime Writers' Association.

LAILAN YOUNG writes on travel and music for *The New York Times* and *The Sunday Times*. She used to work for the BBC World Service. She has written three books: the first, *Secrets of the Face*, has been published in ten languages.

Colour photographs taken for George Weidenfeld and Nicolson Ltd
by Geoff Howard
Designed by Harry Green
Project Editor: Brigid Avison
Picture Researcher: Susan Haskins

Phototypeset by Keyspools Ltd, Golborne, Lancs
Colour separations by Newsele Litho Ltd
Printed in Italy by Printers Srl, Trento
Bound by L.E.G.O., Vicenza

PHOTOGRAPHIC ACKNOWLEDGEMENTS

The publishers would like to thank the following for permission to
reproduce photographs:

John Bethell page 167
The British Library Board 249
Trustees of the British Museum 23, 52, 123, 166, 193, 241, 280, 281
Martin Charles 217
Citisights of London 8
Colnaghi 253
Country Life 170, 188
James Stevens Curl 135
Department of the Environment, Crown Copyright Reserved 53, 94
John Donat 192, 248
John Earl (© Claude Harris) 260
Fotomas Index 159, 207, 232, 233 bottom, 236, 284
John R. Freeman 58, 87 top, 111, 127, 157, 178, 202 top, 233 top, 257,
297 top
Greater London Photograph Library 128, 132, 149 left, 175, 184, 190,
194, 230, 240 bottom, 244, 245, 252, 261, 262, 264
Guildhall Library, City of London 22, 27, 30, 35, 49, 60, 62 top, 70
left, 120, 140 bottom, 180 top, 215, 240 top
Harrods Ltd 254, 303 top
Illustrated London News Picture Library 31, 294, 296, 298
Norbert Ceulemans' City of London map-view reproduced on page
38 with the permission of the copyright holders Inline
International nv, 35 Derbystraat, Ghent, Belgium
The Royal Borough of Kensington and Chelsea Libraries 48, 99, 106,
107, 109, 110, 196, 266, 285
London Transport Executive 187

Mary Evans Picture Library 11, 68, 74 top, 95, 119, 122, 126, 133,
137, 142 bottom, 148, 149 right, 150, 158, 159 top, 172, 195, 198,
211, 214, 220, 226, 256, 269, 270, 272 bottom, 273, 277, 286, 288
The Paul Mellon Centre for Studies in British Art 279
Museum of London 15, 18, 26, 62 bottom, 63, 66, 71, 80, 87
bottom, 91, 115, 134, 144, 146, 152, 153, 160, 165, 179, 181, 206,
228 right, 272 top, 289, 290, 293, 297 bottom
The National Gallery, London 271
National Portrait Gallery, London 302, 303 bottom, 304, 305
Humphrey Nemar (© Hansib Publishing Ltd) 292 right
National Monuments Record 70 right, 102
John Pearson 8
The Photo Source 223 right
Portman Family Settled Estates 162, 163
Private Collection 19
© HM The Queen 54
Royal Commission on the Historical Monuments of England 57, 77,
82, 83, 129, 140 top, 171 left, 174, 183, 203, 228 left, 292 left
British Architectural Library, RIBA, London 118
Royal Opera House, Covent Garden 265
Andrew Saint 237
Spink & Son Ltd 78
The Tate Gallery, London 75
Yale Center for British Art 124
Weidenfeld & Nicolson Archives 64, 74, 86, 156, 180, 182, 186, 202,
223 left, 230
Victoria & Albert Museum, London 142 top
The Worshipful Company of Goldsmiths 222

GEOFF HOWARD thanks the following for assistance with locations for
the colour photographs
For 'Bank'; Chris Jones of Royal Insurance Co.
For 'Temple'; Alister Norbury and Chris–
For 'Bedford Square'; Melanie Ednie of Hodder & Stoughton
For 'Crafts'; Emma Joel and all at The Glasshouse
For 'Rag trade'; Hans Jacoby and Mrs Doreen Rosenwater at
Cojana/Jacoby & Bratt, Mr Schuster at Nat. Union of Garment
Workers
For 'Learning'; Mr Hutt and Sheila Douglas at Linnean Library
For 'Shops'; Ted Jones at Burlington Arcade
For 'Festivals'; Christine Hall of Wardwick Assocs
Various views; Ted Boreham of IPC
For 'Pubs'; Kevin Lee at The Salisbury
For 'Music'; Sussex Camerata and John Mee at St Olaves church
For 'Westminster'; Michael Cummins
For 'Manufacture'; Miss Hickey at Fullers Brewery;
For 'Art gallery'; Andrew Clayton-Payne
For 'Tower'; Liz Broadley and Mr Harding, Chief Yeoman Warder
For 'Money'; Brian Reidy and Michael Brown at LME

Photographed on Canon F-1 cameras, lenses from 20mm–1000mm,
Fujichrome & Kodachrome film.